My God Is The Becoming-One

God Papers

aka: **God: God is the BeComingOne**

Third Edition

by

Walter R. Dolen

Blank page...

MY GOD IS THE BECOMING-ONE

GOD PAPERS

Third Edition

by

Walter R Dolen

President of the Becoming-One Church

"the is, the was, the Coming One, the Almighty"

(Rev 1:8; Mat 11:3)

or in Hebrew: אֱלִיָהוּ

Becoming-One Publications

Pennsylvania USA

Copyright © Walter R. Dolen, 1971, 1977, 1989, 1993, 1999, 2012, 2019

All rights reserved

This book (aka the *God Papers*) is a corrected, rewritten, enlarged version of a written work which was included in part in a 1970-71 non-published work and included in part in the 1977, 1989, 1996, 1999, 2000 and 2012 published books. Included in this 3nd edition is a new Introduction section added after the 2000 and after the 2012 AD edition.

A list of the author's other books can be found at:

www.walterdolen.com

My God is the Becoming-One: God Papers

3rd Edition

2019 Paperback Edition

ISBN: 9781619180550

Printed in the United States of America

Last Printed December 2023

[with typo and format/date corrections]

BeComing-One Publications

http://becoming-one.org/books.htm

May Grace Abound to All

All silencing of discussion is an assumption of infallibility

"**All silencing of discussion is an assumption of infallibility** ... But the peculiar evil of silencing the expression of opinion is, that it is robbing the human race ... If the opinion is right, they are deprived of the opportunity of exchanging error for truth; if wrong, they lose, what is almost as great a benefit, the clearer perception and livelier impression of truth, produced by its collision with error."

(John Stuart Mill, On Liberty,
Chapter 2; see the quote here:
[https://www.beone.ws/resources/OnLiberty-40.pdf])

General Contents

Documentation .... BP 1:17 | Pg 22

BP1: Beginning Papers (Intro & Premises) .... BP 1:1 | Pg 23

    Introduction and Premises .... BP 1:1 | Pg 23

        How can there be an all good God, when there is Evil? .... BP 1:1 | Pg 23

        Typical statement by agnostics/atheists and non-believers .... BP 1:2 | Pg 24

    God or Evolution .... BP 1:2 | Pg 24

        Good and Evil .... BP 1:3 | Pg 25

        Creation or evolution: who or what created the universe? .... BP 1:5 | Pg 27

        Two Views: Earth is old; Earth is young .... BP 1:5 | Pg 27

            Earth is Old Theory .... BP 1:5 | Pg 27

    Foundations for the "Earth Is Old System" .... BP 1:5 | Pg 27

    (1) Theory of Evolution .... BP 1:5 | Pg 27

    (2) Radioactive Dating Methods .... BP 1:5 | Pg 27

        Constant Decay Rates? .... BP 1:6 | Pg 28

        Decay Rates not Constant .... BP 1:7 | Pg 29

        Radiohalos .... BP 1:7 | Pg 29

        Dubious Premises .... BP 1:8 | Pg 30

        Different Methods of Dating Don't Agree .... BP 1:8 | Pg 30

    (3) Great Distances in Space .... BP 1:8 | Pg 30

    Foundation for the "Earth is Young System" .... BP 1:9 | Pg 31

        (1) No Scientific Evidence For Evolution .... BP 1:9 | Pg 31

        (2) Proof that the Earth is Young .... BP 1:9 | Pg 31

        (3) Biblical Chronology .... BP 1:9 | Pg 31

        Your Mindset Limits You .... BP 1:9 | Pg 31

    Earth is Fragile; Life in Danger .... BP 1:10 | Pg 32

        Who can save it? .... BP 1:10 | Pg 32

    Bad News .... BP 1:10 | Pg 32

        Magnetic Fields, Their Disintegration .... BP 1:10 | Pg 32

        Atomic Inferno .... BP 1:11 | Pg 33

        Biological Catastrophe .... BP 1:13 | Pg 35

        Old Age and its Purpose .... BP 1:13 | Pg 35

    New Age .... BP 1:13 | Pg 35

        BP1: Review .... BP 1:14 | Pg 36

BP2: Mindset Paper .... BP 2:1 | Pg 38

    Ptolemy's Mathematical-Geocentric Theory .... BP 2:1 | Pg 38

    Ptolemy and his Treatise .... BP 2:2 | Pg 39

    Mindset, A Brain Cell Problem .... BP 2:5 | Pg 42

BP3: Bible Paper .... BP 3:1 | Pg 43
    Bible's Rich Metaphorical Word Usage .... BP 3:3 | Pg 45
    Bible, an Ancient Text with Abundance of Details .... BP 3:3 | Pg 45
  Typical Criticism .... BP 3:4 | Pg 46
  Three Tests .... BP 3:5 | Pg 47
    Bibliographical Test .... BP 3:5 | Pg 47
    Internal Evidence Test .... BP 3:7 | Pg 49
    External Evidence Test .... BP 3:8 | Pg 50

BP4: Duality Paper .... BP 4:1 | Pg 51
  Type and Antitype .... BP 4:1 | Pg 51
  Visible projects the Invisible .... BP 4:2 | Pg 52
  Examples .... BP 4:2 | Pg 52
    Female and Male Language; Type and Antitype Language .... BP 4:3 | Pg 53
  Look To The Higher Meaning .... BP 4:3 | Pg 53
  Even prophecy is dual .... BP 4:4 | Pg 54

BP5: Premises For Belief .... BP 5:1 | Pg 55
  How To Read These Papers .... BP 5:1 | Pg 55
  Faith .... BP 5:1 | Pg 55
  Premises .... BP 5:2 | Pg 56
    1. There is a God .... BP 5:2 | Pg 56
    2. God Created The Heavens and The Earth .... BP 5:2 | Pg 56
      Design .... BP 5:2 | Pg 56
    3. The Bible Is The Word Of God .... BP 5:2 | Pg 56
      The Bible in its original languages .... BP 5:2 | Pg 56
      How was the Bible written and how was it inspired? .... BP 5:2 | Pg 56
      Any apparent contradiction is just that .... BP 5:3 | Pg 57
      The Bible interprets itself .... BP 5:3 | Pg 57
      The Bible shows its reader HOW to read it .... BP 5:3 | Pg 57
      Here a little, there a little .... BP 5:3 | Pg 57
      Duality .... BP 5:4 | Pg 58
      Spirituality .... BP 5:4 | Pg 58
      Effect of every vision .... BP 5:5 | Pg 59
      The proof of premise 3 .... BP 5:5 | Pg 59
  Creationist Book List Information .... BP 5:5 | Pg 59

My God is the BeComingOne .... GP: Pg 61

God Papers .... GP: Pg 61
  Documentation .... Page 62
  Important Principles to Understand .... Page 63

Premises on the existence of God... Page 63
Introduction.. GP: Page 64
    I believe God did create the universe and here are a few reasons why I do....... GP: Page 65

GP 1: God's Paradoxes and Name .... GP 1:1 | Pg 67

Views and Paradoxes on God.. GP 1:1 | Pg 67
- Gods of Science.. GP 1:1 | Pg 67
- Gods of the Aztecs... GP 1:2 | Pg 68
- Bizarre Gods of Yesterday .... GP 1:2 | Pg 68
- Today's Gods.. GP 1:2 | Pg 68
- Gods, Creation and Science .... GP 1:2 | Pg 68
- Who or What is the Creation Power?... GP 1:3 | Pg 69

Premise for this Study .... GP 1:3 | Pg 69
- 'Problems' with the Bible .... GP 1:4 | Pg 70

Paradoxes on God .... GP 1:4 | Pg 70

Our Goal .... GP 1:4 | Pg 70

Two Basic Laws and One Fact: God Cannot Lie...................................... GP 1:5 | Pg 71
- Law of Contradiction and Law of Knowledge .... GP 1:5 | Pg 71
- God Does Not Lie.. GP 1:5 | Pg 71

Law Of Contradiction... GP 1:5 | Pg 71
What is the Law of Contradiction?... GP 1:5 | Pg 71
- If everything is *and at the same time* is not ... . GP 1:6 | Pg 72
- At the *same time* .... GP 1:6 | Pg 72
- Good and Evil at the *same time* or .... GP 1:6 | Pg 72
- An Example of Paradoxes and Time .... GP 1:6 | Pg 72
- Same time in the *same respect* .... GP 1:7 | Pg 73
- "If everything is and at the same time is not, all opinions must be true"........ GP 1:7 | Pg 73
- Word Games or Lies... GP 1:7 | Pg 73
- Do words have meaning?.. GP 1:8 | Pg 74
- Knowledge cannot exist outside the Law of Contradiction...................... GP 1:8 | Pg 74
- Summarize the Law of Contradiction... GP 1:8 | Pg 74

Attributes Of God .... GP 1:9 | Pg 75
- God Is Life... GP 1:9 | Pg 75
- God Has All Knowledge .... GP 1:9 | Pg 75
- God Is Everywhere .... GP 1:9 | Pg 75
- There Is Nothing Else Besides God .... GP 1:9 | Pg 75
- God Is Invisible.. GP 1:10 | Pg 76
- God Is Almighty .... GP 1:10 | Pg 76
- All Things Possible for God .... GP 1:10 | Pg 76
- Creator Makes All Things .... GP 1:11 | Pg 77

Problem Of Evil .... GP 1:12 | Pg 78
- God's Connection with Good and Evil... GP 1:12 | Pg 78
- Paradoxical Sides of God... GP 1:12 | Pg 78

Right and Left Sides.	GP 1:12 | Pg 78
Right Side or Positive Aspects of God	GP 1:13 | Pg 79
God Is Good	GP 1:13 | Pg 79
God Is Love	GP 1:13 | Pg 79
Love Is	GP 1:13 | Pg 79
Love is Not	GP 1:13 | Pg 79
God Keeps His Word; He Does Not Lie	GP 1:13 | Pg 79
Left Side or Negative Aspects of God:	GP 1:14 | Pg 80
Anger of God or Wrath of God?	GP 1:15 | Pg 81
Anger of God, Destroying Angel, and Satan.	GP 1:15 | Pg 81
Evil Angel's Fate	GP 1:15 | Pg 81
Right and Left Side Metaphor	GP 1:16 | Pg 82
God has Power over Satan	GP 1:16 | Pg 82
Two Sides of God	GP 1:17 | Pg 83
Evil <u>Never</u> a part of the True God.	GP 1:17 | Pg 83
God Predestinates Wrath and Mercy before Creation.	GP 1:17 | Pg 83
Scripture shows God predestinating some to evil and wrath:	GP 1:17 | Pg 83
Some chosen to be good:	GP 1:17 | Pg 83
All generations chosen:	GP 1:18 | Pg 84
Predestination is very difficult to understand	GP 1:18 | Pg 84
The Great Paradox	GP 1:18 | Pg 84
Time Answers The Paradoxes	GP 1:18 | Pg 84
Titles or Names Of God	**GP 1:19 | Pg 85**
Importance of a Name.	GP 1:20 | Pg 86
Personal Names had Meaning	GP 1:20 | Pg 86
Dual Meaning Of Names	GP 1:21 | Pg 87
Great Significance of the Name	GP 1:21 | Pg 87
The Name in Scripture	GP 1:21 | Pg 87
The Name of God.	**GP 1:23 | Pg 89**
What Is God's Name?	GP 1:23 | Pg 89
Exodus 3:12 v. Exodus 3:14	GP 1:24 | Pg 90
Yehowah: God Revealed His Name To Moses.	GP 1:25 | Pg 91
God Restates His NAME.	GP 1:25 | Pg 91
God's NAME is *Emphasized* – He will be!	GP 1:25 | Pg 91
God's NAME is an imperfect verb used as a noun.	GP 1:25 | Pg 91
What is an imperfect verb?	GP 1:25 | Pg 91
Meaning Contrary to "I AM" Doctrine.	GP 1:26 | Pg 92
Hebrew Words Written Without Vowels.	GP 1:26 | Pg 92
Is the Correct Pronunciation of the NAME Possible?	GP 1:26 | Pg 92
Different Spelling of the NAME	GP 1:27 | Pg 93
Gesenius admits the spelling "Yehowah" fits the evidence	GP 1:27 | Pg 93
NAME Pronounced	GP 1:27 | Pg 93
God's Name: BeComingOne.	GP 1:27 | Pg 93
To Review and Conclude.	GP 1:27 | Pg 93

- Name in the New Testament .... GP 1:28 | Pg 94
  - No Problem with the NAME, But with Immutability Theory............. GP 1:28 | Pg 94
- "I Am" Doctrine .... GP 1:28 | Pg 94
  - Grecian Mindset.. GP 1:28 | Pg 94
  - Greek Translation of God's NAME: "The Being" .... GP 1:28 | Pg 94
    - "The Being" was Egypt's God... GP 1:29 | Pg 95
  - Bible Written in Hebrew Not Greek .... GP 1:29 | Pg 95
  - Catholic Church's Bias Toward the Greek Text............................ GP 1:29 | Pg 95
  - NAME Forgotten by Judah .... GP 1:29 | Pg 95
  - Greek Mindset.. GP 1:30 | Pg 96
    - Greek Mindset: God <u>had</u> to be Changeless .... GP 1:30 | Pg 96
  - Hebrew verbs are different from English verbs .... GP 1:31 | Pg 97
  - Didn't Jesus say "I am"? .... GP 1:31 | Pg 97
  - Immutable God Taught by Greeks .... GP 1:33 | Pg 99
  - Immutable God or BeComingOne God? .... GP 1:34 | Pg 100
    - Serious Subject.. GP 1:34 | Pg 100
    - One sense of God's changeability..................................... GP 1:34 | Pg 100
  - Real Unchangeableness of God .... GP 1:34 | Pg 100
    - Immutability: One Conclusion. .... GP 1:35 | Pg 101
- God, Gods... GP 1:35 | Pg 101
  - Elohim Is Plural/Dual.. GP 1:36 | Pg 102
  - God's Name is Yehowah Not Elohim... GP 1:36 | Pg 102
- Israel's Gods is One yhwh .... GP 1:36 | Pg 102
  - One yhwh, Not One Elohim... GP 1:37 | Pg 103
  - One God: Old and New Testament... GP 1:37 | Pg 103
- One Yehowah .... GP 1:38 | Pg 104
  - One in History... GP 1:38 | Pg 104
  - One In Hebrew .... GP 1:39 | Pg 105
  - One In Greek .... GP 1:39 | Pg 105
  - One In English... GP 1:39 | Pg 105
  - One Versus Only.. GP 1:39 | Pg 105
  - Many in One.. GP 1:39 | Pg 105
    - Nation as One Man .... GP 1:40 | Pg 106
    - Birth of One Son, as Birth of New Nation .... GP 1:40 | Pg 106
    - Many in the One Body of Christ .... GP 1:40 | Pg 106
  - Only God .... GP 1:41 | Pg 107
    - Yehowah, Elohim.. GP 1:42 | Pg 108
  - Predestination, Time, Name, and the Paradoxes .... GP 1:42 | Pg 108
  - We Will Use "BeComingOne" in GP .... GP 1:43 | Pg 109
  - I Will Be in Context .... GP 1:44 | Pg 110
- Web Page Links to Biblical Language Aids/Helps (in the digital books): .... GP 1:45 | Pg 111
- **Review of GP 1**.. GP 1:45 | Pg 111

GP 2: God The Father .... GP 2:1 | Pg 112

    Jesus Christ's Father .... GP 2:1 | Pg 112

        First Proof.. GP 2:1 | Pg 112

        Six More Proofs.. GP 2:1 | Pg 112

            God Swore By Himself .... GP 2:1 | Pg 112

            Throne .... GP 2:2 | Pg 113

            Prayer.. GP 2:2 | Pg 113

            God The Father Chose .... GP 2:2 | Pg 113

            YHWH Of Old Testament Is The Father .... GP 2:2 | Pg 113

            "See" The Father?....................................... GP 2:2 | Pg 113

GP 3: Angels, Spirits, and the Word of God .... GP 3:1 | Pg 115

    What are Angels? .... GP 3:1 | Pg 115

        Angels are Spiritual Messengers or Word Carriers .... GP 3:1 | Pg 115

        Two Kinds of Angels: Good & Evil .... GP 3:1 | Pg 115

    Angels Closely Associated with God............................. GP 3:2 | Pg 116

        Angel of the Lord .... GP 3:2 | Pg 116

        Hagar and the Angel .... GP 3:2 | Pg 116

        Abraham and the Angel .... GP 3:3 | Pg 117

        Jacob and the Angel... GP 3:3 | Pg 117

        Moses and the Angel.. GP 3:3 | Pg 117

        Balaam and the Angel... GP 3:4 | Pg 118

        Gideon and the Angel .... GP 3:4 | Pg 118

        Manoah and the Angel .... GP 3:4 | Pg 118

        Jacob and the Angel... GP 3:5 | Pg 119

        Angel of God's Presence... GP 3:5 | Pg 119

        Gabriel and the Angel .... GP 3:5 | Pg 119

        Joshua, Satan, and the Angel................................... GP 3:6 | Pg 120

        Moses. Satan, and Michael the Archangel .... GP 3:6 | Pg 120

        Job, Satan, and the LORD.. GP 3:7 | Pg 121

        Joshua and the Chief-Angel..................................... GP 3:7 | Pg 121

        Review: Angels Close Connection to the BeComingOne........ GP 3:8 | Pg 122

    Angel of the BeComingOne (YHWH) is *not* the BeComingOne (YHWH)......... GP 3:8 | Pg 122

    NAME Given To the Word/Angel .... GP 3:9 | Pg 123

    Cherubs and the Angel between them .... GP 3:9 | Pg 123

    Word of God .... GP 3:10 | Pg 124

        Word of the BeComingOne .... GP 3:10 | Pg 124

        Word: Spoken by an Angel or Spiritual Messenger .... GP 3:10 | Pg 124

    Can we see Spirits?... GP 3:11 | Pg 125

        Analogous to Burning Flames or Wind......................... GP 3:11 | Pg 125

        Satan a spirit had no Form .... GP 3:12 | Pg 126

    Review of GP 3.. GP 3:12 | Pg 126

    General Review .... GP 3:12 | Pg 126

GP 4: Jesus Christ the Man .... GP 4:1 | Pg 128

- Who Was Jesus Christ. .... GP 4:1 | Pg 128
  - His Name .... GP 4:1 | Pg 128
    - Jesus Not Called "Christ" Openly <u>before</u> his Death .... GP 4:1 | Pg 128
    - Meaning of Being Anointed .... GP 4:2 | Pg 129
- Promised Son Of God, Seed Of David, and Eve................................. GP 4:3 | Pg 130
  - Jesus Christ was Prophesied to Come .... GP 4:3 | Pg 130
  - Fulfillment .... GP 4:3 | Pg 130
  - Son of Man Through Mary .... GP 4:3 | Pg 130
  - Virgin Birth .... GP 4:4 | Pg 131
  - Middle Man: Son of God and Son of Man .... GP 4:5 | Pg 132
  - Born of the Seed of David .... GP 4:5 | Pg 132
    - Genealogy of Mary & Joseph .... GP 4:5 | Pg 132
  - Seed of Nathan and Solomon... GP 4:6 | Pg 133
  - Christ's Lineage Review .... GP 4:6 | Pg 133
- God inside Christ The Man .... GP 4:6 | Pg 133
  - Spirit in Jesus was the Angel of God .... GP 4:7 | Pg 134
  - Jesus Christ Came In The Flesh... GP 4:7 | Pg 134
- Jesus Christ The Man Was Not God .... GP 4:8 | Pg 135
  - Came From God .... GP 4:8 | Pg 135
  - They were Two.. GP 4:8 | Pg 135
  - A Mediator is Not God .... GP 4:9 | Pg 136
  - Angel of the BeComingOne Was in Christ the Man .... GP 4:9 | Pg 136
  - Word of God in Jesus .... GP 4:9 | Pg 136
  - Christ Suffered, Can God Suffer?... GP 4:10 | Pg 137
  - God Not As Christ, But *inside* Christ .... GP 4:10 | Pg 137
    - Men as Temples of the Living God. .... GP 4:10 | Pg 137
  - Spirit Did the Works With Jesus .... GP 4:10 | Pg 137
    - Paul is an example. .... GP 4:11 | Pg 138
  - We Are Saved By the Resurrected Christ .... GP 4:11 | Pg 138
  - When Did Christ Receive the Spirit?...................................... GP 4:11 | Pg 138
- God Made Flesh?... GP 4:12 | Pg 139
  - Meaning of, "the Word Was Made Flesh" .... GP 4:12 | Pg 139
- Death of Christ the Man .... GP 4:13 | Pg 140
  - Holy One... GP 4:13 | Pg 140
  - Spirit Leaves Body At Death.. GP 4:14 | Pg 141
  - Why Christ Died .... GP 4:15 | Pg 142
    - Predestinated Before the Foundations of the World .... GP 4:15 | Pg 142
- Jesus Christ the Man, the Son, did not Pre-exist .... GP 4:15 | Pg 142
  - The following is evidence that Jesus Christ the man, the Son, first came into existence when he was conceived in Mary's womb:... GP 4:15 | Pg 142
    - (1) Against the Law of Contradiction.................................. GP 4:15 | Pg 142

- (2) Jesus came into existence in the Flesh .... GP 4:16 | Pg 143
- (3) Prophesied Seed Cannot Exist Before He Genetically Passes through the Fathers and then is Born .... GP 4:16 | Pg 143
- (4) Born of a Woman .... GP 4:17 | Pg 144
- (5) Son Speaks Now, Not in the Old Testament .... GP 4:17 | Pg 144
- (6) Proof of Worshiping Angels .... GP 4:17 | Pg 144
- (7) Spirit and Flesh .... GP 4:17 | Pg 144
- (8) Summarized Evidence against Pre-existence Theory .... GP 4:18 | Pg 145

Pre-existence Theory: Refuting their Evidence .... GP 4:18 | Pg 145
- (1) In the Beginning was the Word, which beginning? .... GP 4:18 | Pg 145
- (2) Whose going forth was from of Old .... GP 4:19 | Pg 146
- (3) Jesus Christ Existed Before He was Born Only in God's Fore-Thoughts .... GP 4:19 | Pg 146
- (4) Jesus Christ Existed in Heaven Before His Birth? How? .... GP 4:20 | Pg 147
- (5) Jesus Christ Created All Things? How? .... GP 4:20 | Pg 147
- (6) Personification of Wisdom .... GP 4:21 | Pg 148
- (7) Jesus Christ Humbled or Emptied Himself? .... GP 4:21 | Pg 148
- (8) Trinitarians' Bias .... GP 4:21 | Pg 148

Melchizedek .... GP 4:21 | Pg 148
- Without Parents, No Beginning of Days? .... GP 4:21 | Pg 148
- Jesus had a Genealogy .... GP 4:21 | Pg 148
- Pre-Existence? .... GP 4:22 | Pg 149
- Mechizedek Prefigured Christ's Perpetual Priesthood .... GP 4:22 | Pg 149

Notes .... GP 4:22 | Pg 149
Genealogy of Jesus .... GP 4:22 | Pg 149
Review of GP 4 .... GP 4:23 | Pg 150

GP 5: Jesus Christ the God .... GP 5:1 | Pg 151

Who He Was/Is/Will Be .... GP 5:1 | Pg 151
BeComingOne's Names And Titles .... GP 5:2 | Pg 152
Christ's Names And Titles .... GP 5:3 | Pg 153
- Glory Not Given to Another .... GP 5:3 | Pg 153
- Was Jesus YHWH in Old Testament Bible? .... GP 5:3 | Pg 153

Spiritual Marriage: Two into One .... GP 5:5 | Pg 155
- Analogy .... GP 5:5 | Pg 155

Marriage Analogy: Two Become One .... GP 5:5 | Pg 155
- God the Husband of Israel .... GP 5:6 | Pg 156
- Spiritual Marriage .... GP 5:6 | Pg 156
- Jesus Christ's New Name .... GP 5:6 | Pg 156
- Jesus Christ's Flesh .... GP 5:7 | Pg 157
- Two, Spirit and Flesh, Became One .... GP 5:7 | Pg 157

Christ in the Image of God .... GP 5:8 | Pg 158
- The Image has Something to do with Two in One .... GP 5:8 | Pg 158
- Male and Female are One .... GP 5:8 | Pg 158

- Spirit and Flesh of Christ Become One ... GP 5:9 | Pg 159
  - Another Sense of the Image of God ... GP 5:9 | Pg 159
  - Word Became Flesh ... GP 5:9 | Pg 159
  - New Creation: Two into One ... GP 5:9 | Pg 159
  - Two Bodies in One ... GP 5:10 | Pg 160
- New Soul ... GP 5:10 | Pg 160
  - Saving of the Soul ... GP 5:10 | Pg 160
  - Angel of the Old Testament Prefigured the New Soul ... GP 5:10 | Pg 160
  - Beginning with Moses Christ was Manifested ... GP 5:11 | Pg 161
  - Spiritually Married ... GP 5:11 | Pg 161
- Christ: Second Adam ... GP 5:11 | Pg 161
- Christ the Man Became and is Becoming the God ... GP 5:12 | Pg 162
- Christ into the Glory of the Father ... GP 5:12 | Pg 162
- Scriptures Now Make Sense ... GP 5:13 | Pg 163
  - Better than Angels ... GP 5:13 | Pg 163
  - Under Christ, not Angels ... GP 5:13 | Pg 163
  - Jesus Christ the BeComingOne ... GP 5:13 | Pg 163
- He was before All in Two Senses ... GP 5:14 | Pg 164
- Trinity, Godhead and the Law of Contradiction ... GP 5:15 | Pg 165
  - Immortality and Death ... GP 5:15 | Pg 165
  - "With God Nothing Shall Be Impossible" ... GP 5:15 | Pg 165
    - Incorrect Translation ... GP 5:15 | Pg 165
    - God of Law, Not of Confusion ... GP 5:16 | Pg 166
    - God's Word Not Impossible ... GP 5:16 | Pg 166
  - Truth Is ... GP 5:16 | Pg 166
- It Follows Thus: ... GP 5:16 | Pg 166
- Trinity Belief Impossible ... GP 5:17 | Pg 167
  - What is the Trinity Belief? ... GP 5:17 | Pg 167
  - What Mystery? ... GP 5:18 | Pg 168
  - Trinitarian Belief against the Law of Contradiction ... GP 5:18 | Pg 168
  - One in Number, but Three in Person ... GP 5:19 | Pg 169
  - Immortal Person Dies? ... GP 5:19 | Pg 169
- God Not the Trinity ... GP 5:19 | Pg 169
- Fourth Person in the Godhead? ... GP 5:20 | Pg 170
  - Four or More Persons in the "Trinity"? ... GP 5:20 | Pg 170
  - How about Five Persons? ... GP 5:20 | Pg 170
  - Metonymy and the Holy Spirit ... GP 5:21 | Pg 171
  - Father is God; Jesus Christ is God; Holy Spirit is God ... GP 5:22 | Pg 172
    - Puzzle of the Godhead ... GP 5:22 | Pg 172
  - Time and Change Play Major Parts in the Answer ... GP 5:22 | Pg 172
- Notes for GP 5 ... GP 5:24 | Pg 174
  - John 1:1-18 ... GP 5:24 | Pg 174
    - Translation and Notes ... GP 5:24 | Pg 174

Symbolic Meaning of the Sun and Moon..................................... GP 5:28 | Pg 178
    Sun.. GP 5:29 | Pg 179
    Moon.. GP 5:29 | Pg 179
Glory of God .... GP 5:30 | Pg 180
    Great Age and Glory... GP 5:31 | Pg 181
Review of GP 5 .... GP 5:32 | Pg 182
General Review .... GP 5:32 | Pg 182

GP 6: All into Christ .... GP 6:1 | Pg 185

Mankind To Be Like Christ .... GP 6:1 | Pg 185
Christ Now Has All The Power....................................... GP 6:1 | Pg 185
All Saved .... GP 6:1 | Pg 185
Jesus Christ's Commission to Save .... GP 6:1 | Pg 185
Great Mystery – Christ Fulfills All .... GP 6:2 | Pg 186
    All in Heaven and Earth .... GP 6:2 | Pg 186
    All into the Church .... GP 6:2 | Pg 186
        Christ's Spiritual "Wife" – the Church .... GP 6:3 | Pg 187
    Great Mystery is Going into Christ .... GP 6:3 | Pg 187
    All Back Into God through Jesus .... GP 6:3 | Pg 187
NAME and the All .... GP 6:4 | Pg 188
    All Power .... GP 6:4 | Pg 188
    All Spirit .... GP 6:4 | Pg 188
    All Glory .... GP 6:4 | Pg 188
    All Name = All BeComingOne .... GP 6:5 | Pg 189
    When All .... GP 6:5 | Pg 189
Angels and Spirits .... GP 6:5 | Pg 189
    Stars and Angels .... GP 6:5 | Pg 189
Our Own Angel .... GP 6:6 | Pg 190
    Two into One .... GP 6:6 | Pg 190
        Engaged – Married Metaphor .... GP 6:7 | Pg 191
        Begotten – Born Metaphor .... GP 6:7 | Pg 191
    An Angel for Everyone .... GP 6:7 | Pg 191
        Stars and Angels .... GP 6:7 | Pg 191
    "You Are Gods"? .... GP 6:8 | Pg 192
    BeComingOne Himself the Gods (Elohim) .... GP 6:8 | Pg 192
    From One to Many .... GP 6:9 | Pg 193
Great Cycle .... GP 6:9 | Pg 193
    All out of the Father; All Back into the Father .... GP 6:9 | Pg 193
New Body, New Soul for All .... GP 6:10 | Pg 194
    Sexuality .... GP 6:10 | Pg 194
    Two Into One .... GP 6:11 | Pg 195
    No Deformities .... GP 6:11 | Pg 195
    Resurrected Young .... GP 6:11 | Pg 195

Spiritual Element.. GP 6:11 | Pg 195
    Memory of Both the Spirit and the Body............................. GP 6:11 | Pg 195
Pleasures of Both the Physical and Spiritual Dimensions................... GP 6:12 | Pg 196

GP 7: The Real Reason Why... GP 7:1 | Pg 197

To Know Good <u>and</u> Evil?.. GP 7:1 | Pg 197
Why Know Evil .... GP 7:2 | Pg 198
    Experience Teaches .... GP 7:2 | Pg 198
Know Evil To Know Good?... GP 7:2 | Pg 198
Law of Knowledge .... GP 7:3 | Pg 199
    The Law of Knowledge can be stated: .... GP 7:3 | Pg 199
    Knowledge of Opposite Qualities .... GP 7:3 | Pg 199
        Blind: Light <u>and</u> Darkness... GP 7:3 | Pg 199
            Knowledge of Each Presupposes Knowledge of Both.................. GP 7:4 | Pg 200
        Sound <u>and</u> Silence .... GP 7:4 | Pg 200
        Hot <u>and</u> Cold, Good <u>and</u> Evil.. GP 7:4 | Pg 200
        Life <u>and</u> Death.. GP 7:5 | Pg 201
        Right <u>and</u> Left & More Examples .... GP 7:5 | Pg 201
        Appreciation .... GP 7:5 | Pg 201
God Has Created Evil? .... GP 7:6 | Pg 202
        Should We Then Seek Evil? .... GP 7:6 | Pg 202
        Light Brings True Knowledge .... GP 7:6 | Pg 202
    Two Forces... GP 7:6 | Pg 202
            Sow in Tears, Reap in Joy .... GP 7:7 | Pg 203
            Light = Good; Darkness = Evil...................................... GP 7:7 | Pg 203
            Time to Love; Time to Hate... GP 7:7 | Pg 203
        Mankind in School... GP 7:7 | Pg 203
        Harmony Means Nothing without Disharmony .... GP 7:7 | Pg 203
    Time & Why Did God Do This? .... GP 7:8 | Pg 204
        What is Time?... GP 7:8 | Pg 204
        Time and Language... GP 7:8 | Pg 204
        Life, Death and Time.. GP 7:8 | Pg 204
Why Physical and Spiritual Dimensions?................................... GP 7:9 | Pg 205
    Another Reason: One-Third / Two Thirds .... GP 7:10 | Pg 206
    Complementary Knowledge.. GP 7:10 | Pg 206
        Man from Satan's Age.. GP 7:10 | Pg 206
        "Ought not Christ to have suffered these things" .... GP 7:10 | Pg 206
        Man from God's Age .... GP 7:11 | Pg 207
        Young Ones .... GP 7:11 | Pg 207
        Two-Thirds and One-Third of Mankind.............................. GP 7:11 | Pg 207
Reincarnation?.. GP 7:12 | Pg 208
Mankind From The 1000 Years... GP 7:12 | Pg 208
Not New Knowledge .... GP 7:12 | Pg 208

More Details on the General Law of Knowledge .... GP 7:15 | Pg 211
   How Children Learn... GP 7:16 | Pg 212
      The Color Green .... GP 7:16 | Pg 212
      GREEN a color is "A" .... GP 7:17 | Pg 213
      What the color green is not (non-A) .... GP 7:17 | Pg 213
   Review of GP 7... GP 7:17 | Pg 213
   General Review .... GP 7:18 | Pg 214

GP 8: Right & Left Hand of God .... GP 8:1 | Pg 217

      Paul and the Cherubs .... GP 8:1 | Pg 217
      Knowledge Not to Stay Hidden .... GP 8:1 | Pg 217
   Christ on the Right Side of The God .... GP 8:2 | Pg 218
   First and Last... GP 8:2 | Pg 218
      First... GP 8:2 | Pg 218
         First or Beginning of the Creation of the God........................ GP 8:3 | Pg 219
      Last and with the Last Ones .... GP 8:3 | Pg 219
   Christ is the BeComingOne .... GP 8:3 | Pg 219
      All Not Yet Under Him .... GP 8:3 | Pg 219
      Not Yet Complete .... GP 8:3 | Pg 219
   Other Offspring in the BeComingOne .... GP 8:4 | Pg 220
      Christ the Individual and the Spiritual Body of Christ .... GP 8:4 | Pg 220
      Many in ONE Body... GP 8:4 | Pg 220
Cherubs.. GP 8:4 | Pg 220
   In The Tabernacle .... GP 8:4 | Pg 220
   Most Holies.. GP 8:5 | Pg 221
      Sanctuary a Type of the Real .... GP 8:5 | Pg 221
      High Priest a Type of the Real .... GP 8:5 | Pg 221
   Christ: Right Cherub .... GP 8:5 | Pg 221
   Two Cherubs: One with Mercy Seat... GP 8:6 | Pg 222
   Christ The Man: Mercy Seat .... GP 8:6 | Pg 222
   Cherubs Face Each Other.. GP 8:6 | Pg 222
   Left Side of God?... GP 8:7 | Pg 223
      Left Cherub?... GP 8:7 | Pg 223
   Three Things to Understand.. GP 8:7 | Pg 223
   Missing Part of the God are the Last Ones .... GP 8:7 | Pg 223
   One Side Good; One Side Evil.. GP 8:8 | Pg 224
      Right and Left Side.. GP 8:8 | Pg 224
   Who is the Left Side of The God?.. GP 8:8 | Pg 224
      Left Cherub.. GP 8:8 | Pg 224
   Right and left Side Join to Create Knowledge................................. GP 8:9 | Pg 225
      Right and Left Hemispheres of the Brain................................. GP 8:9 | Pg 225
   Mercy Seat and Cherubs Prefigured God .... GP 8:9 | Pg 225
   Image of God.. GP 8:9 | Pg 225

Male & Female are One	GP 8:9 | Pg 225
Two in One	GP 8:9 | Pg 225
Two Opposite yet Complementary Qualities	GP 8:10 | Pg 226
From an Imperfect One	GP 8:10 | Pg 226
Christ Fulfills Image of God	GP 8:10 | Pg 226
Different Senses to the Fulfillment	GP 8:10 | Pg 226
Fulfilled within Three Days	GP 8:10 | Pg 226
Fulfillment of the Image of God in Three Orders in Three Days	GP 8:11 | Pg 227
Evil: Who Is To Blame?	GP 8:11 | Pg 227
Blame to All	GP 8:12 | Pg 228
Repentant Evil plus Good are <u>One</u> in Harmony	GP 8:12 | Pg 228
Cherubs Protecting the Garden	GP 8:12 | Pg 228
Why the Contrast Between the God of the Old Testament and the God of the New Testament	GP 8:12 | Pg 228
Satan Cast out of Man	GP 8:13 | Pg 229
God of the New Testament	GP 8:13 | Pg 229
Two in One and the Duality of Elohim	GP 8:13 | Pg 229
Following this logic, what is the *two in one* aspect of the real God?	GP 8:14 | Pg 230
Way to the Tree of Life	GP 8:14 | Pg 230
Scriptures on Satan	GP 8:15 | Pg 231
Satan Does Not Understand Now	GP 8:15 | Pg 231
Satan in Darkness	GP 8:16 | Pg 232
Review of GP 8	GP 8:16 | Pg 232

GP 9: God's Symbolic Throne – Power of God .... GP 9:1 | Pg 234

Outline of Scriptures	GP 9:2 | Pg 235
Throne's Setting	GP 9:2 | Pg 235
Biblical Description of the Four Living Creatures	GP 9:2 | Pg 235
Cherubs	GP 9:3 | Pg 236
Seraphs	GP 9:3 | Pg 236
Throne of God	GP 9:4 | Pg 237
Christ sitting on the throne	GP 9:5 | Pg 238
More Detail on the Throne	GP 9:5 | Pg 238
Putting Scripture Together	GP 9:6 | Pg 239
Throne and the Glory of God	GP 9:6 | Pg 239
Satan's Throne versus God's Throne	GP 9:6 | Pg 239
What is the Meaning of the Throne?	GP 9:6 | Pg 239
Power: All	GP 9:7 | Pg 240
Predestinated Power	GP 9:7 | Pg 240
To Review	GP 9:7 | Pg 240
Review of GP 9	GP 9:8 | Pg 241
General Review	GP 9:8 | Pg 241

GP 10: God Is .... GP 10:1 | Pg 245
    God Is Love .... GP 10:1 | Pg 245
  God, Predestination, and his Essence .... GP 10:2 | Pg 246
    God is the Creator We are the Clay .... GP 10:2 | Pg 246
      Free Will? .... GP 10:2 | Pg 246
    Paul Explained Predestination .... GP 10:2 | Pg 246
    God and Predestination .... GP 10:3 | Pg 247
    Cosmos Created out of Spirit .... GP 10:3 | Pg 247
      Ultimate Building "Blocks" .... GP 10:3 | Pg 247
    Word and Jesus Christ .... GP 10:3 | Pg 247
    Father and Jesus Christ .... GP 10:4 | Pg 248
    Evil Predestinated? .... GP 10:4 | Pg 248
    Should we then be angry with God? .... GP 10:4 | Pg 248
    Time and the God .... GP 10:4 | Pg 248
    God is Omnipresent: Everywhere .... GP 10:6 | Pg 250
    God is Omnipotent: Almighty .... GP 10:6 | Pg 250
    God is Omniscient: Knows All .... GP 10:6 | Pg 250
  Who or What is God? .... GP 10:6 | Pg 250

GP: Appendix .... GP: Appendix | Pg 252
  More Details .... GP: Appendix | Pg 252
  Hebrew Words Written Without Vowels .... GP: Appendix | Pg 252
    Is the Correct Pronunciation of the NAME Possible? .... GP: Appendix | Pg 252
  Yehowah or Yahweh or Jehovah or Lord .... GP: Appendix | Pg 253
    Spelling of the Name of God .... GP: Appendix | Pg 254
    Yehowah or Yahweh .... GP: Appendix | Pg 254
      Yehowah .... GP: Appendix | Pg 254
      Yehwah .... GP: Appendix | Pg 255
    Theory of Yahweh .... GP: Appendix | Pg 255
      Gesenius and Yahweh .... GP: Appendix | Pg 256
        Gesenius admits the spelling "Yehowah" fits the evidence .... GP: Appendix | Pg 256
        Ginsburg lists some evidence for the use of "Yehowah" .... GP: Appendix | Pg 257
    Fourth Letter in God's Name .... GP: Appendix | Pg 257
      Cohortative Verb? .... GP: Appendix | Pg 257
    God's NAME is *Emphasized* – He will be! .... GP: Appendix | Pg 258
    What is a Cohortative Verb? .... GP: Appendix | Pg 258
    Yah .... GP: Appendix | Pg 259
    Hebrew New Testament .... GP: Appendix | Pg 259
    God's NAME in Greek Text Written in Hebrew .... GP: Appendix | Pg 260
    Jehovah .... GP: Appendix | Pg 260
      Yehowah .... GP: Appendix | Pg 261
  Massoretic Text .... GP: Appendix | Pg 261

The Massoretic Text?	GP: Appendix | Pg 261
Written-Read, Kethib-Qere	GP: Appendix | Pg 262
Ben Asher V. Ben Naftali	GP: Appendix | Pg 262
Tiberian Massoretes	GP: Appendix | Pg 262
Vowel-Letters Theory	GP: Appendix | Pg 263
Children Reading the Bible	GP: Appendix | Pg 263
Josephus, Titus, Vespasian, and Severus to the Massorah	GP: Appendix | Pg 263
Massorites	GP: Appendix | Pg 264
More Language Details	GP: Appendix | Pg 264
Yehowah, Similar to Participles	GP: Appendix | Pg 264
Hebrew Participle	GP: Appendix | Pg 265
Yehowah, The Name, is a Verb	GP: Appendix | Pg 265
NAME: An Imperfect Verb	GP: Appendix | Pg 265
NAME: Imperfect Verb, Not Future Tense	GP: Appendix | Pg 266
More on "I will be"	GP: Appendix | Pg 266

Index .... Pg 267

Acknowledgment .... Pg 292

About the Author .... Pg 293

BEGINNING PAPERS

Introduction and Premises

By

Walter R. Dolen

Documentation

When you see, "The God, all in all" (1 Cor 15:28), it means that this is a quote from the New Testament letter called First Corinthians, chapter 15, verse 28. If you see "2 Cor" it would mean the *second* letter of the Corinthians. If you see "2 Cor 11:4" it would mean we quoted from the second letter of the Corinthians, the 11th chapter, and the 4th verse. But sometimes you will see a documentation such as "(1 Pet 2:4)" after a sentence that has no quotes. This kind of documentation is used in order to *support* the previous sentence or sentences, or to *point out other similar or related views* of the previous sentence or sentences, or to *add new light* to the previous sentence or sentences.

When you see reference to "PR7" it means more information can be found in *Prophecy Papers*, Part 7. When you see "GP2" this means more information can be found in the *God Papers*, part 2.

BP	= *Beginning Papers*
NM	= *New Mind Papers*
GP	= *God Papers*
PR	= *Prophecy Papers*
CP	= *Chronology Papers*
cf or cf.	= confer or compare
p. or pp.	= page or pages
w/	= with

BP1: Beginning Papers (Intro & Premises)

Bad News of Old Age

Good News of New Age

Introduction and Premises

How can there be an all good God, when there is Evil?

   bp1» Is there a God – the highest Power, the greatest good, the all powerful, the creator of the universe? Isn't God's power everywhere? Isn't God good? If God is all good, why is there evil? If we look around us it is clear that there is evil, so how can God be all powerful and good, yet allow evil? How can evil be in the universe when God is all powerful and good?

   bp2» Why, if God is good and all powerful, is there suffering? Why do innocent children suffer through no fault of their own. Why do we die? It is said that God made the angels immortal, why didn't he create us immortal? Why do we get diseases? Since he created the world, why did he place the possibility of diseases in the world? Sure, we bring on some of these things ourselves by eating poorly, using poor hygiene or by risky behavior. But what about those diseases caused by mosquitoes or microscopic germs or genetics? Didn't God create mosquitoes, germs and genetics? Didn't God create everything? Isn't God good? Or is the idea of God just some superstitious idea based on fear or naivety, an idea made obsolete by the scientific era? Are people more intelligent if they do not believe in God? Or are atheists 'fools' as the Bible relates (Psa 14:1)? An atheist or an agnostic could say, "you cannot prove there is a God" and, "we do not see anything being created or any miracles by God." While the believers could say, "you do not have any real proof of evolution – where are the billions of missing links?" Today each side would be right – no observable proof exists for either side. Today we do not see any Moses parting the seas or anyone being resurrected from the dead by God as reported in the Bible. Today we don't see any species being made nor do we see the billions of missing links being found. We see many things that are good today and in the past; we also see death, diseases and destruction all throughout history. In addition, we see the hypocrisy of those who claim to believe in God as well as those who do not believe.

Typical statement by agnostics/atheists and non-believers

bp3» Many see the negativity of religion. Mark Twain[1] was disillusioned with Christianity and religion because he only saw the paradoxes and the hell-damnation of religiosity. So he wrote the following in a book not published until after his death:

> "A God who could make good children as easily as bad, yet preferred to make bad ones; who could have made every one of them happy, yet never made a single happy one; who made them prize their bitter life, yet stingily cut it short; who gave his angels eternal happiness unearned, yet required his other children to earn it; who gave his angels painless lives, yet cursed his other children with biting miseries and maladies of mind and body; who mouths justice and invented hell – mouths mercy and invented hell – mouths Golden Rules, and forgiveness multiplied by seventy times seven, and invented hell."
> [Mark Twain, *The Mysterious Stranger*, Chap. 11]

This perception of the inexplicable paradoxes and negativity found in religion, or the emphasis upon such, is one-sided and unfair, for such negativity was superseded by Christ's teaching on the system of Love.

bp4» Jesus Christ, for whom Christianity is named, changed the way some perceived God. Unfortunately, Jesus' words were taken over by those who didn't understand and they changed Christ's teachings of forgiveness and love into those of hell and damnation. Because of this, we are forced to review in detail the doctrines of Christianity because the negativity of the world has been interjected into Christianity. This negativity projects something about man's mind in this age, which we call the "old mind" or the "other mind." But Christ announced a new mind, a new spirit, and a new commandment – the commandment of love.

God or Evolution

bp5» But wait. Doesn't the belief in God, Jesus Christ, or the Jewish Messiah depend on the reliability of the book called the Bible? Yes and no. It also depends on the belief in creation or evolution. Either God or something like evolution "created" the universe and life on the earth. The Bible has been misrepresented or even distorted by many in the name of academia. One reason for this is that academia limits itself to *natural* scientific study, not the study of the invisible-*super*natural. God being spiritual is invisible to the human eyes. But this spiritual Being is not invisible to *indirect* methodological observation. For example, the wind is invisible, but we know it is there by indirect observation – we see the effects of the wind, such as leaves and branches moving. Academia ignores the fact that many of their most famous theories use indirect methods to demonstrate the possibility of their theories. After all, the study of evolution is pre-historical. If it ever occurred, it happened before human eyes, thus before any scientific observation. There is no direct confirmation of evolution through observation, because no intelligent being was alive to observe and record it. Any

---

[1] A pen name for Samuel Clemens, one of America's best known writers

study of evolution uses indirect methods with a lot of conjectures and suppositions. Therefore indirect study pertaining to a supreme God-Being is as valid, if not more so, as the indirect study of evolution. Indirect study of the God-Being can detect God's existence by the great complexity of life (the human cell is as complex as a modern large city), by spiritual revelation, by miracles, by prophecy coming true, by intelligence built into life (DNA) and so forth.

bp6» **Evolution and the big bang?** The big bang theory, is where the universe came into existence out of a huge explosion. It assumes there was gravity, energy and matter before the big bang. This theory relies on billions of years of matter, gravity and energy randomly working together without a design, without intelligence. Intelligence and complexity from random interaction? Isn't this something like saying: if monkeys can bang on a typewriter randomly for a long enough time they can write an intelligent book? But even this example is not realistic. After all, monkeys have brains and intelligence, but evolution does not have intelligence. Evolution is more like rain drops falling on typewriter keys, with millions or billions of keys with different markings on each key, and from that an intelligent book is created. All this before there were any laws of nature, any chemical bonding, any gravity, any energy, any physical matter or molecules.

bp7» **The God choice.** Evolution is not intelligent, but merely random interaction of pre-existing matter. The other option — the God Power — must innately have intelligence and substance, be it that the "substance" is invisible to our eyes. Therefore, the God Being must have created life through its own being and essence. Who or what is this God Being? (We examine this in our *God Papers* book) From the beginning of recorded history people have believed in a higher power(s) that they called God or gods. Why did they believe this? One historical document speaks about this God Being. It's what the Jews, Christians and others call the Bible. The Bible is a complex historical document with thousands of details about God, gods, religious cults, real people, real cities, diverse cultures, kingdoms, kings, genealogy, and chronology. In the last two hundred years important confirmation of these details have been unearthed by archeology, ancient written documents, words carved on stone, and libraries containing thousands of cuneiform clay tablets. They all point out that the Bible records are real history not myth. The Moses of the Bible could write and read; his people could write and read. Some because of this evidence and other evidence believe that the Bible is the very Word of God, as I do. (See the Bible Paper)

bp8» **It is either God or evolution.** Which idea is the winner? The real winner, and proof of, is yet to come. Neither side can claim victory in a provable way that both sides will accept. That real proof for both sides is in the future. But we should ask the real difficult question: why is there anything at all? Or this question: can intelligence come from random interaction of matter (which in fact has the evidence of intelligence within it)? Or this question: can something come from nothing? The Bible says that everything came out of God, not out of nothing as some mistakenly think.

Good and Evil

bp9» **Good and Evil.** To those who believe in the Bible and even those who don't – why did God put the tree of knowledge of good and *evil* in the garden of Eden? And why after Adam and Eve took from this tree of *knowledge* did God say:

"The man has now become like one of us, knowing good *and* evil." So God has the knowledge of good and *evil* and now after the sin in the garden mankind has become like God? How can a God that is supposed to be all good, know about evil? Is there a reason and purpose for evil? Stop. Think. Both good and evil are comparative qualities. Can anyone know good without knowing evil? How can you know what is good without something to compare it to?:

> **bp10**»"There can be nothing more inept than the people who suppose that good could have existed without the existence of evil. Good and evil being antithetical, both must needs subsist in opposition, each serving, as it were, by its contrary pressure as a prop to the other. No contrary, in fact can exist, without its correlative contrary. How could there be any meaning in 'justice,' unless there were such things as wrongs? What *is* justice but the prevention of injustice? What could anyone understand by 'courage,' but the antithesis of cowardice? Or by 'continence,' but for that of self-indulgence? What room for prudence, unless there was imprudence? Why do not such men in their folly go on to ask that there should be such a thing as truth, and not such a thing as falsehood? The same may be said of good and evil, felicity and inconvenience, pleasure and pain. There things are tied, Plato puts it, each to the other, by their heads: if you take away one, you take away the other." [*Chrysippus, Fragment* 1169. On the problem of evil. Barrett, p. 64]

We cover the reason why God allowed evil in this age and all the important ideas about God in our book: *My God is the BeComingOne*. But for now let's move on to other important subjects.

Creation or evolution: who or what created the universe?

bp11» Is the universe billions and billions of years old? Or could it be that our measurement of time is based on a false foundation? Is evolution a fact, or are there thousands of holes in this theory that we are not aware of?

Two Views: Earth is old; Earth is young

Earth is Old Theory

bp12» There are two general views of history that are polarized. One is that the cosmos is old, very old, billions of years old. The other view is that the cosmos is young, very young, only thousands of years old.

bp13» Those who believe that the earth is billions of years old have various theories to "prove" that the earth is billions of years old. They speak of the Uranium to Lead method of dating, or the Thorium to Lead method of dating. They speak of bones that they say are millions of years old. When you are educated in an environment that dogmatically indicates that the earth is billions of years old it is ludicrous to believe that the earth is only thousands of years old. To believe that the earth is thousands of years old is to be uneducated or ignorant, and you are ripe for belittling by the "educated." But every belief system has it foundations. The "earth is old" system of belief is related to the "evolutionary" system of belief. Those who believe in evolution *must* have an old earth. The magic of evolution needs billions of years of "natural selection" in order to work its miracles. But all methods of dating events and materials billions, or even millions of years old, are baseless, illusionary, and arbitrary.

Foundations for the "Earth Is Old System"

(1) Theory of Evolution

bp14» **(1)** The theory of evolution is the first foundation for the "earth is old" theory. Evolution needs an old earth for its development. There are numerous works that examine the theory of evolution (see list later in the *Beginning Papers*). Because the theory of evolution needs an old earth, it found an old earth through selective perception. Any method that indicates a great age is an acceptable method for evolutionists. Any method that indicates a young earth is a rejectable method for evolutionists. Evolutionists don't even feel a need to examine other points of view. Their minds are made up. They have a mindset. Their selective perception reaffirms to them each day that evolution is correct. Thus, any method that proves an old earth is correct; any method that proves the contrary is foolishness.

(2) Radioactive Dating Methods

bp15» **(2)** The radioactive dating method is the second foundation for the "earth is old" theory. All radioactive dating methods start with a parent element which through radioactive decay turns into a daughter element. The decay rate is measured in half lives. The half life of Uranium 238 is said to be about 4.5 billion years. A unit of Uranium 238 turns into ½ lead and ½ Uranium after about 4.5 billion years. The Uranium 238 is the parent element and Lead 206 is the end or final daughter element. There are other daughter elements between Uranium 238 and Lead 206. For example, Uranium 238 first decays into the daughter element Thorium 234 after about 4.5 billion years, and then after about 25 days turns into Protactinium 234, then after 1 minute turns into Uranium 234, then after 300,000 years turns into Thorium 230, then after 80,000 years turns into Radium 226, then after 1600 years turns into Radon 222, then after 4 days turns into Polonium 218, and continues its decay until it reaches Lead 206. (Krauskopf and Beiser, *Fundamentals of Physical Science*, 5th Ed., p. 252, see p. 562)

bp16» If the rate of decay is constant, then we have a clock in which to tell time, **if, and only if**, we know the ratio of Uranium 238 in the earth compared to Lead when the earth was formed/created, either by God or by the magical evolution. Because the decay rate of Uranium 238 is so slow compared to the decay rates of other elements in the series only the amount of the end daughter, Lead 206, is considered when ascertaining the age of the rock. The earth is believed to be about 5 billion years old according to evolutionists. But, of course, 5 billion years ago there was no man to observe the ratio of Uranium in the rocks compared to Lead. It is nothing but guesswork and nothing else when someone arbitrarily says that at the beginning there was such and such ratio of Uranium as compared to Lead. Guesswork is not scientific work.

Constant Decay Rates?

bp17» Furthermore it was believed at first that these decay rates were constant.

"Radioactivity was discovered by Becquerel in 1896. In 1906, Millikan stated, 'Radioactivity has been found to be independent of all physical as well as chemical conditions. The lowest cold or greatest heat does not appear to affect it in the least. Radioactivity seems to be as unalterable a property of the atoms of radioactive substances, as is weight itself.' This state of mind established the modern view, which is quite generally held today.... The electroscope and spinthariscope were used in early study of radioactive alpha-decay rates. The inherent limitations of these early instruments led to erroneous conclusions:

- That radioactive decay rates are constant.
- That these rates cannot be altered by change of the energy state of the electrons orbiting the nucleus.
- That radioactivity results from processes which involve only the atomic nucleus.

Refinements in electronics resulted in the development of sophisticated counting apparatus. The equipment was used in the demonstration by several investigators (1949-73) of rather easily induced changes in the disintegration rates of 14 radionuclides, including ^{14}C, ^{60}Co, and ^{137}Cs. **The observed variations in the decay rates, (changes in the half life) were produced by changes in pressure, temperature, chemical state, electric potential stress of monomolecular layers, etc. ... The decay 'constant' is now considered to be a variable.**" [H.C. Dudley, "Is There Ether?,"*Industrial Research*, Nov 15, 1974, p. 42; my emphasis]

bp18» Even a small amount of variation in the decay rate can make a big difference in the assumed age of the rock:

> "Measurement of nuclear disintegration parameters has been done for about fifty years. To my knowledge no major research effort has been mounted to determine whether nuclear decay parameters vary at all with time [he is speaking of time not pressure, chemical state, etc]. Once values of the decay index for a particular nuclide are obtained and a particular value is agreed upon, this value is generally accepted. Usually no further measurements are taken....
>
> If a small amount of exponential variation occurs in the nuclear decay index, then the half lives of the radiometric nuclides are drastically reduced — orders of magnitude. In the case of U 238 the half life is reduced by a factor of 10^5" (Theodore W. Rybka, *ICR Impact Series* No. 106)

Decay Rates not Constant

bp19» As we see above temperature, pressure, chemical state, and other factors do change the decay rate of radioactive elements, and this drastically changes the so-called clock of radioactivity. Atomic clocks even seem to change their rates of decay by the direction in which they travel in an airplane. Those going westward gained time; those going eastward lost time (Hafele, Keating, 1972, "Around-the-world atomic clocks," *Science* 177 [4044]).

Radiohalos

bp20» Robert V. Gentry's work on radiohalos has cast a shadow on the premise that the decay rates are constant. "Radiohalos" are microscopic, ring-like discolorations caused by radioactivity in certain minerals. Early work seemed to indicate that the radiohalos exhibited dimensions predictable on the basis of modern decay rates. But Gentry who worked at the Chemistry Division of the Oak Ridge National Laboratory in the 1960's "set out to review previous work on the subject, then began his own painstaking study of thousands of halos in rocks from around the world. Almost immediately he found that all was not in order in this long neglected field. Gentry discovered that, although uranium halos, for example, are readily identifiable by the number and relative rough diameters of their rings, their actual dimensions often vary substantially, even within a single crystal" (Ralph E. Juergens, "Radiohalos and Earth History," *Kronos*, III:1, pp 7 ff; read article, and Gentry's articles noted in footnotes). Gentry has shown that the "halos furnish no proof that [the decay constant] is constant" (Gentry, *Science*, April 5, 1974, pp 62-66; Also see Don B. De Young, "The Precision of Nuclear Decay Rates," CRSQ, Vol. 13, No 1 [1976]; and John Lynde Anderson and George W. Spangler, "Radiometric Dating: Is the 'Decay Constant' Constant?," *Pensee*, Vol 4 No. 4 [1974]; *Scientific Creationism*, 2nd Ed., 1985, Chapter VI; Andrew A. Snelling, *Earth's Catastrophic Past: Geology, Creation & the Flood*, Vol 2, chapters 104,111, etc.; and other works).

Dubious Premises

bp21» Evolutionists use the elements with the slowest rates of decay to measure the age of the earth, and they use the highest ratio of the parent element to daughter element at the time of formation/creation in order to give a high age. Remember there were no human observations made at formation/creation to help establish the correct ratio. The ratio may have been low. Thus, even if the Uranium-Lead method is correct, the earth is still young since there was a low ratio at first.

bp22» Also there are other elements that decay at much higher rates. At the far extreme from Uranium 238 is Astatine 216 with a half-life less than a second as is Polonium 214. Why didn't they choose a faster decaying element to clock the earth's age? It is because they assumed a great age for the earth, therefore they arbitrarily chose an element with a slow decay rate along with a high parent to daughter radio instead of a low parent to daughter ratio, so as to self-fulfill their view.

Different Methods of Dating Don't Agree

bp23» There is also the problem of variation of the ages arrived at by using various elements and methods to date the earth. One system of dating gives one date, another gives a contradictory date. Or one set of rocks gives one age, while another set of rocks gives a different age for the earth. What does the believer in the "earth is old" theory do? With the Carbon 14 dating method (C14) they merely pick the result they wanted to begin with, "If a C14 date supports our theories, we put it in the main text. If it does not entirely contradict them, we put it in a footnote. And if it is completely 'out of date,' we just drop it" (T. Save-Soderbergh, "Carbon 14 and Egyptian Chronology," *Nobel Symposium 12 Radiocarbon Variations and Absolute Chronology*, Stockholm, Almquist and Wikwell, p. 35; quotes from R.D. Long, CRSQ, Vol 10, No 1, p. 19; *Science, Scripture, and the Yound Earth*, 1989 Edition, pp.42ff; Andrew A. Snelling, *Earth's Catastrophic Past: Geology, Creation & the Flood*, Vol 2, chapters 104,111 ,etc). This is the way some quote the Bible. If a verse agrees with a belief it is quoted, if not it is ignored. And this is like the "identification game" used in astronomical retro-calculations (see CP2).

(3) Great Distances in Space

bp24» **(3)** Great distances in space is the third foundation for the "earth is old" theory. The "earth is old" group believes in such things as the "big-bang" theory. (Although lately there have been articles critical of this theory.) All matter came from a big explosion and has been spreading out ever since. Since the earth to them *must* be billions of years old, then the matter in the universe has been traveling after the explosion for billions of years. Matter has spread out great distances since the beginning; the larger the universe, the older the universe. Thus they look for methods that "prove" great distances in space. Of course they have come up with methods for great distance and have rejected any method or theory that may show a small universe or young universe. They use the red-shift method of dating, which is partly based on Einstein's relativity theories. But others have shown the shaky foundation of this red-shift method as well as the unstable foundation of the special theory of relativity and consequently the general theory of relativity (See *Science Papers*; Field, Arp, and Bahcall, *Red-Shift Controversy*,1973; Herbert Dingle, *Science at the Crossroads*, 1972; Walter R. Dolen, *Einstein: Light, Time and Relativity*; etc.).

Foundation for the "Earth is Young System"

(1) No Scientific Evidence For Evolution

bp25» The first foundation for the "earth is young" theory is the lack of real evidence that the earth is old. There is sound evidence against the red-shift method for ascertaining distances in space, against radioactive dating methods, and all other methods of dating the earth as old (see my *Science Papers*; Jeremy Rifkin, *Algeny*, 1983; Field, Arp, and Bahcall, *Red-Shift Controversy*, 1973; John C. Whitcomb and Henry M. Morris, *The Genesis Flood*, 1961; etc.).

(2) Proof that the Earth is Young

bp26» The second foundation for the "earth is young" theory are the *many* methods that prove the earth is young. They are at least 76 methods that prove the earth can not be older than 500 million years and of these 24 indicate that the earth is no older than 20,000 years. These methods include such things as the influx of titanium, or cobalt, or zinc, or mercury, or silver, or copper, or gold, or silicon, or nickel into ocean via rivers. If the earth was billions of years old, the ocean would be a soup of pollution without any life in it. And such methods as the influx of meteoritic dust from space, or development of total human population, or lack of vast amounts of ancient cultural debris, the decay of the earth's magnetic field, the decay of C-14 in pre-Cambrian wood, the growth of active coral reefs, the formation of river deltas, decay of short-period comets, and the instability of rings of Saturn show a young earth. These 76 methods are based on the assumption that there were constant rates, no initial daughter components, and all were in a closed system. These methods lead to an even younger age for the earth if, for example, there were some initial daughter components at the beginning (see *Scientific Creationism*, 2nd Ed., Chapter VI; Harold S. Slusher, *Age of the Cosmos*; Henry M. & John D. Morris, *Science, Scripture, and the Young Earth*, 1989 Edition, Chapter 8; Henry M. Morris, "The Young Earth," *ICR Impact Series*, No. 17).

(3) Biblical Chronology

bp27» The third foundation of the "earth is young" theory is the belief in the Biblical chronology, or in creation without mixing the theory of evolution into the picture. And this in turn is based on the proof that the Bible is a sound document, more sound than any other ancient document ("Bible Paper" [BP3]). And this in turn is the belief in a powerful God, not a belief in a powerless and mystical god or the false belief in the magical evolution.

Your Mindset Limits You

bp28» What system you believe in depends on your belief, your research on *both* belief systems, your biases, your world view, and your mindset (perceptual set). The more you research different points of view, the more you see that the world sees through filters that color its perception of reality. To the Evolutionist the world is old. To the Creationists the world is young. It is difficult for either group to prove their case to the other group. Since the only witness to the Beginning (Creation) was either the powerful God or the magic of Evolution, it is only through inductive thinking that we can come to a conclusion. We must piece evidence upon evidence. But for most of us our "mindset" or "world view" interferes with our judgment. We see what we want to see and subconsciously disregard what we do not want to see.

Earth is Fragile; Life in Danger
Who can save it?

bp29» We live on the planet earth which teems with life. The Earth is like a jewel in a desert, for as far as we can look into the universe we see no other life forms. The Earth may in fact be unique in the universe. Yet we are in danger, we are in jeopardy. Life is fragile, amazing, unique, exciting, but sometimes painful. We love life; we sometimes hate it. What is life? Where did it come from? Did it appear through evolution that took billions and billions of years? Or did it suddenly appear? How much proof is there for billions and billions of years of evolution?

bp30» Whether you believe in evolution or creation, we can agree that life is very important. In fact, it is everything. Without life we would know nothing, we would have nothing, we would be nothing.

bp31» But all is not well. There is much danger. It is now possible for mankind to destroy all life on earth, and with it all life in the universe, at least all known life. Atomic weapons, biological weapons, artificial bio-lab creations, and war can now destroy life, even all physical life on earth . This is very important. At no other time has it been possible for mankind to destroy all life on the Earth. We live at the crossroads of mankind. You and I must do all we can to preserve life. But further, you and I must decide if there is more to life than it being a mere chance occurrence. Is there meaning to life? Is there a purpose to life? We believe that there is good news coming. There is purpose and meaning to life. But why is there so much misery, suffering and pain? Before we look at the good news, we will examine some of the bad things.

Bad News
Magnetic Fields, Their Disintegration

bp32» It basically doesn't matter if life is billions of years old or thousands of years old. Life will end on this earth before the year 3900 AD. There is nothing you or I can do about this. I know most of you have not heard of this. Let me quickly explain. There is a magnetic field that protects the earth from harmful solar radiation. If there were not this magnetic field, life on earth would be destroyed by the harmful solar wind and cosmic rays.

> "Perhaps the most drastic impact would come from solar cosmic rays, ultra high energy protons spewed from the Sun during periodic, gigantic eruptions known as solar flares.... Today, Earth's magnetic field deflects the vast majority of these destructive particles.... During a magnetic decline, the onslaught of solar flare particles would be more global, with potentially fatal

consequences for terrestrial organisms" (p. 15, *Frontiers of Time*, Time-Life Books, 1991).

But the magnetic field is decaying in strength. About each 1400 years the magnetic field loses half its strength. A 1967 US government publication concludes that the magnetic field "will vanish in A.D. 3991" (McDonald, Keith L. and Robert H. Gunst. July, 1967. "An analysis of the earth's magnetic field from 1835 to 1965," ESSA Techical Rept. IER 46-IES 1. U.S. Government Printing Office, Washington, D.C., p. 1.). This report was based on a linear decay rate not a more likely exponential decay rate. Even an exponential decay rate would leave the earth with a weak and worthless magnetic field by the year 4000 AD. But far before this, by the year 3000 AD, the earth will be suffering from the effects of increased solar radiation and its consequential mutations.

bp33» "The magnetic field is decaying at a rate of 32 gamma per year at the magnetic poles, 16 gamma per year at the magnetic equator, and at intermediate rates everywhere in between the equator and the poles" (p. 43, *Origin and Destiny of the Earth's Magnetic Field*, by Thomas G. Barnes, D. Sc., 1973).

Atomic Inferno

bp34» There are about 10 thousand atomic weapons on earth today. Most of these can destroy a city. Already two of these weapons have been used against the cities of Hiroshima and Nagasaki in Japan during World War II. They were small weapons compared to today's huge atomic weapons. Today there are atomic bombs 100 to 1000 times larger in power. They can be launched in missiles that can hit cities anywhere in the world in less than half an hour. At no time in history has such destructive power existed. One of today's air bombers has more destructive power than all the armies of the Roman Empire. The great nations of yesterday were weaklings compared to today's nations. Their power was pathetic compared to today's atomic-equipped countries. The USSR's (Russia's) Typhoon nuclear submarine (or newer Borei-class) is said to be able to obliterate any country within 5,000 miles of its position in the ocean. The United States of America also has its nuclear submarines that can do the same thing. The USSR (Russia) and the United States *each* have atomic bombs in their submarines' ballistic missiles equal to 1.4 billion tons of power. It only takes one small atomic weapon to completely destroy a city of 250,000. The city of Hiroshima in Japan was destroyed by a 20-kiloton bomb in 1945. This means that the total nuclear power in the submarines of Russia and the United States' can destroy 140,000 cities of 250,000 people.

bp35» Because of these weapons' frightening destructive power, we try to ignore these weapons, but we must be on guard. The whole earth and maybe life itself is in danger. Today you hear about the theory of the "nuclear winter," which, according to some, may be an effect of an atomic war. But a more threatening and immediate event could occur. Most have not read or even heard of this great danger since the 1950s, not because it can't happen, but because of the head-in-the-sand mentality of humans. Some of today's larger weapons exploded together could conceivably ignite the atmosphere and destroy mankind by burning all of us alive. Horace C. Dudley, a former Professor of Radiation Physics at the University of Illinois Medical Center, wrote in 1975 the book, *The Morality of Nuclear Planning?*, wherein he wrote:

> "During WWII the eminent scientists of that era offered two options to President Roosevelt. These were in effect: Accept the possible slavery of the Nazi Axis or develop and explode atomic bombs.
>
> There was a third option that was kept under wraps, *TOP SECRET*, discussed only behind closed doors, although sometimes guardedly by the lower echelons of 'The Manhattan Project.' This was the possibility of triggering a vast nuclear accident when and if a fission device was detonated" (Dudley p.29).

bp36» Dudley quotes Pearl S. Buck from the *American Weekly* (March 8, 1959) who then wrote:

> "And if hydrogen, what about the hydrogen in sea water? Might not the explosion of the atomic bomb set off an explosion of the ocean itself? Nor was this all that Oppenheimer feared. The nitrogen in the air is also unstable, though less in degree. Might not it too, be set off by an atomic explosion in the atmosphere?
>
> 'The earth would be vaporized?,' I said [Pearl S. Buck questioned]. 'Exactly,' Compton said, and with what gravity! 'It would be the ultimate catastrophe.... If, after calculation, he said, it were proved that the chances were more than approximately three to one million that the earth would be vaporized by the atomic explosion, he would not proceed with the project. Calculation proved the figures *slightly* less — and the project continued" (Dudley p. 29). [Compton here is the Nobel Prize winner Arthur H. Compton]
>
> "What if Oppenheimer, Fermi, Compton *et al.* were right in 1945, and the odds were 3 to one million of a world-wide conflagration? But now the bombs are a thousand times as powerful. Does this lower the odds to 3,000 per one million or properly 3 in 1,000" (Dudley p. 29).

bp37» At the time the first Atomic Bomb was scheduled to go off in New Mexico, S. Groueff writes in *Manhattan Project*, p. 352:

> "There were altogether too many excited people around giving him [Oppenheimer] advice on what he should do. Groves was annoyed, too, with Fermi, who was making bets with his colleagues on whether the bomb would ignite the atmosphere, and if so, whether it would destroy only New Mexico — or the entire world" (quoted by Dudley, p. 30).

bp38» At the end of the 1989 movie called *Fat Man And Little Boy*, just before the atomic device was exploded, the betting about whether the bomb would ignite the atmosphere and destroy New Mexico or the whole world is also mentioned.

bp39» A nuclear winter would be bad enough, but an immediate worldwide inferno would be even more dreadful, and it would be permanent. Life would end on earth. One mad leader could ignite such a war. Scientists do not know how many atomic bombs it would take to ignite the atmosphere, if exploded together. There is a new branch of science called the science of Chaos (James Gleick, *Chaos: Making a New Science*, 1987). The science of Chaos manifests that it may be impossible to predict how huge an atomic explosion would be needed to ignite the atmosphere. Past calculations are obsolete and hampered by naive linear thinking. Enough atomic bombs exploded together may be equivalent to the needle that broke the camel's back. There is a limit to the amount of intense heat that can be applied to the atmosphere before it will ignite and burn up. It may only take a few large explosions in a certain limited area before the atmosphere will ignite. We must not let this happen. But sometimes events take on a life of their own outside of common sense.

Biological Catastrophe

bp40» In the San Francisco Bay Area there are biogenetic laboratories creating new biological forms. It is no leap of imagination to think of new biogenetic materials being created that could exponentially spread throughout the earth and destroy it. There are also biological weapons being created. It may take only one terrorist or one careless laboratory mistake before a dangerous biological form escapes into the environment.

> "Lately, concerns have grown about the potential ecological, social and economic effects of world commerce in engineered seeds, organisms and biotech products.... Some fear that engineered microbes or plants will disrupt local ecologies and undermine traditional farming practices. Others have focused on perceived, albeit unproven, health threats from eating genetically engineered grains or cereals" (*Washington Post*, Feb 14, 1999).

Old Age and its Purpose

bp41» We live in the old age. Not all in this old age is as bad as some of the worst news stories depict, but there is enough of it to make life a bitter pill in many ways. It's an age with a purpose that very few understand. Yes, we believe it does have a purpose. Once it has served it purpose, the old age will end. The purpose and meaning in this age and our life in it, is to obtain the knowledge of good and evil, the understanding of life and death, the appreciation of time and eternity. Everlasting life with no evil would mean nothing if we didn't know its opposite. Actually, what the supreme Being is doing is creating happiness because we will truly understand what happiness is by living in an evil age with confusion, death, disease, war and futility. The Old Age will have a great and rightly deserved end. The *BeComingOne Papers* examines the old age's confusion, its source of confusion, and the coming New Age promised by a spiritual Being we call God.

New Age

bp42» There is good news, and lots of it. Irrespective of the world around you today, the universe is BeComingOne. You and I, our best friends and our worst enemies, are headed towards one goal. That one goal is BeComingOne. We are now in the age of confusion and hate, but a New Age is coming wherein we will all live together in harmony. There is a reason for the present age. The confusion isn't futile, even though it may seem so. You and I aren't perfect now, but we will be. Time is headed towards a goal. The goal is harmony. The goal is BeComingOne.

bp43» This is the "Introduction Paper" [BP1] of The *BeComingOne Papers*. In these papers we seek the answers to the mysteries of life and the answers to the contradictions of religion and science. Yes, we know there are many others who have promised you answers, but how many of them really delivered the answers to you? I have been promised answers to life many times myself, but I have been repeatedly dissatisfied with the answers. Why evil? Is there a God? Who or what is God? Why death? Why pain? Does science have the answers? Does religion have the answers? Does a combination of both have the answer? How can God be good and all powerful, and yet allow evil? Who am I? Where am I going? What is it all about? Is life really meaningless as some say, or is there meaning? What about after death? The *BeComingOne Papers* does its best to answer these questions. The answers make sense even though they are different from traditional answers. Traditional answers have too much mystery and contradiction in them. We do away with mystery and contradictions against the law of contradiction.

bp44» This old age is full of opinion. Everyone seems to have their own opinion on what is and what is not evil. Many call actions evil when in fact the only evil is in the eyes of the beholder. Many call actions right when in fact they are destructive. There are many opinions on what is a good man, a good Christian, a good Islamic, a good agnostic, or a good.... There are so many opinions on who or what is God, or even if there is a God. In other words, in this old age there is much confusion. And with this confusion there is disillusion, cynicism, hate, jealousy, conceit, false-knowledge, and the rest.

bp45» Too many have cried "truth, truth." Too many have wrongly followed. But the truth will stand or fall on its own. There is a goal in the universe: **the universe will Become One**. You won't do it, nor can you prevent it; I can't do it, nor can I prevent it. All will Become One. But, how will all become ONE?

BP1: Review

bp46» Misguided leadership, depraved behavior, murder in its many forms, perceptual blindness, and all other forms of impersonal and dysfunctional behavior happen in one form or other throughout the world in each nation and in all cultures. Everyday throughout the world some husbands physically beat their wives, and wives verbally beat their husbands. Everyday parents, some drunk on wine or drugs, beat their children physically or mentally, and children defy their parents. Everyday some employers mistreat their workers, and workers defraud their employers. Everyday some form of natural catastrophe happens. And maybe even worst of all small children suffer and die each day. There is one word in the English language to describe the aforementioned behavior: *evil*. Contrary to what some say there is evil in the world. This is not to say that all or most of the world's behavior is evil or wrong, but that there is too much wrong behavior. Why? And what about natural catastrophes? And why do young children get sick, get mistreated, and even are killed? Did they do something wrong? Or, if there is a God, and if he is good, and if he is all powerful, then, yes, why do children have to suffer? Why does anyone have to suffer? (1) Is there something behind the world's wrong behavior and is there a reason and a purpose for this behavior? (2) Do natural catastrophes and even the sickness and death of young children also have their purpose? There is a reason for the old age. There is a reason for evil. There is evidence against evolution. There is evidence for a powerful God Being. There is a reason for evil and confusion. Good and evil are opposite qualities that need each other to understand either quality. And thus, the reason for evil is to gain knowledge of good and thus be able to perceive and enjoy the good. What is realy happening is that God is creating happiness. The books belonging to the *Becoming-One Papers* will explore and expain these things. Do read on.

BP2: Mindset Paper

Ptolemy's Theory

Brain Cell Problem

bp47» We are born into a world of traditions. The traditions that we are born into have sets of rules, written and non-written. We are taught or influenced by our parents, teachers, environment, mind(s), the language(s) we speak, and our biology to believe in certain things and act in certain ways. From this we form a belief system, or mindset. A "mindset" is a perceptual set and through this set we perceive the world. A mindset acts like a filter. It filters out any mental conceptions or realities that do not fit our mindset.

A person who strongly believes that victimizers are victims themselves, does not see the crime a victimizer commits in the same way as one who believes that everyone is totally at fault for their crimes, or the way the victim sees the crime, or in the way that I do.

bp48» A person who does not know anything about the game of baseball who overhears someone talking about Smith stealing second base, may think that Smith committed a crime.

bp49» As our knowledge and background filters our perception of the words, "Smith stole second base," so too with almost everything else. Words have different meaning to different people. The word "liberal" means something different to a liberal than to a conservative. The word "communist" means something different to a communist than to a capitalist. The word "Catholic" means something different to a Catholic than to a Protestant. The word "evolution" means something different to an evolutionist than to a creationist. A peaceful countryside, where a nuclear plant is planned, means something different to environmentalists than to the owner or builder of the nuclear plant.

Ptolemy's Mathematical-Geocentric Theory

bp50» One of the biggest examples of a mindset was the geocentric theory in which the earth was the center of the universe. The geocentric theory is the idea that the earth is the center of the universe while the sun, moon, planets, and stars made a complete revolution around the earth each day. This theory was represented well by Claudius Ptolemy. Claudius Ptolemy's work commonly known as the *Almagest* was actually called "Mathematical Systematic Treatise" in the Greek version because it was a mathematical system. Ptolemy believed that mathematics was the highest form of science:

> "that only mathematics can provide sure and unshakeable knowledge to its devotees, provided one approaches it rigorously. For its kind of proof proceeds by indisputable methods, namely arithmetic and geometry" (G.J. Toomer, *Ptolemy's Almagest*, [1984] p 36).

bp51» Today the public makes light of the *Almagest* by thinking of it as some naive theological or church backed doctrine. But instead it was the most scientific work of its day containing abundant mathematical proof with tables and charts, with premises from Greek philosophy, not church doctrine. "One of the most influential scientific works in history, and a masterpiece of technical exposition in its own right" (G.J. Toomer, p. vii). Yes, today the geocentric theory seems preposterous, since after all, we know that the earth is not the center of the universe, and in fact that the earth makes one revolution around the sun each year. We believe this even though it *appears* (empirical evidence) from our eyesight that the sun, planets, and stars revolve around the earth each day.

Ptolemy and his Treatise

bp52» "His name was Claudius Ptolemaeus ... he lived from approximately A.D. 100 to approximately A.D. 175, and that he worked in Alexandria, the principal city of Greco-Roman Egypt, which possessed, among other advantages, what was probably still the best library in the ancient world. ... As is implied by its Greek name, ... , 'mathematical systematic treatise,' the Almagest is a complete exposition of mathematical astronomy as the Greeks understood the term" (Toomer, p. 1). By the "fourth century (and probably much earlier), when Pappus wrote a commentary on it, the Almagest had become the standard textbook on astronomy which it was to remain for more than a thousand years.... It was dominant to an extent and for a length of time which is unsurpassed by any scientific work except Euclid's *Elements*.... " (Toomer p. 2-3)

bp53» "Then, in the second century A.D., came Claudius Ptolemaeus, an Egyptian -- the great Ptolemy who was to be the uncontested monarch of astronomy for a millennium and a half. He restored the harmonious cosmos Hipparchus had shattered. Ptolemy was a theoretician of such superior qualities that only Newton can be considered his peer. A universal mind, he perfected Greek mathematics and Greek natural science in general. His achievement appears all the more impressive when we compare it with the ordinary science of his time, which was hopelessly bogged down in speculation.

bp54» "Ptolemy called his principal work on astronomy the Great System (*Megale Syntaxis tes Astronomias*, later known as *Almagest* from the Arabic translation). This somewhat arrogant title was fully justified, for he had examined every problem in astronomy, and solved every one with Euclidean precision. Ptolemy created the first complete scientific system — a structure so vast and coherent that not even the comprehensive mind of an Aristotle could have conceived it, let alone worked it out.

bp55» "Toward the solution of the chief problem, the apparently irregular velocities of the planets, he made a crucial discovery. Ptolemy drew an overlapping circle near Apollonius' circle.... The second circles came to be known as Ptolemy's epicycles. From the center of the epicycle the motion around Apollonius' eccentric circle appeared to be uniform. The system was extremely complicated, but it worked; Ptolemy could use it to calculate any future position of Mars... Ptolemy could justly boast that he had laid the keystone of Greek astronomy.... Mathematically speaking, this was true; henceforth, everything was calculable.... The planets now traveled in loops, that is to say, around an imaginary point that for unknown reasons itself revolved around the Earth....

bp56» "A man named Kepler, fifteen hundred years after Ptolemy, at last was

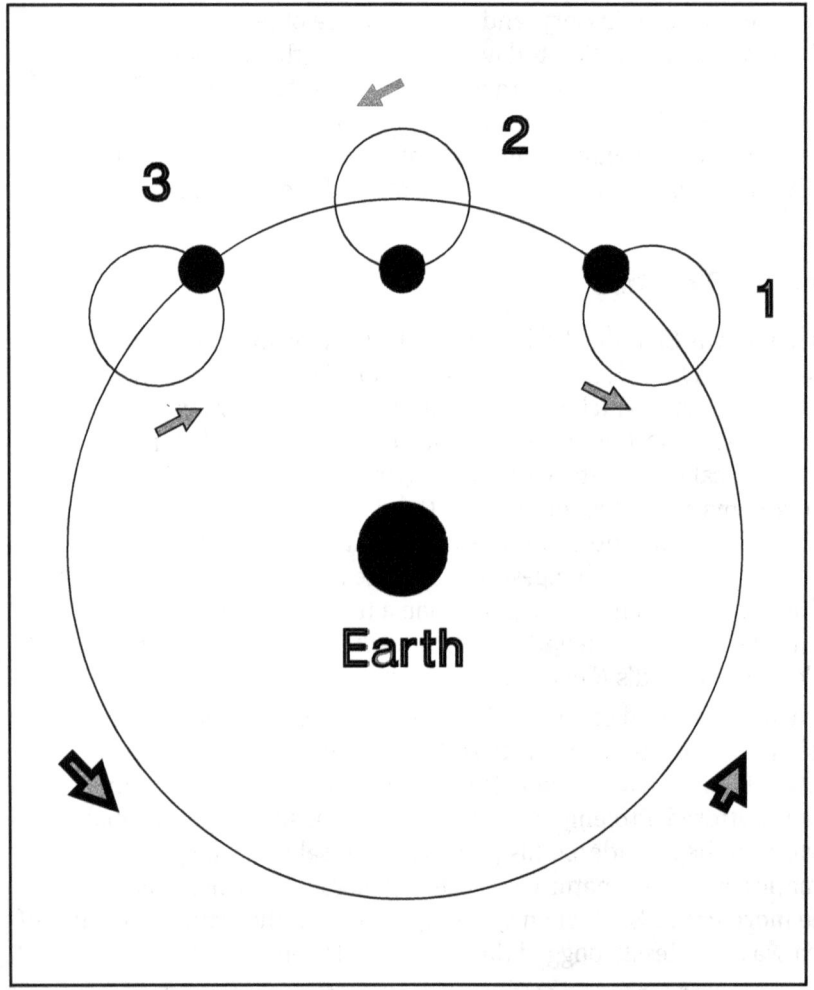

able to refute the last word of Greek astronomy, and overcome the mathematical sovereignty of nonsense by even more exact mathematics, which once more made everything meaningful" (Rudolf Thiel, *And There was Light*, trans. by Richard and Clara Winston, pp. 49-51).

bp57» Ptolemy's system had the earth as the center with the stars, moon, planets, and even the sun circling the earth each day. Ptolemy used the wrong and illusionary concept of epicycles to explain the apparent movement of the planets in the night. He further used mathematics to predict the future movement of planets. His system worked to a remarkable degree. It had a mathematical system to back it up. His book was well written and seemed quite logical. After all even today the planet, sun, moon, and stars do *apparently* circle the earth. Ptolemy system made sense out of wandering stars (planets). It predicted future positions of planets. It was the great system. It lasted for almost 1500 years. Apparently it was the perfect system. It was backed by mathematics. It was apparently backed by observation. But it was wrong. How wrong can you be to think that the massive sun circles the earth *each* day? But because of the prevailing mindset Ptolemy remained king. A mindset can be very compelling. It rules all. Since 1984 English readers have been able to read Ptolemy's work, as translated by G.J. Toomer, *Ptolemy's Almagest*. In this translation you can see the apparent logic to the whole work. You can see the massive amount of tables, observations, and mathematics to back Ptolemy's theory.

bp58» How can a work so logical, based on so many observations, and backed up by mathematics be wrong? It was wrong because it was based on some faulty thinking (the enormous sun going around the smaller earth would have to move at an unbelievable rate), because Ptolemy was a charlatan that cheated on his mathematical figures and cheated on his observations (Newton, *The Crime of Claudius Ptolemy*), and because he had a mindset that told him that all heavenly objects were perfect and god-like, they moved in perfect circles, he thus placed epicycles into his system:

> "The heaven is spherical in shape, and moves as a sphere; the earth too is sensibly spherical in shape ... in position it lies in the middle of the heavens very much like its center.... [Toomer, p.38] The following considerations also lead us to the concept of the sphericity of the heavens....[p. 39] We think that the mathematician's task and goal ought to be to show all the heavenly phenomena being reproduced by uniform circular motions.." (Toomer, p. 140).

Ptolemy got his mindset about the orbits having to be perfect circular orbits from the Greeks such as Aristotle:

> "There must be some substance which is eternal and immutable.... But motion cannot be either generated or destroyed, for it always existed.... But there is no continuous motion except that which is spatial, and of spatial motion only that which is circular... There are other spatial motions – those of the planets – which are eternal (because a body which moves in a circle is eternal...).... for the nature of the heavenly bodies is eternal (Aristotle, *Metaphysics* Book XII [Loeb Classical Lib. No. 287], pp. 141 & 155).

Ptolemy was so overly influenced by the Grecian philosophy that he fabricated a mathematical system to help prove his preposterous belief: "We think that the mathematician's task and goal ought to be to show all the heavenly phenomena being reproduced by uniform circular motions.." (Toomer, p. 140).

bp59» Today math is used extensively to prove likewise absurd theories. (See my book, *Einstein: Light, Time & Relativity*) They do not appear preposterous to most today only because of today's mindsets which filter reality. Mathematics are wrongly used today in this so-called scientific age. Today mathematics are blinding otherwise intelligent people into believing in absolutely paradoxical and nonsensical theories on the cosmos, physics, and biology. Today much of what is called science exists inside of a mindset that shuts out the truth.

Mindset, A Brain Cell Problem

bp60» The main problem with a mindset occurs when you try to communicate with someone with a different mindset. Sometimes it is almost impossible. A Catholic trying to convert a Protestant has a terrible time trying to communicate his point of view, and vice versa. Many times even trying to communicate your different point of view will be met with a harsh reaction and sometimes even a violent reaction. Why?

bp61» One book tried to explain this. Daniel Cohen, in a 1982 book, called *Re:Thinking*, put it this way:

> "Once a pattern — an idea or belief — becomes fixed in our neurological pathways, it is extremely hard to alter it. The more basic the belief, the more we refer to it in our thoughts, the more well worn is that particular neural pathway — and thus the harder it is to change the idea, even when it is wrong" (p. 70).

> "Our memories and beliefs are stored in our brains in the form of nerve cell patterns. When you argue with someone you are pitting your nerve cell patterns against his. The beliefs and opinions you hold are not the result of some abstract intellectual process. They are the result of your total life experience. But your opponent's beliefs and opinions are the same. For both of you, changing these deeply held beliefs is hard and painful.

> Since we all want to avoid pain, we all want to avoid changing these beliefs and opinions. The mind will work very hard to defend them.

> If an argument isn't a means of persuading people, what is it? It's a fight, an attack, and you react to it as such" (p. 118).

bp62» With our mindset we see only what our mindset allows us to see. It acts like a filter and filters out any pattern not belonging to the sets of rules we have etched in our brain cells.

BP3: Bible Paper

Typical Criticism

Three Tests to Give

bp63» The *BeComingOne Papers* uses the Bible. Now to some the Bible is a book full of tales that isn't worth the paper it is written on. But this is a very biased, unfair and incorrect view. It is a view of a mindset. Like other mindsets it is imbedded in brain cells, thus, making it very difficult to change. Just as Ptolemy's geocentric theory of the universe seemed to be very sound to the generations of the past (see "Mindset Paper" [BP2]), today's myths and mistaken theories seem scientific to today's generation. Just because those of Ptolemy's generations believed in his theory, doesn't mean they were less intelligent. Many were quite smart, but nevertheless quite wrong. Irrespective of today's mindsets and biases concerning the Bible, it is a very worthwhile book.

bp64» The Bible is a historical document. Its history goes back to the beginning of mankind. It is an accurate document. Especially in the last hundred and eighty years, archeology has repeatedly confirmed facts recorded in the Bible that previously had no other confirmation. In comparison to other ancient writings, the Bible is by far, let me repeat, the Bible is by far the most accurate historical document in the world, especially considering the volume of words in the Bible.

bp65» The Bible is filled with specific place names, proper names, topographical descriptions, descriptions of ancient customs and nations, descriptions of ancient artifacts, temples, religions, and human behavior. Until the last 180 years the cynics used to call many of the nations, cultures, and customs described in the Bible myth, or just oral traditions that have lost their truth. But archaeological finds have made a mockery out of such outdated skepticism. Mythical books do not have the abundance of specific information as does the Bible. Details after details are abundant throughout the Bible. Today it is ludicrous to call the Bible anything but an accurate historical document. Yet, as a mindset filters a person's perception so does the mindset of anti-Biblical scholars. It is amazing to me how they can ignore the archaeological finds of the last 180 years and still cling to naive views about the Bible. I read in year 1988 a news story about a group of "scholars" voting on various drafts of a revision on what were Christ's real sayings. They refused to believe that the words written in the Bible were really spoken by him, and they had the naivete to *vote* on a new version. This is the height of arrogance, for no other ancient character has more proof for his person or words than Christ (*He Walked Among Us: Evidence for the Historical Jesus*, Josh McDowell & Bill Wilson, 1988). There is far more proof of Christ's existence than Alexander the Great, Julius Caesar, Plato, Aristotle, Homer, etc.

bp66» I have had different mindsets concerning the Bible. First I believed in the Bible because I was reared to believe in it, at least as the church interpreted it for me (the Catholic view). But I never studied it when I had that mindset. Next through reading too many biased liberal books, I thought that the Bible was of little significance. It was only after I had an epiphany in 1969 that I began to study the Bible itself and read other pro-Biblical views that I came to a different view: The Bible is a very important book, an accurate book, a historical book, a revealing book, etc.

bp67» Unlike what cynical people biased by their mindset attest, no other document comes close to the legitimacy of the Bible. The Bible has the oldest manuscripts of any other ancient document of its size. The intra-cohesiveness of these old manuscripts prove that today's Bible very closely, if not exactly, reflects the original documents. Remember there were no copy machines when the manuscripts of the Bible were handed down. The information age is a very recent phenomenon. The copying of old manuscripts was done by hand. Because it is almost impossible to copy a document the size of the Bible without some mistakes, there are some variations between the ancient manuscripts and today's, but most of these variations concern different spelling of words or omission of words or concern words or phrases that were added by scribes so as to clarify the meaning of the text. Very little to none of the variations affect the meaning or doctrine derived from the Bible, especially if you believe that the antitypical sense of the Bible is the real sense of it (see "Duality Paper" [BP4]).

bp68» Among other things, the Bible is a book of the history of man and man's relationship with God up to Israel (Jacob), from there a history of Israel up to Christ, and from there a history of the Church of Christ up to around 40-70 AD. The Bible is mainly concerned with the behavior of mankind and his relationship with God and the coming of the Messiah. In this the Bible is a very different book when compared to most other ancient books, or for that matter contemporary books. The Bible actually thinks there is something called evil in mankind's behavior, and that there is a God or Power that cares about mankind's behavior. The Bible indicates that wrong behavior actually causes grief and death. This is hard for some today to believe. Some who have a humanistic mindset, believe in one form or another that there is no or little real evil in mankind, but just some form of mis-education. To this mode of thinking it is society who is to blame, not the individual.

bp69» The Bible starts out describing the CREATION of the heavens and earth, or as we call it today — the universe. But what about evolution? Did an intelligent Power (God) create or did evolution create? Contrary to what most schools of today teach, the "creation by God" answer is more scientific than evolution. Evolution is nothing but a faith — a faith based on the ludicrous chance that the *complex* universe somehow evolved. I know how dogmatic the scientists seem, but if you read their journals you know that they too have dissimilar views on many aspects of life, and that the foundations of many of their views are very slim and in contradiction to each other. Some of today's most celebrated theories are based on a very thin film of evidence and on a very precarious set of conclusions based on this evidence (see my, *Science Papers*).

bp70» There are forms of mysticism in science today as there are in many if not most religions. But because we are *not* taught to analyze the foundations of branches of science, we have a mindset that cannot perceive the mysticism in science. *In fact there is a close parallel between mysticism, science, and religion.* See the list of Creation books and organizations in the back of this paper if you want greater details on the evolution versus creation controversy. There is more to the idea of Creation than to the mindlessness of evolution.

bp71» Christianity, Judaism and Islam base their belief and knowledge of God on information found in the Bible. The non-believers think the Bible is too legendary and therefore cannot be the word of God. To the disbeliever the Bible is full of exaggerated stories orally passed on through generations.

Bible's Rich Metaphorical Word Usage

bp72» The Bible is a historical document that includes poetry and a rich use of figures of speech. The Bible uses similes, "his eyes were as a flame of fire" (Rev 1:14). The Bible uses metaphors, "tell that fox" (Luke 13:32). The Bible uses metonyms, "if the house be worthy" (Mat 10:13). The Bible uses synecdoches, "all the world should be taxed" (Luke 2:1). The Bible uses personifications, "the earth mourns and fades away" (Isa 24:4). The Bible uses apostrophes, "O death, where is thy sting?" (1Cor 15:55) The Bible uses hyperboles, "the light of the sun shall be sevenfold" (Isa 30:26). The Bible uses allegories, "this Hagar is Mount Sinai in Arabia."(Gal 4:24) The Bible uses parables, "behold, a sower went forth to sow" (Mat 13:3). The Bible also uses irony, riddles, and fables (1Kings 18:27; Rev 13:18; and Judg 9:8 ff & 2Kgs 14:9 ff). So we see that the Bible is rich in its use of language. (The serpent did not literally speak to Eve, only figuratively did the serpent speak to Eve.) Yes, the Bible does have a few fables, riddles and metaphorical serpents talking within its pages. The Israelis were creative writers. Figures of speech are used to draw attention and interest to the meaning of the words, and to aid in the remembrance of the text. A text of poetry is easier to remember than a boring academic document. The fact that the Bible used colorful word usage to convey its message does not mean it does not convey a truthful picture of history and important philosophical and theological messages from God. It may just as well mean that God used man's colorful ways of expression to convey his word so as to better brand the message into the mind of man. Figures of speech can also breed misunderstanding if the hearer/reader takes literally a story that was only meant to teach a lesson. Trees clapping their hands and snakes talking are metaphorical, not literal. Poetry and metaphors grace the Bible throughout.

Bible, an Ancient Text with Abundance of Details

bp73» The Bible's history goes back thousands of years. Especially in the last hundred and eighty years, archeology has confirmed facts recorded in the Bible that previously had no other confirmation. In comparison to other ancient writings, the Bible is as accurate, if not more accurate than any other historical document in the world (See my *Chronology Papers*). Most ancient historians give a skewed view to make their ethnic group look better than they did in reality. Not so with the writers of the Bible. They wrote, not only of the glory, but of the foibles of their people.

bp74» Again, we restate, the Bible is filled with specific place names, proper names, topographical descriptions, descriptions of ancient customs and nations, descriptions of ancient artifacts, temples, religions, and human behavior. Until the last couple of centuries the skeptics used to call many of the nations, cultures, and customs described in the Bible – myth, or just oral traditions that had lost their truth. But archaeological finds have helped to alleviate some of this skepticism.

Typical Criticism

bp75» *Typical criticism: The Bible is a mythological book that contains orally transmitted myths that were passed down through generations until about the time of Ezra who compiled most of the Old Testament. Moses did not write five books of the Bible because for one thing, there were few in his day who could write: the Hebrews used oral tradition and/or he was illiterate and so could not write it.*

bp76» First about Moses: I don't see anywhere in the Bible where it specifically says that Moses wrote every single word of the first five books of the Bible. Of course he compiled sections from other writings and placed them within his books. He may have had scribes helping him; Jeremiah had a scribe to help him. I don't see in the Bible where it states specifically who actually penned each book. Some of the Torah (first five books of the Bible) was composed after Moses' death because it mentions his death and other facts that were impossible for him to write himself. The Torah also included information about the creation, the flood, Abraham, and genealogy that Moses or his scribe (at his direction) copied from older writings. I also don't see any proof that Moses did not know how to read or write, after all, he was brought up by the Pharaoh's daughter in the palace, so of course, he was taught to read and write. Evidence has come forward lately of an alphabetic script and inscriptions on stone that predate the time of Moses and that very much looks like early Hebrew (Douglas Petrovich, *The World's Oldest Alphabet* [2016]; The movie, *Patterns of Evidence: The Moses Controversy* [2019], Etc.). The general criticisms of Moses and the Bible are sometimes petty, merely trying to find fault, and not giving the authors the benefit of the doubt. While others' criticism seems to be mere scholarly exercises, although they do point out apparent paradoxes in the text and in its depiction of the Hebrew God. Books like Richard Simon's, *A Critical History of the Old Testament* [1682, English Trans., (find at www.archive.org)], seem to be anti-Jewish in tone by attempting to prove that the caretakers of the Hebrew text made many mistakes in copying, while the Isaiah scroll from the Dead Sea Scrolls is proof of the immense care they took in preserving the Hebrew Bible. [Go here for info about the Isaiah scroll.] To make his case Simon seems to point out every trivial criticism he could think of (the text repeats itself too many times, the text uses synonyms, it wasn't written in a style he appreciates or understands, laws are written with different words at different places within the text and so forth). Notice that Simon's book goes back two centuries before the 19th century criticism.

bp77» The general criticism is not that solid especially when we examine archaeological finds of the last few centuries. For example, the Ebla tablets, discovered in the 1970's prove that there was written text before Moses at least back to about 2250-2000 BC[2] (see my Chronology Papers). In the 1975 season over 15,000 tablets were found, about 18,000 complete clay tablets were eventually found. The language of the tablets was Sumerian script and the Eblaite language, the earliest known Semitic language. Personal names, geographic names, lists of animals, professions, names of officials, vocabularies, sacrificial systems, rituals, proverbs, hymns, and so forth were found. Most of the tablets dealt with economic matters such as bills of sale, receipts, tariffs, contracts of sale, etc. Among the tablets were copies of treaties, one was between Asshur and Ebla. Asshur is mentioned in the 10th chapter of Genesis. The language of Ebla was Semitic and the closeness to Hebrew is striking. The vocabularies were the oldest found so far in history, about 500 years earlier than any previously known. There are tablets with case law on them. This proves that hundreds of years before Moses there was written law. Moses didn't invent law, he merely put it in a Hebrew form. What is unique about Moses's law is the patterns in it and its God. These tablets named the five cities of the plain mentioned in the book of Genesis of the Bible, proving these cities were not mythological. The tablets reflect the culture of the patriarchal period and even mention people's names that appear in the book of Genesis. (see Beld, Hallo, and Michalowski, *The Tablets of Ebla: Concordance and Bibliography*, 1984; Giovanni Pettinato, *The Archives of Ebla*, 1981; Clifford Wilson, *Ebla Tablets*, 1977; Benner, Jeff A., "The Archives of Ebla and the Bible," http://www.ancient-hebrew.org/bible_ebla.html etc.)

Because these tablets were found in Syria near the modern city of Aleppo, apparently the information that ties these tablets to the Hebrews is being censored by Syria because of the fear of giving any credence to the Jews' rights to the ancient land of Israel.

Three Tests

bp78» There are three tests we can use to determine the reliability of the Bible. **(1) Bibliographical Test**: Not having the original documents of the Bible, how reliable are the copies we have? **(2) Internal Evidence Test**: Is the written record credible? **(3) External Evidence Test**: Does other historical material confirm or deny the material in the Bible?

Bibliographical Test

bp79» How reliable are the copies we have in regard to the number of manuscripts and the interval of time between the original and the surviving copy? Concerning New Testament manuscripts there are about 22,000 copies of manuscripts with at least partial contents of the New Testament. The closest ancient work next to the Bible is the Homer's *Iliad* (700?? BC), but it only has about 643 manuscripts. Such works as Aristotle (c. 340 BC) have only about five manuscripts for any one of his works, the earliest copy is dated about 1100 AD, about 1400 years after he lived and wrote his work. The history of Thucydides (c. 460-400 BC) has just eight manuscripts and the earliest copy is from about 900

---

[2]The contemporary estimate at the time I wrote this.

AD. Pliny the Younger's History has only 7 copies, the earliest copy from about 850 AD. Plato's work has only 7 copies, the earliest from about 900 AD. Livy's work has only 20 copies. Contrariwise the New Testament manuscripts are about 22,000 in number, with one of the earliest (John Ryland MSS) dating from about 130 AD, about a century after Christ. The *Chester Beatty Papyri* located in the Beatty Museum in Dublin has three manuscripts containing major parts of the New Testament. Two of these papyri manuscripts are dated in the second half of the third century (250-300 AD). But manuscript ^{p46}, which was originally dated about 200 AD has since been dated to 100 AD on paleographical grounds (*Biblica* 69:2 [1988], pp. 248-257). "Paleography (literally, old writing) is the study of the manuscripts themselves rather than the text they contain. In attempting to date manuscripts, paleographers are especially concerned with the script, i.e., the style of the letters used. We have so many papyri from Egypt that a definite progression in the style of script from one period to the next can be seen" (Darrell Hannah, "New Testament Manuscripts," *Bible Review*, Feb. 1990, p. 7). [Some of this paragraph's info was taken from Josh McDowell, *New Evidence that Demands a Verdict*, 800 pages, 1999.]

bp80» Until the discovery of the Dead Sea Scrolls the oldest Old Testament manuscript was dated about 900 AD. This was about a 1300-1400 year gap from when the Bible was completed. Because of the reverence for the scriptures, the Jewish community went to great lengths in making new copies of the Old Testament as accurate and perfect as humanly possible. "Besides recording varieties of reading, tradition, or conjecture, the Massoretes undertook a number of calculations which do not enter into the ordinary sphere of textual criticism. They numbered the verses, words, and letters of every book. They calculated the middle word and the middle letter of each. They enumerated verses which contained all the letters of the alphabet ... These trivialities ... had yet the effect of securing minute attention to the precise transmission of the text; and they are but an excessive manifestation of a respect for the sacred Scriptures..." (Frederic Kenyon, *Our Bible and the Ancient Manuscripts*, 1941). Because of this meticulous care of the Jewish caretakers of the Bible, it has been believed the Bible copies were highly accurate. The Dead Sea Scrolls helped to confirm this belief.

bp81» The Dead Sea Scrolls are made up tens of thousands of inscribed fragments from over 900 texts. The texts can be divided into three groups: Biblical manuscripts (copies from the Hebrew Bible) make up about 40% of the total; Apocryphal texts, which make up about 30% of the total; and Sectarian manuscripts. They are dated from about 150 BC to 70AD. One complete scroll of the Old Testament book of Isaiah was found among the Dead Sea Scrolls. According to Gleason Archer, the Isaiah scroll "proved to be word for word identical with our standard Hebrew Bible in more than 95% of the text, but in 1QIs^b [a partial text about 1/3 of Isaiah], (ca. 75 B.C.) the preserved text is almost letter for letter identical with the Leningrad Manuscript. The 5% of variation consisted chiefly of obvious slips of the pen and variations in spelling" (Gleason Archer, *A Survey of the Old Testament*, 1994, p. 29).

Internal Evidence Test

bp82» When you analyze the Bible itself you must be fair. To use what some call Aristotle's dictum:[3] "the benefit of the doubt is to be given to the document itself, and not arrogated by the critic to himself." You should not assume fraud or error unless you find contradictions of known fact.

> "Giving "benefit of the doubt" until further evidence is uncovered and investigation undertaken is hardly incompatible with a healthy skepticism. Extreme incredulity is no more inherently virtuous or useful than extreme credulity. Indeed both represent a mindset not conducive to honest and fair examination of a particular claim....
>
> It is no coincidence that atheists, and skeptics come down on the side of the burden of proof falling upon the document while Conservative Christian scholars come down on the side of the burden of proof falling to the critic.... the burden of proof issue often says more about the person examining a particular text than about the text itself. It often reveals the presuppositions and philosophical assumptions of the contemporary historian.
>
> "Those who accept the empirical claims of a historical text bear the burden of proof just as much as those who assert their falsehood; in the absence of such proof we should suspend judgment. Empirical uncertainty thus forms the middle ground between the claim that empirical claims are certainly true and the claim that empirical claims are certainly false." [Jeff Lowder][4]

bp83» The biggest problem that the secular intellectuals find with scriptures is God and his supernaturalness. According to their system of thinking any supernaturalness is automatically thrown out. But at the same time the magic of evolution, the cosmic non-intelligent soup that by some miracle created the universe, is not thrown out. This is the result of a mindset. The writers of the New Testament were eyewitnesses (Luke 1:1-3; John 19:35; 1 John 1:3; 2 Peter 1:16; etc). They spoke to others who were eyewitnesses (Acts 2:22; 26:24-28; etc.). At first they did not believe in Christ's resurrection, and admitted this very thing in their writings (Mark 16:11; Luke 24:11, 25; John 20:24-29). But later they saw the resurrected Christ and believed (Luke 24:48; John 20:19-20; Acts 1:8; 2:24,32; 3:15; 4:33; 5:32; 10:39, 41; 13:31; 22:15; 26:16; 1 Cor 15:4-9, 15; 1 John 1:2). Later many of them died because of this belief (Acts 7:58-60; 9:1; Rev 6:11; Heb 11:35-12:1). Tradition has it that 11 of the apostles were martyred for their belief. If it was all a lie, if they made it up, why did they allow themselves to die for it? Even when they lived they gained nothing materially from their belief. They must therefore have believed it because they *saw* the things they wrote about.

bp84» Sir William Ramsay, one of the great archaeologists, is another witness to the Bible's accuracy:

---

[3] I could find no evidence that Aristotle actually said this, but the idea is still worthy to note.

[4] www.theologyweb.com, June 22, 2003, by markg

"He was a student of the German historical school that taught that the Book of Acts was a product of the mid-second century A.D. and not the first century as it purports to be. After reading modern criticism about the Book of Acts, he became convinced that it was not a trustworthy account of the facts of that time (A.D. 50) and therefore was unworthy of consideration by a historian. So in his research on the history of Asia Minor, Ramsay paid little attention to the New Testament. His investigation, however, eventually compelled him to consider the writing of Luke. He observed the meticulous accuracy of the historical details, and his attitude toward the Book of Acts began to change. He was forced to conclude that 'Luke is a historian of the first rank ... this author should be placed along with the very greatest of historians.'" (J. McDowell, *He Walked Among Us*, p. 110)

More could be said on the internal evidence, but we will let other books speak on this matter (see book lists below).

External Evidence Test

bp85» Does other historical material confirm or deny the testimony in the Bible? For one thing the names and descriptions of kings, cities, geography, customs, events, wars, and so forth are well attested and confirmed by secular findings such as archeology. In our *Chronology Papers* we give some evidence of this. The books in the book list below as well as the evidence and books referenced within these books also attest to this. Joseph P. Free, in his *Archaeology and Bible History*, said "Archaeology has confirmed countless passages which have been rejected by critics as unhistorical or contradictory to known facts" (p.1). Read the many books available on this subject.

bp86» The following short list [updated 2019] of books will help you in your search:

- Josh McDowell, *Evidence that Demands a Verdict*, 868 pages, 2017
- F.F. Bruce, *The New Testament Documents: Are They Reliable?*, 2013
- Josh McDowell & Bill Wilson, *He Walked Among Us: Evidence for the Historical Jesus*, 1988, 2011
- Merrill F. Unger, *Archaeology and the Old Testament*, 1954, 2009
- J. Pritchard, *Ancient Near Eastern Texts Relating to the Old Testament*, 1969, 2010
- Jack Finegan, *Archaeological History of the Ancient Middle East*, 1979, 1996

Also see all films in the series: *Patterns of Evidence*.

See our website for the latest info on proof that the Bible is a historical document given to man from God: https://beone.ws

BP4: Duality Paper

Type and Antitype

Visible Projects Invisible

Examples

Look to Higher Meaning

For God speaks once, yet twice, though people do not perceive it (Job 33:14).

gp87» All of the papers in the *BeComingOne Papers* project the duality of the Bible. **If there is a secret to understanding the Bible, it is the duality of the Bible or the type and antitype of the Bible.** There are events and words in the Bible that have dual meanings. One meaning is the physical meaning; the other meaning is the spiritual meaning. The physical meaning is the typical rendition. The spiritual meaning is the antitypical rendition. By the time you read all the *BeComingOne Papers* you will understand, or should understand, what we mean when we say the Bible is dual. But in this short paper we will give you a beginning towards an understanding of the duality of the Bible.

Type and Antitype

bp88» The duality of the Bible consists of "types" and "antitypes." A "type" is an event, person, thing, or symbol in the Bible that represents some Spiritual Truth. The Spiritual Truth is the antitype of the type. For example, in the Old Testament it describes the Passover lamb. In the New Testament it tells us the True or Real Passover lamb is Jesus Christ. (1 Cor 5:7) The Old Testament's Passover lamb is a type of the New Testament's lamb Passover, which is Jesus Christ. (see "God's Appointed Times" paper [NM16]) The Old Testament's Passover foreshadowed the New Testament's Passover.

bp89» Paul of the New Testament, in his letter called Hebrews, tried to explain the duality of the Bible. He didn't use the word "duality" when he tried to explain it, but nevertheless he was explaining the duality of the Bible. Paul in Hebrews speaks of a "sanctuary that is a copy and shadow of what is in heaven. This is why Moses was warned when he was about to build the tabernacle: 'See to it that you make everything [in the tabernacle] according to the pattern shown you on the mountain.'" (Hebrews 8:5; Exo 25:9, 40) Paul is saying that the tabernacle that Moses built was a *pattern* of the tabernacle in heaven. What does this mean?

bp90» When you see the word "heaven" used in the Bible, you can think of it as *spiritual*, for both "heaven" and "spiritual" are used interchangeably in the Bible. (compare "heaven" and "spiritual" in 1 Cor 15:44-49) Thus Paul is saying that Moses made his tabernacle (the physical one) according to the pattern of the heavenly or spiritual tabernacle.

bp91» Paul explains that Christ didn't go into the physical tabernacle, but the "true tabernacle" or the "more perfect tabernacle that is not man-made," "for Christ did not enter a man-made sanctuary that was only a copy of the true one; He entered heaven itself [the spiritual dimension itself], now to appear for us in God's presence" (Hebrews 8:2; 9:11, 24). The physical tabernacle built by Moses was merely a copy of the Real or True tabernacle. Paul tells us that "the law [much of the Old Testament is called the law] is only a shadow of the good things that are coming — not the realities themselves" (Heb 10:1). The law and things of the Old Testament were merely shadows of the good things, the real things, to come. The Old Testament and the things in it are only the *types* of the *antitypes*. The antitype being the Real and True — the Spiritual fulfillment of the type. Paul tells us that the things written in the Old Testament were *types* or *examples* for us, that is, types or examples for us Christians. (1 Cor 10:11)

Visible projects the Invisible

bp92» Paul tells us that the invisible qualities of God can be understood by the things that God has made. (Rom 1:19-20) And in our papers you will see how many aspects of this world, like males and females, which God made, are types of the antitype. Marriage, being born, women, water, stars, and so forth all have higher meaning: they all point to the Spiritual plan of God; they are all types of the Real or True, which is the antitype. For example, "stars" are representative of angels. (see Rev 1:20) And even "water" foreshadows the Spirit (John 7:38-39).

Examples

bp93» Even New Testament rituals like water baptism are types of the antitypes. Water baptism represents spiritual baptism. (see "Baptism Paper" [NM4]) All of the Bible is dual: type and antitype. This includes the Old as well as the New Testament. Even the physical creation is representative of a higher or spiritual meanings. (Rom 1:20) The physical creation (the type) is representative of the spiritual creation (the antitype). For example the days of the week are seven. The week was instituted right after the creation. (see Genesis, chapter 1) But this week is a type. It represents the antitypical week. To God each day is 1000 years. (2 Pet 3:8) God, Who is Spiritual, has a week that lasts seven 1000 year periods, for each of His days lasts 1000 years. Therefore the week (the type) is representative of the 7,000 year week (the antitype). The first seven days of creation, which are described in the book of Genesis, are the physical or typical rendition of the creation. But since the Bible is dual, we know that these seven days of creation have corresponding antitypical or Spiritual days. According to Peter a day of God is 1000 years. (2 Peter 3:8) God being Spiritual has different days than us. God's days are each 1000 years. Therefore, with the awareness of duality, we know that the seven days in Genesis was speaking *first* of the typical seven physical days of creation, and *second* was speaking of the seven Spiritual days of creation, which are each 1000 years long.

bp94» Thus, we see that from Peter's mentioning that a day to God was like 1000 years, we can ascertain the antitypical meaning or higher meaning of the week. This is duality. The typical week is our week of seven literal days. But the antitypical week has 1000 years to each day.

Female and Male Language; Type and Antitype Language

The two sexes use the same language and understand the same language in slightly different ways. The same words or sentences have different meanings to each sex *(Male/Female Language,* by Mary Ritchie Key, 1996) because of their biosocial differences (see my book, *Male & Female*). Just as women and men can get two different meanings from the same words (a sex/gender difference), people also understand the Bible in two different ways: its physical and its Spiritual meaning. In all my books pertaining to the Bible I manifest this and attempt to explain this phenomenon.

Look To The Higher Meaning

bp95» Even such things as "salt" and "light" have higher or antitypical meaning. (Matt 5:13-16) "Clean" and "unclean" have a higher meaning (Matt 15:2,11,15-20). "Yeast" has a higher meaning. (Matt 16:5-12) In fact, Christians are to look for the higher meanings. The enemies of Christ have their minds or thoughts on earthly things. (Phil 3:19) But Real Christians are to have their thoughts on the things above — the heavenly or Spiritual thoughts and meanings. As explained in the "Other Mind Paper" [NM21] all of us in this old age have the other-mind in us misleading us towards confusion. This other-mind is actually another living being — a spiritual being of confusion and evil. Peter had "Satan" inside of him. (Mark 8:33) That is, Peter had the spiritual influence of Satan inside of him. (see the "Other Mind Paper" [NM21]) When Christ spoke to this "Satan" inside of Peter, He said: "You do not have in mind the things of God, but the things of men" (Mark 8:33). That is, Satan has in his mind the things of men — the physical — instead of the things of God, which are the Spiritual. Satan and his spiritual power look on the lower things instead of the higher things. But Christians are to look upon the higher, or Spiritual things, which are the antitypical things.

bp96» Christians have in their mind the Real or True tabernacle when they read about the tabernacle in the Old Testament. Christians have in mind the Real or True water (the Spirit) when they read about the water baptism or living waters in the Bible. Christians have in mind the Real or True bread (Christ, His Spirit) when they read about the breaking of bread or the bread of life in the Bible. Christians think about the Real or True circumcision (being Spiritually circumcised) when they read about circumcision in the Bible. Christians think about the Real or True faith (Faith of the Spirit) when they read about faith in the Bible. Christians think about the Real or True light (God's Spirit) when they read about light in the Bible. Christians are those with the New Mind, which is called by some the Spirit of God, that is, they have the mind of God, they think like the God thinks. With this mind of God Christians look upon the *higher* meaning of people, events, and things they read about in the Bible. They just don't look to the physical things, they look upon the higher or Spiritual meaning of the physical things.

bp97» Christians have the New Mind — the Spirit of God leading them. As Paul said: "God has revealed it to us by his Spirit. The Spirit searches all things, even the deep things of God . . .. This is what we speak, not in words taught us by human wisdom but in words taught by the Spirit, expressing spiritual truths in spiritual words. The man without the Spirit does not accept the things that come from the Spirit of God, for they are foolishness to him, and he cannot understand them, because they are Spiritually discerned" (1 Cor 2:10,13-14). You have to have the Spirit of God to truly understand the higher meanings (the Spiritual meanings) that the Bible has hidden in its words. When you have the Spirit of God, you can see the type and antitype of the Bible. You can see the physical as well as the spiritual. You can see the duality of the Bible.

Even prophecy is dual.

bp98» As you can see by reading our *Prophecy Papers*, there is type and antitype in prophecy. All the ceremonial laws of the Old Testament have higher or Spiritual meaning. (see book of Hebrews) Even the things Christ did had dual meaning. Christ did most, if not all, of his healing on the Sabbath. The higher meaning of this is that Christ will do his True healing on the antitypical Sabbath, which is the 1000 years. Do read the rest of the papers we have to offer you. Look up the scriptures and begin to understand the duality of the Bible. If there is a secret to the Bible, it is the duality of the Bible.

BP5: Premises For Belief

How to Read These Papers

Premises of Belief

Creationist Book List

bp99» The *BeComingOne Papers* were written to inform. All "Papers" were written in one form or another over the last 47 years (1970-2017). Together they are called — *BeComingOne Papers*. To every set of beliefs there are premises. In this paper we amplify on our premises.

How To Read These Papers

bp100» Because tradition is so strong and because each of us has a "mindset," we must be deliberate when reading the *BeComingOne Papers*. The *BeComingOne Papers* concern serious matters and must be read with this in mind. First, read the papers through once. Next, read them looking up our documentation. After this, read all the papers again. When you follow these three steps you should have a good idea what we are trying to convey to you.

bp101» Be careful. Because you have learned your views on God, the Bible, Evolution, Christianity, Science, and the meaning to life from tradition, you will be shocked by some of the papers in the *BeComingOne Papers*. Think. Question. There is something happening on earth. There is a reason for evil. God, the Power, is much more powerful than most think: "Jesus said to them, You err, not knowing the Scriptures, nor the POWER of God" (Matt 22:29). The might of the Power, the God of the universe, will make all *become one*.

bp102» "*Faith* is the substance of things hoped for, the evidence of things not seen." (Heb 11:1) Real *faith* is not naive, but based on substance. We seek real *faith* based on evidence.

How can we believe in the Bible? How can we know there is a God who created the universe? What can we base this faith on?

Premises

1. There is a God

bp103» **A.** The evolutionary Theory always starts with laws like those of heat, energy, motion, gravity, etc. Law projects order and intelligence. The genetic code of life found in our DNA also projects this high intelligence. *How can law evolve?* The laws of the universe must have come from somewhere. God is the creator of law. (Isa 33:22)

bp104» **B.** The law of biogenesis says that life comes from life. You can't get life from dead matter. God is the life giver. (Gen 1:20-31)

bp105» **C.** The fact of radioactivity indicates there was no eternity of matter. If matter always existed, without a starting point, then the "life" period of the radioactive elements would have long ago run its course, that is, the radioactive elements would have run down and there would not be any radioactive elements left. Thus, there was a *beginning* of matter. God created matter. (Gen 1:1)

bp106» **D.** The ecosystems of the earth, sea, and heavens indicate everything was planned, for the theory of evolution maintains that life was a hit and miss adventure ("natural selection" or "mutation," etc.). If this was so, then the universe would be filled with the misses (the inferior products of the evolutionary process) that were not superior enough to continue. There should be fossils of the inferior products of the evolutionary process. In other words, the rejections of the evolutionary process should be polluting the universe. But there are NO fossils of inferior or half-made species. Yet when one studies the ecosystems, one sees that all the substances in the ecosystem are needed in order to maintain these ecosystems even though some may seem at first observation to be not needed.

2. God Created The Heavens and The Earth.

Design

bp107» One proof of creation is that the theory of evolution can't be proven — it is full of contradictions. But what the Bible reveals about creation answers all the problems about the origin of life. How can life come from a mindless soup? The intelligence or mind or order of the universe presupposes or manifests a great Mind Power, the Great God. See the Creationist Book List for more details on creation.

3. The Bible Is The Word Of God That Reveals The Purpose Of The Creation.

bp108» **A.** *The Bible in its original languages* is a doctrine given to mankind through spiritual influence in the minds of many individuals over approximately a 1500 year period. (Heb 1:1-2; 2 Peter 1:20-21; 2 Tim 3:16; see "Bible Paper" [BP3]; see below)

bp109» **B.** *How was the Bible written and how was it inspired?* It was written by humans in situations that were planned and predestined [see NM8 & NM9]. The writers' languages (with its vagueness) their societies (with their complexities), their environments (micro and macro), and their biology (with its direct and indirect influences) were all planned, predestined, and carried out by The Power. Each complete thought written had its type and antitype. They may have only intended the physical or typical meaning, but The Power predestinated its antitypical meaning (note 1 Cor 9:9-10; see "Duality Paper" [BP4]; etc.). The Power made it possible for the writings to be copied and passed down to our time in an accurate enough form (not too accurate so as to make it obvious that we were being manipulated, yet accurate enough). The Power is in *full* control because he is *all powerful*. He thinks of and controls many trillions of things and their interconnections. We think of a few interconnecting things. No cosmic soup can produce intelligence. We must be intelligent about this. There is something going on. Life and death have their purposes.

bp110» **C.** ***Any apparent contradiction is just that***, it only appears at first examination to be a contradiction. A total understanding of the Bible answers all apparent contradictions in a logical way. God is a God of logic: "Come now, and let us reason together says the LORD" (Isa 1:18).

bp111» **D.** ***The Bible interprets itself***; it interprets its own symbols.

(1) For example, the Bible interprets the symbolic meaning of stars by telling us that stars are symbolic of angels. (Rev 1:20)

(2) A second example is how the Bible interprets the symbolic heads on the beast of Revelation 17: "the seven heads are seven mountains" (Rev 17:9). Then it describes these seven mountains as seven kings. (Rev 17:10) Thus, these seven heads or mountains are seven kings.

(3) Notice that the beast of the book of Revelation has ten horns. (Rev 17:7) What are "horns" symbolic of? "And the ten horns ... are the ten kings" (Dan 7:24).

bp112» **E.** ***The Bible shows its reader HOW to read it*** in order to understand it. The Bible says it is "profitable for doctrine, for reproof, for correction, for instruction" (2 Tim 3:16). But one must know how to read it to get this information. There are *four* principles to know about when reading the Bible before one can understand it.

bp113» **(1)** ***Here a little, there a little***. "Whom shall he teach knowledge? and whom shall he make to understand doctrine? them that are weaned from the milk, and drawn from the breasts. For precept must be upon precept, precept upon precept; line upon line, line upon line; here a little, and there a little: For with stammering lips and another tongue will he speak to this people" (Isa 28:9-11).

bp114» A most important principle of the Bible is "here a little, and there a little." God has spoken to man in a stammering tongue. God through his Word (the Bible) speaks in a strange tongue to the world. Readers have noticed that the Bible in places puts information together in no apparent order. It seems that some of the writers of the Bible were in some kind of dream when they wrote. The Bible speaks on almost every subject, but it never totally gives all the information about that subject in one place in the Bible. A person must search throughout the Bible if he wants to find the complete information about any one subject.

bp115» An example of the principle shown in Isaiah 28:9-11 is if someone wants to ascertain exactly what happened shortly after Christ was resurrected from the dead. To find this information one must compare *all* four of the books of Matthew, Mark, Luke, and John with each other, *and* any other book of the Bible that may have any information in it concerning the resurrection of Christ. Only when you put all these scriptures together ("here a little, and there a little") will one have the correct information about Christ's resurrection (*Chronology Paper* [CP4]).

bp116» There is a reason why God is not going out of his way to "save" people or to inform people of his plan. Jesus Christ said he spoke in parables so people would *not* understand, but only those who had Spiritual ears would understand (Matt 13:10-17). God is not trying to save everyone Spiritually now, that comes later (see "All Saved Paper" [NM13] and the *New Mind Papers*).

bp117» (2) *Duality*. Next one must know that the Bible is DUAL — type and antitype. There are types of the real; or shadows of the real; or foreshadows of the real events; or symbols of the real. The REAL of these types *is* the antitypical thing or event.

bp118» An example of the type and antitype is that the physical is a *type* of the Spiritual. But the Spiritual is the *antitype* of the physical. The holy days mentioned in the Old Testament like the Passover are fore-shadows of the real or antitypical event. The physical Passover pictured the sacrificed lamb, which prefigured Christ, the Lamb of God — the real Passover. Another example is stars which are symbols of the antitype — the angels. (Rev 1:20)

bp119» God does things in twos: "the dream was doubled unto Pharaoh *twice*; it is because the thing is established by God" (Gen 41:32). God created male and female, he created the spiritual and the physical dimensions. He used a new and old Covenant when dealing with mankind (Hebrew, chaps. 8, 9, & 10). He even had Moses design the tabernacle as a shadow of the heavenly one.

bp120» God made "the law having a shadow of the good things to come, and not the very image of the thing" (Heb 10:1). He even created the physical world so that we could understand the spiritual dimension. (study, Rom 1:19-20) The physical is a *type* or shadow of the Spiritual dimension. God works in twos — type and antitype. This is duality. See "Duality Paper" [NM13] in the *New Mind Papers*.

bp121» (3) *Spirituality*. Knowing then that the Bible is a creation of God through his influence, we must learn how to read the Bible besides taking "here a little, and there a little," and besides understanding that the Bible is dual — type and antitype.

bp122» God says through his Word that : "God is Spirit: and they that worship him must worship him in Spirit and in truth." (John 4:24) And, "the words that I speak unto you, they are Spirit, and they are life" (John 6:63). Thus, God's words are Spiritual. They have a Spiritual meaning. They are not just physical words, they have a higher or antitypical meaning. There is actually a Spiritual language in the Bible.

bp123» And through God's Word it tells us to look away from the earthly (the physical) meaning *to* the higher or heavenly or Spiritual meaning. (Phil 3:19;

Col 3:1-2; see "Duality Paper" [BP4]) We compare "Spiritual things with Spiritual" (1 Cor 2:13).

bp124» **Important:** The Spiritual or antitypical meaning of the Bible is the aspect of the Bible that is 100 % accurate all the time in every respect. The physical or typical meaning of the Bible is as close to accurate as human languages gets. But the typical language or meaning uses hyperboles, metaphors, and other language phenomena that may not be "literally" 100% true.

bp125» **(4)** *Effect of every vision*. The last principle we need to know is the one shown in Ezekiel 12:22-23: "Son of man, what is the proverb that you have in the land of Israel, saying, the days are prolonged, and every vision fails? Tell them therefore, Thus says the Lord GOD; I will make this proverb to cease, and they shall no more use it as a proverb in Israel; but say unto them, *the days are at hand, and the effect of every vision.*"

>**bp126»** This means that the prophecy up to "the days are at hand" has not come true to its fullest degree. The visions have failed. Israel has not been completely restored, Christ (the Messiah) has not returned, etc. But when the "days are at hand," then will come "the effect of every vision." If we can locate when "the days are at hand," then we will know when the effects of every vision will happen, and then we will know when prophecy will be fulfilled to 100% of the words uttered in the Bible.
>
>**bp127»** Now in Revelation 1:3 it indicates that when someone finally comes to rightly read the mysterious book of Revelation, then the "time is at hand."

bp128» *The proof of premise 3* ("the Bible is the word of God that reveals the purpose of creation") is that logical answers concerning the creation and its purpose have been ascertained. And these solutions remove all apparent Biblical contradiction. For example, it explains how God, who is love (1 John 4:8), can also be a killer. (Deut 32:39) Love has nothing to do with killing, and since God is love, how can he also be a killer? That is surely a Biblical contradiction. How can God be love and a killer? The fact is that people do not know something about God that explains this "contradiction." The True God is love and won't and can't kill, but God is a killer! Now what kind of nonsense is that? Read the *God Papers* to find out who or what is God, and how this Biblical "contradiction" is logically removed. There is something most people don't know about God and the creation that easily explains this and other apparent contradictions concerning God's nature and person.

Creationist Book List Information

- *Scientific Creationism*, Edited by Henry M. Morris (Master Books, San Diego, CA, 1974)
- *Modern Creation Trilogy* (3 vol.) by Henry M. Morris & John D. Morris (Master Books, 1996)
- *The Creation - Evolution Controversy*, by R.L. Wysong (Inquiry Press, Box 1766, East Lansing, Mich., 1976)
- *Earth's Catastrophic Past: Geology, Creation, & the Flood*

bp129» These books will give you a good idea why Creationism is a better explanation than evolution. Book two is more technical than book one, but goes much deeper into the question. Book three gives a refutation on Evolution from someone who is not a creationist.

Also see Web Sites such as: Institute for Creation Research; Creation Research Society; Creation Science.

Go to http://becomingone.org/creation.htm for Internet links to creation sites.

bp130» I am not saying that everything in these publications is correct. I am saying these publications give good evidence on the side of creation in the creation-evolution debate.

MY GOD IS THE BECOMINGONE

God Papers

aka: **God: God is the BeComingOne**

by

Walter R. Dolen

"the is, the was, the Coming One, the Almighty"
(Rev 1:8; Mat 11:3)

or in Hebrew: אֱלִיָהוּ

Documentation

When you see, "The God, all in all (1 Cor 15:28)," it means that this is a quote from the New Testament letter called First Corinthians, chapter 15, verse 28. If you see "2 Cor" it would mean the *second* letter of the Corinthians. If you see "2 Cor 11:4" it would mean we quoted from the second letter of the Corinthians, the 11th chapter, and the 4th verse. But sometimes you will see a documentation such as "(1 Pet 2:4)" after a sentence that has no quotes. This kind of documentation is used in order to *support* the previous sentence or sentences, or to *point out other similar or related views* of the previous sentence or sentences, or to *add new light* to the previous sentence or sentences.

When you see reference to "GP7" it means more information can be found in *God Papers* (aka *God*), chapter 7. When you see "GP2" this means more information can be found in the *God*, chapter 2. When you see gp283, it means the information can be found in the *God* paragraph #283.

BP = Beginning Papers (found on web site)

NM = *New Mind Papers* (aka: *New Mind and Christianity*)

GP = *God Papers* (aka *God: God is the Becoming-One*)

PR = *Prophecy Papers*

CP = *Chronology Papers* (*Chronology of the World*)

cf or cf. = confer or compare

p. or pp. = page or pages

w/ = with

Important Principles to Understand

Logic: "The most certain principle of all is that regarding which it is impossible to be mistaken; for such a principle must be both the best known ... and non-hypothetical. For a principle which every one must have who understands anything that is, is not a hypothesis; and that which every one must know who knows anything ... Evidently then such a principle is the most certain of all ... **It is, that the same attribute cannot at the same time belong and not belong to the same subject and in the same respect.**"
[Aristotle in *Metaphysics*]

Good and Evil: "There can be nothing more inept than the people who suppose that good could have existed without the existence of evil. Good and evil being antithetical, both must needs subsist in opposition, each serving, as it were, by its contrary pressure as a prop to the other. No contrary, in fact can exist, without its correlative contrary. How could there be any meaning in 'justice,' unless there were such things as wrongs? What *is* justice but the prevention of injustice? What could anyone understand by 'courage,' but the antithesis of cowardice? Or by 'continence,' but for that of self-indulgence? What room for prudence, unless there was imprudence? Why do not such men in their folly go on to ask that there should be such a thing as truth, and not such a thing as falsehood? The same may be said of good and evil, felicity and inconvenience, pleasure and pain. There things are tied, Plato puts it, each to the other, by their heads: if you take away one, you take away the other." [*Chrysippus, Fragment* 1169. On the problem of evil. Barrett, p. 64]

Premises on the existence of God

- *There is something* — the universe and life therein;

- *Something cannot come from nothing* — there must have *always been something*;

- *Randomness cannot create intelligence* — intelligence is highly complex and ordered, randomness is disorder and chaos;

- Because of the second law of thermodynamics and the phenomenon of radioactivity, we know that the universe did not always exist and must have been created;

- **Therefore** the "something" that created the universe must be an *Intelligent-Being* who must have existed *before* the universe existed;

- That "intelligent-Being" is **God**: he was before the universe; he exists now; he-will-be always. He is life itself.

Knowing that there is a God does not explain why the God Being created the physical universe or why he created it the way it is with its good and evil. Thus this is the reason for writing the *God Papers*, which explains who or what God was, is and will be. We use the Bible to find information on God because of the reasoning in *BP3: Bible Paper*. This paper is included in the *Beginning Papers*, which is included in the five-book volume of the *Becoming-One Papers*. [ISBN 9781619180451]

Introduction

This book attempts to demonstrate in a logical way who or what God is, assuming a few premises. Although most people believe in God or gods, some do not. Why, if God is good and all powerful, is there suffering? Why do innocent children suffer through no fault of their own. Why do we die? God made the angels immortal, why didn't he create us immortal? Why do we get diseases? Since he created the world, why did he place the possibility of diseases in the world? Sure, we bring on some of these things ourselves by eating poorly, using poor hygiene or by risky behavior. But what about those diseases caused by mosquitoes or microscopic germs or genetics? Didn't God create mosquitoes, germs and genetics? Didn't God create everything? Isn't God good? Or is the idea of God just some superstitious idea based on fear or naivety, an idea made obsolete by the scientific era? Are people more intelligent if they do not believe in God? Or are atheists 'fools' as the Bible relates (Psa 14:1)? An atheist or an agnostic could say, "you cannot prove there is a God" and, "we do not see anything being created or any miracles by God." While the believers could say, "you do not have any real proof of evolution – where are the billions of missing links?" Today each side would be right – no observable proof exists for either side. Today we do not see any Moses parting the seas or anyone being resurrected from the dead by God as reported in the Bible. Today we don't see any species being made nor do we see the billions of missing links being found. We see many things that are good today and in the past; we also see death, diseases and destruction all throughout history. In addition we see the hypocrisy of those who claim to believe in God as well as those who do not believe.

I believe in a powerful God. With all the suffering and pain in this world, how can I or anyone believe in the good almighty God? How can such a being be good, if he allows so much misery? My answer is, I do not believe in the stereotypical gods of most religions because they fail to answer the hard questions and paradoxes pertaining to their gods. After years of study I wrote this book to explain the results of my study. Instead of describing God in a few words, I had to use tens of thousands of words because of the confusing and self-contradictory ideas people have about God. I do not *have* to believe in God merely because I was raised to believe in God. I was also reared as a member of a certain religious group which I no longer believe in or follow. I have a relatively independent mind. If there is no God, why would I have to believe in him?

I believe in the scientific method. In my research for this book I used the scientific method as far as possible. I studied contrary ideas on God; I formed new hypotheses; I tested and analyzed each hypothesis with all available facts: I was looking for the answer that would solve the paradoxes pertaining to God that would make logical sense and that would be in harmony with available evidence. Since God is invisible, I could only use indirect methods. But, whether you know it or not, modern Science also uses indirect methods to study the universe and its origin (See my Science Papers). Fundamental and extensive 'scientific' theories important to science (the big bang theory, the age of the universe, the quantum theory, the string theory, and the special and general theory of relativity) were formed through indirect methods using mathematical formulas and thought experiments – not through direct observation. Since God is invisible (spiritual) we cannot see God, except indirectly, and only as much as he wishes us to "see" him. People do not need to know if God exists; humans also do not need to know how the universe came into existence. But something inside of many of us needs to know, as we need to know who our parents were, or where our ancestors came from, or who invented the first watch, or who first discovered America, etc. An orphan has an inner need to know who his parents were; many of us have an inner need to know where the world/universe came from. Why, or how, is there life? Is death permanent? How can God, if there is one, be all powerful, all good, yet allow evil, misery and suffering?

Although we cannot yet prove (as some define proof) in a scientific manner that there is an all powerful God who created the universe, we also cannot prove or show in a scientific method any other alternative for the genesis of the universe. No one can prove in a scientific manner that evolution created the universe because, apparently, we have no witnesses (observers) for the beginning of the cosmos. (The Bible mentions that the angels witnessed the creation [Job 38:7[5]].) Evolution is really a historical theory based on insufficient evidence, not a scientific theory based on observation.

I believe God did create the universe and here are a few reasons why I do

Law. The evolutionary theory always starts with, and assumes, the eternal existence of laws like those of mass, energy, motion, gravity, conservation, chemical bonding and so forth. Laws, in and of themselves, *are* systematic order and project intelligence and power outside of the law itself. The genetic code of life found in DNA also projects high intelligence and power. *How can* the *code of DNA evolve* or any law such as gravity or chemical bonding evolve? How can any code or law itself have any power? What gives a code power? I am speaking about the code itself, the order of the elements within the code. How can the *arrangement* of the code itself have power? The apparent connection between the code and its effect on a body or plant projects, or strongly suggests some kind of force or power *behind* the law. The code itself doesn't do anything, just as the letters in this book don't do anything by themselves. If you change the arrangement of the letters of the code or a word, it has a different result or may not have any. A seed grows into a certain kind of flower, not because of the code per se, but because of the power behind the code. The basic laws of the universe must have come from somewhere and the power behind these laws must have some connection to the law. Evolution has yet to explain the source of the power behind the universal laws. Science can only *describe* gravity (through mathematical formulas) and partially *describe* the code of life, but it has no idea how the power of gravity works or how or where the code of DNA gets its power. I believe that God, as described in this book, is the creator and power behind all universal laws. And I believe it is more naive to believe in a cosmic soup theory (evolution) than in a powerful God, although I agree that common descriptions of God are naive and do not explain the paradoxes pertaining to God.

Beginning. Radioactivity and laws of thermodynamics indicate there was no eternity of matter and it corollary: there was a beginning of matter. If matter always existed, without a starting point, then the "life" period of the radioactive elements would have long ago run its course and the whole universe would be the same temperature (thermodynamic laws). The radioactive elements would have run down and there would not be any radioactive elements left; the whole universe should be the same temperature. Thus, there was a *beginning* of matter, and it wasn't that long ago, since there are still radioactive elements. The "science" of evolution cannot explain energy or matter or its source nor will it ever because it has no witnesses and has no real explanation for their beginning. A mathematical description of energy doesn't explain it, it only describes what it does in a quantitative manner in *our* solar system. God created matter and energy and in some way God is matter and God is energy as we attempt to explain in this book.

---

[5] Compare Greek text with Hebrew cf. metaphorical usage of 'sons of God'

Life. The relative harmonic-symbiosis of the ecosystems, from the biochemical cell to the earth-sea-heavens, projects design. There is a co-operation, interaction and mutual dependence among life forms; one species cannot live well, or at all, without mutual-beneficial interaction of the whole: the flowers need the birds and insects for pollination in order to continue to exist and vis versa; the seed needs its DNA, the dirt with its nutriments, water and the power behind the DNA for it to grow. Our bodies need a heart, lungs, liver, intestines and so forth in order to exist: we need our whole factory of body parts and a compatible earth in order to live. The whole cannot live without the parts; the parts cannot exist without the whole. The theory of evolution maintains that life is arbitrary, for life came from a hit and miss adventure ("natural selection" or "mutation," etc.). If life is arbitrary, then the universe would be filled with the inferior products of this evolutionary process, and the inferior and half-made life-forms would greatly outnumber the surviving species. There should be fossils of the inferior products of the evolutionary process in all strata, in the rocks everywhere. In other words, the rejections of the evolutionary process should be polluting the universe. Where are the fossils of these inferior life-forms? For that matter, where are the masses of missing links in the evolutionary process? Where? Life came from God, not from the mindless soup of evolution.

The Proof. The big bang theory and other theories need to explain where the material and energy for the big bang theory came from. God, the all powerful Being, by definition, must have always been there, or else there is nothing and we are nothing and so this dialogue doesn't exist. Either the all powerful god of Evolution (mindless soup) was there at the beginning or the all powerful Being was there. Of course we cannot prove God by definition, but there is a way to settle this disagreement:

- The evolutionists can prove the universe came into existence through evolution by physically demonstrating evolution. For example, a new species being spontaneously 'created' before our eyes, or at very least finding the massive amount of missing links in the fossils record and logically explaining where laws get their power;

- The believers in the God can prove to others that there is an all powerful God by people seeing God create a new heaven and earth or by seeing God resurrect the dead back to life. Such is the prophecy recorded in the Bible: all will see the resurrection of the dead and the creation of the new heaven and earth, as apparently the angels witnessed the creation of the present universe at the beginning of the present heaven and earth.

> "For out of Him [God], and through Him, and into Him, all things"
> (Rom 11:36)

> "And Beginning at Moses and all the prophets, He expounded unto them in all the Scriptures the things concerning Himself" (Luke 24:27)

GP 1: God's Paradoxes and Name

Views on God

Paradoxes on God

Law of Contradiction

Attributes of God

Problem of Evil

Titles / Names of God

The Name of God

"I AM" Doctrine

Unchangeableness of God

God, Gods

One God (YHWH)

Views and Paradoxes on God

Gods of Science

gp1» God, gods, and idols come in all sizes, shapes, and powers. All cultures have their gods. Even science has its god. In Robert Wright's *Three Scientists and Their Gods* (1988), Wright writes:

> Some people find it hard to believe that a heartless, brainless, spineless bacterium floating around in the primordial ooze could have evolved into a multi-billion-celled animal... Given enough time ... unlikely things will come to pass—such as strands of DNA that make copies of themselves. But other scientists ... think that the first form of life owed its existence to some as-yet-undiscovered law of thermodynamics... This unformed law, says Bennett, has "taken over one of the jobs formerly assigned to God" (pp 205-206).

The god of science is the theory of evolution with its life-creating "black holes" and its invisible "anti-matter." Evolution does everything that the religious god does.

Science thinks of itself as holy and worthy of praise, but it and its priests have created city-killing bombs, experimented on live humans, injected animal and human victims with drugs, diseases, plagues, and even theorized extermination of whole sets of people in the name of science.

Gods of the Aztecs

gp2» In the past most were "religious." To appease their gods, mankind built great stone altars. On these altars, sometimes located on high hills or pyramids, they built fires. In these fires some sacrificed their children and virgins. According to eyewitnesses with Cortez,[6] in the Aztecs' barbaric culture, on top of the pyramid the high priest dressed in black would cut open a live human victim pull out the live, bloody and beating heart, extend his bloody hand to the heavens while squeezing out all the heart's blood. Then the victim was pushed down the pyramid, the heartless body would tumble over pointed and jagged rocks that ripped it all the time it fell to the ground where others would cut off the victims arms and legs, which were later eaten by the populace, and then the priests discarded the remaining flesh of the victim to the waiting half-starved animals, who were kept near the bottom of the pyramid, to eat the bloody remains that the populace would not or could not eat.

Bizarre Gods of Yesterday

gp3» In contrast, some more "humane" societies only sacrificed animals: sheep, goats, and birds. Around their holy hills they sold animals for sacrifices. Temple prostitution was present in many cultures. Some walked on fire, wrapped poisonous snakes around their necks, and beat and disfigured themselves with whips and knives. Others prayed in various ritualistic ways to their gods with pious and disfigured faces, hoping that their gods would listen to them and grant their request. Kings assumed for themselves godhood and had their subjects worship them as gods. In their kingship they robbed and humiliated their subjects. These god-kings started wars, raped, killed, and destroyed cities and nations.

Today's Gods

gp4» Today there are many theories on who or what is God. Depending on your education and mindset, some of the explanations of God are serious while others are chaotic, if not ludicrous. Although there are few remnants of killing-sacrifices today, there are financial sacrifices, jihad, ritual prayers, asceticism, hedonism as well as plenty of rituals for the gods: free-form to rigid-formal as well as masochistic/sadistic rituals (ritual whipping).

Gods, Creation and Science

gp5» Did evolution, with its cosmic and non-intelligent soup, create the universe, did the god of modern religiosity create it, or did the all-powerful Being create it? The cosmic-soup theory (evolution) is omnipotent; it is like God: it creates matter; from it all life evolved; it's all-powerful. Although some theologians speak of God as all-powerful, for many God needs the magic of the cosmic-soup to create the universe and mankind. And for many God's power is tempered in someway because he is struggling for good against a surprisingly powerful anti-god, the Devil. For this "all-powerful" god of religiosity, there is the "problem of evil."

But there is evidence against both the magical cosmic-soup, and against the weak god of religions. The intelligence, design and complexity of the cosmos cannot come

---

[6] (Bernal Diaz, *The True History of the Conquest of New Spain*, Pub. 1568; Francisco Lopez de Gomara, *Cortes: The Life of the Conqueror by His Secretary*, Pub. 1552)

from a non-intelligent soup or a weak god. The genetic code of life that exists in each of our cells is one proof of the intelligence of life, complexity of life and design of life. This code of life and the complexity of life **must** have come from a highly intelligent Power not from a non-intelligent cosmic soup. I find the arguments against 'design' naive, since any man-made design has intelligence behind it. We assume intelligence behind all our design (inductive logic). Yet the design and complexity of the universe has no intelligence behind it? A non-intelligent soup created our universe? The vastness, complexity and design of the universe are evidence for a *powerful* and *intelligent* creative being. A great intelligent Power must have created the universe, not a non-intelligent soup. Science cannot and never will acknowledge a powerful God, because the very definition of Science rules out the supernatural: "science" was instituted to negate the overbearing influence of religion on knowledge, but if the true answer to origins includes the acts of an invisible Power, "science" by its very definition[7] will be blind to this truth. See my *Science Papers* for my analysis and critique of Science.

Who or What is the Creation Power?

gp6» Considering the improbability of life coming from a non-intelligent soup, the question should be: who or what is the Power that created the universe? If this power is God, then where did God come from? Why should there be anything at all? Why not nothing? Of course there is something, there is life. We are the proof. We are the witness to life as well as to death. What is God? Is it even possible to know? Why is this power invisible? Or is he invisible? Why is there evil? Isn't God supposed to be good? If so, why is there evil? Doesn't the creator have responsibility for his creation? Is God a he, a she or an it? Do these terms even apply?

Premise for this Study

gp7» If an intelligent Power created the universe did he leave us a way to ascertain his essence? Is it even possible to prove his existence? Wouldn't you think in some manner he may have revealed his essence or presence to us? I have come to the conclusion that the Power *has* revealed his essence. In this book, *God Papers*, we (the reader and I) will examine God, the great Power, scripturally. This means, we will use the Bible to study God because I believe the Bible reveals the essence of God. I believe the Bible reveals the essence of God because of the Bible's uniqueness, its history, its inner cohesiveness, its fulfilled prophecy,[8] its continuing confirmation by archeology, and its honesty in pointing out the hypocrisy and fallibility of mankind and the paradoxes[9] pertaining to God. Remember science, in and of itself, will always rule out the supernatural because science is only the study of the natural. If the true answer to origins includes the acts of a invisible God, 'science' by its very definition and practices will ignore a *super*natural God.

---

[7] The activity encompassing the systematic study of the structure and behavior of the physical and natural world through observation and experiment.

[8] see *Prophecy Papers, Encyclopedia of Biblical Prophecy*, etc.

[9] We will see in this paper, there can be no 'good' God/Power without the apparent paradoxes.

'Problems' with the Bible

The main problem with finding truth in the Bible is that it wasn't written as a scholarly text, but as a collection of writings that included history, poetry, ritual, fables, prophecy,[10] written in different styles by different people, often with metaphorical word usage, describing events and peoples over thousands of years, showing the foibles of humans as well as describing their unique view of their God and their hope for the coming messiah. There is an uniqueness and greatness to the Bible. After studying the Bible it was of great interest to me, not only what the Bible said about God, but what the religions that were supposedly based on the Bible chose not to teach. God in the Bible shows his other side, so to speak, through Biblical paradoxes. Religions do not admit these paradoxes. They ignore and even hide and deny them, sometimes even mistranslating words to hide them. For example, the word translated "forever" throughout the Bible does not mean forever, but merely a time of unknown length. This mistranslation, in of itself, changes the whole picture of doctrine taken from the Bible (see *Age Paper* NM7). The paradoxes pertaining to God were some of the evidence that helped to convince me that the Bible was written to manifest the real God, not the God of religiosity. There can be no *all powerful* God without these paradoxes. So what are these paradoxes?

Paradoxes on God

gp8» The Bible *seems* to be highly contradictory. How can God be love (1John 4:8), and also a killer? In scripture the LORD says, "I kill and I make alive; I wound, and I heal" (Deut 32:39; 1Sam 2:6). Yet the Bible says that God is good to all (Psa 145:9). How can God be good to all and also a killer? How can God predestinate some to wrath and destruction (Rom 9:21-23; Jude 1:4; Prov 16:4; 1Peter 2:8), and some to mercy and glory (Rom 9:21-23; Eph 1:4-5; etc.)? Not only is God love, but He is all-powerful (Gen 17:1; Rev 1:8). In his all-powerfulness He even *created* evil: "I make peace, and create evil: I the LORD do all these things" (Isa 45:7). These are some of the Biblical paradoxes of God. Just how can God be love and also a killer, or how or why has He created evil? According to the Biblical definition of love (1Cor 13:4-8), killing or evil isn't one of the qualities of love. Yet, according to the Bible, God is love and in someway has killed and in someway has created evil.

Many attempts to negate these paradoxes of God have failed. Some call the problem of these paradoxes, the "problem of evil." But the only true description of the true God must explain these paradoxes.

Our Goal

gp9» **The goal of this book** is to <u>define</u> God through scripture without real contradictions using the paradoxes of God to help illuminate and explain. But this will not be easy. Christ even said: "no one knows who the Son is, but the Father; and who the Father is, but the Son, and to whom the Son reveals" (Luke 10:22). Theologians have for almost 2,000 years been studying the essence of Jesus and his Father and have come up with differing views, even more paradoxical and self-contradictory views (Trinity). Are contradictions the proof that people's views about God are mistaken? Or are the contradictions a key in ascertaining the truth?

---

[10] some say one-third of the Bible is prophecy

Two Basic Laws and One Fact: God Cannot Lie

Law of Contradiction and Law of Knowledge

gp10» There are two basic laws of reasoning and knowledge. These laws are so elementary that most people know them only intuitively. Only a few such as Aristotle and the stoic writer Chrysippus have attempted to put these laws into words. By amplifying these two laws we project a logical reason why the all-powerful Being, the Real God, has "allowed" evil to exist in his creation, or in His own words why He, "created evil" (Isa 45:7).

- One law, the **Law of Contradiction**, shows us the only sure way of ascertaining the truth from known facts.
- The other law, the **Law of Knowledge**, shows us *why* God has allowed evil to exist.

We will explain the Law of Contradiction now; in GP 7 of this book we will explain the Law of Knowledge.

God Does Not Lie

gp11» Along with these two laws of reasoning and knowledge must go the important fact that the true God does not lie. God cannot go back on his word (Isa 46:11). In fact, it is *impossible* for God to lie (Heb 6:17-18; 1John 5:18; etc.). With these three things we will be able to understand who or what God was/is/will-be.

Law Of Contradiction

What is the Law of Contradiction?

gp12» There is no greater principle in thinking than the Law of Contradiction. You cannot know anything, I repeat, you cannot know anything if the Law is not true. What is the Law?:

- "Now the best established of all principles may be stated as follows: The same attribute cannot at the same time belong and not belong to the same subject in the same respect ... This I repeat, is the most certain of all principles...." [Aristotle in *Metaphysics*]
- "There is a principle in existing things about which we cannot make a mistake; of which, on the contrary, we must always realize the truth — that the same thing cannot at one and the same time be and not be, nor admit of any other similar pair of opposites...." [Aristotle in *Metaphysics*]
- "The most certain principle of all is that regarding which it is impossible to be mistaken; for such a principle must be both the best known ... and non-hypothetical. For a principle which every one must have who understands anything that is, is not a hypothesis; and that which every one must know who knows anything ... Evidently then such a principle is the most certain of all ... **It is, that the same attribute cannot at the same time belong and not belong to the same subject and in the same respect.**" [Aristotle in *Metaphysics*]

Aristotle is reported to have written this in his *Metaphysics*. Aristotle further said that "everyone in argument relies upon this ultimate law, on which all others rest." He said this principle or law of logic "must be known if one is to know anything at all." He also said, "if everything is and at the same time is not, all opinions must be true."

If everything is *and at the same time* is not ...

gp13» Aristotle was right. There is no greater principle in thinking than the Law of Contradiction. Something cannot be all black and at the same time be all white. But a wall can be all white at noon time, and be all black at one hour past noon, because it was painted black shortly after noon time. Or for that matter, something cannot appear to be *all* white to a certain individual, and *at the same time* appear to the same certain individual as any other color. Either the object at that time was *all* white or it was not. But for those who ignore the Law, they say without blinking their eyes:

- the wall is all black at the same time it is all white, or the wall is simultaneously all black and all white.

You protest. You say, no one would say that a wall can be simultaneously all black and all white? Do read on.

At the *same time* ...

gp14» A man cannot be legally married and *not* be legally married at the same time. But a man named Joseph can be married at noon time on Tuesday, and not be married at two minutes past noon time because his wife died at one minute past noon. But this Joseph was not: married and not married *at the same time.* Although you can say that on Tuesday Joseph was single, he was married, and he was widowered; Joseph was not single, married, or widowered *at the same time* even though on the same day he was all three.

Good and Evil at the *same time* or ...

gp15» A man cannot be good (in the truest sense of the word) and yet *at the same time* commit murder. But John could *have* killed Joseph last year, yet today be good because he has changed from his former behavior. He is a reformed murderer. In the English language, you can still call this John a killer because in the *past* he killed Joseph, and you at the same time could call John, "good," because he has reformed. But you cannot say that John was good *when* he murdered Joseph. **Time** has an important part to play in the Law of Contradiction. Your general behavior cannot be good and evil at the same time, but your general behavior could have been bad in the past, and yet you have now changed your general behavior to that which may be called good.

An Example of Paradoxes and Time

gp16» In testimony at a trial, three witnesses testified that they saw illegal drugs being sold from a certain house on a certain day. (All houses on the block looked the same, had no street numbers, but did have different colored garage doors.) Each witness described the house, but each witness described the color of the garage door at the house as being a different color. One said it was brown, one said it was red, and one said it was green. This contradiction almost led to the home owners (husband and wife) being freed, except for the last witness. The last witness, who lived across the street from the house in question, explained that the normal color of the garage door was brown, but at 11 am on the day in question the owner came out and sprayed it red. His wife came home from shopping that same day at 12 pm and the witness could hear the man and woman arguing. She apparently didn't like the color. So the husband at 1 pm that same day came out of the house and sprayed the garage door green. On the same day the color of the garage door was brown, red, and green, but never was the garage door all three colors at the same time.

gp17» What at first appeared to be a real contradiction, later just turned out to be explainable. Time played an important part in this story. At one time the garage door was brown. Later it became red. Still later it became green. The garage door was **not** brown, red, and green at the same time even though on the same day the door was all three colors. On this same day, in time, the door **became** different colors. **Time** played a significant role in this story, as does time play an important role in the understanding of the apparent paradoxes pertaining to God.

Same time in the *same respect*

gp18» Because of the Law of Contradiction, you cannot be physically present on First Street in San Jose, California at 1:30 PM on April 20 and *at the same time* be physically present on First Street in New York, New York. Of course those who play word games could say that at the same time you were *mentally* in San Jose, you were *physically* in New York. Notice the change in the sense of *being* in a place. For those who play word games, Aristotle qualified his statement: "the same attribute cannot at the same time belong and not belong to the same subject *in the same respect*." His qualification, "in the same respect," means that you cannot be, in the *same* sense, in San Jose and New York at the same time.

"If everything is and at the same time is not, all opinions must be true"

gp19» *If* the Law of Contradiction is not correct, you could say that John murdered Joseph at 1:30 PM, or just as truthfully say that the same John did not murder the same Joseph at 1:30 PM on the same day. Both of these contrary statements can be truthful at the same time, *if* the Law of Contradiction is not true. Again, *if* the Law of Contradiction is not valid, you could say and be 'correct': "I am alive physically, yet in the same sense and at the same time that I am alive — I am also dead." But you protest again. No one you say in their right mind would say he is alive and dead at the same time in the same respect. But –

Word Games or Lies

gp20» The Law of Contradiction is so obviously valid that few say it isn't true, yet there are many who act as if the Law of Contradiction is not true by their belief in contrary theories. In fact, impossible contradictions are taught as truth each day in the fields of religion, politics, law, and "science." If contradictions are taught by "respected" people, they are accepted by some, even though at some level of thought they see the contradiction. Authority and tradition are strong — so strong that real contradictions are taught as the absolute truth. Many dogmas use obviously false statements such as claiming:

- "The simultaneity of Jesus's death and immortality" (Hugh Ross, *Beyond the Cosmos*, p. 108).

gp21» How can Jesus be immortal and simultaneously experience death? There is a way to move beyond the paradox of Jesus being God, yet Jesus dying, without tossing out the Law of Contradiction. In order to know anything we must hold on to the Law of Contradiction. The theologians are making a mistake in their beliefs that force them to ignore and degrade the Law of Contradiction. You cannot find the Truth without using the Law of Contradiction.

Do words have meaning?

gp22» Look again at the statement from the astronomer Hugh Ross, a person with a Ph.D in a astronomy:

- "The simultaneity of Jesus's death and immortality" (Hugh Ross, *Beyond the Cosmos*, p. 108).

Ross is not simple. But because Ross and others believe that Jesus is God, and that God is not mutable or changeable,[11] then in order for Jesus to die on the cross, he must have been dead and alive at the same time. Instead of examining their immutable theory they insist on saying that God was alive and dead at the same time.

gp23» Do words have meaning? Apparently not for some theologians. Berkhof wrote:

- "In view of all this [scripture] it may be said that, according to Scripture, physical death is a termination of physical life by the separation of body and soul. It is never an annihilation... Death is not a cessation of existence, but a severance of the natural relations of life. Life and death are not opposed to each other as existence and non-existence, but are opposites only as different modes of existence. It is quite impossible to say exactly what death is. We speak of it as the cessation of physical life, but then the question immediately arises, Just what is life? And we have no answer." [Berkhof, *Systematic Theology*, p. 668].

I do not believe that Berkhof does not understand what death is. He merely doesn't want to believe it because of some view he holds. In order for some to believe in certain theories they must either change the normal meaning of words (death is not death) or diffuse its meaning. How can death be a different mode of *existence* as Berkhof maintains? He completely negates the meaning of death by asserting this. This is a ploy used by those who do not wish to look the truth in the eye. When their theory on the nature of God cannot hold up, they merely change the meaning of words, or make preposterous statements that claim and maintain:

- "The simultaneity of Jesus's death and immortality" (Hugh Ross, *Beyond the Cosmos*, p. 108).

Knowledge cannot exist outside the Law of Contradiction

gp24» The Law of Contradiction is true. Once explained and understood it is the most obvious law. It is the basis on which we judge what is true and what is not true. It is the basis on which courts judge whether a person committed a crime or not. Either the murderer was at the crime scene at the same time as the crime or he was not. He could not, be there *and* not be there, at the same time in the same respect.

Summarize the Law of Contradiction

gp25» The Law of Contradiction is the basis from which we reason:

- something or some specific action cannot *at the same time* be and not be.

But there are some, as Aristotle noted, that foolishly argue against this law. But I ask, how can anyone not believe in this law? If someone does not believe in this law, he cannot prove or disprove anything (at any one time something could be or could not

---

[11] See "Unchangeableness of God" in this part for more information

be true); he cannot believe in anything (for what he believes in could just as well not be true).

Attributes Of God

Now that we know the importance of the Law of Contradiction, we now can continue with our search for the real essence of God by studying the main attributes attributed to God. How is God described in the Bible? Are there contradiction? If so, how can they be explained?

God Is Life

gp26»

- 'For as *the Father has life in Himself*, so He has granted the Son to have life in Himself' [John 5:26 NKJV]

    - " 'For *in Him we live and move and have our being*,' as also some of your own poets have said, 'For we are also His offspring.' " [Acts 17:28 NKJV]

God Has All Knowledge

gp27»

- Great is our LORD, and mighty in power; *His understanding is infinite.* [Psa 147:5 NKJV]:

    - For if our heart condemns us, God is greater than our heart, and *knows all things.* [1 Jo 3:20, NKJV].

God Is Everywhere

gp28» But will God indeed dwell on the earth? Behold, heaven and the heaven of heavens cannot contain You. How much less this temple which I have built! [1Ki 8:27, NKJV]

- "Can anyone hide himself in secret places, so I shall not see him?" says the LORD; "do I not fill heaven and earth?" says the LORD [Jer 23:24, NKJV].

- Where can I go from Your Spirit? Or where can I flee from Your presence? 8 If I ascend into heaven, You are there; If I make my bed in hell, behold, You are there. [Psa 139:7, NKJV]

- So that they should seek the LORD, in the hope that they might grope for Him and find Him, though He is not far from each one of us; 28 for in Him we live and move and have our being, as also some of your own poets have said, 'For we are also His offspring.' [Acts 17:27, NKJV]

There Is Nothing Else Besides God

gp29» "That they may know from the rising of the sun to its setting that there is none besides Me. I am the LORD, and there is no other." [Isa 45:6, NKJV]

gp30» This scripture does not say there is not any *like* God, but it does say there is none besides God, "I am YHWH, and there is no other." Of course, if there is none besides God, then it follows there is also none *like* God. In a sense, the true God is everything; there is nothing beside Him. This may make little sense now, but after you read *all* this book, you may come to understand.

God Is Invisible

gp31» As we have just seen, God's presence and/or spirit and/or power is everywhere. But up to the present, most, if not all, have not seen God in a physical way (Although some can "see" God in a Spiritual sense. See Chap2). This is because God in this age is invisible to human eyes:

- When he [God] passes me, *I cannot see him*; when he goes by, I cannot perceive him. [Job 9:11, NIV]

- He is the image of the *invisible God*... [Col 1:15, NIV]

- No one has ever seen God... [John 1:18]

See GP 2 and the rest of this book to further understand this.

God Is Almighty

gp32»

- When Abram was ninety-nine years old, the LORD appeared to Abram and said to him, 'I am *Almighty God*; walk before Me and be blameless.' [Gen 17:1, NKJV]

- Both riches and honor come from You, and You reign over all. In Your hand is power and might; in Your hand it is to make great and to give strength to all. [1Ch 29:12, NKJV]

- and said: "O LORD God of our fathers, are You not God in heaven, and do You not rule over all the kingdoms of the nations, and in Your hand is there not power and might, so that no one is able to withstand You? [2Ch 20:6, NKJV]

- Thus says the LORD, your Redeemer, and He who formed you from the womb: I am the LORD, who makes all things, Who stretches out the heavens all alone, Who spreads abroad the earth by Myself; [Isa 44:24, NKJV]

- You will say to me then, "Why does He still find fault? For who has resisted His will?" [Rom 9:19, NKJV]

All Things Possible for God

gp33»

- And He [Christ] said, "Abba, Father, all things (are) possible for You. Take this cup away from Me; nevertheless, not what I will, but what You will" [Mar 14:36, NKJV]

This "all things (are) possible" is qualified by Matt 26:39, Luke 22:42, and Mark 14:35. It is qualified by, "if it were possible" and "not as I will, but as you will." Everything *was* possible *before* God sent forth his will, or his word. But once God wills something, God does not go back on his word (See below under "God Keeps His Word."). Also notice that in Mark 14:36 there is no verb ("are") in the Greek text; therefore, all things *were* possible (to take away the death of Jesus) to the true God *before* he gave his word or before God predestinated Jesus Christ's death as the true Lamb of God (Acts 4:27-28; 2:23; 3:18).

See chapter 5, Jesus Christ the God, under "With God Nothing Shall Be Impossible" for more detailed information on this subject.

Creator Makes All Things

gp34» God has all the power in the whole universe. In fact God is the creator of the whole universe.

- In the beginning God created the heavens and the earth [Gen 1:1, NKJV].
- As you do not know what is the way of the wind, or how the bones grow in the womb of her who is with child, so you do not know the works of *God who makes all things* [Ecc 11:5, NKJV].

Problem Of Evil

gp35» The scripture we just studied tells us that God is almighty. With His great power God created all. God made all things. But do you understand what *all* includes? "All" not only includes the good, but "all" also includes the wicked, their evil, and even the waster or spoiler and his destruction (Isa 54:16). It is Impossible for the God to have created good without in some way also having created evil, for good and evil are comparative qualities which need each other in order for anyone to know either quality (See GP 7; NM19; NM9). *All* power not only includes all the power of good, but also, somehow or in someway, all the power of evil. Therefore God cannot be almighty without having power over evil. Yet at the same time God cannot be good and still execute evil. This is "the problem of evil" that the theologians write about. The power over evil is somehow included in God's power as scripture indicates, for God (YHWH) in someway or somehow even kills and wounds (Deu 32:39, see below), and even created evil (Isa 45:7).

God's Connection with Good <u>and</u> Evil

gp36» Job said to his wife: "shall we receive good at the hand of God, and shall we not receive evil? In all this Job did not sin with his lips." (Job 2:10)

- The LORD has made everything for its purpose, even the wicked for the day of trouble. [Prov 16:4]

- I form the light and create darkness, I make peace and create evil [Hebrew - *ra* Strong's # 7451]; I, the LORD, do all these things.' [Isa 45:7]

- Behold, I have created the blacksmith who blows the coals in the fire, who brings forth an instrument for his work; and I have created the spoiler to destroy. [Isa 54:16, NKJV]

- Now see that I, even I, am He, and there is no God besides Me; I kill and I make alive; I wound and I heal; nor is there any who can deliver from My hand. [Deu 32:39, NKJV; also note 1Sam 2:6]

Paradoxical Sides of God

Right and Left Sides

gp37» Notice that not only did the God create light, but he also created darkness (Isa 45:7; Gen 1:1-4). Notice that not only did God create peace, good, and life (Isa 45:7; Gen 1:31; 1Sam 2:6; Gen 1:24), but he also created evil and killed (Isa 45:7; Gen 1:1-2; Deut 32:39; 1Sam 2:6). There are two opposite aspects of God. You can call these two facets of God, **God's right and left hand <u>or</u> sides**. The Hebrew word for right hand (*yamin*) also means right side; the Hebrew word for left hand (*semovl*) also means left side.

Right Side or Positive Aspects of God

God Is Good

gp38» First let us look at the positive aspects of God – God is good.

- So He said to him, "Why do you call Me good? *No one is good but One, that is, God….*" [Mat 19:17; Mark 10:19; Luke 18:19]
- God's Name, Word, Spirit is good (Psa 54:6 [8]; Isa 39:8; Jer 29:10; Heb 6:5; Psa 143:10)

Not only is the one true God good, but God is or will be good to all:

- The LORD (is) good to all, And His tender mercies are over all His works. [Psa 145:9, NKJV]

When is God good to <u>all</u>:

- God (YHWH) for good and mercy in olam [see Hebrew text:1Ch 16:34; 2Ch 5:13; 7:3; Ezra 3:11; Psa 100:5; 106:1; 107:1; 118:1,29; (135:3)136:1; Jer 33:11]

God Is Love

gp39» He who does not love does not know God, for *God is love.* [1John 4:8, NKJV]

Love Is

gp40» Love suffers long and is kind; love does not envy; love does not parade itself, is not puffed up; 5 does not behave rudely, does not seek its own, is not provoked, thinks no evil; 6 does not rejoice in iniquity, but rejoices in the truth; 7 bears all things, believes all things, hopes all things, endures all things. 8 Love never fails. But whether there are prophecies, they will fail ['become ineffective' — because they will have been completed]; whether there are tongues, they will cease; whether there is knowledge, it will vanish away. [1 Co 13:4-8]

- The entire law is summed up in a single command: "Love your neighbor as yourself." [Gal 5:14]

Love is Not

gp41»

- Among other things Love is not: fornication, impurity, licentiousness, 20 idolatry, sorcery, enmities, strife, jealousy, anger, quarrels, dissensions, factions, 21 envy, drunkenness, carousing, and things like these. I am warning you, as I warned you before: those who do such things will not inherit the kingdom of God. [Galatians 5:19-21]

God Keeps His Word; He Does Not Lie

gp42» It is impossible for God to lie (Heb 6:18, NIV; see, Titus 1:2):

- So is my WORD that goes out from my mouth: it will not return to me empty, but will accomplish what I desire and achieve the purpose for which I sent it (Isa 55:11, NIV).
- What I have said, that will I bring about; what I have planned, that will I do (Isa 46:11, NIV).

- The WORD is gone out of my mouth in righteousness, and shall not return (Isa 45:23).
- My covenant I will not break, Nor alter the word that has gone out of My lips (Psa 89:34, NKJV).

gp43» God does not lie, therefore all that comes out of his mouth, or all his words, are the truth. God's words are found in the Bible. Thus,

- For assuredly, I say to you, till heaven and earth pass away, one jot or one tittle will by no means pass from the law [Old Testament books] till all is fulfilled (Matt 5:18, NKJV).

[This scripture does not mean that in our copies of the Hebrew text that there would not be any variant (even the smallest) when compared to the originals, but it means that it would be easier for heaven and earth to pass away than for the smallest word of God to fail. Note *Figures of Speech Used in the Bible*, by Bullinger, page 678, 1984 Baker printing.]

If what God has said has yet to happen, it *will* happen. The scripture cannot be broken (John 10:35).

Left Side or Negative Aspects of God:

gp44» An honest reading of the Bible manifests to us negative aspects of God. Here follows some of them:

- killing kings [Psa 135:10; 136:18; 145:20]
- of bringing evil on Job [Job 42:11; 1:6-12; 2:1-8]
- somehow causing drought, or floods [Job 12:15]
- destroying nations, and making the leaders of the world go mad [Job 12:23-25; Dan 4:28-35; Deut 28:28]
- sending curses and confusion; He plagues some with diseases, and so on [Deut 28:15-68]
- killing Er, Onan, the firstborn of Egypt, the Pharaoh and his army, Korah his family and men, Israelites, Amorites, Uzzah, and so forth for various reasons [Gen 38:7; 38:9-10; Exo 12:29; 14:16-19, 24-27; Num 16:1-35; Num 16:41-50; 2Sam 24:1-15; Josh 10:6-12; 2Sam 6:6-7]
- And God said to Noah, 'The end of all flesh has come before Me, for the earth is filled with violence through them; and behold, *I will destroy them* with the earth.' [Gen 6:13]
- The "**anger** of the LORD" or the "**wrath** of the LORD," or the "**jealousy**" God, or some "**angel** of the LORD" destroyed the people and are pictured in the Old Testament scripture as bringing "all the curses that are written in this book [the Bible]," and destroying such cities as Sodom and Gomorrah and even destroying 70,000 Israelites [Deut 29:20; Gen 19:24-29 with Deut 29:23,20; 2Sam 24:1, 15-16; Nah 1:2; see "God's Wrath" paper (PR 4)].

gp45» Outside of the question of natural disasters, some of the evil God somehow brings upon mankind is because of mankind's behavior (Deut chap 28; Josh 24:20; "God's Wrath" PR4 to PR6; etc.). We are not saying here that the evil brought on each man is directly proportional to each man's sin (Luke 13:1-5).

Anger of God or Wrath of God?

gp46» We just saw a list of negative facets of God, and in it we saw the "anger of God" ("his anger"), or the "wrath of God" ("his wrath"), or "jealousy of God" ("his jealousy") that destroyed Sodom and Gomorrah and others (Gen 19:24-29; Deut 29:23,20). What does the Bible mean when it speaks about the "anger of God" or the "wrath of God"? First look at 2Samuel 24:1,15-16:

- "Now again the **anger of the LORD burned against Israel**, and it incited David against them to say, "Go, number Israel and Judah.... So the LORD sent a pestilence upon Israel from the morning until the appointed time, and seventy thousand men of the people from Dan to Beersheba died. 16 When the **angel stretched out his hand toward Jerusalem to destroy it**, the LORD relented from the calamity and said to the angel who destroyed the people, "It is enough! Now relax your hand!" And the **angel of the LORD** was by the threshing floor of Araunah the Jebusite."

gp47» Notice that it was an **angel of the LORD** (YHWH) that did the destroying. By doing a computer search for the words "anger of the LORD" we see the following verses also speak of the anger or wrath of LORD destroying and killing (Ex 4:14; 32:11,22; Num 11:1,10,33; 12:9; 25:4; 32:13,14; Deut 6:15; 7:4; 9:19; 11:17; 29:20; 29:23,27; 31:29; Joshua 1; 23:16; Jud 2:14,20; 3:8; 10:7; 14:19; 2Sam 6:7; 24:1; 1Kings 16:7; 22:53; 2Kings 13:3; 24:20; 1Chron 13:10; 12:12; 25:15; 28:11; Psa 6:1; 21:9; 106:40; Isa 5:25; 30:27; 66:15; Jer 4:8; 7:20; 12:13; 23:20; 25:37; 30:24; 42:18; 51:45; 52:3; Lam 1:12; 2:1,6; Ezek 25:14; 38:18; Zeph 2:2-3; 3:8; Zech 10:3; etc.).

Anger of God, Destroying Angel, and Satan

gp48» From the Bible we know there are two kinds of angels: one good; one evil (GP3). What kind of angel of God, destroys? Who is the destroyer? There is a parallel verse to 2Samuel 24 found in 1 Chron 21:1,12:

- "Then **Satan stood up** against Israel and moved David to number Israel.... pestilence in the land, and **the angel of the LORD destroying** throughout all the territory of Israel." (1Chron 21:1,12)

gp49» It is Satan that moved David to Number the Israelites against God's will (cf. 2Sam 24:1-2 with 1Chron 21:1-2). By comparing both versions and other scripture in the Bible, we see that the "anger" of the LORD is an angel called Satan, who goes about destroying, "the devil, prowls around like a roaring **lion**, seeking someone to devour" (1Pet 5:8).

gp50» Look at another verse that says the same thing:

- Because he [Balaam] was going, began burning the anger of God, and **an angel of the LORD** took his stand in the way as **an adversary [Satan] against him**. Now he was riding on his donkey and his two servants were with him." (Num 22:22; see Hebrew text)

In some way Satan is an "angel of the LORD" who destroys (1Chron 21:1,12). How can Satan be an "angel of the LORD"?

Evil Angel's Fate

gp51» It is this evil angel and his angels, who are on the left hand or side of God, that will be put in the fire at the end of the age for their evil deeds:

- "But when the Son of Man comes in His glory, and all the angels with Him, then He will sit on His glorious throne. 32 "All the nations will be gathered before Him; and He will separate them from one another, as the shepherd separates the sheep from the goats; 33 and **He will put the sheep on His right, and the goats on the <u>left</u>**. 34 Then the King will say to those on His right, 'Come, you who are blessed of My

Father, inherit the kingdom prepared for you from the foundation of the world.'... Then **He will also say to those on His left**, 'Depart from Me, accursed ones, **into the aeonian fire which has been prepared for the devil and his angels.**" (Matthew 25:31-34,41)

- "**And angels** who did not keep their own domain, but abandoned their proper abode, He has kept in eternal bonds under darkness **for the judgment of the great day**," (Jude 1:6)

- "Then I saw an angel coming down from heaven, holding the key of the abyss and a great chain in his hand. 2 And **he laid hold of the dragon, the serpent of old, who is the devil and Satan**, and bound him for a thousand years; 3 and **he threw him into the abyss**, and shut *it* and sealed *it* over him, so that he would not deceive the nations any longer, until the thousand years were completed; after these things he must be released for a short time." (Revelation 20:1-3 cf 20:10)

Right and Left Side Metaphor

gp52» By comparing various verses we see that the abyss is the great lake of fire, and it is this fire that will burn up the evil of the world (Mat 3:10-12; 13:40; NM24). As the above scriptures indicate this evil is so to speak on the "left hand" or "left side" of God. In other words, the Bible uses a metaphor that compares the right side or hand of God with goodness, and conversely compares the left side or hand of God with evil. It is the left hand that is cut off and sent to the fire. Notice the principle of the following pertinent verse:

- "If your **hand** causes you to stumble, cut it off; it is better for you to enter life crippled, than, having your two hands, to go into hell, into the unquenchable fire." (Mark 9:43)

gp53» The all powerful God has the power of all good and all evil, or else he is not all powerful. What Mark 9:43 is telling us along with Matthew 25:41 and other verses, is that the God will cut off the power of his left hand or side at the end of the age and put it in the hell-fire for punishment of sins.

God has Power over Satan

gp54» Notice that the LORD does indeed have power over Satan:

- Job 1:6 – Now there was a day when the sons of God came to present themselves before the LORD, and Satan also came among them. 7 The LORD said to Satan, "From where do you come?" Then Satan answered the LORD and said, "From roaming about on the earth and walking around on it." 8 The LORD said to Satan, "Have you considered My servant Job? For there is no one like him on the earth, a blameless and upright man, fearing God and turning away from evil." 9 Then Satan answered the LORD, "Does Job fear God for nothing? 10 "Have You not made a hedge about him and his house and all that he has, on every side? You have blessed the work of his hands, and his possessions have increased in the land. 11 "But put forth Your hand now and touch all that he has; he will surely curse You to Your face." 12 **Then the LORD said to Satan, "Behold, all that he has is in your power**, only do not put forth your hand on him." So Satan departed from the presence of the LORD. (Job 1:6-12)

- "And the Lord said to Satan, Behold, he [Job] is in your hand; but save his life" (Job 2:6).

So the LORD does have power over Satan, as He must, if He indeed is all powerful. The scriptures we are studying are hints, from which we will be able to understand and answer the "problem of evil."

Two Sides of God

gp55» As we are seeing there are two sides of God, or two facets of God that work together to create good and evil: one side creates good; one side evil. Both sides work together to create as the right and left side of our brain work together to form our knowledge, our speech, and our personality.

Evil Never a part of the True God

gp56» Does this mean that the real God now is in some way evil? No! God cannot be good and evil at the same time. Since the one true God is good, the real God can never be evil. Since God is all powerful, God in someway does have control over evil. But the real God now, is not doing evil. It is what we call the left side of God that is now doing evil. This evil "side" is not now the one true God. Evil will never be a part of true God. But evil is being "allowed" in this age through predestination as we will see. As we will see in this book, predestination, time, and God's real Name answer the paradoxes pertaining to God. Do read on.

God Predestinates Wrath and Mercy before Creation

Scripture shows God predestinating some to evil and wrath:

gp57» (Remembering that predestination occurred before creation [(See nm170ff; Compare 1 Pet 1:19-20; John 1:29; Rev 13:8; Isa 53:7-8; Matt 12:18; 1Pet 2:4; Isa 49:7; John 14:10; Rom 1:4]):

- Does not the potter have power over the clay, from the same lump to make one vessel for honor and another for dishonor? 22 What if God, wanting to show His wrath and to make His power known, endured with much longsuffering the *vessels of wrath prepared for destruction*, 23 and that He might make known the riches of His glory on the vessels of mercy, which He had prepared beforehand for glory, [Rom 9:21-23, NKJV]

- For *certain men* have crept in unnoticed, who long ago *were marked out for this condemnation*, ungodly men, who turn the grace of our God into licentiousness and deny the only Lord God and our Lord Jesus Christ. [Jud 1:4, NKJV]

- The LORD has made all things for Himself, Yes, even the wicked for the day of doom. [Pro 16:4, NKJV]

- And a stone of stumbling and a rock of offense. They stumble, being disobedient to the word, to which *they also were appointed*. [1 Pe 2:8, NKJV]

Some chosen to be good:

gp58»
- Eph 1:4 -- Just as He chose us in Him before the foundation of the world [cosmos], that we should be holy and without blame before Him in love, 5 *having predestined us to adoption as sons* by Jesus Christ to Himself, according to the good pleasure of His will [Eph 1:4-5, NKJV; see Rom 9:21-23 above and "Predestination" paper (NM8)].

All generations chosen:

gp59»
- (from Hebrew text): [LORD] who has appointed and done, calling forth the generations from the beginning. [Isa 41:4]

Predestination is very difficult to understand

gp60»
- Paul said: "It does not, therefore, depend on man's desire or effort, but on God's mercy. For the Scripture says to Pharaoh: 'I raised you up for this very purpose, that I might display my power in you and that my name might be proclaimed in all the earth.' Therefore God has mercy on whom he wants to have mercy, and he hardens whom he wants to harden. One of you will say to me: 'Then why does God still blame us? For who resists his will?'" [Rom 9:16-19, NIV]

No one resists God's will. As we said this is very difficult to understand. But after you have read all of this book, it will be easier for you to understand.

The Great Paradox

gp61» God has ALL the power. This all-powerfulness must somehow include all the powers of evil. If God does not have in someway the power of both good and evil, then of course he does not have *all* the power.

gp62» But the true God does have <u>all</u> the power. Thus, he has in someway both the power of good and the power of evil. Yet somehow God is good and God is love, and God will give good to all. This is a great paradox. How can one be <u>good</u> and *at the same time* predestinate some to evil? How can God be <u>good</u> and yet *at the same time* kill and destroy? How can God be <u>love</u> and *at the same time* kill and destroy? It would be impossible for God to be <u>love</u> and *at the same time* kill and destroy. Or it would be impossible at the same time God is love to also predestinate some to destruction. It would be impossible because it would be against the most fundamental law of reasoning: the Law of Contradiction (see Law of Contradiction above). But it is within the Law of Contradiction for God to predestinate some for mercy and some for destruction, if they were predestinated <u>before</u> creation (as we know it), <u>before</u> time (as we know it), <u>before</u> good (as we know it), <u>before</u> evil (as we know it), <u>before</u> law (as we know it), and consequently <u>before</u> sin (as we know it).

Time Answers The Paradoxes

gp63» The key to these paradoxes and most, if not all, paradoxes concerning the true God has to do with predestination, time, and God's Name. There is a secret to understanding God. When you know this secret the paradoxes concerning God are answerable in a logical way. The answer to these paradoxes has to do with the phenomenon of **time**, as well as **when** God planned and gave power for evil in his creation, and lastly the fact that the one true God cannot be good and evil **at the same time**. All this plus the meaning of God's Name, which carries time within it (the was, is, will be one), is the answer to the paradox about God being love and God creating evil. The secret of "time" is hidden in God's NAME. There is a time element in God's Name. This will not make sense now, until you understand the meaning and significance of

God's NAME. But before we learn about his NAME of names, we should learn about some of his other names and titles.

Titles or Names Of God

gp64» Names or titles of God:

- Holy One [Isa 43:15; 48:17; 49:7]
- Creator [Isa 45:18; 48:13; 51:13]
- Savior [Isa 45:15, 21; 49:26; 60:16]
- Father [Isa 63:16]
- Husband of Israel [Isa 54:5; Jer 3:14; Hos 2:19]
- Shepherd [Psa 23:1]
- Redeemer [Isa 48:17; 49:7, 26; 60:16]
- Rock [Isa 26:4; Deut 32:4]
- First and Last [Isa 44:6; 48:12]
- Mighty One [Isa 49:26; 60:16]
- God Almighty [Gen 17:1]
- King [Psa 10:16; 89:18; 5:2]
- King of Israel [Isa 43:15; 44:6; 1Sam 12:12]
- King of Kings (that is, King of the whole earth) [Psa 47:2, 7; Zech 14:9]
- King of Glory [Psa 24:10]
- King of *olam* [Psa 29:10; Jer 10:10]
- King above all gods [Psa 95:3]
- Lord of kings [Dan 2:47]
- God of gods [Josh 22:22;"Gods of gods" in Hebrew; see Psa 136:2 & Deu 10:17]
- The Great God [Deu 10:17]
- Lord(s) of lords [Deut 10:17; Psa 136:3]
- Lord(s) above all gods [Psa 135:5]
- Most High [(Heb, *'elion* or *'lyown*) is used as a title of God (Gen 14:18-22; Num 24:16; Deut 32:8; etc.). But this Hebrew word (*'elion*) is also used when not speaking about God. It is translated as "uppermost" in Gen 40:17; "upper" in 2Kings 18:17; "high" in 2Chron 23:20; etc.]

These could be called titles or names of God. These are not all of God's titles or names. But none of these are the real God's NAME. God has one NAME he has chosen to best represent himself.

gp65» There is something very important that we must know about God. By knowing the true NAME of God we will be able to understand God much better, and we will better understand the paradoxes concerning God. The true NAME of the God allows TIME to negate the paradoxes concerning God, and helps to answer the problem of evil.

Importance of a Name

Personal Names had Meaning

gp66» Names of people in the Bible had more meaning to them than personal names have for us. To Israel personal names generally expressed some personal characteristic, some incident connected with birth, some hope, desire, or wish of the parents. The Biblical Hebrews had a tendency to play on names and find analogies or contrasts in them (see Ruth 1:20; 1Sam 25:3, 25; Rom. 9:6; etc.). For example the following play on the name "Dan."

- "Dan ['judge'] shall judge his people" (Gen 49:16).

gp67» Personal names given at birth were sometimes changed later in life for various reasons. Sometimes the names given at birth expressed the time of birth, Hodesh (new moon). Sometimes the names indicated the place of birth, Zerubbabel (born in Babylon). Sometimes the condition of the mother called for a certain name for the child, Benoni (son of my pain). Sometimes the name of the child indicated the appearance of the child, Esau (hairy). Religious names were frequently given, the most simple being expressive of thanks to God for the gift of a child, Mahalaleel (praise to God).

gp68» Some names of people were changed by God to indicate what God was going to do with or through that person:

- Abram's name ("exalted father") was changed to Abraham ("father of many") because God was going to make him a father of many nations (Gen 17:5);

- Sarai's name ("Jah is Prince") was changed to Sarah ("princess") because God was going to make her a mother of nations and kings of peoples would come from her (Gen 17:15-16);

- and Jacob's name ("supplanter" or *heel* catcher) was changed to Israel ("ruling with God" or "contender or soldier or prince of God") after he struggled with the angel (Gen 32:28).

The word "Israel" comes from two words: Sarah ("prince" or ruler or commander) and el ("god"). Princes had their names changed on their accession to the throne (2Kings 23:34; 24:17; note information under "name" in Unger's Bible Dictionary, The International Standard Bible Encyclopaedia, etc.).

gp69» In the New Testament names also were of a more distinctive nature than they are today. Names in the New Testament times, at least among the Biblical Jews, represented certain aspects of the person. For example, "Jesus" is the English translation of the Greek word "Iesous" which is the equivalent of the Hebrew "Joshua" (Jehoshua) meaning: "Jehovah (is) salvation." Thus, "she shall bring forth a Son, and thou shalt call his name Jesus, for he shall *save* his people from their sins" (Matt 1:21).

gp70» In the New Testament names were also changed during one's life time for various reasons. For example, Simon's name was changed to Peter and Saul's name was changed to Paul.

Dual Meaning Of Names

gp71» A name of a single person or quality can also refer to a whole nation or all those with that single quality:

- *Israel*, the individual, or Israel, the nation (see "Seed Paper" [PR 1]).
- *Christ*, the individual, or Christ, the whole Body of Spiritual people in Christ's Spirit (see *New Mind Papers*).
- *Seed*, the individual (Christ), or Seed in the sense of all those in the true Seed (see "Seed Paper" [PR 1]).
- *God's Spirit*, as individually distinctive versus other kinds of spirit, or any to all Spirits of the same nature as God's.
- *Satan*, as the individual, or any to all the spirits or angels of the same nature as Satan's.
- *Beast*, the individual, or the system of the Beast (see Beast Papers [PR 2, PR 3]).

A name of a person can also have a physical and Spiritual meaning: There is a physical Israel and a Spiritual Israel (see "Seed Paper" [PR 1]).

Great Significance of the NAME

The Name in Scripture

gp72» In the Bible there was a great significance placed on the Name of the true God. God revealed His NAME to Moses when Moses asked Him for His name (Ex 3:13-16). His NAME was a memento or memorial to all generations (Exo 3:15). Moses spoke in God's NAME (Exo 5:23). God spoke to Moses and told him that Abraham, Isaac, and Jacob knew God as "God Almighty" for God had not revealed His NAME to them (Exo 6:2-3). God declared His NAME to the people of the earth (land) by showing His great power against Egypt during the Hebrews' exodus from Egypt (Exo 9:13-16). God warned the Hebrews about taking His NAME in vain (Exo 20:7). God said He would bless the Hebrews in every place in which He caused His NAME to be remembered (Exo 20:24). God proclaimed His NAME to Moses (Exo 33:19; 34:6).

gp73» Before the Hebrews went into the promised land God instructed them to seek the place where God shall choose to put His NAME (Deut 12:1-5). The Levites were chosen by God to stand and to minister in the NAME of God (Deut 18:1, 5). Aaron and his sons were to put God's NAME on the Israelites (Num 6:27). God's NAME is called on Israel (Deu 28:10; 2Chron 7:14; Isa 56:5; Dan 9:19). False prophets caused Israel to forget God's NAME and use the name of Baal ("Lord") instead (Jer 23:27). Israel would profane the NAME of God among the other nations (Ezek 36:21-22). Jews in Egypt would also forget God's NAME (Jer 44:26). But the God delivers for his NAME's sake (Psa 23:3; 25:11; 143:11; Isa 48:9). Since God's NAME was called on Israel, if Israel was totally destroyed, God's NAME would not have remained (Josh 7:9; Isa 48:9). Therefore, God for his holy NAME's sake, promises to give Israel a new heart and a new spirit so they can keep God's law and thus not profane God's NAME (Ezek 36:21-27). God told Moses that He was going to raise up a prophet to the Israelites from among their brothers, and that God would put His words in the month of the prophet (note, John 12:49), and that this prophet would speak in God's NAME (Deut 18:15-19).

gp74» God told David through a messenger that David's seed would build a house for God's NAME (2Sam 7:1-13). Solomon gave directions for the construction of the house for God's NAME (1 Kings 5:5-6). After Solomon finished building the house, God appeared to him and said to Solomon that His NAME would be put there (1 Kings 9:3). The temple was the house for God's NAME (1Kings 8:15-20). God's NAME was on Jerusalem and its temple (Jer 3:17; 2Kings 21:4, 7). The NAME was on mount Zion (Isa 18:7).

gp75» Jesus Christ came in his Father's NAME (John 5:43; John 10:25; Mat 21:9; etc.). Jesus Christ in a Spiritual sense was the true temple of God (note John 2:19, 21; compare with 1Cor 6:19; 3:16-17; etc.). Jesus Christ's Father is God (John 8:54; see GP 2). God the Father gave His NAME to Jesus (John 17:11-12, NIV, see Greek text; see Jer 23:5-6; 33:14-16). This is Jesus Christ's *new* NAME (Rev 3:12). Jesus Christ's *new* NAME is better than the angels (Heb 1:3-4). Jesus did his work in his Father's NAME (John 10:25). Jesus said that whatsoever a follower of him should ask in his NAME He would do it (remember Jesus was in his Father's NAME) (John 15:16).

gp76» After Jesus died, and then rose up to life again, it was said that those believing that Jesus was the Christ (the Messiah) would have life in Jesus' NAME (John 20:31). After this, people were baptized in the NAME of Jesus Christ (Acts 2:38; 8:16). Those who were baptized in the NAME of Jesus are in effect in the NAME of Jesus and are said to be in the NAME of Jesus (1 Cor. 5:4). Those in God's NAME are saved, have life, are justified, preach boldly, their sins are forgiven and they receive God's Spirit, and signs and wonders are done by them (Acts 4:12; John 20:31; 1Cor 6:11; Acts 9:27, 29; Acts 2:38; 10:43; 1John 2:12; Acts 4:30). These are called in a Spiritual sense the "temple of God" (1Cor 6:19; 3:16-17; 2Cor 6:16).

gp77» The Father, the Son, and the Holy Spirit have the same NAME (Matt 28:19). The 144,000 have the NAME written on their foreheads (Rev 14:1). *Remember* those in the NAME of Jesus Christ are in the NAME of God because God gave His NAME to Jesus Christ (John 17:11-12, NIV; Phil 2:9; see Jer 23:5-6; 33:14-16).

gp78» God is taking out of the nations a people for his NAME (Acts 15:2, 12-14; Amos 9:11-12). In fact all nations shall be gathered to the NAME (Jer 3:17; 4:2). God has sons and daughters from the ends of the earth who will be called by His NAME, "whom I [LORD, YHWH] created for my glory, whom I formed and made" (Isa 43:6-7, 21, NIV). After God's judgment he will change the people's speech and call all of them by the Name of God: "For then will I turn to the people a pure language, to call them all by the name of the LORD [YHWH], to serve Him with one consent (Zeph 3:9, see Hebrew text; see YLT; see Eph 3:15). All people will be in His Name, and call or pray in His Name. If you can call in someone's name, you can be called by that name.

gp79» All through the Bible one can find where people call upon the NAME of God and trust in His NAME. By looking "name" up in Young's concordance or in Strong's concordance you can see how important God's NAME was to His people.

But what is God's NAME?

THE NAME OF GOD

gp80» As we've just seen there is great significance placed on God's NAME in the Bible. The importance placed on God's NAME has little to do with the pronunciation of the NAME. Unlike today in many nations, the Hebrews placed more significance on the *meaning* of names. This is very important. We must not only take care to understand what is God's NAME, more importantly we must understand the real meaning of God's NAME. The paradoxes of God and the problem of evil can only be understood by knowing the true meaning and significance of God's NAME.

gp81» For some persons what follows is too detailed and repetitive, for others it is not detailed enough. We will repeat some things many times in order to make our point as clear as possible because we must break through a prevalent mindset imposed by tradition. See "More Details" at the end of GP in the GP: Appendix for more specific information on some topics.

What Is God's NAME?

gp82» We must go back to the book of Exodus to find God magnifying and revealing His NAME to Moses:

- Then Moses said to God, "Indeed, when I come to the children of Israel and say to them, 'The God of your fathers has sent me to you,' and they say to me, **'What is His name?'** what shall I say to them?" (Exo 3:13)

And God answered the question:

- **"I will be** that **I will be"** (Exo 3:14).

[Hebrew = אֶהְיֶה אֲשֶׁר אֶהְיֶה]

gp83» This is the literal English translation from the Hebrew text. But in the *King James Version* it reads: "**I am** that **I am**." The majority of English Bibles translates it this way. But this traditional translation is incorrect (See "I am" below). I repeat, the "I am" translation is incorrect. Look at the following examples:

- In the note for Exodus 3:14 in the *American Standard Version* it correctly says the verse is: **I will be that I will be.**
- In a footnote for *The NIV Study Bible*, it has **I will be what I will be.**
- In most Hebrew lexicons it shows that this phrase in Exodus 3:14 should be translated, **I will be that I will be,** or **I will be who I will be.**
- In the *Englishman's Hebrew-English Old Testament*, by Joseph Magil (printed by Zondervan in 1974), Exodus 3:14 reads: **I will be that I will be.**
- According to *The Pentateuch And Haftorahs: Hebrew Text, English Translation And Commentary*, edited by Dr. J. H. Hertz, C. H (former Chief Rabbi), published by Soncino Press, London (1956), in its commentary it states: "Most moderns follow Rashi in rendering [Hebrew - *ehyeh asher ehyeh*] '**I will be what I will be.**'"

  [But even though this is close to how Exodus 3:14 should be translated J. D. Hertz still allowed the traditional rendering of Exodus 3:14 to be used in the book's English translation of the verse.]

- According to The *International Standard Bible Encyclopedia* (1915 Edition) under "God, names of," page 1266, we see that it should be translated: **I will be that I will be.**
- By looking up the Hebrew words in The *Analytical Hebrew and Chaldee Lexicon*, by Benjamin Davidson we see that the correct translation is: **I will be that I will be.**
- Even the Bible in *Today's English Version*, published by the American Bible Society in 1976, has in a note for Ex 3:14, **I will be who I will be.**
- And in the *New International Version* (1978) it has a note for Exodus 3:14, "**I will be what I will be.**"

- And from the *Brown, Driver, Briggs, Gesenius Hebrew and English Lexicon*, "**I shall be the one who will be**."

gp84» The "that," or "who," or "what," in "I will be ... I will be" is a relative pronoun, *'asher* (# 834), which can be translated in several ways such as: "that" or "who," or "what" or "when," etc (see Lexicon).

Exodus 3:12 v. Exodus 3:14

gp85» To transliterate **I will be that I will be** from Exodus 3:14 into English without the vowels we get:

- 'hyh 'shr 'hyh.

[Hebrew = אֶהְיֶה אֲשֶׁר אֶהְיֶה]

gp86» The root form of the Hebrew verb translated into **I will be** in Exodus 3:14 is *hyh*, a *to be* verb (Strong's # 1961). With the addition of ' [א] to *hyh* [היה] the word becomes, *'hyh* [אֶהְיֶה], and is now in the imperfect, first person, and singular form (*Analytical Hebrew and Chaldee Lexicon*, note Table N; *Gesenius' Grammar*, §40a-c; *The Essentials of Biblical Hebrew*, by Yates, p.41).[12]

gp87» This is the same verb as in Exodus 3:12: "**I will be** with you." Most English versions of the Bible translate Exodus 3:12 as, **I will be**, even the versions that translate Exodus 3:14 as, **I am**. This is important, so I'll repeat:

- **'hyh** [אֶהְיֶה] appears in both Exodus 3:12 and 3:14. In 3:12 it is translated, "**I will be** with you." But for some reason it is translated as, "**I am** " in Exodus 3:14 when pertaining to God's NAME. In most other places in the Bible in most translations it is translated, "I will be." In fact, in 41 other places in the Bible in most English translations it is mostly translated as, "I will be." (See below, "I will be in Context," gp180)

gp88» Notice the *Kings James Version* of Exodus 3:12 as compared to Exodus 3:14:

- And he said, Certainly **I will be** [אֶהְיֶה] with thee; and this shall be a token unto thee, that I have sent thee: When thou hast brought forth the people out of Egypt, ye shall serve God upon this mountain. [Exodus 3:12]
- And God said unto Moses, **I am that I am** [אֶהְיֶה אֲשֶׁר אֶהְיֶה]: and he said, Thus shalt thou say unto the children of Israel, **I am** [אֶהְיֶה] hath sent me unto you. [Exodus 3:14]

gp89» Do you see it? The same Hebrew word translated into ***I am*** in Exodus 3:14 is translated ***I will be*** in Exodus 3:12. Furthermore, this same word is translated into ***I will be*** dozens of other times in the Bible (See "I will be in Context" below). But why is it traditionally translated **I am**? Yes, something very strange is going on here with this common mistranslation of **I am**, and that something has to do with the influence of Grecian philosophy on Biblical study, as well as the real reason — the "other-mind." We'll examine more on Grecian philosophy later.

---

[12] The Hebrew *hyh* is a *to be* verb (Strong's # 1961). The Hebrew **'hyh** *perfectly* conforms to the rules of an imperfect verb when a verb is united with its personal pronoun fragment. When the first-person-pronoun fragment (א) is attached to the verb היה (*hyh*) together (אהיה) they mean, *I will-be*.

Yehowah: God Revealed His NAME To Moses
God Restates His NAME

gp90» Right after God told Moses that his NAME was **I will be that I will be**, and for Moses to tell Israel that **I will be** had sent him (Exo 3:14), God rephrased his NAME and said unto Moses:

- "You shall say to the children of Israel that **Yehowah** [יְהֹוָה] ... has sent me [Moses] to you [Israel]" (Exo 3:15).
- "and say to them, '**Yehowah** [יְהֹוָה] the God of your fathers, the God of Abraham, of Isaac, and of Jacob, appeared to me [Moses]'" (Exo 3:16).

gp91» After Moses asked God his NAME, He answered with **I will be** repeating it twice, then He told Moses to tell Israel that his NAME was *I will be*, and right after this He told Moses to tell Israel that his NAME was **Yehowah** [יְהֹוָה]. Going back 1000s of years, in an ancient Hebrew script, the spelling of God's NAME without the vowels looked something like this:

𐤄𐤅𐤄𐤉

God's NAME is *Emphasized* – He will be!

gp92» It is known that when words are repeated in Hebrew it has the effect of ***emphasizing*** the word (see Introduction in the *Emphasized Bible*, and *Gesenius' Hebrew Grammar*, § 133 *k,l*). For example in Genesis 2:17, the Hebrew word for "death" is repeated twice, and can be literally translated, "dying, you shall die." But when translated into English it becomes "you shall *surely* die." Or in Exodus 26:33 in Hebrew it has, "holy of the holies," and is translated as "the most holy" or "the most holy place." Therefore when God repeated his NAME twice (**I will be** that **I will be**), He was giving *emphasis* to his NAME.

gp93» God repeated his NAME twice, He again says that his NAME is **I will be**. He then changes it to **Yehowah** only because this is the only grammatically correct way for Moses or anyone else to address God. Moses couldn't grammatically say, "**I will be** has sent me," but he could correctly say, "**Yehowah** has sent me." Because **Yehowah is** an imperfect *to be* verb in the masculine gender, except that it is in the 3rd person (see *BDBG Hebrew and English Lexicon* pp. 217-218; *Gesenius' Gram.* § 40 & § 75*s*; see below), **literally God was telling Moses to say to the nation of Israel:**

"***He (who) will be*** has sent me."

God's NAME is an imperfect verb used as a noun.

gp94» In Hebrew verbs were used as nouns. Without its vowels, Yehowah is spelled YHWH. **Yehowah** as with "I will be" of Exodus 3:14 is an imperfect *to be* verb in the masculine gender, except that it is in the 3rd person (see *BDBG Hebrew and English Lexicon pp.* 217-218; *Gesenius' Gram.* § 40 & § 75*s*; see below). It is not a noun *per se*, but because it is used in the Bible as a proper noun because it is God's NAME as manifested in Exodus 3:14-16 (*Gesenius' Gram.* §125*d*; §§ 79, 83*a*, 116*f*).

What is an imperfect verb?

gp95» Hebrew has two different verbs: perfect and imperfect. God's NAME is in the imperfect. To understand what an imperfect verb is in Hebrew, we will contrast it with the perfect. Some call the Hebrew imperfect verb a future tense word, but this is not correct. From *Gesenius' Hebrew Grammar* (Oxford, 1980 reprint) we see that:

- "The Hebrew (Semitic) **Perfect** denotes in general that which is **concluded**, **completed**, and **past**, that which is *represented* as accomplished, even though it is continued into present time or even be actually still future. The **Imperfect** denotes, on the other hand, the **beginning**, the **unfinished**, and the **continuing**, that which is just happening, which is conceived **as in process of coming to pass**, and hence, also, that which is yet future; likewise also that which occurs repeatedly or in a continuous sequence in the past (Latin Imperfect)" (*Gesenius* § 47.1, note 1).

gp96» More on the Hebrew Imperfect verb from S.R. Driver's *Hebrew Tenses*:

- "It emphasizes the process introducing and leading to completion, it expresses what may be termed ***progressive*** **continuance**" (Driver, p. 27).

Meaning Contrary to "I AM" Doctrine

gp97» The meaning of God's NAME (beginning, unfinished, continuing, or coming to pass; see also Rev 1:8) is contrary to the "I AM" doctrine and the immutability doctrine. We will examine these traditional doctrines later. But for now remember that God's NAME is a verb, used as a noun, in the imperfect tense. For more information on this see read further in this chapter and see GP: Appendix in the back of this book.

Hebrew Words Written Without Vowels

gp98» At first the Hebrew language was written only with consonants and was written from right to left. When the Hebrews read, they added the vowels in their mind to the words. In Moses' time there was apparently no method of writing vowels in Hebrew. Two thousand years after Moses a system of vowel points was developed that was added below, between, and sometimes on top of the letters:

- "The present pronunciation of this consonantal text, its vocalization and accentuation, rest on the tradition of the Jewish schools, as it was finally fixed by the system of punctuation (§ 7 *h*) introduced by Jewish scholars about the seventh century A. D." [*Gesenius' Hebrew Grammar*, p. 12]

Therefore when Moses wrote down God's NAME he did not write any vowels.

Is the Correct Pronunciation of the NAME Possible?

gp99» As we have just manifested, Moses did not write down the vowels for God's NAME, since in his time there was no method to write vowels. But it is said that the correct vowels for God's NAME were passed down orally through the years and are preserved in today's vowel point system. But it is unlikely that the exact sound of the Biblical Hebrew has been preserved for us today because there were different schools with different methods and interpretations, and there were Jews with different ways of pronouncing the Hebrew words (*Gesenius' Grammar*, p. 38, footnote 2; see § 7 *i*; § 8 "Preliminary Remark"; p. 42 footnote 3; etc.).

gp100» Because the Jews themselves pronounced words differently, depending on where they lived, it is debatable how one should pronounce God's NAME. It is only a guessing game. In order to write something with vowels we shall pick the spelling of **Yehowah**, which is the spelling found in some Jewish-Hebrew texts of the Old Testament (See "More Details" in Appendix). But Nehemia Gordon makes good arguments for Yehovah as maybe the original spelling.

(www.nehemiaswall.com/nehemia-gordon-name-god)

Different Spelling of the NAME

gp101» Now the Hebrew word "Yehowah" is sometimes translated into English as Jehovah or as the LORD (small caps). Some even translate the Hebrew word into Yahweh, Jehovah, LORD, and Yahweh, etc. The spelling of the Hebrew word YHWH as recorded in some Hebrew texts with vowel points is **Yehowah** (#3068) except when it is found with *'adhonay* (#136), then it is spelled, **Yehowih** (#3069). One text from about 1000 A.D. has it, **Yehwah**. As of the end of 2020, no Hebrew text that Nehemia Gordon has examined has it **Yahweh**.

gp102» The spelling of *Yehowah* for God's NAME is found in *The Pentateuch and Haftorahs*, edited by J.H. Hertz, Chief Rabbi, and published by the Soncino Press, 1956; the spelling is found in the *Interlinear Hebrew-English Old Testament* (Genesis-Exodus), by George R. Berry; the spelling is found in the C.D. Ginsburg's Hebrew Bible; the spelling is also found in some verses of the *Biblia Hebraica Stuttgartensia* (BHS), such as Gen 3:14; 9:26; Ex 3:2; 13:3,9,15; 14:1,8; etc. For the reason Yehowah is translated into LORD in some English translations, and for sufficient and qualifying details on the vowels used in God's NAME, you must read, "Yehowah or Yahweh or Jehovah or LORD." This is included in GP: Appendix of this book.

Gesenius admits the spelling "Yehowah" fits the evidence

gp103» Gesenius, the famous 19th century expert in Oriental literature, apparently popularized the theory that Yahweh was the true spelling of God's NAME instead of Yehovah or Yehowah. But at the same time Gesenius made this argument for the spelling, being Yahweh, he also wrote, "**Also those who consider that Yehowah was the actual pronunciation, are not altogether without ground on which to defend their opinion. In this way can the abbreviated syllables Yeho and Yo, with which many proper names begin, be more satisfactorily explained.**" As the editor of *Gesenius' Hebrew and Chaldee Lexicon* [1949, Eerdmans Pub] said, "This last argument goes a long way to prove the vowels **Y**eh**ow**ah to be the true ones" (p. 337). See GP Appendix for more info on this subject

NAME Pronounced

gp104» Keeping the above qualifications in mind, the NAME is pronounced with the vowels, **yᵉ hō wäh** [the "o" is a long o]. Or **Yᵉho vah**. The "w" in Yehowah came from *Gesenius's Grammar*, German language, but since the Germans pronounce their "w" like the English pronounce their "v," then Yehovah may be correct.

[More information - *https:////www.youtube.com/watch?v=wRsbSLU9oFA* and *https://nehemiaswall.com/nehemia-gordon-name-god*]

God's NAME: BeComingOne
To Review and Conclude

gp105» As shown above, God said that his NAME was, "I will be." He repeated it twice in a row for emphasis. But to others God's NAME is "He-will-be" or "He (who) will be" or thus "Yehowah" or "Yehovah." We do not address God as, "I will be." To be grammatically correct we must call Him, "Yehowah" or "He (who) will be." As shown above, the Hebrew word "Yehowah" is from a verbal stem. "Yehowah" if used as a verb means, He-will-be, or He-will-become, or He-will-come-to-be. But when used as a noun "Yehowah" means, He-(who)-will-be, or He-(who)-will-become, or the **Becoming-One**. In The *Emphasized Bible*, page 26, it says the "Becoming-One" is a proper translation for YHWH. Many translations insist on using "LORD" in translating YHWH even though it is based on a mistaken Greek translation that used *Kurios* ("Lord") when the Hebrew YHWH was translated into Greek.

gp106» **BeComingOne** is a better translation than "He-(who)-will-be" since it indicates that "Yehowah" exists now, but somehow is not yet perfected or completed or fully finished: He is *Becoming*. Since "Yehowah" is an imperfect verb (used as a noun), it signifies an incomplete state, it indicates something that is becoming, it indicates something that is in the process of coming-to-be, it indicates something that will be, yet is somehow now in existence. Thus, the translation, "BeComingOne," fits the Hebrew word "Yehowah" best for the English language. The meaning of God's NAME indicates that at some point in time the BeComingOne will come to be, or at that time will have become, or at that time will exist in his truest form or meaning.

NAME in the New Testament

gp107» In the New Testament please note the Lord God Almighty is the one "who is, and who was, and *who is to come*" (Rev 1:4, 8; 4:8; 11:17; 16:5). **The BeComingOne (YHWH) is the almighty God, the one "who is, and who was, and who is to come."** This is a good translation of the meaning of the Hebrew imperfect verb Yehowah, which is God's NAME. Or we can translate Revelation 1:8: "Lord, the God, the is, the was, and the coming-one, the almighty." God Almighty is to come, or He is the COMING-ONE, who is now, and who was; He is the BeComingOne.

gp108» With our knowledge that God's NAME was an imperfect verb, and that it was in the cohortative form, we can conclude that:

- **YHWH means one existing in someway in an incomplete state who yet will, without any doubt, come to be, or come to exist, in the fullest sense.**

Hereafter in this book we will use the correct translation of YHWH — BeComingOne — instead of "LORD."

No Problem with the NAME, But with Immutability Theory
Yes I know that God's NAME is against the immutability theory, but the problem is not with His NAME, but with the false immutability theory.

"I Am" Doctrine
Grecian Mindset

gp109» The Hebrew word translated "**I Am**" in many of today's translations of Exodus 3:14 is an incorrect translation because the Hebrew word is a verb in the *imperfect* tense. The translation of "I am" doesn't give the full meaning of God's NAME. The translation, "I am," does not take into consideration that it was translated from a Hebrew *imperfect* verb. The "I am" translation is not only a wrong translation from the Hebrew text, but also was influenced by a mistaken Greek translation (*Septuagint*) made in Egypt.

Greek Translation of God's NAME: "The Being"

gp110» The much used Greek translation of the Old Testament, called the *Septuagint* (LXX or seventy), because it was translated by about 70 translators, was translated in Egypt in the third century BC for Ptolemy II, a king of Egypt. In this Greek translation, instead of "**I will be** that **I will be**," the Greek (*Septuagint*) has "**I am the Being**" and "**The Being** has sent me to you" for Exodus 3:14.

- LXE Exodus 3:14: And God spoke to Moses, saying, **I am The Being**; and he said, Thus shall ye say to the children of Israel, **The Being** has sent me to you. [English of Greek text]

"The Being" was Egypt's God

gp111» It is important to point out the Greek version, the *Septuagint*, was made in Egypt and a notable Egyptian's god, Osiris, was addressed in their prayers as "the Being":

- "At a later period, however, the Egyptians put their trust in Osiris himself, and addressed their prayers directly to him as **the Being**." (p. 151, *The Gods of the Egyptians*, Vol 1, by W.A. Wallis Budge, emphasis mine)

From this corruption of the Hebrew Bible, later translations intermingled the Hebrew and Greek translation in order to get: "I am that I am."

Bible Written in Hebrew Not Greek

gp112» But the Old Testament was written in Hebrew, not Greek. Besides the mistranslation of Exodus 3:14, the *Septuagint* mistranslates the Hebrew word, YHWH. For YHWH it substitutes the Greek word for "Lord," which is *Kurios* (# 2962). From this early Greek translation we see many translations that use "LORD" instead of "Yehowah" or as commonly misspelled, "Jehovah" or "Yahweh."

Catholic Church's Bias Toward the Greek Text

gp113» It was the "fathers" of the Catholic Church such as Augustine that were insistent on using translations from the Greek text instead of the Hebrew text:

- "There have, of course, been other translations of the Old Testament from Hebrew into Greek. We have versions by Aquila, Symmachus, Theodotion, and an anonymous translation which is known simply as the 'fifth edition.' Nevertheless, the Church [Catholic] has adopted the Septuagint as if it were the only translation.... From the Septuagint a Latin translation has been made, and this is the one which the Latin churches use. This is still the case despite the fact that in our own day the priest Jerome, a great scholar and master of all three tongues, has made a translation into Latin, not from Greek but directly from the original- Hebrew. The Jews admit that his [Jerome's] highly learned labor is a faithful and accurate version, and claim, moreover, that the seventy translators [Septuagint] made a great many mistakes in their version. Christ's Church [Catholic], however, thinks it inadvisable to choose the authority of any one man [Jerome] as against the authority of so many men — men hand-picked, too, by the high priest Eleazar for this specific task. [Augustine here speaks of the myth of the 70 or so translators of the Greek text (*The Canon of Scripture*, F.F. Bruce, pp 43ff).] For, even supposing that they [the 70] were not inspired by one divine Spirit, but that, after the manner of scholars, the Seventy merely collated their versions in a purely human way and agreed on a commonly approved text, still, I [Augustine] say, no single translator should be ranked ahead of so many. The truth is that there shone out from the Seventy so tremendous a miracle of divine intervention that anyone translating the Scriptures from the Hebrew into any other language will, if he is a faithful, translator, agree with the Septuagint; if not, we must still believe that there is some deep revealed meaning in the Septuagint." [*City of God*, by Augustine, book 18, chapter 43]

NAME Forgotten by Judah

gp114» It is very significant that Judah was prophesied to not pronounce God's NAME:

- "Behold, I have sworn by My great NAME, says Jehovah, that My NAME shall no more be named in the mouth of any man of Judah in all the land of Egypt." [Jer 44:26, King James II Version]

gp115» The *Septuagint* translation was done in Egypt, and it was in Egypt that the Jews were to forget God's NAME: they began to use the Greek equivalent for "Lord" instead of the Hebrew YHWH or Yehowah ("Jehovah"). *The International Standard Bible Encyclopaedia* (1915 A.D.) speaks about the translation:

- "It is one of the outstanding results of the breaking-down of international barriers by the conquests of Alexander the Great and the dissemination of the Greek language .... The Jewish commercial settlers at Alexandria forced by circumstances to abandon their language, clung tenaciously to their faith; and the translation of the Scriptures into their adopted language, produced to meet their own needs, had the further result of introducing the outside world to a knowledge of their history and religion.... The LXX [Septuagint] was also the Bible of the early Greek Fathers, and helped to mold dogma; it furnished proof-texts to both parties in the Arian controversy." [under "Septuagint"]

Greek Mindset

gp116» If God's Being is what or like what others say it is, then God's very NAME should have been written or spoken with a *perfect* verb.

- "A Hebrew perfect verb is "concluded, completed [they say that nothing can be added to God, he is eternal, not changeable, etc] ... even though it is continued into the present time or even be actually still future." [*Gesenius' Gram*, § 47.1, note 1]

gp117» But God's NAME was written and spoken with an *imperfect* verb, "I will be."

- "The imperfect does not imply *mere* continuance as such ... it emphasizes the process introducing and leading to completion, it expresses what may be termed *progressive* continuance." [Driver, *Hebrew Tenses*, p. 27]

gp118» If God's Being is what others say it is, then God's NAME should have been written with the Hebrew *participle active*, which indicates *mere* continuance and not *progressive* continuance (Driver, p. 27, 35ff; *Ges. Gram.*, §116a,c). The Hebrew imperfect indicates progressive continuance. (See "More Details" in GP: Appendix)

Greek Mindset: God <u>had</u> to be Changeless

gp119» According to the Grecian mindset, which was influenced by Plato and Aristotle, God's NAME and its meaning could never, no *never* be from an imperfect verb, because an imperfect verb is one that is beginning, unfinished, and continuing. Plato in *Timaeus* makes the distinction between that which has existed always and that which is becoming:

- "We must in my opinion begin by distinguishing between that which always is and never becomes from that which is always becoming but never is....In addition, everything that becomes or changes must do so owing to some cause; for nothing can come to be without a cause." [Plato: Timaeus and Critias, trans. Desmond Lee, Penguin Classics, p. 40; see also *Plato*, volume IX in the Loeb Classical Library (No. 234), which gives a slightly different translation, p. 49 & p. 113]

gp120» God to the Grecian mindset could not be **becoming** in any sense, since He must be the First Cause, the One that cannot be caused in anyway; He must have existed always; He must have been perfect and complete always.

- "Moreover, life belongs to God. For the actuality of thought is life, and God is that actuality; and the essential actuality of God is life most good and eternal. We hold, then, that God is a living being, eternal, most good; and therefore life and a continuous eternal existence belong to God; for that is what God is." [Aristotle, *Metaphysics*, Loeb Classical Lib. #287, p. 151]

gp121» To the Greek philosophers it was God who was "the Cause wherefor He that constructed it constructed Becoming and the All" (*Plato*, volume IX in the Loeb Classical Library, p. 55). God in no way could have been in anyway "becoming" to the Greek mindset.

gp122» Their Grecian mindset was unable to translate the Hebrew imperfect word for God into a Greek imperfect. Instead they translated Exodus 3:14 into, "the Being," which is a present participle in the Greek translation. Plato's God was:

- "the ever-existing God"
- someone who "existed always"
- had "no beginning of generation"
- He must have "constructed Becoming and the All"
- "'Was' and 'will be' on the other hand, are terms properly applicable to the Becoming ... but it belongs not to that which is ever changeless." [pp. 65, 51, 55, 77, Plato's *Timaeus*, Loeb Classical Library, No. 234, Harvard Univ. Press]

gp123» According to Plato, God was eternal, always existed, and since he was good, then any change must be change for the worse (Plato, *Republic*, Book II, 381B). Because God to the great Grecian philosophers was changeless, his special NAME could not have been translated, "I will be" or "He will be," but had to have been translated, "I am" and "The Being." Yet in Revelation 1:8 it reads, "Lord the God, the is, the was, and the Coming-One" or "the one who is, who was, and who is coming." The real NAME for God and its meaning is absolutely contrary to the Grecian mindset.

gp124» Because this Grecian mindset of a changeless God was passed on to the "fathers" of the Catholic Church, and from them to our day through tradition, modern translations of God's NAME as revealed in Exodus 3:14-15 are faulty.

Hebrew verbs are different from English verbs

gp125» Not only did the Greek culture make it difficult for some to translate God's NAME correctly, but the differences between Hebrew and other languages also make it difficult to translate God's NAME correctly. It should be noted here that it is difficult, if not impossible, to translate verbs from Hebrew to English:

- "There is no tense [past, present, future] in the Hebrew verb. The student is only kidding himself when he continually translates the Hebrew perfect into the English past, and the Hebrew imperfect into the English future. After a while, he unconsciously begins to believe it. The perfect state is really talking only about an action which is completed. The imperfect state speaks of an incomplete action. Both of these actions (completed and incomplete) can occur in the past, present or future. The only way you can tell the tense [past, present, future] in the Hebrew language is by the context.... So, when you find the tenses in your English Old Testament, don't lean too hard on them. You might be counting on what might be a translator's precarious guess. Don't blame the translators for putting those tenses in, however; you cannot write English without them." [*Do It Yourself Hebrew And Greek*, by Edward W. Goodrick, Pub. 1976, pages 15.4 & 15.5; *Hebrew Tenses*, S. R. Driver, ch. 1]

Didn't Jesus say "I am"?

gp126» According to the Trinitarians, because Christ said "I am" [ἐγώ εἰμι] (John 8:58; 4:26; 6:35; 8:12; 10:7; 10:11; 11:25; 13:13; 14:6 15:1; 18:8), "He thus identified Himself with the covenant name of Jehovah in the Old Testament" (p. 39, *All the Messianic Prophecies of the Bible*, Herbert Lockyer). The problem here is that God's NAME is not, "I am." God's NAME is, "I will be," as we have seen in chapter 1 of this book. First the Trinitarians use a false name for God ("I am") obtained from a false Old Testament translation of Exodus 3:14, then to prove their falsehood they quote a few times from the New Testament of the Bible where Jesus said the words, "I am."

gp127» Since God's real NAME is not "I am" [ἐγώ εἰμ] it means nothing that Jesus said "I am" a few times in the New Testament. Others in the New Testament also said, "I am." [ἐγώ εἰμ]:

- The apostles said the same "I am"[13] when asking a question, "I am Lord?" In English we would say, "am I he Lord? (Mat 26:22).
- Judas said the same "I am"[1] when asking a question, "I am Master?" In English we would say, "am I he Master?" (Mat 26:25).
- The healed blind man said the same "I am"[1] when identifying himself, while we would say, "I am *he*."(John 9:9)
- Peter said the same "I am"[1] when identifying himself, but in English we would say, "I am *he*."(Acts 10:21).
- Paul said the same "I am"[1] when identifying himself as a Jew, "I am [exist] as a male Jew (Acts 22:3) or when identifying the way he existed, "such as I am [exist]" (Acts 26:29).
- Paul said, "by the grace of God <u>I am what I am</u>" (1Cor 15:10)

This last verse is almost exactly how most English translations translate Exodus 3:14. Does this mean Paul is God? Of course not, but it further proves the nonsense of those who believe in the "I am" theory.

Thus to the Trinitarians' mode of thinking, the apostles, including Judas and Paul, are "I am."[14] Of course, this is nonsense, since Christ was not saying he was the very Jehovah when he said "before Abraham was, I AM" (John 8:58).

gp128» By studying how "I am"[1] is used in the New Testament, we see that it may mean either:

- (1) "I am *he*"
- or (2) "I exist" or "I existed"

What Jesus Christ was saying in John 8:58 was that he existed before Abraham: **before Abraham was, I existed**." In some way he existed before Abraham. This was true because the *Spirit* (not the flesh) of Christ did exist before Abraham (see, GP 3-5). In this scripture Christ was **not** saying he was the Jehovah or YHWH, by saying, "I am," even though we know through other scripture that he indeed is Jehovah (YHWH) after he went to the Father.

gp129» When Christ said he came in his Father's NAME ("I come in my Father's name," John 5:43), he was saying he was coming in the real NAME of God; he was coming in the NAME of the One who said his NAME was, "I will be." But the places in the New Testament where Christ said "I am" (John 8:58, etc.) had nothing to do with identifying Christ with Jehovah, for one reason God's NAME is not "I am," and for another reason others in the New Testament also said "I am" or used the phrase similarly to the way that Christ used it. Unchangeableness of God

gp130» God's NAME tells us that God is in someway moving and changing towards his completed "state," for God is the BECOMINGONE, for God said his NAME is, *I will be that I will be*, He is Yehowah — He (who) will be. But the book of Malachi said that Yehowah does not change (Mal 3:6). Others speak about the "immutability" of God.

- "The immutability of God is a necessary concomitant of His aseity [self-existence]. It is that perfection of God by which He is devoid of all change, not only in His Being, but also in His perfections, and in His purposes and promises. In virtue of this attribute He is exalted above all becoming, and is free from all accession or diminution and from all growth or decay in His Being or perfections. His knowledge and plans, His moral principles and volitions remain forever the

---

[13] ἐγώ εἰμ

[14] ἐγώ εἰμ

same. Even reason teaches us that no change is possible in God, since a change is either for better or for worse. But in God, as the absolute Perfection, improvement and deterioration are both equally impossible." [*Systematic Theology*, Berkhof, p. 58]

The fathers of the Church took the "immutability of God" theory from Greek philosophers like Plato and Aristotle. Plato believed that God was always perfect and any change was for the worse. Aristotle thought that God could not change because it would prove that God was not completely actualized in all His potentialities (Note *Logic and the Nature of God*, by Davis, pp. 41-42). But as noted by Davis, "now the 'God' Plato speaks of in his writings is different in several respects from the Christian God ... Again, Aristotle's God is not the same thing as the Christian God" (pp. 41 & 42). The immutability of God doctrine has more to do with Grecian philosophy than with the Bible.

gp131» The champions of the immutability of God theory say, "this immutability of God is clearly taught in such passages of scripture as Ex 3:14; Ps 102:26-28; Isa 41:4; 48:12; Mal. 3:6; Rom 1:23; Heb. 1:11,12; Jas. 1:17" (Berkhof, p. 58-59). Yet when you study these scriptures you do not see anything that compares with the descriptions of the immutability doctrine just quoted from Berkhof's book (p.58). Shockingly, we see the immutability doctrine is described in almost the same words used by Plato and Aristotle when they characterize their God(s).

Immutable God Taught by Greeks

gp132» Plato's God was:

- the ever-existing God.
- one who existed always,
- one who had no beginning of generation.
- one who must have constructed Becoming and the All.
- 'Was' and 'will be' on the other hand, are terms properly applicable to the Becoming ... but it belongs not to that which is ever changeless (pp. 65, 51, 55, 77, Plato's *Timaeus*, Loeb Classical Library, No. 234, Harvard Univ. Press).

gp133» Aristotle wrote in his *Metaphysics*:

- "Moreover, life belongs to God. For the actuality of thought is life, and God is that actuality; and the essential actuality of God is life most good and eternal. We hold, then, that God is a living being, eternal, most good; and therefore life and a continuous eternal existence belong to God; for that is what God is. Those who suppose, as do the Pythagoreans and Speusippus, that perfect beauty and goodness do not exist in the beginning ... are mistaken in their view." [Aristotle, *Metaphysics*, Loeb Classical Lib. #287, p. 151]

gp134» Plato wrote in his *The Republic*:

- "But think, God and what is God's is everywhere in a perfect state... if he does alter. Does he change himself for the better and more beautiful, or for the worse and more ugly than himself? He must change for the worse...." [Book II, 381B]

Therefore, according to this way of thinking, God does not change because he is already perfect, and any change would have to be "for the worse." But the theory ignores the Law of Knowledge among other things and limits what God can do. For one thing, change in and of itself is not negative. With the immutability theory God cannot create something new or change at all. Anything that cannot change is actually dead. Those who propagate an immutable God are describing a dead god, not the live God of the Bible. The immutability theory, when you understand the Law of Knowledge, is nothing but a naive theory, not very well thought out. But we cannot explain this until you yourself understand the fundamental Law of Knowledge, which we cover in chapter 7 of this book.

Immutable God or BeComingOne God?

gp135» **This unchangeable or immutable "God" of the great Grecian thinkers is not the one found in the Bible.** The Grecian mindset could not and did not admit that God in any way at all could be **becoming**. Thus they refused to translate God's NAME correctly. But God said His very NAME was "He (who) Will-Be" or the "BeComingOne." The true God emphasized His NAME over and over in scripture. Names in the Bible were used to describe certain important aspects of people. The true God said He was **He will be**, that he was **Yehowah**, or the **BeComingOne**. Some important aspect of Him is becoming. As explained previously, the real God used an imperfect Hebrew verb for His NAME:

- "The *Imperfect* denotes ... the *beginning*, the *unfinished*, and the *continuing*, that which is just happening, which is **conceived as in process of coming to pass**, and hence, also, that which is yet future" (*Gesenius' Hebrew Grammar*).

Serious Subject

gp136» If God is becoming, then He is not immutable in the sense that the Grecian mindset taught. What the Bible teaches about God is not what the Grecian mindset teaches about God. The essence of God is called a "mystery" because hundreds of scriptures are being overlooked that would teach us what God's essence really is. Do we wish to believe what the Bible teaches about the essence of God, or do we wish to continue being blinded by the Grecian mindset? This is serious. We must pay attention to scripture, not to the theological courses taught inside the Grecian mindset.

One sense of God's changeability

gp137» One sense of God's changeability is that throughout the Bible it shows God changing his actions toward people depending on the people's good or bad behavior (Psa 18:25-26; Prov 3:32-35; Lev 26:3ff, 14ff, 40ff; Exo 32:9-13; Jer 18:7-10; etc). If Israel follows God's commandments they receive a just reward. If Israel does not follow God's commandments, they receive a judgment (note Deut chap 28; etc.). The same applies to others besides Israel, for the true God is the God of all (Rom 3:29; Eph 4:6). The true God judges according to the *ways* of people: "the soul that sins, it shall die ... the righteousness of the righteous shall be upon him, and the wickedness of the wicked shall be upon him" (Ezek 18:20). Another sense of God's changeability is manifested in this book. But this change in no way diminishes the Power of God. We cannot speak of this change yet. Do read on.

Real Unchangeableness of God

gp138» Scripture indicates that the unchangeableness of God is his unchangeable words, his **unchangeable truth** (Isa 31:2; Heb 6:17-18; Isa 46:11; Isa 55:11; etc.) and his **all mighty power** (Gen 17:1; 1Chron 29:12; Isa 44:24; etc). God gave his Word that he will not totally consume Israel (note Isa 65:8-9; Exo 32:13, 9-13; 33:1; Lev 26:44-45), because it is through Israel that the true Seed or Savior was to come, so for the sake of His word and His NAME Israel is not consumed (note Ezek 36:21-22ff; Isa 48:9). The statement of Malachi ("I change not; therefore ye sons of Jacob are not consumed") merely indicates that God's *word* does not change, for he has promised that the true SEED would come from this nation. The word translated "change" in Malachi 3:6 is Strong's #8138 which has more to do with duplicity or changing one's promises than changing one's nature or power. To keep his word, to not lie, God must not consume the nation before the SEED came. Read the "Seed Paper" [PR 1] to understand more about God's promises to Israel and how God kept these promises.

gp139» Jesus Christ is not the same "forever" as Hebrews 13:8 in some English translations say, for this is incorrectly translated since it should be "Jesus Christ the same [or the very one], and into the ages" (see Greek text; see "Age Paper" [NM7]). What is unchangeable about God (or Jesus Christ) is his words, his love, his promises, and his power. These things are unchangeable because God does not lie, and he has all the power and life in his hands. In fact God is life (John 5:26; Acts 17:28). The fact that God is life does not change. The fact that God is all-powerful does not change. The fact that God does not lie does not change. But since God is the BeComingOne, then something about God is now changing. What is changing about God was manifested in the Bible. This book will also manifest the becomingness of God. Do read on.

gp140» In Psalm 55:19 it speaks of those who do evil as not changing: "they do not change" (NKJV). Does this mean they are immutable? Of course not. Those who use the "I change not" in Malachi 3:6 to prove their immutability of God theory are taking scripture out of context and using it to infuse the Greek theory of immutability into Christianity. They are not using scripture to find out who or what the God is, but want to hold on to myth instead of finding the truth. The very NAME of God is "He (who) Will-Be." Thus, in some way God is changing. This book will expound on this.

Immutability: One Conclusion.
gp141» In Stephen T. Davis's *Logic and the Nature of God*, he admits,

- I believe the route for the Christian philosopher to follow is happily to admit that there are senses in which God does indeed change, i.e. alter.... . In fact, it is not easy to read the Bible without forming the strong impression that the God revealed there does indeed change in some senses. To pick an obvious case, very typically God is at one moment angry with someone (the person has sinned) and at a later moment forgives that person (the person has repented)....What was the classical doctrine of divine immutability designed to protect? I believe the answer is this: as I noted earlier, it was designed to preserve the view that God is faithful in keeping his promises.... [p.47]

This "classical doctrine of divine immutability" that Davis is writing about is the Grecian influenced ideas, which are not Biblical.
There are ways in which God changes over time, but one thing that does not change is His power and the fact that God cannot lie (Heb 6:17-18; 1John 5:18; Isa 46:11). The true God has all the power. But in someway God does change. This book will amplify on the nature of these changes.

God, Gods

gp142» *In English*, most use the word "God" to describe the supreme being. But the word "god" in English can mean either: the almighty, supreme being; or "any of various beings conceived of as supernatural, immortal, and having special powers over lives and affairs of people" (*Webster's New Word Dictionary*). There can be one god, or many gods. The word "god" is not a proper name for the Supreme Being. The word "god" is a *generic* name for God: it can represent a *class* of beings. In Hebrew and Greek the same applies.

gp143» *In Hebrew*, "elohim," "eloah," "elah," and "el" are the Old Testaments words for god or God. As with the English word "god" these Hebrew words are generic names for god or God.

gp144» *Elohim* was translated into the English word "god" about 2555 times in the KJV. In about 2310 instances "elohim" is translated into "God," thus indicating the supreme God. For example in Genesis 1:1, "In the beginning *elohim* created...." But in some 245 cases "elohim" is translated into lower senses of the word. "Elohim" has been translated in the KJV into such words as:

- *gods* (Gen 3:5);
- strange *gods* (Gen 35:2,4);

- "I have made you [Moses] a *god* to Pharaoh" (Exo 7:1);
- *gods* of Egypt (Exo 12:12);
- *gods* of silver, *gods* of gold (Exo 20:23);
- *judges* (Exo 22:8[7], 9[8]);
- their *gods* (Exo 34:15);
- molten *gods* (Exo 34:17);
- *goddess* (1Kings 11:5,3);
- "I have said, you, *gods* and all of you sons of the most high, but you shall die as man.." [Psa 82:6-7; see John 10:34-36]

gp145» We see that the Hebrew word, *elohim* was translated in many different ways beside being translated as "God." *Elohim* can indicate *gods*, *gods* of silver and gold, *judges*, a *goddess* (like the female god, Ashtoreth) even indicate *Moses* (Exo 7:1) or *mankind* (Psa 82:6-7; see John 10:34-36). Notice that *elohim* is translated in the singular AND plural (god and god*s*). WHY?

Elohim Is Plural/Dual

gp146» The Hebrew word *elohim* is a plural noun as the lexicons indicate and as some of the translations above indicate. "*Elohim*" has the ending "*im*." This indicates that it is a simple plural word (§ 87(a), *Gesenius' Hebrew Grammar*, 1910; re: Holy of Holies – 2 cherubs). The correct nominal suffix is used for the plural *elohim*.

[Compare in the Hebrew text *their gods* (elohim), *my God* (elohim), and *our God* (elohim) in Exo 34:15; Isa 25:1,9 with table A, section I in the Tables of Paradigms of the *Analytical Hebrew and Chaldee Lexicon*.]

Thus the Hebrew word "elohim" itself is an ordinary plural noun.

God's NAME is Yehowah Not Elohim

gp147» The other names or titles of God can refer to others, but the NAME Yehowah only refers to the true God (*Gesenius' Gram.* §125d). "And let them [God's enemies, v.2] know that you, your NAME, Yehowah, you alone the Most High over all the earth" (Psa 83:18; see Exo 6:3). From *Girdlestone's Synonyms of the Old Testament* we read:

- "The Hebrew may say *the* **Elohim**, the true God, in opposition to all false Gods; but he never says *the* **Jehovah**, for Jehovah is the name of the true God only. He says again and again *my God*, but never *my* **Jehovah**, for when he says 'my God' he means Jehovah. He speaks of *the God of Israel*, but never *the* **Jehovah** *of Israel*, for there is no other Jehovah. He speaks of *the living God*, but never of *the living* **Jehovah**, for he cannot conceive of Jehovah as other than living." [pp. 36-37, Jehovah = Yehowah]

Yehowah is the God's proper NAME. In Hebrew "Yehowah" means the BECOMINGONE, or He who will be. Thus, God is the BeComingOne.

Israel's Gods is One YHWH

gp148» But why is *elohim*, an ordinary plural word, translated into the English singular "God" when representing the TRUE God? The main reason for this is that the plural *elohim*, when referring to the TRUE God, is used as if it where a singular noun. "Although plural in form, the name is generally used with a singular verb when it refers to the true God" (p. 19, *Synonyms of the Old Testament*). Gesenius called this phenomenon the *plural of majesty* or *plural of excellence* (Ges. Heb. Gram. § 145h, § 124g).

gp149» When the Old Testament was written, the nations around Israel worshiped *god*S, deitie*S*, and idol*S*. These nations did not worship just ONE God, but many god*S*; their religion was not monotheistic. When the nations around Israel spoke of their deity, they called them "our gods," and they meant more than one kind of god; they spoke of gods who had different attributes. There were gods of fire, of heaven, of the sea, of love, of fertility, of maternity, of the moon, of the sun, of planets, etc (see *Unger's Bible Dict.*, under "gods false"; *The Gods of the Egyptians*, by E.A. Wallis Budge; etc.).

One YHWH, Not One Elohim

gp150» *One Yehowah.* But to Israel there was only ONE deity, and his NAME was/is Yehowah (YHWH) or as popularly spelled today, Jehovah or Yahweh or LORD.

- "Here Israel, Yehowah our *elohim*, Yehowah (is) ONE." [Deut 6:4, literal trans.]

gp151» *One NAME.* As we see, it is Yehowah (YHWH) who is ONE, not *elohim* (gods) who are ONE. But as Deut 6:4 says, Yehowah was Israel's Gods (elohim): "our Gods." But it is Yehowah who is ONE; his NAME one:

- "In that day there shall be ONE Yehowah, and his NAME ONE." [Zech 14:9]

gp152» **Israel's Gods** (elohim) was Yehowah and He was ONE; He had ONE NAME. Thus, Moses calls Yehowah, *our Gods*:

- "Yehowah, Gods [*elohim*] of Israel." [1Kings 8:20]
- "Moses began to explain this law, saying: *Yehowah, our Gods* [elohim] spoke to us in Horeb....." [Deut 1:5,6]

gp153» Yehowah, himself, tells Israel:

- "and you shall be afraid of your Gods, for *I Yehowah, your Gods*." [Lev 25:17, see Hebrew text]

gp154» What kind of Gods are or is Yehowah?:

- "God [el] of gods [elohim] (is) Yehowah." [Josh 22:22]

The expression "god of gods" means: greatest god. Thus, Yehowah is the greatest God, or the great God:

- For the LORD [YHWH] your Gods [elohim] is Gods of gods and Lords of lords, the great God [el]... [Deut 10:17]

gp155» Not only is Yehowah the greatest God, the God of Gods, but He *alone* dwells as or sits as *the* cherubim and *the* Gods, and he *alone* created the universe:

- "And Hezekiah prayed before Yehowah, and said, Yehowah, Gods [elohim] of Israel, who dwells [or sits as] the cherubim [plural], you alone the Gods [elohim], by yourself alone, for all the kingdoms of the earth, you have made the heavens and the earth." [2Kings 19:15]

וַיִּתְפַּלֵּל חִזְקִיָּהוּ לִפְנֵי יְהוָה וַיֹּאמַר יְהוָה אֱלֹהֵי יִשְׂרָאֵל יֹשֵׁב הַכְּרֻבִים אַתָּה־הוּא הָאֱלֹהִים לְבַדְּךָ לְכֹל מַמְלְכוֹת הָאָרֶץ אַתָּה עָשִׂיתָ אֶת־הַשָּׁמַיִם וְאֶת־הָאָרֶץ׃

gp156» In Malachi 2:10 it speaks of the one Father the one God who created us. The "God" here is "el" the singular case of the Hebrew "elohim." Remember the One YHWH is the God of Gods, or the greatest God. It is YHWH who is the true God, the real God, the greatest God.

gp157» Therefore, the nations around Israel had their gods (*elohim*), but *each* of these gods had different qualities or attributes. But Israel's God(s) (*elohim*) was one — there was a oneness to Israel's God(s). And the ONE NAME of Israel's God(s) was "Yehowah."

One God: Old and New Testament

gp158» The New Testament also speaks of One God, but the New Testament does not use God's NAME as manifested in the Old Testament. There is some evidence that at least some of the New Testament was written in Hebrew or Aramaic (Jerome, see "God's NAME in Greek ..." below). There also have been Greek texts of the New Testament found that had God's NAME written in Hebrew or Aramaic instead of the word "Lord" as we see in today's New Testament's translations. One place where "Lord" should be translated into Yehowah is in Mark 12:29. In this scripture it speaks about the One Lord, but since it is a quote from the Old Testament (Deut 6:4) it should read, One Yehowah. So even in the New Testament it is One Yehowah when speaking of the true One God. In Mark 12:32 it should not read "for there is one God," but "for there is one." Other places in the New Testament Bible where it speaks of "one Father, the God," or "one the God," or "no one, but God," or "God is one," or "one God and Father of all," or "one God," or "the God is one,"[15] all point to the Old Testament God, who was/is/will be, He is the BeComingOne (YHWH). It was in the Old Testament that God revealed his NAME and said it was the NAME that was one; it was Yehowah that was one (Deut 6:4; Zech 14:9). It is Yehowah who is God of gods, the great God, the true God.

One Yehowah

gp159» As we have just seen Israel's deity is the most powerful God, he is the Great God, He is Yehowah (YHWH), He is ONE. How is he *one*?

One in History

gp160» In the past "one" was not even considered a number, but "unity." Plato even put unity (one) and numbers into separate categories: "To what class do unity and number belong?" (Smith, *History of Mathematics*, Vol II, p. 27, quoting Plato's *Republic*). Smith in his *History of Mathematics* lists numerous other mathematicians that agree that one (unity) was not a number (pp. 26-29).

- "Not until modern times was unity considered a number. Euclid defined number as a quantity made up of units, and in this he is followed by Nicomachus. **Unity was defined by Euclid as that by which anything is called 'one'** " (Smith, *History of Mathematics*, Vol II, p. 26-27). Euclid who wrote the famous book on Geometry called *Elements* lived around 300 B.C.
- "Number is a multitude brought together or assembled from several units, always from two at least, as in the case of 2, which is the first and the smallest number. **Unity is that by virtue of which anything is said to be one**" (*The First Printed Arithmetic*, Treviso, Italy, 1478).
- "A Living Creature perfect and whole, with all its parts perfect; and next, that it might be One, inasmuch as there was nothing left over out of which another Creature might come into existence... He fashioned it to be **One single Whole, compounded of all wholes**, perfect and ageless... Now for that Living Creature which is designed to embrace within itself all living creatures...."

[From *Timaeus* found in, *Plato* volume IX in the Loeb Classical Library [No. 234], p. 61; see also, Plato: *Timaeus* and *Critias*, trans. Desmond Lee, Penguin Classics, p. 43, which gives a slightly different translation]

This last item shows that even Plato believed that One equaled wholeness or unity, especially when speaking of the "one universe." One question here is at the time the Trinity doctrine was formulated, what was the prevailing idea of one? Was it also unity? Yet as seen by studying Augustine's almost 1600-year-old book called, *On the Trinity*, the Trinitarian belief indeed had something to do with three in one, not three in unity, even though they spoke of the "unity of the Trinity." You can see Augustine struggling with this problem and that is why he (and all of the Trinitarians) calls it a mystery.

---

[15] John 8:41; Rom 3:30; 1Cor 8:4, 6; Gal 3:20; Eph 4:6; 1Tim 2:5; James 2:19

One In Hebrew

gp161» The *Hebrew* word translated One in Deut 6:4 and Zech 14:9 is *'echad*. It means *one* as well as *united* or *unified*.

[Strong's number 259, 258; also Gesenius (7) under, *'echad*; note use in Judges 20:8 & 1Sam 11:7, KJV; *"in one"* translated as "together" in Ezra 2:64; 3:9; 6:20; and "alike" in Ecc 11:6]

One In Greek

gp162» The Greek word one (*heis*) means according to *Thayer's Greek Lexicon*:

- "a cardinal numeral, *one* ... in opposition to a division into parts ... to be united most closely (in will, spirit) ..."
- According to the *Analytical Greek Lexicon* "heis" means: one, one virtually by union, etc.
- The Greek text of the Old Testament used the Greek word *heis* for the Hebrew *'echad* in Deut 6:4.

One In English

gp163» In English the word "one" means according to *The Synonym finder*, by Rodale under "one": "single person or thing, unit...," and under "oneness," "has quality of being one, unity, singleness, sameness..."

- In *Webster's Collegiate Thesaurus* under "unity," we find "the condition of being or consisting of one."
- In *Roger's International Thesaurus*, 3rd ed. we find under, "89. Unity,": "state of Being One. — Nouns 1. unity, oneness, singleness..."
- In a translation of Aristotle's *Metaphysics* by John Warrington (Everyman's Library No 1000) the words "unity" and "one" are used interchangeably (p. 117).
- In *Webster's New Word Dictionary*, College Edition, under "unit": "1. the smallest whole number; one." And under "unity": "1. the state of being one; oneness; singleness; being united." The English word "unity" comes from the Latin word *unitas* which means: oneness.

One Versus Only

gp164» Thus we see in three different languages that "one" has very similar meanings. One means one, as in **singular** (one thing), and one means **unity**. "One" does not mean "only." Hebrew has a special word for only, *yachiyd* (Strong's #3173). This Hebrew word is mostly translated as "only" in the Old Testament (Gen 22:2, 12, 16; Jud 11:34; Zech 12:10; etc.). In Greek there is also a word for only, *monos* (Strong's #3441). And of course English has a word for only.

Many in One

gp165» The ONE Yehowah does *not* mean only or alone. Scriptures such as "let **US** create man in **OUR** image" (Gen 1:26) indicate, there are more than a single person or entity in Yehowah. Other scripture project to us the same thing that there are more than one (single in number) in Yehowah (YHWH). The following plurals are correctly translated from the Hebrew and project the many-in-oneness of the God:

- "Yehowah, God**S**, look! the man has become like one of **US**" — Gen 3:22
- "Come, let **US** go and mix up their language" — Gen 11:7
- "the voice of the Lord**S** saying, Whom shall I send and who will go for **US**" — Isa 6:8
- "Yehowah, our God**S**, one Yehowah" — Deut 6:4
- "Yehowah, he, the God**S**" — Deut 4:35, 39; 7:9; 1Kings 18:39
- "Yehowah, you the God**S**" — 2Sam 7:28

- "Yehowah, he is GodS in heaven above and earth below, there is none else" — Deut 4:39
- "that great (is) Yehowah and our LordS above (#4480) all gods" — Psalm 135:5
- "your CreatorS" — Eccl 12:1
- "Let Israel rejoice in his MakerS" — Psalm 149:2
- "For your husband, your MakerS, Yehowah of hosts" — Isa 54:5
- "knowledge of the HolieS" — Prov 9:10; 30:3
- "Yehowah GodS, HolieS is he" — Joshua 24:19
- "AlmightieS" or "PowerS" — Gen 17:1; etc.
- "most HighS" — Dan 7:18, 22, 25, 27
- "my lordS, Yehowah" — Isa 10:23; 25:8; 40:10; Jer 2:22; see Amos 5:14; Gen 18:27; Exo 4:10; Isa 6:1; *'adonay*="my lords"

Nation as One Man

gp166» The fact that in the Bible nations and groups of people are looked upon "as one man" helps us to understand the God's many-in-oneness:

- Then all the people of Israel came out, from Dan to Beersheba, including the land of Gilead, and the congregation assembled **as one man** to the LORD at Mizpah (RSV Judges 20:1).
- So all the men of Israel gathered against the city, united **as one man** (RSV Judges 20:11).
- When the seventh month came, and the sons of Israel were in the towns, the people gathered **as one man** to Jerusalem (RSV Ezra 3:1).
- And all the people gathered **as one man** into the square before the Water Gate; and they told Ezra the scribe to bring the book of the law of Moses which the LORD had given to Israel (RSV Nehemiah 8:1).

Birth of One Son, as Birth of New Nation

gp167» The fact that the Bible looks upon the birth of one male child as the birth of a whole nation helps us to understand the many-in-oneness of the God:

- "[7] Before she was in labor she gave birth; before her pain came upon her **she was delivered of a son.** [8] Who has heard such a thing? Who has seen such things? Shall a land be born in one day? **Shall a nation be brought forth in one moment?** For as soon as Zion was in labor she brought forth her sons (RSV Isaiah 66:7-8).

Many in the One Body of Christ

gp168» This above mentioned use of ONE in "one Yehowah" and its meaning of, "unity" — or of many being united in the same spirit or quality, is also manifested to us in scripture about the **ONE body of Christ**:

- For as the body is one and has many members, but all the members of that one body, being many, are one body, so also is Christ. 13 *For by one Spirit we were all baptized into one body* — whether Jews or Greeks, whether slaves or free — and have all been made to drink into one Spirit. [1Cor 12:12, NKJV]
- Now you are the body of Christ, and members individually [1 Cor 12:27, NKJV]
- There is neither Jew nor Greek, there is neither slave nor free, there is neither male nor female; *for you are all one in Christ Jesus.* [Gal 3:28, NKJV]

gp169» This use of the word ONE also explains how Jesus Christ and God the Father are ONE and how real Christians are ONE in God and ONE in Christ:

- *I and My Father are one.* [John 10:30, NKJV]
- At that day you will know that I am in My Father, and you in Me, and I in you. [John 14:20, NKJV]
- And the glory which You gave Me I have given them, that *they may be one just as We are one*: [John 17:22, NKJV]

- If we love one another, *God abides in us* ... [1John 4:12, NKJV]
- God is love, and he who abides in love abides in God, and God in him.. [1John 4:16, NKJV]
- By this we know that we abide in Him, and He in us, *because He has given us of His Spirit*. [1John 4:13, NKJV]
- "But by ONE Spirit we were all baptized into one body ... Now you are the body of Christ ...." [1Cor 12:13, 27]
- "But to us ONE God the Father, out of whom the all and we into Him, and ONE Lord Jesus Christ, through whom the all and we through him." [1Cor 8:6, from Greek text]
- "ONE Lord, ONE Faith, ONE baptism, ONE God and Father of all, the one upon all and through all and in all." [Eph 4:5-6, from the Greek]

Therefore: God, Jesus Christ, and Christians are ONE because they have the ONE Spirit of God — they are *united* (one) with the same Spirit.

gp170» Today, as in those days, we use "one" to mean "one in unity" as well as one as in singular of number. Yet because of tradition the so-called theologians seem to be unable to perceive the "one" Yehowah in any other way than singular of number. Because of this there is confusion concerning the nature of the God. But as we have seen there is some form of plurality in the unity or oneness of the true God, YHWH, the BeComingOne, who is our God(s).

Only God

gp171» Notice that Jesus Christ the man called his Father [YHWH, see GP 2] the "*only* true God" (John 17:3). But how is it that Jesus Christ is now the "*only*" God? (1Tim 1:17, Jude 1:4, 25) Jesus Christ in his own times will be the "*only*" ruler (1Tim 6:15) and now he is he "who *alone* ['only' — *monos*] has immortality" (1Tim 6:16). But also Jesus Christ was/is the "*only begotten* son" of God (John 1:18; see John 3:16, 18; 1John 4:9), but this should be translated, *one-of-a-kind* Son, because its first meaning is: *1) single of its kind*. Jesus was "unique" or "one-of-a-kind" because he is represented in the Holy of Holies, which was set apart (most holy) from all other aspects of God's temple. As we see in the *New Mind Papers*, and as most Christians believe, there will be others who have and will obtain immortality and be born or begotten of God. Christ may at this time (2021) be the only one with immortality, but in time all others will be given immortality. The "only" aspect of God has meaning only in time and one's definition of who or what God is. Christ may be "only" now in some sense, but in **time** the Only One will share his qualities, so the only God will be all in all (cf 1:Cor 15:28). Remember, Jesus Christ is the "firstborn of all creation" (Col 1:16), he is the "firstborn from the dead" (Col 1:18 see 1Cor 15:20), he is the "beginning of the creation of the God" (Rev 3:14), he is "the beginning" (Col 1:18), he is the "first fruits Christ" (1 Cor 15:20, 23), and he is the "firstborn among many brethren" (Rom 8:29). Thus, Jesus was the first of many to come (GP 6). **Yet Jesus Christ the man, who was separate in a sense from his Father when he was a man on earth before his going to the Father (GP 4), is NOW the "only God"** (uniquely born– GP 5). Jesus Christ NOW is the only God. But look:

- "Jesus answered them, Is it not written in your law, I said, You are Gods? If he called them Gods, unto whom the word of God came, and the scripture cannot be broken..." [John 10:34-35; cf. Psa 82:5; 97:7]

gp172» There are/will-be more than one individual in the only ONE true God:

- "Yehowah" is the God(s). He is ONE. That is, ONE in Spirit. This ONE is the only true God (John 17:3). But He is not singular in number or as one individual. He is many in ONE Spirit. As Jesus Christ the man went into his Father (GP 5), who was, and is, and will-be the "only true God" (John 17:3; 1Cor 8:4, 6), and Jesus became *one* with that only true God, and thus became the only God (1Tim 1:17), so too will Christians and all others go into the Father and thus into the Son, at their appointed times (GP 6). Thus, all will go into the Spiritual Body of Christ and into the ONE Yehowah so that God will be all in all (1 Cor 15:28; Eph 1:23, 10; Phil 3:21; Col 1:20; see GP 6). Yehowah (YHWH) is the only true God (John 17:3 w/ GP 2; 2Kings 19:15). He alone knows the hearts of mankind (2Ch 6:30). He alone created the universe and everything in it and gave them life (Neh 9:6). He alone has the NAME Yehowah (Psalm 83:18). He alone dwells the cherubs (Isa 37:16). But he is not just single or alone as scripture in the Old Testament clearly point out in its original language: He is many in ONE. He is many in Unity as the Body of Christ is many in One. He is Yehowah the Gods (See above).

This may make little sense to you now, but after you read the rest of this book you will understand, especially with the New Mind.

Yehowah, Elohim

gp173» Before we continue let me explain something about the use of *Elohim* and *Yehowah* in the Bible. Remember, the Hebrew word "elohim" is the simple plural word for "el." The word elohim means godS. Most of the places in the KJV English Bible where you see "God," should read "Gods" since it was translated from the Hebrew word "elohim" which means godS. The first scripture in the Bible is, "In the beginning Gods created the heavens and earth," *not* "God created the heavens and the earth." But since in other verses of the Bible it says that Yehowah (LORD or Jehovah) created the heavens and earth (Isa 40:28; Ex 20:10), then the Hebrew word *elohim* has something to do with Yehowah.

gp174» In Christian D. Ginsburg's *Introduction to the Massoretico-Critical Edition of the Bible*, pages 368 to 369, he shows that in parallel verses in 2Samuel 5 and 1 Chronicles 14 that the words Yehowah ["LORD"] and Elohim [Gods] are interchangeable. 2Samuel 5 uses "Yehowah" while 1 Chronicles 14 uses "Elohim." Also in the book of Psalms the same phenomenon is detectable. And we can see throughout the Old Testament Yehowah ["LORD"] and Elohim are used together as follows: "LORD God" (KJV), but in the Hebrew it reads *Yehowah Elohim*. The literal translation of this would be the "*BeComingOne (of) Gods*," or "*He-(who)-Will-Be, Gods*."

gp175» We thus see that the "BeComingOne" is somehow connected with Gods. Now Gesenius, the great Hebrew grammarian, insisted that these two words (Yehowah Elohim) should not be translated as "Yehowah *of* Elohim" (Gesenius' Lexicon, under "YHWH"). But we see little difference between this usage and "Yehowah of HostS," or as in some English translations, "LORD of HostS," and "Yehowah of Elohim" or "BeComingOne of Gods."

gp176» As we mentioned above, Israel's *elohim* (gods) were/was the ONE Yehowah (YHWH). This is another reason the Hebrew word *elohim* (gods) is closely associated with Yehowah (YHWH).

gp177» The reason we are discussing this whole subject of God's names may not be clear to you now, but as you read on you will come to understand it, and by the time you finish this book it should make more sense.

Predestination, Time, NAME, and the Paradoxes

gp178» As mentioned earlier in this Part [GP 1], our awareness of predestination, time, and God's NAME gives us the secrets to understanding the paradoxes of God. Because of the Law of Contradiction we know that God cannot *at the same time* be love and also a creator of evil or a killer. We have learned that God's NAME — the BeComingOne (YHWH) — is from an imperfect or incomplete Hebrew verb. God's NAME tells us that the God is Becoming, that He-will-be, that His full essence is not yet complete. Therefore, in <u>time</u> the true God will come to be; and in <u>time</u> all that is said about the YHWH (the BeComingOne) in the Bible **will-be**, or will happen. Thus, it is possible, because of the true meaning of God's NAME, that God has/will have created evil and was/is/will-be all good without being evil and without being all good *at the same time*. God's NAME allows God, through his predestinated power, to create evil before creation and separate it through time as different sides of God until the end when the BeComingOne has become, or until the BeComingOne has been made complete, or until the full essence of God comes to be, or until God is all in all (GP6). Remember it is the scriptures that have said that YHWH made evil, killed, etc. But it is also scripture that says God predestinated events before the cosmos (Eph 1:4; 1Pet 1:19-20; 2Tim 1:9; Titus 1:2) and therefore before time (as we know it), before good (as we know it), before evil (as we know it), before law (as we know it), and consequently before sin (as we know it). So before creation (as we know it) when God predestinated good things and evil things, there was no sin because there was no law and no creation. You therefore cannot put sin on God because of predestination. Do read on.

We Will Use "BeComingOne" in GP

gp179» Before we begin the next part of this book let me mention first something about the NAME of God. The NAME of God as we have shown was *Yehowah* from the Hebrew, which has the meaning of, the "BeComingOne." In many English translations of the Bible it has the "BeComingOne" translated as either "LORD" or "Jehovah." For example in the King James Version (KJV) of the Bible it translates God's NAME as "LORD" (usually small capital letters). Since this book uses the King James Version for some of its quotation of Biblical scriptures, when you see "LORD," instead of "Lord," in this paper you know it is the very NAME of God, that is, it was translated from the Hebrew word *Yehowah*, which means: the BeComingOne. Hereafter, in this set of papers we will translate God's NAME as the "BeComingOne." We thus translate the *meaning* of God's NAME, for the meaning of God's NAME is the secret in answering the paradoxes of God. Do read on!

I Will Be in Context

gp180» From the Hebrew text, the Hebrew word, אֶהְיֶה, should always have been translated into English as, "I will be." The following English quotes were taken from the King James Version (KJV) of the Bible which proves that most of the time this word was translated as "I will be" except in Exodus 3:14. Never was it translated in the KJV as "I am" except in Exodus 3:14.

Exod 3:12 "I will be" אֶהְיֶה
Exod 3:14 "I am" or "I am that I am" [should be, "I will be that I will be"]
         אֶהְיֶה אֲשֶׁר אֶהְיֶה
Exod 4:12 "I will be" אֶהְיֶה
Exod 4:15 "I will be" אֶהְיֶה
Deut 31:23 "I will be" אֶהְיֶה
Jos 1:5 "I will be" אֶהְיֶה
Jos 3:7 "I will be" אֶהְיֶה
Jdg 6:16 "I will be" אֶהְיֶה
Jdg 11:9 "I will be" אֶהְיֶה
Ruth 2:13 "I am not" from the Hebrew "not I will be" לֹא־אֶהְיֶה
1Sam 18:18 "I should be" אֶהְיֶה
1Sam 23:17 "I shall be" אֶהְיֶה
2Sam 7:14 "I will be" אֶהְיֶה
2Sam 15:34 "I will be" אֶהְיֶה
2Sam 16:18 "I will be" or "will I be" אֶהְיֶה
2Sam 16:19 "will I be" אֶהְיֶה
1Chr 17:13 "I will be" אֶהְיֶה
1Chr 28:6 "I will be" אֶהְיֶה
Job 3:16 "I had not been" from the Hebrew "not I will be" לֹא־אֶהְיֶה
Job 10:19 "I had not been" from the Hebrew "not I will be" לֹא־אֶהְיֶה
Job 12:4 "I am" from the Hebrew "I will be" אֶהְיֶה
Job 17:6 "I was" from the Hebrew "I will be" אֶהְיֶה
Ps. 50:21 "I will" אֶהְיֶה
Cant 1:7 "should I be" אֶהְיֶה
Isa 3:7 "I will not" from the Hebrew "not I will be" לֹא־אֶהְיֶה
Isa 47:7 "I shall be" אֶהְיֶה
Jer 11:4 "I will be" אֶהְיֶה
Jer 24:7 "I will be" אֶהְיֶה
Jer 30:22 "I will be" אֶהְיֶה
Jer 31:1 "I will be" אֶהְיֶה
Jer 32:38 "I will be" אֶהְיֶה
Ezek 11:20 "I will be" אֶהְיֶה
Ezek 14:11 "I may be" אֶהְיֶה
Ezek 34:24 "will be" אֶהְיֶה
Ezek 36:28 "I will be" אֶהְיֶה
Ezek 37:23 "I will be" אֶהְיֶה
Hos 1:9 "I will not" from the Hebrew "not I will be" לֹא־אֶהְיֶה
Hos 14:5 "I will be" אֶהְיֶה
Zech 2:5 "I … will be" אֶהְיֶה
Zech 8:8 "I will be" אֶהְיֶה

Web Page Links to Biblical Language Aids/Helps (in the digital books):

Link to S.R. Driver's Hebrew Tenses (2rd Ed)

    Note: The 3rd Ed. was used in this book; page numbers are different

Link to Gesenius' Hebrew and Chaldee Lexicon

Link to Gesenius' Hebrew Grammar

Link to International Standard Bible Encyclopedia

Link to Hebrew Bible Biblia Hebraica Stuttgartensia

Link to Hebrew Bible Westminster Leningrad Codex

Link to Introduction to the Masoretico-Critical Edition of the Hebrew Bible

    by Christian D. Ginsburg

Review of GP 1

gp181» In GP 1 we started our search: who or what is God? From the Bible we learned about the apparent paradoxes of God: "I make peace, and create evil: I the LORD do all these things" (Isa 45:7). God who is Love (1John 4:8) has somehow and for some reason created evil; He has even killed (Deut 32:39). But how can God be Love and also a killer?

We next learned that there are two basic laws and one basic fact we must understand in order to rightly perceive the true nature of God: the Law of Contradiction and the Law of Knowledge plus the fact that the God cannot lie.

We then went on and explained the Law of Contradiction.

We further showed the many attributes and titles of God and put forth that "time" is very important in our understanding of the paradoxes of God.

We also showed you the very NAME of the true God: YHWH, or Jehovah, or Yehowah, or He (who) will-be, or the BeComingOne, or the One who was, who is, and who is coming. God's NAME and its meaning is the real secret in revealing the answer to the Paradoxes of God. God's NAME is an *imperfect* (incomplete) verb and not as would be expected a *perfect* (complete) verb or a noun. Names are very important in the Bible and many times describe some facet of a person. The true NAME of the true God is important for it is the secret in explaining the apparently unexplainable scriptures about God.

In GP 1 we also looked into the meaning of "with God all things are possible," the "*one* Yehowah," the so-called unchangeableness of God, and other matters concerning the God. What GP 1 does is set the stage in our search for who or what is God.

GP 2: God The Father

Jesus Christ's Father

gp182» Who is the BeComingOne (YHWH) of the Old Testament, and who is God the Father? We must note again that the translation of "LORD God" in the Kings James Version of the Bible and other translations of the Bible is incorrect. Transliteration from Hebrew should read *Yehowah Elohim* in most cases. A translation of the literal meaning would be the "*BeComingOne* (of the) *Gods*," or "*BeComingOne, (the) Gods*," or "He (Who) will-be, (the) Gods" (see GP 1).

First Proof

gp183» Jesus was speaking to some Jews who had accused him of being possessed with a demon and making himself greater than Abraham by his words. Christ's answer is significant, for he reveals something important in it:

- "Jesus answered, If I honor myself, my honor is nothing: it is my Father that honors me; of whom you say, that he is your God" (John 8:54).

gp184» Notice Christ says his Father is the God that they, the Jews, say is their God. Now the Jews believe that their God was the "BeComingOne God(s)" or "Yehowah Elohim" or as mistranslated by some "LORD God" of the Old Testament (Psalm 140:6; Lev 18:30; 1Chron 29:10). And Jesus said his Father is that God (John 8:54; cf. Rom 15:6; 1Cor 8:6; 2Cor 1:3; 11:31; Eph 1:17; Phil 2:11; 1Peter 1:3). Therefore Jesus Christ's Father was the God of the Jews, and the Old Testament called the God of the Jews, Yehowah (YHWH).

Six More Proofs

gp185» Let's continue to prove that the BeComingOne of the Old Testament was the Father and is the ONE BeComingOne (Deut 6:4). We will give six more proofs besides John 8:54 that show that the BeComingOne of the Old Testament is Christ the man's Father.

God Swore By Himself

gp186» **(1)** "For when God made promise to Abraham, because he could swear by no greater, he swore by himself" (Heb 6:13). Now the God Paul was speaking about here was the BeComingOne (Gen 22:16; Isa 45:23). Paul said there was no greater than the BeComingOne of the Old Testament. He, the BeComingOne, was the greatest. Of course the BeComingOne was the greatest, for he was Jesus Christ the man's Father (John 8:54). Jesus Christ the man said his Father was the greatest of ALL, even greater than Jesus the man: "my Father who has given them to Me is greater than all ... I am going to the Father, for my Father is greater than I" (John 10:29; 14:28).

Throne

gp187» **(2)** Christ the man by a statement in Matthew 5:34 said God's (implying his Father's) throne was heaven, and in Isaiah 66:1 we see the BeComingOne calling heaven his throne. This is another proof that Christ's Father and the BeComingOne of the Old Testament were one and the same.

Prayer

gp188» **(3)** Now Christ taught that we should pray to our Father in heaven (Matt 6:6, 9-15). And Christ said his Father was the God of the Old Testament (John 8:54). Thus, we see Daniel praying to the BeComingOne, "And I [Daniel] prayed unto the BeComingOne my God and made my confession..." (Dan 9:4). Daniel and the rest of the others of the Old Testament prayed to the BeComingOne (note Jer 32:16-18), for he was in a sense their Father (Isa 63:16). We (Spiritual Israel) pray to our Father, who is the BeComingOne, the true God mentioned in the Old Testament, as physical Israel prayed to the BeComingOne, who was their Father (see # 5 below).

God The Father Chose

gp189» **(4)** In the New Testament it speaks of God the Father choosing people to be his sons through Jesus Christ (Eph 1:3-5). And since it is the Father who chooses, so does the BeComingOne of the Old Testament, for both the Father and the BeComingOne are the same being (note Isa 44:1-2; 43:10; 49:7; Psa 89:3; 105:43; 106:4, 5, 23; see "Predestination Paper" [NM8]).

YHWH Of Old Testament Is The Father

gp190» **(5)** The BeComingOne is called the Father in the Old Testament, and calls himself the Father: "You, O BeComingOne, art our *Father*, our Redeemer"(Isa 63:16). "For I am a *Father* to Israel, and Ephraim is my first-born" (Jer 31:9). "But now, O BeComingOne, you art our *Father*; we are the clay, and you our potter; and we all are the work of your hand" (Isa 64:8). "Thus, says the BeComingOne, the Holy One of Israel, and his Maker, Ask me of things to come concerning my *sons*, and concerning the work of my hands command you me" (Isa 45:11). "And David said, Blessed be you, BeComingOne of Israel our *Father*, from the age and to the age"(1 Chron 29:10). "He shall cry unto me [the BeComingOne], You art my *Father* my God, and the rock of my salvation" (Psa 89:26). Compare this with such verses as John 20:17. "I will be his *Father*" (2Sam 7:14, 1-29). Compare in context Psalms 2:7 with Hebrews 1:1, 5 and Psalms 110:1 with Hebrews 1:1, 13.

"See" The Father?

gp191» **(6)** Now some will say that God the Father could not be the God of the Old Testament, for scripture says that no one has seen the Father (John 1:18; 5:37). Since some did "see" the God of the Old Testament (Moses "saw," Deut 5:4; 34:10), this is proof that Jesus Christ's Father is not the BeComingOne of the Old Testament. But this is wrong, for did Christ say *no* one had seen his Father?

gp192» "And the Father himself, which has sent me, has borne witness of me. *You* have neither heard his voice at any time, nor seen his shape. And you have not his word abiding in you: for whom He has sent, him you don't believe" (John 5:37-38).

gp193» Notice verse 38 that the ones ("You") Jesus was speaking to didn't have the word abiding *in* them. Now in 1 John 2:14 we see that real Christians do have the word of God in them. John is writing to Spiritual Christians and says, "I have written unto you, young men, because you are strong, and the word of God abides *in you*" (1John 2:14). Hence, we know that Jesus was speaking to non-Spiritual people when he spoke in John 5:37-38.

gp194» Notice carefully: "Not that any man has seen the Father, except he which is of God, he has seen the Father" (John 6:46). "If you had known me, you should have known my Father also: and from henceforth you know him, and have seen him" (John 14:7). "He that is of God hears God's words: you therefore hear them not, because you are not of God" (John 8:47). We see that those of God are able to "see" the Father, at least in a Spiritual sense. Because God is spirit, then those of God can/will "see" God at least Spiritually. And soon they will see God as he is, and in the truest possible sense (see GP 10). Those who "saw" God in the Old Testament saw him in a vision or transfiguration (Deut 34:10; Num 12:8).

Outside of visions, no one had seen the true God in a physical sense (except to see Jesus Christ, who is the image of God, see GP 5, GP 10), because the true God is Spiritual and because the true God is the BeComingOne [He (who) Will-Be], whose completeness is yet to be manifested. Also see "Can we see spirits?" in GP 3. Eventually the true God will incorporate the entire new creation into Himself (1Cor 15:28).

gp195» God the Father is the BeComingOne (YHWH) of the Old Testament as shown herein.

GP 3: Angels, Spirits, and the WORD of God

What are Angels?
Two Kinds of Angels
Angels Closely Associated with God
NAME given to the Angel
Cherubs and the Name
Word of God
Can we see Spirits?

gp196» In order to continue our study on God we need to know something about angels, spirits, and the WORD of God. What are angels? What is spirit? Can we see spirit? What was the WORD (John 1:1) in the age before the resurrection of Jesus Christ? We say what was he before Christ's resurrection, for after it a new dimension was added to the WORD's make-up (GP 5).

What are Angels?

Angels are Spiritual Messengers or Word Carriers

gp197» The word "angel" is translated from a Hebrew word (*malak* # 4397) that means *messenger* and from a Greek word (*aggelos* # 32) that means *messenger*. An angel is a messenger. An angel brings the words of someone else. An angel or messenger is a spiritual being (Heb 1:7). An angel is a spiritual being who brings messages or words from someone else. All angels or spirits were created by God the Father (Psa 148:2,5; Col 1:16; Heb 12:9). A few verses seems to indicate that the angels ("sons of God") existed at the beginning of creation (Job 38:4-7; Gen 1:14-19; Rev 1:20).

Two Kinds of Angels: Good & Evil

gp198» There are two kinds of angels:

- **Good Angels:** The good angels are holy angels (Mat 25:31; Mark 8:38). They are called elect angels (1Tim 5:21). They cannot die (Luke 20:36). They have great power and serve God's will by listening to his voice and carrying out his commandments (Psa 103:20-21). The age before Christ was subjected to angels (Heb 2:2,5; Acts 7:53) and they spoke through the fathers and prophets of Israel (Heb 1:1). They are spirit, or that is, made from spirit (Heb 1:7) and thus are invisible (Job 4:15-16), except when seen in visions (see below). They will come with Christ at the end of the age to resurrect God's saints (Mat 25:31; 24:31; Mark 8:38; Luke 9:26; Rev 14:3-4). There was a special angel mentioned in the Bible that carried the very words of the BeComingOne (see below).

- **Evil Angels:** There are evil angels who carry words and thoughts of evil and they are testing mankind in the old age (NM20, "Other Mind"). These angels were appointed to a hell-fire judgment before the cosmos began (Mat 25:41; Jude 1:6,13; Rom 9:22; Prov 16:4; 1Pet 2:8; 2Pet 2:4; NM8; NM9; NM24). Adam and Eve were tested by an evil angel (Gen 3:4-7; Rev 20:1-2; 12:9). An evil angel called Satan destroyed Israel and tested Job (1Chron 21:1,12; Job 1:6-12; 2:6). For some reason this evil angel is called "angel of the LORD" (1Chron 21:12). Satan even tries to pass himself off as "an angel of light" (2Cor 11:14). But this angel is associated with God's anger or God's wrath, and as shown in chapter 1 and the God's Wrath Papers (PR4 to PR5) This angel is in some way the "left side" of God who was predestinated before creation began, and in that sense he is an "angel of the LORD" carrying out the works of the "left side" of God. As the good angels are invisible, so are the evil angels (Num 22:22-31).

gp199» Before we continue our study on angels we need to remember that "angels" were associated with the WORD of God in the Old Testament including the giving of the Ten Commandments (Heb 2:2; Acts 7:38,53, Gal 3:19). Apparently the old world before Jesus Christ was subject to angels (Heb 2:1-5). In the new age we are to be subjected to Christ (Heb 2:5-8). As of now (before Christ's return) all are not yet subjected to Christ (Heb 2:8), but in the near future all will be put under Christ and his rule (Psa 110:1; Acts 2:32-36; Heb 2:8-10; 1Cor 15:23-28; see GP6). There is confusion about this. We need to understand how the WORD was given through angels in the Old Testament, and the connection of these angels to the LORD, or Jehovah, or the BeComingOne of the Old Testament.

gp200» There was a very close connection between the angels of the Bible and the BeComingOne (YHWH) or the "LORD" of the Bible. Sometimes it is very difficult to see the difference between the "angel of the BeComingOne and the BeComingOne himself.

Angels Closely Associated with God

Angel of the Lord

gp201» Who was the "angel of the LORD [YHWH]" or more correctly the "angel of the BeComingOne" in the Old Testament, and in a few places in the New Testament of the Bible, the "angel of the Lord"? In the New Testament, the word "Lord," the Greek *Kurios*, is the word used instead of the "BeComingOne" or YHWH. The "angel of *Kurios*" translated as the "angel of the Lord" in many versions of the New Testament equals the "angel of the BeComingOne" of the Old Testament. One of the reasons *Kurios* was used in the New Testament instead of YHWH, was because of the *Septuagint* (See GP 1 under "More Details").

Hagar and the Angel

gp202» Now the *angel* of the BeComingOne was talking to Hagar, and right after the angel had spoken to her the verse reads: "And she called the name of the BeComingOne [YHWH] that spoke to her, *You God sees me*: for she said, Have I also here looked at him that sees me?" (Gen 16:13) Check the English translation like the Moffatt, NEB, etc. and the Greek Septuagint versions, they all say the same thing. Literally from Hebrew, "she called the NAME, YHWH, the one speaking to her: you God [el] of vision."

gp203» After the angel spoke to her, Hagar called the NAME of the BeComingOne who spoke to her *El roi* or "God of seeing," and asked herself if she had looked on the God of seeing or vision. She also named the well she was standing by, "*Beerlahairoi*," or "the well of the living one who sees me." In these scriptures the angel of the BeComingOne, the God of sight, and the NAME of the BeComingOne are closely connected. Why?

gp204» "And God [elohim] heard the voice of the lad; and the *angel* of God [elohim] called to Hagar out of heaven, and said unto her, What ails you, Hagar? fear not; for God [elohim] has heard the voice of the lad where he is" (Gen 21:17). The angel of God? God heard, and the angel of God called. In these verses the angel of God and God are closely connected.

Abraham and the Angel

gp205» "And the *angel* of the BeComingOne called unto Abraham out of heaven the second time. And said, By myself I have sworn" (Gen 22:15, 16). What? The angel of the BeComingOne called to Abraham and said, "By myself I have sworn." Notice in the New Testament where Paul describes the same event: "For when God made promise to Abraham, because he could swear by no greater, he swore by himself" (Heb 6:13). Does Paul call this *angel* of the BeComingOne, God? The answer is no, as we will see. But by comparing both verses it <u>appears</u> that way. Here again the angel and God are closely connected.

Jacob and the Angel

gp206» Now Jacob was blessing Ephraim and Manasseh when he said: "the *angel* which redeemed me from all evil bless the lads" (Gen 48:16). Jacob is asking an angel to bless his lads; he says this angel is "the redeemer." Genesis 48:16 in the KJV is a mistranslation. It should read: "*the* angel *the* redeemer of me from all harm, may he bless *the* boys." "The redeemer" in Gen 48:16 is the same Hebrew word as Isa 49:7, "Thus says the BeComingOne, (the) Redeemer of Israel," except with the additional article, "the." But who is *the* redeemer? "I have mercy on you says the BeComingOne your Redeemer" (Isa 54:8). "I will help you [Jacob], says the BeComingOne, your Redeemer, the Holy One of Israel" (Isa 41:14). Jacob in Gen 48:16 apparently spoke of an angel which redeemed him from evil, but the BeComingOne said in Isaiah 41:14 that He was that redeemer. Since the BeComingOne is the redeemer (Isa 41:14; 49:7; 54:8), then the angel (the messenger or agent) of the BeComingOne is the agent *of* the redeemer and his redemption.

Moses and the Angel

gp207» "And the *angel* of the BeComingOne appeared to him in a flame of fire out of the midst of a bush: and he [Moses] looked, and, behold, the bush burned with fire, and the bush was not consumed" (Ex 3:2). (In other words this "angel of the BeComingOne" looked like he was on fire much like Christ's face appears in the pictures of his glory, Matthew 17:2.) "And when the BeComingOne saw that he turned aside to see, God called to him out of the midst of the bush, and said, Moses, Moses ... Moreover he said, I am the God of your father, the God of Abraham, the God of Isaac, and the God of Jacob. And Moses hid his face, for he was afraid to look upon God" (Ex 3:2, 4, 6). Do not these verses seem to say the *angel* of the BeComingOne appeared in the midst of the bush (V. 2), and he who called out of the bush was God (V. 4). In fact, this angel of the BeComingOne was apparently the God (elohim) of Abraham, Isaac, and Jacob. There is a very close connection between the angel and the BeComingOne.

gp208» This is confirmed in Acts 7:30-33: "And when forty years had passed, an *Angel* of the Lord [YHWH] appeared to him in the desert of Mount Sinai, in a flame of fire in a bush. And Moses saw and wondered at the sight. And as he was coming near to look, a voice of the Lord came to him: 'I am the God of your fathers, the God of Abraham and the God of Isaac and the God of Jacob.' " Here it says Moses drew near to a bush where an angel of the Lord appeared, and the *voice* of the BeComingOne (YHWH) came out of it, and said that he was the God of Abraham, Isaac, and Jacob. Furthermore in an inspired speech by Stephen we read, "This is he [Moses], that was in the church in the wilderness with the *angel* which spoke to him in mount Sinai, and with our fathers: who received the lively oracles [Ten Commandments] to give unto us" (Acts 7:38). Notice that Stephen had already spoken about an angel of the Lord who appeared in a bush in verse 30, but now he says it was an angel who *spoke* to Moses in mount Sinai when the commandments were given.

Balaam and the Angel

gp209» Notice that the Bible's rendition of the angel and Balaam's ass. In Numbers 22:22, 23, 24, 25, 26, and verse 27 it shows the *angel* of the BeComingOne standing in the way of the ass that Balaam was riding. Then in verse 28: "and the BeComingOne opened the mouth of the ass...." And verse 31, "then the BeComingOne who was there with the ass and Balaam, and he opened the eye of Balaam and the mouth of the ass."

gp210» Notice verse 35, "and the *angel of the BeComingOne* said unto Balaam, Go with the men: but *only the word that I shall speak unto you, that you shall speak.*" And, "and the BeComingOne put a word in Balaam's mouth..." (Num 23:5). And again, "must I not take heed to speak that which the BeComingOne has put in my mouth?" (V. 12) Further, "and the BeComingOne met Balaam, and put a word in his mouth.." (V. 16). Compare Numbers 22:35 with Numbers 23:5, 12, and 16. The "angel of the BeComingOne" and the "BeComingOne" are used interchangeably in these verses because the angel is the agent of the BeComingOne as the messenger of a general is the agent for that general. Also notice that this angel is somehow "for an adversary [Satan] against" Balaam. This cannot be understood without knowing the significance of the cherubs in the holy of holies, which we discuss in later chapters of this work. Again we see the close connection between the angel of the BeComingOne and the very BeComingOne.

Gideon and the Angel

gp211» "And the *angel* of the BeComingOne appeared unto him [Gideon], and said unto him, The BeComingOne is with you" (Judges 6:12). Notice the angel of the BeComingOne appeared. "And the BeComingOne looked upon him" (V. 14). And again, "and the BeComingOne said unto him" (V. 16). The angel of the BeComingOne appeared, but the BeComingOne looked and talked. And further in verse 20 it says: "and the angel of God said unto him." And again, "then the angel of the BeComingOne put forth the end of the staff that was in his hand... Then the angel of the BeComingOne departed out of sight. And when Gideon perceived that he was an angel of the BeComingOne, Gideon said, Alas, O Lord(s) BeComingOne [YHWH — not 'GOD']! for because I have seen the angel of the BeComingOne face to face" (V. 21, 22). Again the angel or messenger of the BeComingOne and the BeComingOne (YHWH) are closely connected.

Manoah and the Angel

gp212» "And an *angel* of the BeComingOne appeared unto the woman ... then the woman came and told her husband, saying, A man of God [thus, the angel of the BeComingOne, looked like a man] came unto me and his countenance was like the countenance of an angel of the God ... the angel of the God came again unto the woman ... her husband was not with her. And the woman ... ran, and showed her husband ... And Manoah [her husband] arose and went after his wife, and came to the man [or angel, V. 6] ... And the angel of the BeComingOne said unto Manoah ... And Manoah said unto the angel of the BeComingOne" (Judges 13:3, 6, 9, 11, 13, 15).

gp213» Remember this angel of the God/BeComingOne looked like a man with an appearance like the angel of God. In verse 15 Manoah asks the "man" to stay and he will fix him something to eat. In verse 16 the angel of the BeComingOne declines the offer, but tells the husband to offer the food to the BeComingOne, "for Manoah knew not that he [the 'man'] was an angel of the BeComingOne" (V. 16). Next the husband asks the "man's" name, but the angel says it is secret (V. 17 & 18). Then Manoah offers his kid of the goats to the BeComingOne, but at that time the angel of the BeComingOne did an amazing work, for he ascended as a flame into heaven (V. 19 & 20). In the Greek translation, the *Septuagint*, of the Old Testament, the Greek words indicate that the angel disunited or separated in form when he did this amazing act of ascending in a flame. This must have amazed Manoah and his wife for they didn't know it was an angel since he looked like a man. "But the angel of the BeComingOne did no more appear to Manoah and his wife. Then Manoah knew that he (the 'man') was an angel of the BeComingOne. And Manoah said unto his wife, We shall surely die, because we have *seen God*. But his wife said unto him, If the BeComingOne were pleased to kill us..." (v. 21-23). Again the angel or messenger of the BeComingOne and the BeComingOne (YHWH) are closely connected.

Jacob and the Angel

gp214» "And Jacob was left alone; and there wrestled a *man* with him until the breaking of the day" (Gen 32:24). In Hosea 12:2, 4 it identifies this "man" Jacob wrestled with as an *angel*. Thus, Jacob was wrestling an angel (in a dream?) who looked like a man. Jacob asks this angel his name, but the angel asks a rhetorical question and then blesses him (Gen 32:29). Jacob then calls the place where he wrestled with the angel/man — *Peniel*, which means "the face of God." Jacob calls this angel/man, *Peniel*, for he saw God face to face: "I have seen God face to face, and my life is preserved" (verse 30, cf Ho 12:3, 4). This event is of a dual significance because it also prophesies of Jacob [Israel, the true Church] until the breaking of the great day of the Lord when Jacob will be redeemed and see God as he is (1 John 3:2). Again the angel or messenger of the BeComingOne and the BeComingOne (YHWH) are closely connected.

Angel of God's Presence

gp215» In Isaiah it speaks of "the angel of his [the BeComingOne's] presence" who saved Israel, and with his love and pity he redeemed them and carried them all the days of old (Isa 63:9, 7-8). Now the angel of the BeComingOne's presence redeemed Israel. Jacob [Israel] spoke of this same angel (Gen 48:16), a redeeming angel who blesses. This same angel is described in Genesis 32:24-30, and is the angel who changed Jacob's name to Israel. As explained before, this angel looked like a man, but Jacob said he saw the face of God. Further we've shown in Judges 13:1-23 that Manoah and his wife had seen an angel of the BeComingOne who looked like a man, who then transformed himself into the flame of fire and ascended into heaven, *and* they said that seeing this angel of the BeComingOne/God, who looked like a man, was like seeing God. We've also shown that the redeemer is the BeComingOne of the Old Testament who is Jesus Christ's Father: "said the BeComingOne, and your Redeemer, the Holy One of Israel" (Isa 41:14).

gp216» Who is this angel of His presence? The angel of the BeComingOne is the answer. The Hebrew word translated in the King James Version as "presence" (*paniym*, # 6440) is in the plural form, but is used as if it were in the singular form. It means, face(s). It was the angel of the BeComingOne who led Israel out of Egypt and appeared to Moses (Exo 32:34; 33:14, 15; Isa 63:9; etc.). The angel of the BeComingOne's presence is the angel of the BeComingOne/God. He is described again in the New Testament as Gabriel.

Gabriel and the Angel

gp217» Now "Gabriel" means, *man of God*. Notice in Judges 13:1-25, that the angel of the BeComingOne/God that appeared to Samson's parents, was called God (V. 22), but he looked like a man (V. 11). Now Samson's mother, the wife of Manoah, called this angel of the BeComingOne, "a man of God" (V.6). The very word Gabriel means, man of God.

gp218» We have shown that the "angel of his presence" in Isaiah 63:9 is the angel of the BeComingOne. Further the angel Gabriel is the angel of the BeComingOne as we will show. As Satan is called many names in the Bible and as each name helps to describe some characteristic of Satan, so too is the angel of God called many names.

gp219» Note in Luke's first chapter that an angel of the Lord appears to Zechariah, the father of John the Baptist (V. 11, 12). This angel of the Lord in answering a question by Zechariah (V. 18), says to him: "I am Gabriel ["man of God"], that stand in the presence of God..." (V. 19).

gp220» The angel of the Lord (YHWH) says he is Gabriel. And Gabriel means, "man of God." And the angel of the BeComingOne/God of the Old Testament is called "a man of God" (Judges 13:6) because he looks like a man (Gen 32:24; Jud 13:6, 11). Furthermore, it is Gabriel who stands in the presence of God as does the angel of Isaiah 63:9. Let's go back to the Old Testament for a moment to further help connect the BeComingOne of the Old Testament with the angel of the BeComingOne.

Joshua, Satan, and the Angel

gp221» Notice in Zechariah 3:1 that Joshua was standing before the angel of the BeComingOne and Satan was there too. Verse one tells us Joshua and Satan were standing before the angel of the BeComingOne. But in verse two, "and the BeComingOne said to Satan, The BeComingOne rebuke you, O Satan." And in verse three it again tells us they were standing "before the angel." And in verse six it is the angel of the BeComingOne speaking, but in verses seven and nine it says the BeComingOne spoke. Reading this, one has to almost conclude, that the "angel of the BeComingOne" and the "BeComingOne" are one and the same person. The Bible doesn't say the angel of the BeComingOne each time but alternates with either angel of the BeComingOne or BeComingOne. With what has already been shown you, we know that there is a very close connection between the angel of the BeComingOne, and the BeComingOne.

Moses. Satan, and Michael the Archangel

gp222» Notice the BeComingOne or the angel of the BeComingOne says to Satan, "The BeComingOne rebuke you, O Satan" (Zech 3:2). Compare this with: "Yet Michael the archangel, when contending with the devil [Satan] ... said, the Lord rebuke you" (Jude 1:9). Now Satan in Jude is contending over Moses while in Zechariah, Satan was contending about Joshua. But where in the Bible does it say Satan comes before a regular angel of heaven? In Job it says "there is a day when the sons of God came to present themselves before the BeComingOne and Satan came also among them" (Job 1:6; 2:1). Notice Satan is before the BeComingOne in Job, and is contending against Job at that time (V. 1:9, 10). While in Zechariah, it was Joshua he contended against, and in Jude it was Moses. Actually as Gabriel is another name for the angel of the BeComingOne, so too is Michael. The word "Michael" means, "who is God."

gp223» Notice Jude calls Michael the archangel. The word in Greek means, *chief* angel. The prefix of the Greek word translated "archangel" means, *chief*, or *beginning*, or *headship*, or *first* in place or time, or *prince*. Thus, Michael is the head-angel, or first-angel, or beginning-angel, or chief-angel, or prince angel. Notice what Michael is called elsewhere in the Bible, the "great prince" (Dan 12:1), and "your prince" (Dan 10:21). Michael is the great-angel, the prince-angel, the first-angel, the head-angel, the archangel. It is Michael who "stands for the children of your [Daniel's] people" (Dan 12:1). Who are the children of Daniel's people? By verses 2 and 3 of the 12th chapter of Daniel and the *New Mind Papers*, we can perceive that these children are those who are resurrected at Christ's coming. Michael is the angel who will stand up and deliver the Spiritual Christians at the end of the age of Satan's misrule (See the *New Mind Papers*). The angel of the BeComingOne is Michael, the first-angel. Could another angel be above the angel of the BeComingOne. No, the angel of the BeComingOne is the chief-angel, the archangel.

gp224» In Daniel 12:1 it says that Michael will stand up for the children of God. But in Isaiah 40:10 it says the "BeComingOne will come with strong hand, and his arm shall rule for him: behold, his reward is with him...." Again there is a very close connection between the BeComingOne (YHWH) and the angel of the BeComingOne.

Job, Satan, and the LORD

gp225» A comparative survey of the phrase "sons of God" indicates that this expression is used in the Bible as not only meaning physical sons of God (those who are sons of Adam, for Adam was a "son," so to speak, of God), but also spiritual sons of God, or angels. Notice the following where the LORD spoke to Satan and even in some way directed or gave Satan permission to do certain things to Job:

- Job 1:6 Now there was a day when the sons of God came to present themselves before the LORD, and Satan also came among them. 7 The LORD said to Satan, "From where do you come?" Then Satan answered the LORD and said, "From roaming about on the earth and walking around on it." 8 The LORD said to Satan, "Have you considered My servant Job? For there is no one like him on the earth, a blameless and upright man, fearing God and turning away from evil." 9 Then Satan answered the LORD, "Does Job fear God for nothing? 10 "Have You not made a hedge about him and his house and all that he has, on every side? You have blessed the work of his hands, and his possessions have increased in the land. 11 "But put forth Your hand now and touch all that he has; he will surely curse You to Your face." 12 Then the LORD said to Satan, "Behold, all that he has is in your power, only do not put forth your hand on him." So Satan departed from the presence of the LORD. (Job 1:6-12)

- Job 2:1 Again there was a day when the sons of God came to present themselves before the LORD, and Satan also came among them to present himself before the LORD. 2 The LORD said to Satan, "Where have you come from?" Then Satan answered the LORD and said, "From roaming about on the earth and walking around on it." 3 The LORD said to Satan, "Have you considered My servant Job? For there is no one like him on the earth, a blameless and upright man fearing God and turning away from evil. And he still holds fast his integrity, although you incited Me against him to ruin him without cause." 4 Satan answered the LORD and said, "Skin for skin! Yes, all that a man has he will give for his life. 5 "However, put forth Your hand now, and touch his bone and his flesh; he will curse You to Your face." 6 So the LORD said to Satan, "Behold, he is in your power, only spare his life." 7 Then Satan went out from the presence of the LORD and smote Job with sore boils from the sole of his foot to the crown of his head. (Job 2:1-7)

In the book of Job it has the Lord speaking to Satan and directing him or giving him permission to do certain bad things to Job. We can look upon this as the BeComingOne's (YHWH) "predestinating permission" for Satan to do certain things in this age, things predestinated before the cosmos, before law, and before sin. This may be hard to understand, but a thorough reading of this book should help you to understand.

Joshua and the Chief-Angel

gp226» When Joshua was near Jericho he "saw a man" with a sword drawn who said he was the commander of the army of the BeComingOne (YHWH) (Josh 5:13-15). Joshua put his face down to the ground (a sign of worship) and asked, what my lord(s) is the message for his (YHWH) servant.

gp227» Who is this "commander of the army of the LORD" (NIV); or the "captain of the host of the LORD" (KJV); or the "prince of Jehovah's host" (Young's Literal Translation)? The Hebrew word translated commander or captain or prince is *sar* (# 8269) which means prince, head, chief, captain, general, etc. This is the same Hebrew word translated "*prince* of the host" (KJV) in Daniel 8:11, or "*prince* of princes" (KJV) in Daniel 8:25, or "prince" (KJV) in Daniel 11:21 and 12:1. This great prince of Daniel was Michael the angel.

gp228» The Hebrew word translated army or host by some is *Tseba* (Tsaba, # 6635) which means a "mass" of things, people, solders, angels, etc. It is the Hebrew word in such translations as "LORD of *Hosts*" (KJV) in such books of the Bible as Isaiah and Jeremiah.

gp229» Thus, this "man" that Joshua saw was the prince of the host of Yehowah, or the prince of the host of the BeComingOne. With the information shown to you in chapter 3, we see this "man" was the great chief angel of the BeComingOne: Michael.

Review: Angels Close Connection to the BeComingOne

We have seen angels closely associated with the BeComingOne in the cases of Hagar, Abraham, Jacob, Moses, Balaam, Gideon, Manoah, Gabriel ("man of God"), Joshua, Michael, and Job. So close are these associations that it is difficult to see if there is any difference between the angels and the very BeComingOne. But since we know that the true God was, is will be all in all (Rev 1:8; 1Cor 15:28), whose spirit is everywhere (Psa 139:7; Jer 23:24; 1Kings 8:27), and since we know that angels occupy location (a place in the cosmos versus all the cosmos), and are *messengers* of another one, then we know for these reasons and others that the angel of the BeComingOne is not in the truest sense the true God, the "BeComingOne" or the YHWH.

Angel of the BeComingOne (YHWH) is *not* the BeComingOne (YHWH)

gp230» So far in GP 3 we have seen the very close connection between the BeComingOne (YHWH) and the angel of the BeComingOne. In some scriptures they appear to be the same. But there are scriptures that indicate they are not the same.

(1) Notice that the "word of the BeComingOne" came to Zechariah (Zech 1:1). Now notice the prayer of the *angel* of the BeComingOne:

- ZEC 1:12: Then the Angel of the BeComingOne answered and said, "O BeComingOne of hosts, how long will You not have mercy on Jerusalem and on the cities of Judah, against which You were angry these seventy years?" 13 And the BeComingOne answered the angel who talked to me, with good and comforting words.

The angel of the BeComingOne prayed to the BeComingOne (YHWH) and asked Him a question, and the BeComingOne answered. This is proof that the angel of the BeComingOne (YHWH) and the BeComingOne (YHWH) are not exactly the same.

(2) Another proof that the angel of God AND God are not exactly the same is that God is Spirit (John 4:24) and God's spirit fills all (Jer 23:24). Angels also are spirits (Heb 1:7), but do not fill all. Angels appear in locations and thus are not the fullness of God. No single angel in himself can be the true God, because the true God fills all. But angels can and do represent God, or speak for God: they are agents of God.

gp231» The very Hebrew word translated into angel in the Old testament, and the very Greek word translated into angel in the New Testament means, "messenger." The angel of the BeComingOne (YHWH) is the agent or ambassador of the BeComingOne (YHWH). A messenger of God brings the words of God. A messenger of a king brings the words of the king. The words that a messenger speaks in the name of a king, are the very words of the king. The message or words of the messenger (angel) of God are the very *words* of God. This is why there is a close connection in the Bible between the angel of God or the angel of the BeComingOne and the BeComingOne, for the angel of the BeComingOne brought the WORD of the BeComingOne.

Name Given To the Word/Angel

gp232» One very important fact we need to know is that the angel of the BeComingOne (YHWH) was given the NAME of the true God:

- "Behold, I send an angel before you, to keep you in the way, and to bring you to the place which I have prepared. Beware of him and obey his voice, provoke him not; for he will not pardon your transgressions: FOR MY *NAME* IS IN HIM" (Exo 23:20-21, KJV).

- "See, I am sending an angel ahead of you to guard you along the way and to bring you to the place I have prepared. Pay attention to him and listen to what he says. Do not rebel against him; he will not forgive your rebellion, since my NAME is in him" (Exo 23:20-21, NIV).

gp233» This angel had the NAME (YHWH) in him. This angel with the NAME in him was the angel of the BeComingOne (YHWH) (compare Isa 63:9 and proof in GP 3). This angel spoke in the NAME of God; he spoke the BeComingOne's WORD. Remember here that God's very Name is a verb, a verb in the imperfect tense – God very Name tells us that God is <u>Becoming</u> (GP1). This is the great hint that God's Name carries: He is BeComing. He is, He (who) will be. He is the BeComingOne.

Cherubs and the Angel between them

gp234» As we learn in Part 16 of the *New Mind Papers*, Moses' tabernacle was made according to the pattern of the heavenly tabernacle (NM16; Heb 9:1-9, 23-24). In the tabernacle there was a place called the holy of holies. The typical most holy of holies had two cherubs in it, and *between* these cherubs the BeComingOne used to appear and speak to Moses:

- "There I will meet with you; and from above the mercy seat, from <u>between the two cherubim</u> which are upon the ark of the testimony, I will speak to you about all that I will give you in commandment for the sons of Israel. (Exodus 25:22)

- Now when Moses went into the tent of meeting to speak with Him, he heard the voice speaking to him from above the mercy seat that was on the ark of the testimony, from <u>between the two cherubim</u>, so He spoke to him. (Numbers 7:89)

- The LORD said to Moses: "Tell your brother Aaron that he shall not enter at any time into the holy place inside the veil, before the mercy seat which is on the ark, or he will die; for <u>I will appear in the cloud over the mercy seat</u>. (Leviticus 16:2)

Since we know the BeComingOne is Spirit and his spirit fills all (or will fill all), then we know that the BeComingOne <u>himself</u> did not appear between the cherubs, but the angel or messenger or agent of the BeComingOne appeared. How do we know this? As we are seeing in GP3, there is an angel that is closely connected to the BeComingOne. So close, it is difficult sometimes to differentiate between them. This angel went with Israel and gave them the law through Moses (Ex 23:20ff; Acts 7:30, 38; Heb 2:2, 5; see all of GP 3). "The angel the one speaking to him [Moses] in the Mount Sinai" (Acts 7:38, Greek text). This angel was the one that spoke to Moses in the bush and with the fathers of Israel, and this angel is the one who gave the commandments to Moses in Mount Sinai (Acts 7:30,35,38). This angel is the angel with God's Name (YHWH) in him (Ex 23:20-21). The Spirit in Paul told us that in the past God had put mankind under angels (Heb 21-2, 5), but now he has put us under his Son (Heb 1:2; 2:5,8-10; 1Cor 15:23-28). God spoke to mankind through his angels in the Old Testament. Once we understand that the Spirits in the prophets, were Spiritual messengers or angels (Heb 1:1), then we further understand how angels ruled before Jesus Christ. This angel who spoke to Moses represented the God who is becoming, for he was the angel who spoke between the cherubs over the mercy seat. The cherubs and the mercy seat represent the BeComingOne (GP8).

Word of God

Word of the BeComingOne

Word: Spoken by an Angel or Spiritual Messenger

gp235» "For if the word [logos] spoken through angels proved steadfast, and every transgression and disobedience received a just reward ... For He has not put the world to come, of which we speak, in subjection to angels" (Heb 2:2, 5 ,NKJ).

gp236» The word or logos was spoken through angels. As Acts 7:38, 53 indicate, the ten commandments were also given through an angel. And this world was in subjection to angels as Hebrew 2:5 indicates. But this angel(s) spoke the very message or word of God, with the power that goes with these words. The words of God have power because all God's words come true (Isa 46:11, etc.).

- In Genesis 15:1, "the *word* of the BeComingOne came to Abram."
- In Exodus 24:3, 4, "And Moses came and told the people all the *words* of the BeComingOne ... And Moses wrote all the *words* of the BeComingOne ..."
- In Deuteronomy 5:4, 5, "The BeComingOne talked with you face to face in the mount out of the midst of the fire (I stood between the BeComingOne and you at that time, to show you the *word* of the BeComingOne ....") But as Exodus 3:2 and Acts 7:30ff say, it was the *angel* who appeared in the bush that appeared on fire. Therefore Moses gave Israel the word of the BeComingOne that Moses received from the *angel* of the BeComingOne.
- In Judges 2:4, "And it came to pass when the angel of the BeComingOne spoke these *words* ...."
- In Isaiah 1:10, "Hear the *word* of the BeComingOne."
- In Jeremiah 1:2, "To whom the *word* of the BeComingOne came ...."
- In Ezekiel 1:3, "The *word* of the BeComingOne came expressly to Ezekiel ...."
- In Hosea 1:1, "The *word* of the BeComingOne came to Hosea ...."
- In Joel 1:1, "The *word* of the BeComingOne came to Joel ..."
- In Jonah 1:1, "Now the *word* of the BeComingOne came to Jonah ...."
- In Micah 1:1, "The *word* of the BeComingOne came to Micah ...."
- In Zephaniah 1:1, "The *word* of the BeComingOne which came to Zephaniah ...."
- In Haggai 1:1, "...came the *word* of the BeComingOne by Haggai ...."
- In Zechariah 1:1, "... came the *word* of the BeComingOne to Zechariah ...."

gp237» In Zechariah 1:1 we see the Hebrew word *debar* translated "word" in English is also *logos* in the Greek translation. The same applies to Haggai 1:1, Zephaniah 1:1, Micah 1:1, Jonah 1:1, Joel 1:1, Hosea 1:1, Ezekiel 1:3, Jeremiah 1:2, and Isaiah 1:10.

gp238» The LOGOS or the WORD of the Old Testament was the *angel* of The BeComingOne (YHWH). **The messenger (or angel) of the BeComingOne (YHWH) is**

the WORD of the true God. This Word was also described in the New Testament by John:

- "In the beginning was the WORD, and the WORD was with God, and the WORD was God. 2 He was in the beginning with God. 3 All things came into being through Him, and apart from Him nothing came into being that has come into being. 4 In Him was life, and the life was the Light of men." (John 1:1-4)

This translation is not literal, and it should read:

- John 1:1 In [the] beginning was the WORD, and the WORD was toward the God, and God was the WORD. 2 He was in the beginning toward the God.[16] 3 All things have being [aor] through him, and outside of him have being not one [thing] which have received being. 4 In him was life, and the life was the light of men. (John 1:1-4, BCB; see Notes GP5)

Therefore the WORD, or angel of the BeComingOne, was <u>toward</u> the true God. The angel was the messenger of the great coming one, the BeComingOne, and so his WORD was in reference and toward this great coming God, the God that will be all in all (GP6). Power was given to this WORD, this angel, to create the cosmos.

Can we see Spirits?

gp239» But can spirit ever be seen? Or is spirit absolutely invisible to physical eyes? What is vision anyway? Is it possible that angels or spirits cannot be seen by any kind of eye? Could it be that angels or spirits have no form? Could it be spirits are intelligent modes of energy or power?

Analogous to Burning Flames or Wind

gp240» Now spirits themselves have no flesh and bones (Luke 24:39). Further, spirits or angels are represented by burning flames (Heb 1:7). Burning flames have no particular form, but they do have position — they exist in a certain area. And Job 4:15-16 shows us spirits or angels have no form: "Then a spirit passed before my face ... but I could not discern the form thereof: an image was before mine eyes." He could not comprehend any form, yet there was a spiritual image before his eyes. In verse 8 of John 3 Jesus made an allegory between Spirit and the wind and says as one cannot see the wind so also he cannot see the spirit. Something that is spiritual is something that is not easily detectable by sight, touch, smell, or by our other senses. Spirit is analogous to air: you cannot see air but we see the effect of its wind; spirit is invisible but we see the effects on mankind's behavior: either good or bad.

gp241» Thus, it is impossible to actually physically see the *spiritual* essence. Remember God through Paul said we could figure out the invisible by what appears (Rom 1:20). God used burning flames to represent angels or spirits, thus from this typical representation we should be able to learn something. And the something we learn, with the verses of Job 4:15-16, is that spirits or angels have no particular form, but are modes of energy or life or power. *Spirits or angels are physically formless modes of energy, or powers, with spatial location, with self-consciousness, and with mental ability.*

---

[16] "toward the God" cf John 13:3; "toward the Father" cf John 16:17; 16:28; 20:17, the Father being the God; see Greek text

Satan a spirit had no Form

gp242» Notice where it describes Satan, in an antitypical way, that it says, "you were perfect *in your **ways*** from the day you were created, till iniquity was found in you" (Ezek 28:15). Satan was beautiful (Ezek 28:12) in his *ways* before his first sin; he was not beautiful in his physical appearance, for spirits have no physically manifestable form.

Review of GP 3

gp243» The Word (logos) of God before Christ's resurrection was a spirit, the chief-spirit, the chief-angel, the angel of the BeComingOne. Since "angel" is translated from the Hebrew word *malak*, which means messenger, then the angel of the BeComingOne is the messenger of the BeComingOne. A messenger brings words from someone else. Thus, the messenger of the BeComingOne is the "WORD of the BeComingOne," for he brought the very words of the BeComingOne. Since the BeComingOne (YHWH) is the proper NAME of the true God, then the WORD is the WORD of *the* God. The angel of the BeComingOne had the NAME of *the* God in him (Exo 23:20-21). The WORD of God or the angel of the BeComingOne represented and stood in the NAME of *the* God. The age before Jesus Christ was subjected to angels, even the commandments given on Mount Sinai were from an angel (Acts 7:38).

General Review

gp244» Now let's clarify what we have learned so far.

In GP 1 we started our search: who or what is God? From the Bible we learned about the apparent paradoxes of God: "I make peace, and create evil: I the LORD do all these things" (Isa 45:7). God who is Love (1John 4:8) has somehow and for some reason created evil; He has even killed (Deut 32:39). But how can God be Love and also a killer?

We next learned that there are two basic laws and one basic fact we must understand in order to rightly perceive the true nature of God: the Law of Contradiction and the Law of Knowledge plus the fact that the God cannot lie.

We then went on and explained the Law of Contradiction.

We further showed the many attributes and titles of God and put forth that "time" is very important in our understanding of the paradoxes of God.

We also showed you the very NAME of the true God: YHWH, or Jehovah, or Yehowah, or He (who) will-be, or the BeComingOne, or the One who was, who is, and who is coming. God's NAME and its meaning is the real secret in revealing the answer to the Paradoxes of God. God's NAME is an *imperfect* (incomplete) verb and not as would be expected a *perfect* (complete) verb or a noun. Names are very important in the Bible and many times describe some facet of a person. The true NAME of the true God is important for it is the secret in explaining the apparently unexplainable scriptures about God.

In GP 1 we also looked into the meaning of "with God all things are possible," the "*one* Yehowah," the so-called unchangeableness of God, and other matters concerning the God. What GP 1 does is set the stage in our search for who or what is God.

In GP 2 we learned that Jesus Christ's Father was the BeComingOne (YHWH) of the Old Testament: He was the Jews' God.

In GP 3 we learned that the angel of the BeComingOne and the BeComingOne of the Old Testament were closely connected. Since angels are messengers, this means the angel of the BeComingOne is a messenger of the BeComingOne or this angel is the WORD of the BeComingOne. Therefore, the words that the angel of the BeComingOne spoke belonged to the Great BeComingOne Power — the true God. This angel stood in the NAME of the true God (Exo 23:20-21); he represented the great NAME. This angel was in a sense the very WORD of God. The Word (logos) of God before Christ's resurrection was a spirit, the chief-spirit, the chief-angel, the angel of the BeComingOne. The age before Jesus Christ was subjected to angels, even the commandments given on Mount Sinai were from an angel (Acts 7:38).

GP 4: Jesus Christ the Man

His Name
Promised Seed
God Inside
God Made Flesh
Death of Christ the Man
Jesus' Pre-existence Doctrine
Melchizedek
Genealogy of Christ

Who Was Jesus Christ

gp245» Who or what is Jesus Christ? Is he God, man, or man/God? Was he spirit, or human? Did he pre-exist before he was born? What does the Bible mean by saying he is the Son of God?

His Name

gp246» Let's begin with Christ's name. The Bible uses a name not only to point out a person among others, but also to describe that person. For example "Satan" means the hater, or accuser, or adversary. The name "Christ" tells us also something about him. "Christ" in the New Testament is a translation from a Greek word (*Christos*, # 5547) that is equivalent to "Messiah" of the Old Testament, and the Greek word means "*anointed*" as with oil, and implies to consecrate for an office or religious service. The word "Jesus" is from a Greek word (*Iesous*, # 2424) that means "*Jehovah* ('s or is) *salvation*." The meaning of Jesus Christ's name speaks of Jehovah's [the BeComingOne's] anointed savior which Jesus Christ was and is and will be.

Jesus Not Called "Christ" Openly *before* his Death

gp247» Although we call Jesus Christ, "Jesus Christ," he was not called "Jesus Christ" by his acquaintances before his death, but he was called "**Immanuel**" and/or "**Jesus**" because that was the name(s) he was given:

- "Behold, a virgin shall be with child, and shall bring forth a son, and they shall call his name **Immanuel**, which is interpreted, God with us" (Matt 1:23; see Isa 7:14).

- "and he [Joseph] called his name **Jesus**" (Matt 1:25).

- "and, behold, you shall conceive in your womb, and bring forth a son, and shall call his name **Jesus**" (Luke 1:30; see 2:21).

gp248» Before Jesus' resurrection, he was *not* openly called the "Christ" (Matt 16:15-16, 20; Luke 9:20-21). Only after his resurrection was he called Christ by his disciples and by his apostles. By some of his enemies Jesus was called such names as, *impostor* or *deceiver* (Matt 27:63). The New Testament writings were written *after* Jesus's resurrection, and thus the writers used "Jesus **Christ**" because at that time they knew he was the Messiah — the Christ, or the one anointed the YHWH. (See later in this book for details.)

gp249» This is similar to two in marriage. A woman named Mary Jones marries Joseph Smith, so after their marriage she is called Mary Smith. Later in life some may say Mary Smith moved from Seattle to San Jose when she was seven years old, even though Mary Smith was not known as "Smith" when she was seven; she was known as Mary Jones when she was seven. So when the writers of the New Testament say Jesus Christ did this and did that before his death, it did not mean that he was called Jesus Christ at that time. It was only after his death and resurrection (when the New Testament was written) that his followers openly called him, Jesus Christ.

Meaning of Being Anointed

gp250» "Christ" which means *anointed* has a special meaning in context of its usage in the Bible. When one is anointed it represents something, "then Samuel took the horn of oil, and anointed him [David] in the midst of his brethren: and the spirit of the BeComingOne came upon David from the day forward" (1Sam 16:13). And, "but you are an anointing from the Holy One, and you know all things ... But the anointing which you have received of him lives in you, and you need not that any man teach you: but as the same anointing teaching you all things, and is truth, and is no lie, and even as it has taught you, you shall live in him" (1 John 2:20, 27).

gp251» Note that after David was anointed, the spirit came to him. And also notice that with the true anointing, "you know all things," the anointing "lives in you," and the anointing "is truth." Now to be spiritually anointed in the highest sense is to receive God's Spirit and that anointing from the Holy One leads you into truth so you know all things concerning the Spiritual (1 John 2:20, 27).

gp252» To confirm that Spiritual anointing is anointing with the Spirit, compare 1 John 2:20, 27 with: "the Spirit of truth, is come, he will guide you into *all* truth..." (John 16:13). And, "the Comforter, which is the Holy Spirit, whom the Father will send in my name, He shall teach you all things" (John 14:26).

gp253» Thus, Christ's own name tells us he is anointed with the Spirit. "The Spirit of the Lord [= YHWH of OT] is upon me, because he has anointed me [Jesus] to preach the gospel to the poor" (Luke 4:18). Hence, Christ is anointed with the Spirit to preach the gospel. This is one of Christ's commissions from God.

gp254» Remember that the word "Jesus" is translated from a Greek word, *Iesous*, the equivalent of the Hebrew, *Jehoshua* [Yehoshua], which means, The BeComingOne (is) savior, or the BeComingOne's savior. This could be written as, "Yehowah's Savior," or "Jehovah's Savior." Jesus Christ's name has the meaning that is equivalent to the English's, *"The BeComingOne's savior, anointed"* or *"anointed The BeComingOne's savior."* "For unto you is born this day in the city of David a *Savior*, which is Christ (the) Lord" (Luke 2:11). This could be translated :"... a Savior which is anointed Lord." "The Father sent the Son to be the Savior of the World" (1 John 4:14). "And she shall bring forth a son, and you shall call his name Jesus: for he shall *save* his people from their sins" (Matt 1:21). Jesus Christ is Jehovah's anointed Savior of the world. "Savior" also indicates one who sets free or delivers those captured or enslaved. Jesus Christ will and is setting the world free from the slavery and confusion of this age through the New Mind of the New Spirit (John 8:31-36; Rom 8:2).

Promised Son Of God, Seed Of David, and Eve

Jesus Christ was Prophesied to Come

gp255» In the Old Testament it *foretold* the birth of Jesus Christ: "he shall cry unto Me, you art my Father, my God, and the rock of my salvation. Also I will make him My first born, higher than the kings of the earth" (Psa 89:26-27). "For unto us a child is born, unto us a son is given: and the government [rulership of God] shall be upon his shoulder: and his name shall be called Wonderful, Counselor, the mighty God, the duration Father, the Prince of Peace" (Isa 9:6). "I will declare the decree: the BeComingOne has said unto me, You art my Son; this day have I begotten you" (Psa 2:7; Heb 1:5).

gp256» "The BeComingOne came unto Nathan, saying, Go and tell my servant David, Thus says the BeComingOne ... and when your days be fulfilled, and you shall sleep with your fathers, I will set up your *seed* after you, which shall proceed out of your bowels, and I will establish his [Christ's] kingdom. He shall build a house for my NAME and I will establish the throne of his kingdom for olam. I will be his [Christ's] father, and he shall be my son" (2Sam 7:4, 5, 12-14).

Fulfillment

gp257» The Bible also shows the fulfillment of these prophesies. "This is my beloved Son, in whom I am well pleased" (Matt 3:17). "And I saw, and bare record that this is the Son of God" (John 1:34). "I come in my Father's name [the son of YHWH, thus Jesus had His NAME]" (John 5:43). "Concerning his [God's] Son Jesus Christ our Lord, which was made of the seed of David according to the flesh" (Rom 1:3; Acts 2:30).

gp258» Thus, Jesus is the Son of God as well as the seed of David as promised (Luke 3:23-38). Further Christ is the seed of Eve that was promised to bruise the head of Satan (Gen 3:15; Rom 16:20; Psa 91:13; see The "Seed Paper" [PR 1]).

Son of Man Through Mary

gp259» Jesus Christ is called Son of God, but also he is called Son of man (Acts 7:56). Now to be a son of mankind, one needs to be human. Jesus was human for he was a son of Mary (Mark 6:3). "And Joseph also went up from Galilee, out of the city of Nazareth, into Judea, unto the city of David, which is called Bethlehem (because he was of the house and lineage of David) to be taxed with Mary his *espoused* wife [notice not wife, but espoused wife; for Joseph hadn't consummated the marriage, see Matt 1:24-25], being large with a child ... And she brought forth her first-born son" (Luke 2:4-5, 7). Thus another prophecy about Christ came true, "but you Bethlehem ... out of you shall he come forth unto me that is to be ruler in Israel" (Micah 5:2). Jesus was born in Bethlehem as prophesied in Micah and confirmed in Luke. "Therefore the BeComingOne himself shall give you a sign; Behold, a virgin shall conceive, and bear a son, and shall call his name Immanuel" (Isa 7:14).

gp260» As we've shown you Joseph hadn't consummated the marriage, and after Gabriel had told Mary about the son that she was to bring forth, "said Mary unto the angel, How shall this be, seeing I know not a man?" (Luke 1:34) Mary was a virgin mother. "But when the fullness of the time was come, God sent forth his Son, *made* of a woman" (Gal 4:4).

gp261» Notice in Galatians 4:4 that God's Son was "made" (KJV) or was "born" (NIV) of a woman. This word "made" is translated from a Greek word *ginomai* (# 1096) which means: "to become, i.e. to come into existence, begin to be, receive being" (*Thayer's Greek-English Lexicon*). From the Greek Gal 4:4 reads:

- "But when had come fullness of the time, the God sent forth the Son of Him, *coming into existence* from [or "out of"] a woman."

It says that God's Son was made out of a woman. This same Greek word, *ginomai*, is also found in two other closely related verses:

- "Concerning his Son Jesus Christ our Lord, which was made [*ginomai*] of ['out of' — Greek] the seed of David according to the flesh" (Rom 1:3; Acts 2:30).

- "And the Word was made [*ginomai*] flesh" (John 1:14).

The Son of God *first* came into existence from a woman, who was flesh ("according to the flesh"), who was also a seed of David.

gp262» Furthermore, these verses are related in meaning to 1John 4:2:

- "By this you know the Spirit of God: Every spirit that confesses that Jesus Christ *has come* in the flesh is of God" (NKJV).

The word translated "has come" is a Greek verb in its participle *perfect* tense (The Analytical Greek Lexicon). Christ *did* come in the flesh as the above verses indicate. In fact, he first came into existence through a woman. He had no pre-existence. The word "pre-existence" is a self contradiction. Scriptures prove that Jesus Christ the man did not exist *before* he was born from a woman (see later).

gp263» Jesus Christ was a Son of mankind, not a product of man through a male and female union, but from mankind through his mother. Mary was Christ's mother, but Joseph was not his real father, for Joseph didn't "know" Mary. At that time Mary was a virgin. Thus, Jesus is a son of man or mankind through the medium of Mary only.

Virgin Birth

gp264» Let's understand this virgin birth, and see how Jesus is a Son of God through being born from a woman:

- "And the angel [Gabriel] said unto her, Fear not, Mary: for you have found favor with God. And, behold, you shall conceive in your womb, and bring forth a son, and shall call his name JESUS ... Then said Mary unto the angel, How shall this be, seeing I know not a man? And the angel answered and said unto her, The Holy Spirit shall come upon you, and the power of the Highest [BeComingOne] shall overshadow you: therefore also that holy thing which shall be born of you shall be called the Son of God" (Luke 1:30-31, 34-35). And, "for that which is conceived in her is of the Holy Spirit" (Matt 1:20).

gp265» This is why the Bible calls Christ the Son of God. God, the highest power, the power of the Holy Spirit, conceived Jesus Christ in the womb of Mary. In this way, Christ is a Son of God. (In another way Christ is the Son of God, as Christians are sons of God, because he had the Spirit of God in him.) Through the power of God, Mary conceived, not through the power of a male's sperm. Basically, what the male's sperm does when it contacts a female's ovum (egg-cell) is to initiate a chemical-biological chain reaction. Through this chemical reaction the egg-cell grows into a child. Jesus Christ began as any other child from an ovum. But this egg-cell was fertilized *not* by a male's sperm, for Mary was a virgin. It was the power of God that fertilized this egg-cell that became Christ. How? God by merely duplicating the chemical code of a male's sperm conceived Jesus. Since God designed the ovum and sperm, he knows how they work and thus is able to initiate the chemical reaction in an ovum needed to produce a child. Through the power of God the Father, Mary conceived. In this way, God is the physical father of Jesus; Joseph is not the physical father of Jesus. Mary was a virgin to man, but not to God, for in a sense God "knew" Mary.

Middle Man: Son of God and Son of Man

gp266» This is why Jesus Christ is called a mediator, "for there is one God, and one mediator between God and men, the MAN Christ Jesus" (1 Tim 2:5). Notice it was the *man* Jesus who was the mediator, *not* the resurrected Christ. Now "mediator" means middle man or middle one. The man Jesus Christ is the middle one between God and mankind. He was "Jesus of Nazareth, a *man*" (Acts 2:22). This offspring of Mary and God was the beginning of a union of man back to God.

Born of the Seed of David

Genealogy of Mary & Joseph

gp267» Matthew 1:1-17 and Luke 3:23-38. Notice that Christ was born "of the seed of David according to the flesh" (Rom 1:3). In order for Jesus to be the Messiah, he must be from David, that is from the seed of King David. Since Mary's husband, Joseph, was not the physical father of Christ (Mary was a virgin), then Joseph's genealogy as listed in Luke 3:23-38 is irrelevant. Jesus' genealogy must come through Mary.

gp268» Matthew 1:1-15 is Jesus Christ's real genealogy because it says specifically in verse one, that it was the "book of the generation of Jesus Christ, Son of David, son of Abraham."

gp269» In most translations Matthew 1:16 reads, "Joseph was the husband of Mary, out of whom was born Jesus." Most translations in English come from Greek texts, and in these texts Joseph is said to be the husband of Mary. But the book of Matthew was first written in Hebrew. In at least two Hebrew texts found recently by a Hebrew scholar named Nehemia Gordon, it says for verse 16 that Joseph was the father of Mary. How can Joseph be the father and also the husband of Mary? It is because both genealogies are not speaking about the same Joseph, but two different Josephs. Those who translated Matthew did not understand this and so they "corrected" the Hebrew text from Joseph being the father of Mary to Joseph being the husband of Mary.

gp270» Notice in Matthew 1:16 that it specifically says Jacob begat Joseph: Jacob was the father of Joseph. But the wording in Luke 3:23 has Heli as the father of Joseph: "Joseph of Heli."(Luke 3:23, 24). There are **two different Josephs** being spoken about: one whose father was Jacob and one whose father was Heli.

gp271» Examine both of these genealogies in Matthew and Luke, they are different. Can Joseph have two genealogies with different fathers? No. The simple answer is that there were two Josephs. The proof is the use of the **format formula of three 14 generations' lists** in the Matthew genealogy:

> "all the generations, therefore, from Abraham to David were **fourteen** generations; and from David until the carrying away to Babylon, **fourteen** generations; and from the carrying away from Babylon unto the Messiah, **fourteen** generations" [Matt 1:17].

The first two lists of 14 generations in the book of Matthew have 14 generations each, but the third list in the Greek/English texts has only 13. This is because these mistaken translations have Joseph as the *husband* of Mary instead of the *father* of Mary. Matthew didn't make a mistake in his original text written in Hebrew, but the translators did make a mistake and thus were left with only 13 generations in their third list instead of 14 generations.

Seed of Nathan and Solomon

gp272» Mary's lineage came from David's son Solomon (2Sam 5:14). Nathan was also a son of David as shown in 2 Samuel 5:14, and Joseph's (Mary's husband) lineage came from Nathan. Notice this in Zechariah 12:12, "and the land shall mourn [in verses 10 and 11 it prophesies of people: first looking on Jesus on the cross; and second looking on Jesus when he returns, Rev 1:7], every family apart ['I am come to set a man at variance against his father, and daughter against her mother,' Matt 10:35]; the family of the house of David apart [Mary's], and their wives apart; the family of the house of Nathan [Joseph's family, Luke 3:31] apart, and their wives apart" (Zech 12:12).

[NOTE: Christ was on the cross, and possibly Christ's brothers were apart from their wives, and Joseph was apart from Mary (Joseph isn't mentioned at the end of the accounts of Matthew, Mark, Luke, and John — he could have been dead or separated from his wife). The Nathan Family was apart because some of them believed in Christ while others didn't. There is also a Spiritual meaning here. Christ had the Spirit of God and was apart from his brethren Spiritually up until the time they received the Spirit.]

gp273» Mary came from Solomon's lineage, but Joseph came from Nathan's, yet both from David since Nathan and Solomon were sons of David. Notice that in Joseph's and Mary's genealogy from David back to Abraham and beyond is the same, although not all of the generations are listed.

Christ's Lineage Review

gp274» We have proved from scriptures that Jesus was a descendant of David as promised David (2Sam 7:4-5, 12-14). Further, we saw that Jesus was the son of God. God (YHWH) begot Jesus the man through the power of the Holy Spirit (Luke 1:30-35). Thus, God is Jesus' physical Father (Psa 2:7; Heb 1:5; Psa 89:26-27; 2Sam 7:4, 12-14). Therefore, Jesus is at once the Son of mankind and the Son of God.

gp275» Jesus is the middle one between man and God, "one mediator between God and men, the MAN Christ Jesus" (1 Tim 2:5). Jesus was flesh and blood, born of woman (Gal 4:4). And his physical birth was initiated through the power of God.

God *inside* Christ The Man

gp276» But Jesus had another facet about him: he had God's Spirit inside him. God's Spirit was not him, but inside him. This is very important:

- "The BeComingOne has called me [Christ] from the womb; from the bowels of my mother has he made mention of my name [see Luke 1:26-32]. And he [BeComingOne] has made my mouth like a sharp sword [word of God, cf Eph 6:17; Rev 1:16] ... the BeComingOne that formed me [Christ] from the womb His servant, to bring Jacob again to Him ... and my God shall be my strength ... I [the BeComingOne] will also give you [Christ] for a light to the Gentiles" (Isa 49:1-2, 5-6; cf Luke 2:32).

gp277» God gave Jesus a "sharp sword" (word of God) and God was Christ's strength. It was God who gave his strength and words to Christ. Christ didn't speak *his* own words or use *his* own power. Notice, "behold my [the BeComingOne's] servant, whom I uphold; mine elect, in whom my soul delights; *I have put my spirit upon him*: he shall bring forth judgment to the Gentiles" (Isa 42:1). "And the *spirit of the BeComingOne shall rest upon him*, the spirit of wisdom and understanding, the spirit of counsel and might, the spirit of knowledge and of the fear of the BeComingOne" (Isa 11:2). This "spirit of wisdom" is the same "wisdom" pictured in Proverbs 8:22ff. The "spirit of wisdom" is God's Spirit.

gp278» Jesus was prophesied to receive the BeComingOne's spirit of wisdom, knowledge, and so on. Did he receive it? "The words that I speak unto you I speak not of myself: but the Father that lives in me, he does the works" (John 14:10). Notice that the Father, the BeComingOne's Spirit, was inside him and this Spirit, did the works. Even the words of knowledge that Christ spoke were from the BeComingOne as Isaiah 11:2; John 14:10,24; 12:49-50; 8:38 prove. Jesus was set forth distinctively from men, not merely by his resurrection (Rom 1:4), but by his works; Jesus says his Father did the works (John 14:10).

Spirit in Jesus was the Angel of God

gp279» But since angels are spirits (Heb 1:7; compare Heb 1:13 w/1:14), since angels are messengers, and since messengers are word carriers, then the Spirit in Christ was an angel. In fact it was the very angel of the BeComingOne (YHWH). It was this angel who was the WORD of God, who carried the words of the BeComingOne (see GP 3).

gp280» It was the Spirit or the angel of God *in* Christ the man that did the good works. Jesus was sinless (John 8:46) and it was the Spirit in him that did these works. Jesus was a human being, but he had the BeComingOne's Spirit or mind inside him. He was not Spirit himself, for if he were spirit, one could not see him (John 3:8). The man Jesus was flesh and blood, he was human, with the BeComingOne's Spirit inside him. "God was manifest in the flesh" of Christ (1Tim 3:16). "That God was in Christ" (2Cor 5:19).

gp281» "And she [Mary] shall bring forth a son, and you shall call his name Jesus for he shall save his people from their sins. Now all this was done, that it might be fulfilled which was spoken of the Lord [BeComingOne] by the prophet, saying, Behold, a virgin shall be with child, and shall bring forth a son, and they shall call his name Immanuel, which being interpreted is, GOD WITH US" (Matt 1:21-23). Names are used in the Bible to identify characteristics of people. Immanuel, one of Jesus's names, means, "God with us." INSIDE Christ, God was with the world. Christ the man was not God, but God was inside him. Jesus was *man* only, until his resurrection from the dead and his ascension to the Father.

Jesus Christ Came In The Flesh, Anointed by the Spirit

gp282» Notice, "by this you know the Spirit of God: every spirit that acknowledges that Jesus Christ *has* come in the FLESH, is of God" (1 John 4:2, see NKJV & Greek). John gives those reading the Bible a test: IF someone does agree that Christ Jesus came in the flesh, then he is of God's Spirit. But further John says: "and every spirit [in man] that acknowledges that Jesus is not come in the flesh, is not of God: and this is the spirit of antichrist" (1 John 4:3). Jesus was the Christ; He was the Messiah. Jesus was thus the promised anointed one. He was anointed by the Spirit of God. He was anointed by the very Word of God. **If Jesus the man was the very Word of God, then how could he have been anointed by the Spirit?** If Jesus was already Spirit why would he be anointed again with the Spirit again? Was he anointed by himself? No Jesus came in the flesh, as a human being, and then was anointed by the Spirit. The Savior of mankind came in the flesh with the Spirit of God inside him. But this does not mean he saves us in or by his former state as a man. We are saved by his resurrected life, not by his human life or death, but by his new life.

Jesus Christ The Man Was Not God

gp283» Jesus was *not* God before his resurrection. Jesus was a man with God's Spirit inside him as many scriptures prove (John 14:10; 1Tim 3:16; John 10:38; etc.). Jesus Christ before his resurrection was a *man*: "the *man* Christ Jesus" (1 Tim 2:5).

Came From God

gp284» "He [Christ] came from God, and went to God" (John 13:3). The literal translation from the Greek of this verse reads: "and that from God he came *out of* and to the God goes." Jesus Christ came out of God. He was a physical offspring of God, as shown before, through the power of God. And, "I came out from God. I came forth from the Father, and am come into the world; again, I leave the world, and go to the Father" (John 16:27-28). By the fact that God was Christ's "physical" father, by the power of the Father, Christ indeed come *out of* the Father in the same sense that a son comes from his father's physical seed. (There is a dual sense here, see later.) "Now are we sure that you know all things, and need not that any man should ask you: by this we believe that you came forth *from* God" (John 16:30). If one is *from* or *out of* something, he is not that thing. Christ the man was from God, he was not God.

They were Two

gp285» There is an abundance of scripture that indicates that Jesus Christ the man and His Father were two distinctive individuals or beings at one time:

- **sender-sent:** The fact that Jesus was sent by his Father means he is someone other than the sender (John 4:34; 6:38-39, 57),

- **two wills:** the fact that he came not to do his will but the will of him who sent him shows two wills (John 6:38),

- **two witnesses:** the fact that Jesus Christ the man spoke about the law of *two* witnesses and that he was not alone (*monos*), comparing himself as one witness and his Father as the other witness indicates two (John 8:16-18),

- **not alone:** the fact that Jesus Christ spoke about himself *not* being alone (*monos* or only) because his Father who sent him was with him indicates two (John 8:29; 16:32),

- **not his words:** the fact that Jesus doesn't say his own words ("not from myself") but his Father's words indicate he was not the Father (John 12:49; 14:24),

- **"we":** the fact that Jesus spoke of himself and his Father as "we" indicates two (John 14:23),

- **from-going back:** the fact that Jesus came from the Father and was going back indicates two (John 16:28),

- **"nor me":** the fact that Jesus said that men didn't know his Father "nor me [Christ]" indicates two (John 16:3),

- **Father greater:** the fact that Jesus called the Father greater than himself indicates two (John 14:28),

- **sent by the only God:** the fact that Jesus Christ said he was sent by the only (*monos*) true God indicates two (John 17:3),

- **prayed to the Father:** the fact that Jesus Christ the man prayed *to* his Father indicates two (John 14:16; 17:1 ff),

- **resurrected by God:** If he was raised by God (Acts 2:24, 2:32; 13:33-37), at the time he was raised by God, how could he be God? No there were two, the one resurrecting, and the one resurrected,

- **not yet returned to the Father:** the fact that Jesus said he had yet to return to his Father and called his Father "my Father and your Father"indicate that Jesus Christ the man and God the Father were *two* (John 20:17),

- **God made him both Lord and Christ:** this speaks of two, the who made Jesus Lord and Christ, and Jesus who was made by God, both Lord and Christ (Acts 2:36).

All the above and other scripture indicate that Jesus Christ the man and his Father were two before Jesus was resurrected and went to the right side of his Father. Yet other scripture indicates somehow they were one (John 10:30) in a way similar to the way Christians are one in God (John 17:21-23, 11; see 1Cor 12:12ff). When Jesus Christ the man was on earth before his resurrection he was separate *from* his Father, yet he was ONE in a Spiritual sense, since Christ the man acted as his Father directed (John 12:49-50).

A Mediator is Not God

gp286» "For there is one God, and one mediator between God and men, the MAN Christ Jesus ... Now a mediator is not of one, but God is one" (1 Tim 2:5; Gal 3:20). Jesus Christ the man as a mediator was not God, but God was inside him, for the Spirit lived inside him.

Angel of the BeComingOne Was in Christ the Man

gp287» *Word of God in Jesus.* Jesus was a Spiritually begotten Son of God through the Spirit inside him. Jesus had inside him the very Spirit or the angel of the BeComingOne. The BeComingOne being the Father because the Power of the BeComingOne predestinated all, thus in this sense the BeComingOne is the Father, while the angel was the messenger and agent of the Father. The archangel (as the messenger of the Father) was actually inside his mind Spiritually leading him. Since Spirit takes up no space (as some imagine space), it can and does live anywhere, including inside a human mind. Since "angel" is a translation from a word meaning "messenger," then the Spiritual Messenger of God the Father was inside Jesus the man's head giving him Spiritual messages that enabled him to fulfill God's will. In a sense, this angel was the WORD of God — the WORD of the BeComingOne.

gp288» And again, here is some proof that this Spirit or angel of God the Father was inside Jesus the man:

- One of Christ's names tells us this: "Immanuel" means *God with us*. God was with man, by the fact His Spirit was *inside* Christ.

- Paul said God was manifested *in* the flesh (1Tim 3:16). This means by the context of the chapter that God was *in* Christ, not as the flesh of Christ. If God was as the flesh of Christ, it means God died with Jesus on the cross. But since God is immortal, then God could not and did not die on the cross (see GP 1). To refute this is to say that God lied when through scripture he said that spiritual beings like angels cannot die (Luke 20:36). How can an immortal being die? How can someone that cannot die, die?

- Jesus said "the son of man shall give you, because God the Father has set His seal on Him" (John 6:27). Jesus was sealed by the God with the Holy Spirit as Christians are sealed: "And do not grieve the Holy Spirit of God, with which you were marked with a **seal** for the day of redemption" (Eph 4:32; see Eph 1:13; 2Cor 1:22).

- "That is, that God was in Christ, reconciling the world unto himself" (2Cor 5:19). God's mark or seal was on Christ the man. He had God's Spirit, God's angel, God's WORD, in him. Again God was *in* Christ.

Christ Suffered, Can God Suffer?

gp289» Jesus Christ the man, from a regular ovum in Mary, grew into a man who was sinless (Heb 4:15) because of the power of the Spirit in him. He was only given what was needed for his commission as the man Jesus Christ. He was given God's Spirit that produced the wisdom of Christ the man (Isa 11:2-4) and the great works (John 14:10). But he was given only just enough to do this. He "who in the days of his flesh, when he had offered up prayer and supplications with strong crying and tears unto Him that was able to save him from death, and was heard in that he feared" (Heb 5:7). Jesus had to cry aloud to his Father for help, "but was in all points tempted like as we are, yet without sin" (Heb 4:15). Because of this, the resurrected Christ, "in that he himself has suffered being tested, he is able to help them that are tested" (Heb 2:18). Can God suffer or was God inside of Christ, not as Christ?

gp290» We will explain later how Jesus became God, or we should say was infused into the true God, after being resurrected to the right side of the true God. This may be confusing until you understand who or what is the true God. But for now let's go into more details to prove God's Spirit was inside Christ the MAN.

God Not As Christ, But *in*side Christ

Men as Temples of the Living God

gp291» God was manifested in the flesh of Christ (1Tim 3:16). And one of Jesus Christ's names ("Immanuel") meant "God with us" (Matt 1:23). But we have shown you that Jesus before his death was not God, but God was inside him. Human beings are called temples of God and God lives inside these temples, if these individuals are Spiritual Christians. "For we are the temple of the living God" (2Cor 6:16). Even Jesus the man was the temple of his Father's Spirit: "Jesus answered them. 'Destroy this temple, and I will raise it again in three days.' The Jews replied, 'It has taken forty-six years to build this temple, and you are going to raise it in three days?' But the temple he had spoken of was his body" (John 2:19-21).

gp292» Although God the Father through his Spiritual messenger initiated the chemical process in one of Mary's eggs that produced Christ, God didn't put himself or transform himself *with or as* the flesh of Christ. God in a sense begot Christ, through a chemical process (created sperm) to produce the MAN Christ in the womb of Mary. At that time, God was not man, thus he did not have physical sperm with genes in it. No physical genes from God went into the ovum that produced Christ, for God being Spirit had no human sperm when he produced Christ the man. Nor did a Spiritual "sperm" enter the ovum, or else Jesus would have been part Spirit. But God did put his Spirit *into* the mind of Christ. And it is this Spirit of God that led Christ as it leads all sons of God (Rom 8:14) that are sons in the Spiritual or antitypical sense.

Spirit Did the Works With Jesus

gp293» And it was through this Spirit in him that Jesus did the great works (John 14:10). Yet just because it was the Spirit inside him that did the great works, this doesn't mean the man Jesus did nothing. The Spirit in him worked and produced Christ's good Spiritual fruit as the sap in trees produce the fruit. Yet, as the sap needs the branches and the leaves to produce the fruit, so does the Spirit need a body to produce the good fruit. As the leaves and the branches help with the work, so did Christ the man help the Spirit produce the good fruit. Yet without the Spirit no one can produce good fruit, as no branch can produce fruit without the sap from the trunk and roots of the tree. The Spirit is the energy needed to produce the good fruit, as the sap is the energy needed to produce the fruit. They need each other to produce. The Spirit in Christ worked and led Jesus just enough for Jesus the man to be sinless. God gives enough Spiritual power for a person to do what is asked of him (Rom 8:28ff; see *New Mind Papers*).

Paul is an example.

gp294» Paul was "appointed a preacher, and an apostle, and a teacher of the Gentiles" by God (2Tim 1:11; Acts 9:15). And what did God answer Paul about a problem he had: "my Grace is sufficient for you" (2Cor 12:9). "But by the grace of God I am what I am: and his grace which was bestowed upon me was not in vain; but I labored [he did his appointed work] more abundantly than they all: YET NOT I, but the grace of God which was with me" (1Cor 15:10). The grace of God did Paul's work, as the grace of God, or the Spirit of God, or the New-Mind did the works of Christ (John 14:10).

We Are Saved By the Resurrected Christ

gp295» "And if Christ is not risen, then is our preaching futile, and your faith is also futile ... For if the dead don't rise, then Christ is not raised ... If in this life [our human life] only we have hope in Christ [the MAN], we are of all men most miserable. But now Christ is risen from the dead" (1Cor 15:14, 16, 19-20). Christ must be alive and resurrected or our faith is just plain stupidity. "WE SHALL BE SAVED BY HIS LIFE" (Rom 5:10). The Savior of mankind came in the flesh as a human, but we are saved by his new resurrected life.

When Did Christ Receive the Spirit?

gp296» Jesus the man was unique, he was a physical Son of God (through God's power over the ovum) and a Spiritually begotten Son of God (through the Spiritual power in his mind). Romans 8:9-17 and elsewhere manifests to us that to be a Spiritual son of God, you must have God's Spirit in you.

gp297» In the New Testament, it doesn't say *when* Christ received God's Spirit in his mind, but it was probably from his birth (Isa 49:1-2, 5-6, "from the womb"; cf Luke 2:32; see above), for during his childhood he had the Spirit and the grace of God upon him (Luke 2:40, 46-47). Therefore when Christ was baptized in water by John, the "Spirit of God descending like a dove," was representative of Christ having the Spirit. People saw a dove land on Jesus which fulfilled a sign that Christ was the one who baptized with the Spirit; John merely baptized with water (John 1:33). Those John baptized didn't receive the Spirit (Acts 18:24-25; 19:1-6). Christ received the Spirit at birth. The water baptism by John of Jesus was symbolic only, for Christ already had the Spirit (Luke 2:40). Christ only got water baptized to fulfill prophecy and righteousness and to show a physical example or sign to Israel (Luke 2:40; Matt 3:11-16; Luke 3:15-16; John 1:30-33).

God Made Flesh?

gp298» Now some say that Jesus Christ the man and the BeComingOne (Jehovah) of the Old Testament were one and the same person. They, believing that the *Word* of God, God, and Jesus Christ are one and the same, point out, "In the beginning was the Word ... and the Word was made flesh" (John 1:1,14). Therefore they say God somehow became flesh, but they have a problem since they believe God is immutable or not changeable. Part of the gymnastics that they go through because of their impossible theory is written about in *Trinity v. BeComingOne* paper.[17] But as we have shown with many proofs in GP 3, the WORD of the Old Testament was the *angel* of the BeComingOne. It was through this angel or messenger that God — the BeComingOne — spoke. This angel spoke for the Coming Power: the God all in all; the BeComingOne that will finally become. The BeComingOne spoke (Isa 52:6) in the Old Testament of the Bible, but he spoke through His agent — the angel, the very WORD of God. The BeComingOne was one and the same being as Christ's Father (GP 2). One of the proofs of this came from Christ's own lips. Since the Jews' God is the God of the Old Testament, then when Christ tells them his Father is the same God, we know that the BeComingOne is the Father (John 8:54).

gp299» Now *if* it was true, that the very God became flesh, and that he became Christ the man, then it means the BeComingOne, the Father, died when Christ died. We ask, if this is true, WHO RESURRECTED CHRIST THE MAN? Scripture plainly shows us God the Father (through His predestinated Power) raised Christ the man from death (Acts 2:32, 24; Rom 8:11; 1Cor 6:14). Thus, they were separate. God inside Christ the man, not God as Christ the man. God was in Jesus Christ because His Spirit, that is His Angel, or His WORD (and the Power of His WORD), was in Jesus Christ. Angels or spirits do not die (Luke 20:36). God is immortal, unable to die (1Tim 1:17). Jesus said scripture could *not* be broken (John 10:35), therefore the BeComingOne or his angels do not die. Before the resurrection God or His angel did not become Christ the man. God in some way was living inside Christ the man. Since the Father is the BeComingOne of the Old Testament, we know that God was with man because he was somehow *in* Christ the man. God was in Jesus through His Spirit, His Angel, His Spiritual messenger.

Meaning of, "the Word Was Made Flesh"

gp300» Let's see what the scripture means by "the Word was made flesh." From the Greek text this sentence reads, "and the Word became Flesh" (John 1:14). The real sense of this verse is that the WORD became flesh *after* the resurrection, for these words were written by John *after* the resurrection (GP 5). But there is another sense to this verse. By other scriptures which we shall show you, we can in light of these make this verse clear as following, "and the Word became [in] flesh." For the antitypical or higher or real meaning of this verse see GP 5.

gp301» "God who at different times and divers manners spoke in time past unto the fathers by the prophets, Has in these last days spoken unto us in his Son" (Heb 1:1-2; cf. Heb 2:2-3). God did not speak in the past (before Christ the man) through His Son because he did not exist then. God spoke by or inside his Son during his days on earth:

- "The words that I speak unto you I speak not from myself: but the Father that lives in me, he does the works" (John 14:10).

---

[17] See http://becomingone.org/gp/gp10b.htm

- "For I have not spoken out of myself; but the Father which sent me, he gave a commandment, what I should say, and what I should speak ... whatsoever I speak therefore, even as the Father said unto me, so I speak" (John 12:49-50).

- "The word which you hear is *not* mine, but the Father's which sent me" (John 14:24). And again, "I speak that which I have seen with my Father" (John 8:38).

Notice the prophecy of this, "I [the BeComingOne, Deut 18:15] will raise them up a Prophet from among their brethren, like unto you [Jesus came in the flesh, 1 John 4:2-3, by the seed of mankind not angels, Heb 2:14, 16], and *will put my words in his mouth*; and he shall speak unto them *all that I shall command him*" (Deut 18:18).

gp302» Jesus spoke the Words of his Father because the angel or messenger of the BeComingOne was inside Jesus and was leading him. In this way the Father was *in* Jesus the man leading him with God's Spirit (Isa 42:1; Rom 8:14). The Word was *in* the flesh, the Word was made and manifested *in*side the flesh, but was *not* the same as the flesh before the resurrection. The BeComingOne or the Father didn't become flesh, for if he did then God or His angel died on the cross with and as Christ. But since immortal beings cannot die, then God or His angel was not transformed into Christ in order to die.

Death of Christ the Man

Holy One

gp303» Let's look at Christ's death, for by it we can prove positively what we have put forth herein (For details see CP 4). Notice what is quoted in Acts from the 16th Psalm, "because you [the BeComingOne] will not leave my [Christ's] soul in hell, neither permit your Holy One to see corruption" (Acts 2:27).

gp304» Who is the Holy One? He is the God of the Old Testament. In other words, Christ's Father. "BeComingOne of hosts (is) his name, the Holy One of Israel" (Isa 47:4). "Thus says the BeComingOne, the Holy One of Israel" (Isa 45:11). There are about 40 places in the Old Testament where the BeComingOne identifies himself as the Holy One. The BeComingOne will not permit the Holy One (the BeComingOne himself) to see corruption. Corruption is used by the Bible to indicate death. Thus God will not die on any cross, as some make Him by having Jesus Christ the man joined to their Trinitarian God.

gp305» Christ the man died according to scripture (1Cor 15:3), and was buried for three days (Matt 12:40). And they buried his body in the grave (John 19:40-42). Now Christ the man was resurrected after exactly three days and three nights in the grave (see CP 4). But notice, "of the resurrection of Christ that his soul was not left in hell [the grave], neither his flesh did see corruption" (Acts 2:31). What?

gp306» If Christ the man died, how could his flesh not see corruption? Scripture as we have shown you said specifically Christ died. Since he was flesh, that means his flesh died. But Acts 2:31 said his flesh didn't see corruption. Notice the verse is speaking of the resurrection, and that his soul was not *left* in the grave. He wasn't left in the grave. He was resurrected, and after this resurrection his flesh didn't and won't see corruption *again*.

gp307» Notice the proof of this rendition, "and as concerning that he [God] raised him [Christ the man] from the dead, now no more to *return* to corruption" (Acts 13:34). Acts 2:31 must be read in context of Acts 13:34. Christ's flesh did see death, but after his resurrection his flesh will not see corruption *again* (NOTE: the resurrected Christ does have a flesh and blood body, Luke 24:39). Thus in context of Acts 13:34, Acts 2:31 means "his flesh did see corruption no more after his resurrection." And Acts 13:37 means in context, "whom God *raised*, saw no [more] corruption."

gp308» "You shall not permit your Holy One to see corruption" (Acts 13:35). Acts repeats this twice in Acts 13:35 and Acts 2:27. The "Holy One" is the BeComingOne or the Lord God of the KJV, an immortal being. He cannot die according to scripture. Those who say Christ is the BeComingOne of the Old Testament or the LORD or Jehovah of the Old Testament, say he became flesh and died. But scripture says God will not permit the Holy One (the BeComingOne [YHWH] himself) to die. Of course not, for the BeComingOne is the Holy One. He is Christ's Father. He lived inside of Christ the man through His angel who carried God's WORD.

gp309» But Acts does use a similar word formation as in Psalms 16:10 and Acts 2:27. Notice Acts 2:31 and Acts 13:37. It seems to say Christ the man is the Holy One by the word formation. But it does not speak of the Holy One. It uses Christ's name, thus, fooling those who are not discriminating enough to notice the difference. Those who do not know there is a difference between the Holy One and Christ the *man* conclude that Christ didn't really die when they look at Acts 2:31. When they see "neither his flesh did see corruption," they conclude he didn't really die. But as shown, they leave out Acts 13:34 which clears up Acts 2:31.

Spirit Leaves Body At Death

gp310» Therefore Christ died, but the Holy One (the Father's Spirit) inside Christ the man did not die. Notice where the Holy One left Christ the man's body, "Father, into your hands I commend my spirit" (Luke 23:46). At that same time "he gave up the breath." The Bible uses this last expression to indicate dying, for life came at first from the breath of life (Gen 2:7). At the losing of this breath of life, one loses his life. Also, at death, the man Christ gave up his spirit or angel. And since his Spirit was what made the God *in* him, it was at this point that the Holy One's Spirit left Christ's body. This fulfills prophecy that the Holy One would not see corruption, but that Christ the man died.

gp311» Now some will probably point to Acts 3:14 in order to prove (they think) that the *man* Jesus was the Holy One, "but you denied the Holy One and the Just, and desired a murderer to be granted unto you" (Acts 3:14). But HOW did they deny the Holy One? "If you had known me, you should have known my Father also: and from henceforth you know him, and have seen him ... Don't you believe that I am in the Father, and the Father in me? the words that I speak unto you I speak not of myself: but the Father that lives inside me, he does the works" (John 14:7, 10). "It is the Spirit who gives life; the flesh profits nothing. The words that I speak to you are spirit, and are life" (John 6:63). Christ's good works and his words came from the good Spirit inside him. "God was manifest in the flesh" (1Tim 3:16). They denied the Holy One because Christ was a shadow or image of the Holy One (Col 1:15), for Christ did exactly as the Holy One in him led him.

gp312» The angel of the BeComingOne did not die on the cross with Christ the man. Jesus the *man* died. Jesus came in the flesh (1 John 4:2-3). He was made just like his brothers, as flesh and blood, as a human (Heb 2:14, 16). Jesus the man was commissioned before the world began to be sinless, to die for sin, and to be resurrected into God.

Why Christ Died

Predestinated Before the Foundations of the World

gp313» Jesus the man is the Spiritual Lamb of God who *before* the foundations of the world was chosen to be a spotless or sinless "lamb" through the power of God's Spirit inside him (Compare John 1:29; Rev 13:8; Isa 53:7-8; Matt 12:18; 1Pet 2:4; Isa 49:7; John 14:10; Rom 1:4).

gp314» It was by the death of one spotless, sinless *human* being, that God is going to reconcile the world to himself (Rom 5:18; 2Cor 5:19; 1Tim 2:5-6). God who through his Spiritual power begot Jesus physically as well as Spiritually, has given his own physical Son as a sacrifice for all man's sins (1 Tim 2:6). Jesus as a man was a physical son of God as explained before, but a Spiritually begotten son not yet born. After Christ the man was resurrected, he became a Spiritually *born* Son of God as opposed to a Spiritually *begotten* son of God. To understand the difference between being begotten and being born, see the "Begotten, Born Paper" [NM5] in the *New Mind Papers*.

gp315» Notice the proof of Christ's commission, "for as by one man's [Adam's] disobedience many were made sinners, so by the obedience of one [Jesus] shall many be made righteous ... for if, when we were enemies, we were reconciled to God by the death of his Son, much more, being reconciled, we shall be saved by his life" (Rom 5:19, 10). "Christ was without sin, but for our sake God made him share our sin [or share the effects of our sins] in order that in union with him [Jesus] we might share the righteousness of God ... he [Jesus] bore the sin of many, and made intercession for the transgressors" (2Cor 5:21, TEB; Isa 53:12, NIV). "For there is one God, and one mediator between God and men, the *man* Christ Jesus; Who gave himself a ransom for *all*, to be testified in due time" (1 Tim 2:5-6). God the Father gave his physical Son, the man Christ, to be a sacrifice for the transgressions of *all*.

Jesus Christ the Man, the Son, did *not Pre-exist*

gp316» How can someone "pre" exist? It is against the Law of Contradiction to say that Jesus the promised Messiah and Son of God existed before he existed. But since the "pre- existence" of Jesus Christ the man is a popular theory today, we are going to show you the evidence that he *first* came into existence when he was conceived or begotten in the womb of Mary. We will also look at the so-called scriptural evidence used by others to "prove" that Christ the man existed as some kind of "god" or "angel" before he was born.

The following is evidence that Jesus Christ the man, the Son, first came into existence when he was conceived in Mary's womb:

(1) Against the Law of Contradiction

gp317» The biggest proof that Jesus Christ did not exist before he was born, is the evidence given in GP1 of this book: it would be against the very Law of Contradiction for an immortal being (a being not capable of death) to be changed into a being that is mortal in order for that being (Jesus Christ) to die, or for the being to be simultaneously immortal, yet capable of death (see GP 1).

(2) Jesus came into existence in the Flesh

gp318» "By this you know the Spirit of God: every spirit that acknowledges that Jesus Christ *has* come in the FLESH, is of God" (1 John 4:2, see NKJV & Greek). John gives those reading the Bible a test: IF someone does agree that Christ Jesus came in the flesh, then he is of God's Spirit. But further John says: "and every spirit [in man] that acknowledges that Jesus is not come in the flesh, is not of God: and this is the spirit of antichrist" (1 John 4:3). Christ did not come as a transformed spirit, angel, or God, but he "has come in the *flesh*."

gp319» And it was the "man Christ Jesus; who gave himself a ransom for all" (1Tim 2:5-6). It was not the Spirit of Christ that gave himself for mankind, but the "*man* Jesus Christ." The Spirit of Christ the man was inside Christ before his death; thus, Christ the man gave up his Spirit when he died (note Luke 23:46; Matt 27:50; Mark 15:37; John 19:30).

(3) Prophesied Seed Cannot Exist Before He Genetically Passes through the Fathers and then is Born

gp320» "The BeComingOne came unto Nathan, saying, Go and tell my servant David, Thus says the BeComingOne ... and when your days be fulfilled, and you shall sleep with your fathers, I will set up your *seed* after you, which shall proceed out of your bowels, and I will establish his [Christ's] kingdom. He shall build a house for my NAME and I will establish the throne of his kingdom for olam. I will be his [Christ's] father, and he shall be my son" (2Sam 7:4, 5, 12-14).

Look at this carefully. This is a prophecy of the Messiah. He must be a seed or offspring of David, but also the son of the God. How can he be a son of man and a son of God at the same time?

gp321» This prophecy of God's Seed coming out of David who would also be God's son ("my son") pointed to the future when God would make his Son through the means of Mary. It was through Mary that God's one-of-a-kind son was made, not at some previous time:

- "And the angel said to her, Do not be afraid, Mary, for you have found favor with God. And behold, *you will conceive* in your womb and *[will] bring forth* a Son, and *shall call* his name Jesus. He *will be* great, and *will be called* the Son of the Highest" (Luke 1:30-32).

gp322» Notice these emphasized words are in the *future* tense (see Greek text). God's Son did not exist before this time, and was not great before this time (except in the forethought of God). The angel was announcing the coming Son being born by a woman with the help of the Holy Spirit. The Son did not exist before these events.

- "And Joseph also went up from Galilee, out of the city of Nazareth, into Judea, unto the city of David, which is called Bethlehem (because he was of the house and lineage of David) to be taxed with Mary his *espoused* wife [notice not wife, but espoused wife; for Joseph hadn't consummated the marriage, see Matt 1:24-25], being large with a child ... And she brought forth her first-born son" (Luke 2:4-5, 7).

gp323» Joseph hadn't consummated the marriage, for after Gabriel had told Mary about the son that she was to bring forth, "said Mary unto the angel, How shall this be, seeing I know not a man?" (Luke 1:34) Mary was a virgin mother. And with the help of the Holy Spirit Mary conceived a son (Luke 1:35, see above). "But when the fullness of the time was come, God sent forth his Son, made of a woman" (Gal 4:4).

(4) Born of a Woman

gp324» Notice in Galatians 4:4 that God's Son was "made" (KJV) or was "born" (NIV) of a woman. This word "made" is translated from a Greek word *ginomai* (# 1096) which means: "to become, i.e. to come into existence, begin to be, receive being" (Thayer's Greek-English Lexicon). From the Greek Gal 4:4 reads: "But when had come fullness of the time, the God sent forth the Son of Him, *coming into existence* from [or 'out of'] a woman." It says that God's Son was made out of a woman. It did not say that before this event God existed with the Son. God's Son was made or came into existence from a woman by the power of the Holy Spirit (note earlier in this chapter).

(5) Son Speaks Now, Not in the Old Testament

gp325» God didn't speak through the Son in "time past," but to the fathers of Israel by the prophets, but in the last days He speaks in his Son (Note Heb 1:1-2). God did not speak by His Son in the Old Testament times because, His Son did not exist at that time.

(6) Proof of Worshiping Angels

gp326» "But again WHEN He [God] brings the firstborn into the world, He says: Let all the ANGELS of God worship Him" (Heb 1:6; Deut 32:43, Greek text). God brought His Son into the world by having him being made by a woman with the power of the Holy Spirit (see above). But *when* the Son came into the world *angels* were present to worship him. Thus, after the Son was born:

- "*Today* in the town of David *a Savior has been born to you*; he is Christ the Lord. This will be a sign to you: You will find a baby wrapped in strips of cloth and lying in a manger. *Suddenly a great company of the heavenly host [angels] appeared with the angel*, praising God and saying, Glory to God in the highest, and on earth peace to men on whom his favor rests. And when the *angels* had left them and gone into heaven..." [Luke 2:11-15, NIV].

gp327» With Heb 1:6 and Luke 2:11-15 we see *when* (at Jesus's physical birth) and *how* (with the angels worshiping him) the first born of God came into the world; He (the man Jesus) did not exist before Mary conceived him in her womb, except in the forethought of God

(7) Spirit and Flesh

gp328» All the so-called "pre-existence" scriptures can be shown to refer to Christ the man's Spirit or angel existing before Christ the man. The Spirit of Christ the man was the angel of the BeComingOne or the angel of Jehovah (YHWH) as we have so far explained (GP 3). The Spirit of Christ and the fleshly Christ the man are just as different as a man and a woman in marriage even though according to the Bible they are ONE in marriage. That is why Paul said that our fathers passed through the sea, baptized unto Moses in the cloud and in the sea, by the spiritual rock: "and that Rock was Christ" (1Cor 10:1-4). The "spiritual Rock" (1Cor 10:4) was Christ even though Christ himself was not even born yet during Moses' time because:

- (1) Paul was talking about the "spiritual Rock that <u>followed them</u> [the fathers]" (1Cor 10:4)

- and (2) Paul was talking about Christ in an *ex post facto* manner as one uses a married woman's marital name even when speaking about some event that happened before she was married (see gp313).

(8) Summarized Evidence against Pre-existence Theory

gp329» Jesus Christ the man was/is the *one-of-a-kind* Son of God (John 1:18; 1John 4:9; monogenes=unique). The scriptures we covered above indicate when and how this Son was born: He did not exist before he was begotten; He was not begotten twice for He is the *one-of-a-kind* Son of God. (There are two senses to Jesus being the only one-of-a-kind Son — physical and Spiritual. We speak here of the special physical sense as explained in this chapter.)

gp330» Again, we repeat, there is no way for an immortal being to die. Most, if not all, of those who believe that Jesus Christ existed before he was a man have him existing as an immortal being (an angel or God). There is no way an immortal being can die, for if he ever does die he proves he was never immortal, but mortal.

gp331» Some, but not all, who argue for the so-called "pre-existence" of Christ the man are not thinking through their beliefs and are unknowingly participating in the "big lie":

- "The coming of the lawless one will be in accordance with the work of Satan displayed in all kinds of counterfeit miracles, signs and wonders, and in every sort of evil that deceives those who are perishing. They perish because they refused to love the truth and so be saved. For this reason God sends them a *powerful delusion* so that they will believe the lie and so that all will be condemned who have not believed the truth but have delighted in wickedness" (2Thes 2:9-12).

gp332» It is a powerful delusion to believe in the contradiction of the Trinitarian theory. But since most, if not all of us, at least subconsciously, act in our daily lives as if they know the Law of Contradiction, then we are in a sense knowingly participating in the "big lie" if we believe in the contradictory Trinitarian theory. At one time I "believed" in the Trinitarian theory, but was puzzled by it: on a certain level I believed; on a different level I did not believe. This is not the only delusion we are under. There are just as big contradictions in various fields of "science."

Pre-existence Theory: Refuting their Evidence

Let's look at some of the scripture others use to "prove" their "pre-existence" theory:

(1) In the Beginning was the Word, which beginning?

gp333» "In the beginning was the Word ... the Word was toward the God ... All things were made through him ... In him was life ... And the Word became flesh" (John 1:1-4, 14, see Greek).
But which beginning was John speaking about?:

- (1) the beginning of the Good News of Jesus Christ (Mark 1:1) as witnessed by the disciples of Jesus (Luke 1:2; John 15:27; 1John 1:1); or (2) the beginning of the creation (Gen 1:1) Since John spoke about the "beginning" in his Gospel and letters, it is John's meaning in (1) above that should clarify this verse. Yet the Genesis' "beginning" also applies, being true through the *Spirit* of Jesus, but not true through the flesh of Jesus, for the flesh of Jesus only existed after his birth from Mary.

gp334» The word, "Word," was translated from the Greek word, *logos*. This Greek word means, "something *said* (including the thought)." "Logos" not only indicated the word spoken, but can also indicate the reason or thought behind the word. But a word is *spoken*, that is, a word is spoken by someone. The "Word" in the beginning was spoken by the God through His angel or messenger for it was through angels that God spoke in the Old Testament times (cf Heb 1:1-2 w/ 2:2-5):

- "And God said, let there be light: and there was light" (Gen 1:3).

This is some proof that the Word and the true God are not one and the same in the fullest sense: the Word comes from God, and is spoken ("God said") from God, but is not the God. We have explained already in the Word chapter that the Word was carried by the angel of God. Also in the Greek it says, "the Word was *toward the* God" not the Word was "with" God (John 1:1; cf. John 13:3). And the Greek says, "and God was the Word," not the Word was God. The Word cannot be *toward* the God and at the same time be the true God in the fullest sense. As shown in the Word chapter (GP 3) there is a very close relationship between the Word or angel of God and the God, and as we will show in a later chapter, the Word is indeed *toward* the true God, but is not the God in the fullest sense of God all in all. The Word of God was/is closely related to God, for it carries with it the power of God, for what God says will happen. God does not lie (see GP 5 for more details on John 1:1-18 and the rest of this book).

gp335» The Word became flesh in the truest sense after the death of Christ the man (see GP 5). Another sense of John 1:14 ("And the Word became flesh") is that during Christ the man's life on earth the Word was inside the flesh (see this chapter, GP 4)

(2) Whose going forth was from of Old ...

gp336» This verse is speaking about the place of the birth of Jesus, and is mostly incorrectly translated into something like this:

- "And you Bethlehem Ephratah... out of you shall he come forth unto me to be Ruler in Israel: whose going forth are from of old, from the days of eternity" (Micah 5:2).

It looks like the Messiah comes from past eternity. The problem is that "eternity" should be translated *olam* which as explained in the "Age Paper" (NM7) means an age of unknown length. In one sense Jesus Christ's going forth was from the very old days, for since the beginning God had been prophesying his coming. And the second meaning is that the Spirit in Christ was from the old days, since the Spirit in Christ existed from the beginning of creation. In fact this very Spirit created the universe. The man, the Messiah born in Bethlehem, did not exist in the old days, for he first came into the world through Mary, but his "going forth" by prophecy was from even before the very beginning for he was predestinated before the cosmos (1Pet 1:19-20) and he was the seed prophesied in Genesis (Gen 3:15).

gp337» Other scriptures such as Proverbs 8:22-23 and John 8:58 can be explained in this way: Christ's Spirit existed before the man Jesus was born. This is the same for us. Our own Spirit has existed since the beginning, but we were born in this age, a long time after the beginning. After we are infused with our Spirit in the resurrection, we can say in a sense that we existed from the beginning since our own Spirit existed from the beginning even though there were many years after the beginning before we were born.

(3) Jesus Christ Existed Before He was Born Only in God's Fore-Thoughts

gp338» "And now, Father, glorify me in your presence with the glory I *had* with you before the world began" (John 17:5). The Greek word translated "had" here is an imperfect Greek verb that means "to possess" or "to hold." Christ possessed in some imperfect or incomplete sense (remember the verb is in the imperfect or incomplete tense) glory *before* the world began.

gp339» Christ was predestinated to possess the glory of God *after* he was born and thereafter was to obtain the Kingdom of God and its glory; in the Old Testament it *foretold* the birth of Jesus Christ:

- "He shall cry unto Me, you art my Father, my God, and the rock of my salvation. Also I will make him My first born, higher than the kings of the earth" (Psa 89:26-27).

- "For unto us a child is born, unto us a son is given: and the government [rulership of God] shall be upon his shoulder: and his name shall be called Wonderful, Counselor, the mighty God, the duration Father, the Prince of Peace" (Isa 9:6).

- "I will declare the decree: the BeComingOne has said unto me, You art my Son; this day have I begotten you" (Psa 2:7; Heb 1:5).

- "The BeComingOne came unto Nathan, saying, Go and tell my servant David, Thus says the BeComingOne ... and when your days be fulfilled, and you shall sleep with your fathers, I will set up your *seed* after you, which shall proceed out of your bowels, and I will establish his [Christ's] kingdom. He shall build a house for my NAME and I will establish the throne of his kingdom for olam. I will be his [Christ's] father, and he shall be my son" (2Sam 7:4, 5, 12-14).

- "And behold, you will conceive in your womb and bring forth a Son, and shall call his name Jesus. And he will reign over the house of Jacob for aeonian, and of his kingdom there will be no end" (Luke 1:31,33).

gp340» Just as Jeremiah was known *before* he was born, and was ordained a prophet *before* he was born (Jer 1:4-5), just as Paul was "appointed" an apostle *before* the world began (2Tim 1:11, 9), just as Christians are chosen *before* the world began (2Tim 1:9; 1 Per 1:2; 2Thes 2:13; see "Predestination Paper" [NM8]), is how Jesus Christ possessed the glory of God before the world began. Before the world began Jesus possessed the glory in an imperfect or incomplete sense: thus the use of the imperfect Greek verb ("I had" — KJV) in John 17:5. It was in an incomplete sense because he at the beginning did not yet have the glory, but was predestinated to have it.

gp341» But when Jesus Christ the man was predestinated before the world began he did not at that time possess the glory because at that time he did not exist as the Son of God, nor did the great glory of God exist before the world began: the great glory of God is coming, not here yet. In the truest sense, the glory of the God will exist when the BeComingOne (YHWH) has come (see GP 6, "Glory of God," and rest of this book). Such verses as Micah 5:2 can be explained in the way we explained John 17:5.

(4) Jesus Christ Existed in Heaven Before His Birth? How?

gp342» The scriptures that apparently say that Jesus Christ the man existed in heaven before his birth can be explained by the fact that Christ the man spoke the words of God, it was the Word of God or the angel of God *inside* Jesus the man that existed before Christ was born (see above under, "God Inside Christ"). Such verses as John 1:30; 3:13, 31; 6:33, 38, 51; 8:23, 42, 58; 1Cor 10:4; Col 1:17 and so forth can be explained in this way. As we will learn in GP 6 we also have a spirit or angel that existed before we were born. Does that mean we existed before we were born just because our spirit existed before we were born?

(5) Jesus Christ Created All Things? How?

gp343» The scriptures that seem to say that Jesus Christ the man created all things can be explained by the fact the Word or Spirit of the God was *inside* Christ the man, and it was this Word of God that created the present universe (Psa 33:6; Gen 1:1, 3 ["and God *said*"]). Another sense of Jesus Christ creating all is explained in the next chapter. Read all this book to understand still more fully the meaning of the verses that seem to indicate that Christ did/will create all. Some of these verses are John 1:1-4, 10; Col 1:16; Heb 1:2.

(6) Personification of Wisdom

gp344» The scripture in Proverbs 8:22-31, concerning the personification of Wisdom, where "The BeComingOne possessed me [Wisdom] in the beginning of his way before the works of old" can be explained by the fact Jesus the man had the Spirit or angel of Wisdom *inside* him (see above under, "God Inside Christ," note Isa 11:2; 42:1).

(7) Jesus Christ Humbled or Emptied Himself?

gp345» The scriptures that seems to say the "pre-existent" Christ "emptied himself" or "humbled himself" of his pre-birth glory or power to be born or transformed or incarnated as Christ the man can be explained by the fact that *inside* Christ the man was the Word or angel with the NAME of God. It was the Spirit *inside* Christ the man that humbled himself by being restricted inside a human being while that being was being humbled by the ignorant around him. And it was the man Jesus Christ the coming king who was also humbled, for he knew he was predestinated by God to be king of the whole world, yet he was treated with irreverence. These scriptures are Phil 2:6-8 and 2 Cor 8:9.

(8) Trinitarians' Bias

gp346» Most, if not all, who point to the scriptures that seem to say that Christ the man existed before he was born, speak of that pre-existent Christ as God (i.e. in the "Trinity" God), or a God, or an angel. But God is immortal and angels do not die (Luke 20:36). Therefore such an immortal being cannot be converted or transformed or incarnated into a being that can die. This is foolishness (See GP1 under, "Law of Contradiction").

Melchizedek

Without Parents, No Beginning of Days?

gp347» Some use the scriptures on Melchizedek to try and prove that Jesus Christ had no beginning of days, that he has always existed, and that Melchizedek (or Melchisedec) and Jesus Christ are one and the same person. They quote from Hebrews:

- "Without father, without mother, without descent, having neither beginning of days, nor end of life; but made like unto the Son of God; abides a priest continually." [Heb 7:3]

They point out that Melchizedek had "neither beginning of days, nor end of life, but made like unto the Son of God." So they conclude wrongly that Melchizedek was Jesus Christ, and that this is proof that Jesus had no beginning of days. But this misunderstands what Paul was saying and misunderstands type and antitype in scripture.

Jesus had a Genealogy

gp348» All one has to do to disprove that Jesus Christ and Melchizedek are not one and the same person is to read Hebrews 7:14, "For *it is* evident that our Lord sprang out of Judah; of which tribe Moses spake nothing concerning priesthood." Jesus, our Lord, was an offspring from Judah. Jesus had a genealogy and it is found in the Bible (Mat 1:1-17). Jesus was born "of the seed of David according to the flesh" (Rom 1:3). All through the Old Testament it predicted Christ's coming in the flesh (GP 4). It is the spirit of the anti-Christ that will not admit that Christ came in the flesh (1John 4:3). Jesus Christ came in the flesh with a clear genealogy. Where Christ differs from others is that his Father was God, not a human father (GP 4). It is clear that Jesus had a father and had a mother: he had a genealogy; he had a beginning. But Paul said that Melchizedek was without father, without mother. So it is clear from this alone that Melchizedek and Jesus are not one and the same person.

Pre-Existence?

gp349» Jesus Christ did not pre-exist as some say, but nevertheless his Spirit did exist before he was born (GP 3), as did my Spirit, as did your Spirit, and as the Spirit of everyone else did exist before they were born (GP 6). Just because Christ or you or I have a Spirit that existed before we were born doesn't mean we pre-existed. We came into existence only when we were physically begotten.

Mechizedek Prefigured Christ's Perpetual Priesthood

gp350» But why did Paul say that Melchizedek was without father or without mother, "having neither beginning of days, nor end of life." Was Melchizedek an angel who always existed? No, for Paul said Melchizedek was a man (Heb 7:4). And as a man he was born, and he also died, even though the Bible did not record this fact. Look at what a study Bible had to say about this point:

- *"Without father ... or end of life.* Genesis 14:18-20, contrary to the practice elsewhere in the early chapters of Genesis, does not mention Melchizedek's parentage and children, or his birth and death. That he was a real, historical figure is clear, but the author of Hebrews (in accordance with Jewish interpretation) uses the silence of Scripture about Melchizedek's genealogy to portray him as a prefiguration of Christ." [*NIV Study Bible*, footnote for Heb. 7:3]

Just because the Bible doesn't mention Melchizedek's genealogy doesn't mean he had none. Paul shows in the book of Hebrews that the high priest Melchizedek prefigured the priesthood of Christ (Heb 6:20). Christ's high priesthood did not come from him being genealogically linked to the Levites (who were priests by the Law), but through the "order of Melchizedek" (who was without genealogical linkage to the Levites):

> "For it is evident that our Lord was descended from Judah, a tribe with reference to which Moses spoke nothing concerning priests. 15 And this is clearer still, if another priest arises according to the likeness of Melchizedek" (Heb 7:14-15, 99-15).

But just because Melchizedek prefigured Christ in some way doesn't mean he was Christ. The Passover lamb prefigured Christ. Does this mean the lamb was Christ? Of course not. Other real persons in the Bible prefigured Christ, does it mean they were Christ just because they were a type of Christ. To get the "type" mixed up with the "antitype" is to show one does not know what type and antitype mean.

Notes

Genealogy of Jesus

gp351» Notice that there is something strange in Mary's and Joseph's genealogies. During the time of the Babylon captivity there is again a common ancestor to Joseph and Mary's side of the family. "And after they brought to Babylon, Jechoniah begat Shealtiel; and Shealtiel begat Zerubbabel" (Matt 1:12). And, "Zerubbabel, which was the son of Shealtiel, which was the son of Neri" (Luke 3:27). Now in Matthew 1:12 it says Jechoniah begat Shealtiel. This is impossible for Jechoniah had no sons who lived to produce offspring (see 2Kings 24:12, 15; Jer 22:24, 30; note Jechoniah=Coniah=Jehoiachin). But he had wives (2Kings 24:15). The scriptures said Jechoniah begat Shealtiel, yet scriptures say he would have no sons. Thus, the Bible contradicts itself? No! "If brethren [brothers or near of kin] live together, and one of them die, and have not child [Jechoniah had no sons], the wife of the dead [Jechoniah or Jehoiachin died without offspring, see 2Kings 24:12; Jer 52:31-34; Jer 22:24, 30] shall not marry without unto a stranger: her husband's brother [or near of kin] shall go in unto her, and take her to him to wife, and perform the duty of a husband's brother [or near of kin, see Book of Ruth, especially 3:11-13; 4:10, 13-14, this proves one doesn't have to be a brother, but be the nearest of kin willing and able to perform this duty] unto her. And it shall be, that *the first-born which she bears shall succeed in the name of his brother* which is dead, that his name be not put out of Israel" (Deut 25:5-6).

gp352» Therefore, a near of kin to Jechoniah performed his duty as described in Deuteronomy 25:5-10 and married one of Jechoniah's wives. The first-born of this relationship is accounted to the name of Jechoniah *not* the name of the near of kin who married one of Jechoniah's wives. Hence according to the laws of Israel Jechoniah begat Shealtiel even though physically he didn't, but a next of kin did.

gp353» The physical father of Shealtiel was Neri (Luke 3:27), but the *legal* father (for the genealogy of David) was Jechoniah (Matt 1:12). Therefore Neri was the near of kin who married one of Jechoniah's wives to conform to the law of Deuteronomy 25:5-10.

Review of GP 4

gp354» We have shown in this part that *before* Jesus Christ was resurrected, he was a human being because he was born from a woman. Jesus the man was not just any human being. Christ was also a Son of God, both physically (through the Holy Spirit's union with Mary) and Spiritually (through the medium of God's Spirit inside of him). Christ was also a Son of man, for he was born through the means of Mary his mother. Christ was a mediator between man and God; he was the Son of God and the Son of man. Jesus Christ the man actually had the Spirit or Angel of the BeComingOne (YHWH) inside him leading him in the right way. It was because of this Spirit that Christ the man became sinless. God was not Jesus Christ the man, but God was inside of Christ the man. When Jesus Christ the man died, his Spirit was then separated from him. The Spirit or angel of God did not die *as* Christ the man or *with* Christ the man, for Spirit cannot die. The angel of the BeComingOne separated himself from Christ the man when Christ died.

GP 5: Jesus Christ the God

Same Titles and Names
Spiritual Marriage
Image of God: Two into One
Before All
Trinity, Godhead and the Law of Contradiction
John 1:1-18
Sun and Moon
Glory of God

Who He Was/Is/Will Be

Resurrection

gp355» After Jesus Christ the man was dead and in the grave for three days and three nights, he was resurrected by his Father's power, that is, he was brought back to life again.[See *Chronology Papers*]

gp356» But before this resurrection we know that Jesus was *not* God when he lived on earth. He was a son of God, both physically and Spiritually, as just explained in GP 4. The very angel/Spirit of the BeComingOne (YHWH) was inside Christ. This angel/Spirit was in a sense the WORD of God of the Old Testament, for he carried the very words of God (see GP 3). Jesus was anointed by this very angel/Spirit. Jesus was the Messiah because he was anointed by this angel/Spirit. Jesus, you might say, was a shadow of the Spirit or angel inside him. Christ spoke what the Spirit inside him directed him to speak (Isa 59:21; John 14:10). Therefore in a sense he was a reflection of the true light. In fact, a symbol of Jesus Christ the man is the moon (see Notes). To ones on the earth, the moon is the reflection of the light from the sun, so too is Christ the man the reflection of the true Light of the Father to those on the earth. The Spiritual light in Jesus Christ the man came from the Father, the YHWH, the BeComingOne.

BeComingOne's Names And Titles

gp357» The BeComingOne of the Old Testament had such titles as:

- **Lord of lords** (Psa 136:3);
- **Lord and God** (Psa 68:19-20; 68:32);
- **Lord of kings** (Dan 2:47);
- **King of Glory** (Psa 24:7-10);
- **Almighty God** (Gen 17:1; 28:3; Exo 6:3);
- **Creator** (Isa 45:18; 48:13);
- **Rock** (Deut 32:4; Psa 18:2; 28:1; Isa 26:4);
- **Father** (Isa 63:16);
- **Husband of Israel** (Isa 54:5);
- **Savior** (Isa 45:15; 49:26);
- **Redeemer** (Isa 47:4; 49:26; 54:5; 60:16);
- **Word**, the one who speaks through an angel (Isa 52:6, see GP 3 & 4);
- **True God** (Jer 10:10);
- **"I am the first, I also the last"** (Isa 44:6);
- **Only God** (I am YHWH, none else... no God beside me[Isa 45:5])

gp358» But God's proper NAME is YHWH, pronounced Yehowah or traditionally as Jehovah (lately as Yahweh). It means "He-(who)-will-be" or the "BeComingOne" (see GP 1).

gp359» We have shown in GP 4 that the angel of the BeComingOne was not the man Jesus. Jesus the man was born from an ovum as flesh, but born to be Savior of the world (see Matt 1:21; 1John 4:2-3; Luke 9:56; 1John 4:14). Christ the *man* saved no one. The BeComingOne through His Spirit was inside Christ the man, and He (YHWH) is the true Savior of all (Isa 49:26; 45:21).

gp360» The Savior came inside the flesh of Jesus Christ the man. Jesus Christ the man was the real sacrificial Lamb of God who died for mankind's sins. Christ the man lived his commission by revealing his Father's way (John 17:6; 14:10) and then dying as a sacrificial offering for sin (1Pet 1:18-19; Isa 53:10).

Christ's Names And Titles

gp361» But in the New Testament we see that the *resurrected* Christ is called:

- **Lord of lords** (Rev 19:6);
- **Lord and God** (John 20:28);
- **King of kings** (1Tim 6:15; Rev 17:14; 19:16);
- **King of Glory** (1Cor 2:8);
- **Almighty** (Rev 1:8);
- **Creator** (John 1:3; Col 1:16, 17; Eph 3:9);
- **Rock** (1Cor 10:4);
- **Father**, through prophecy, (Isa 9:6; 22:21);
- **Husband of Spiritual Israel** (Rev 21:2; Eph 5:22-23);
- **Savior** (2Tim 1:10; Titus 2:13; 3:6);
- **Redeemer** (Gal 3:13; 1Tim 2:6; Titus 2:14; Rev 5:9);
- **WORD of God** (Rev 19:13);
- **True God** (1John 5:20);
- **First and the Last** (Rev 22:13);
- **Only God** (Jude 1:25; 1Tim 1:17; 1Cor 8:4)

gp362» We see that the resurrected Christ is called by the same names as the BeComingOne of the Old Testament. Christ the man was *not* called by these titles.[18] Only after Christ was resurrected was he called by these titles. The first time Jesus was called God was *after* he was resurrected (John 20:28), not before. But how can this be? Does this mean the BeComingOne gave his titles to Christ after the resurrection?

Glory Not Given to Another

gp363» "I am the BeComingOne: that is my name: and my glory will I *not* give to another, neither my praise to graven images" (Isa 42:8; Isa 48:11). The BeComingOne will not give his glory to another, yet we see the BeComingOne's titles on Christ, and we see that Jesus Christ will come in the glory of his Father (Note Mark 8:38).

Was Jesus YHWH in Old Testament Bible?

gp364» Because many have seen the titles of the BeComingOne on Jesus Christ, they have assumed that Jesus Christ was the BeComingOne of the Old Testament or was inside the God of the Old Testament as some kind of "Trinity." But at the same time they ignore other scriptures that indicate Jesus Christ the man was not the same as God (see GP 4), or not the same as God the Father (GP 2). You can read books that assert false evidence that Jesus Christ belongs to some type of "Trinity." You can also read books that pretend to show evidence that Jesus Christ was/is only a man. You can also read so-called evidence that seems to show that Jesus Christ existed *before* he was born as a human (his so-called pre-existence). All this can get confusing even for the theologians.

gp365» Why did Christ after the resurrection have the same titles as the BeComingOne? How can this be when the BeComingOne said he would not give his glory to another? (Isa 42:8; 48:11) Can there be two Saviors, or two who are Almighty?

---

[18] Qualification: He was called "king of Israel" in John 1:49 as YHWH was called the king of Israel in the OT (Isa 44:6). But Christ at the time Nathanael called him king of Israel was only king in the sense that Christ was born to be king and born to be savior (John 18:37; Mat 1:2).

Some may try and say that the BeComingOne could have given these titles to the resurrected Christ, but He said he would not give His glory or honor to another. Remember God does not lie; He keeps His Word. There is an answer to this paradox. The answer is all around us. Much of creation shouts to us the answer to this puzzle.

Spiritual Marriage: Two into One

Analogy

gp366» God tells us through Paul that we can know "the invisible things of him from the creation of the world." He is "understood by the things that are made" (Rom. 1:20). Through *analogy* of events or persons in the Bible Paul taught some of the New Testament Christians the truth about God. Paul used the analogy between Christ and Adam (1Cor 15:21-22, 45, 47; Rom 5:14, 18). Paul used analogy between Christ and Melchizedek and the high priest (Hebrews chap 7 & 8). Paul used analogy between the seed of Abraham and the true Seed, and between Abraham's faith and the Faith of Christians (Rom chap 4; Gal 3:16; etc.). Paul used analogy between old Israel (physical Jews) and new Israel (Spiritual Jews) [Rom 2:28-29; etc.]. Paul used analogy between a woman in marriage and the Church in marriage (Eph 5:22-33). Paul used analogy between the old physical Jerusalem and the new Spiritual Jerusalem (Gal 4:25-26). John, Paul, James and others from the New Testament used analogy to help explain doctrine. We will also use analogy to help prove doctrine. Paul spoke about the law having a shadow of good things to come, not the very image of the things (Heb 10:1). Paul spoke of events in the Old Testament happening as types or examples for Christians (1Cor 10:11; see "Duality of The Bible" in Intro).

gp367» Through analogy we will be better able to understand the paradox concerning Jesus Christ and the BeComingOne (YHWH) and we will be better able to understand how: "the WORD became flesh" (John 1:14).

Marriage Analogy: Two Become One

gp368» Notice how the physical marriage union was described in scripture? "Therefore a man shall leave his father and his mother and shall cleave to his wife, and they shall become one flesh"(Gen 2:24). And again, "For this cause a man shall leave his father and mother, and the two shall become one flesh; consequently they are no longer two but one flesh" (Mark 10:7-8). According to scripture, when two marry they are no longer two, but they are one. Two become one, not only sexually, but as a union in their work, finance, families, pleasure, hope, life, and name. And through the sexual act of two becoming one a new creation (a child) is born. From two a newborn is created with the physical traits and genes of both parents. There is a higher meaning to the various aspects of sex especially sexual intercourse. **The sexual act of two becoming one is used in a spiritual sense throughout the Bible**:

- **1)** In a good sense of the Church and God: 2 Cor 11:2; Rev 21:2; Eph 5:23-32; Matt 22:1-14; 25:1-13; or Israel and God, Isa 54:5;

- **2)** or in the evil sense of mankind and Satan: Ezek 16; Exo 34:15-17; Jud 2:11, 17; Jer 3:6-14; Hosea 1:1-3; 2:19-20; 4:10-19; Rev 2:14, 20-22; 17:1-2ff

Therefore, there is a another meaning to sex in the scriptures and when we understand this higher meaning we will understand the mystery of the BeComingOne (YHWH) and Jesus Christ having the same titles even though the BeComingOne said he would not give his glory to another.

God the Husband of Israel

gp369» In the Old Testament the BeComingOne is pictured as the husband of the Israelite people, "for your maker is your husband; the BeComingOne of hosts is his name" (Isa 54:5; see Jer 3:14; Hos 2:19-20; etc.). The BeComingOne is pictured as the husband of Israel. Jesus Christ the man was an Israelite, the true seed of Abraham (Heb 2:16; Gal 3:16). He fulfilled Israel's promise not to sin and thus is the real Israel (Ex 19:5-6). We also see that Christ the man is the true Israel of God by comparing Matthew 2:15 with Hosea 11:1. So following this analogy since God was the husband of Israel, then God is the "husband" of Christ, the true Israel of God.

Spiritual Marriage

gp370» The BeComingOne of the Old Testament was connected closely with an angel as shown in GP 3. In fact, the BeComingOne (YHWH) said his NAME was *in* the angel or messenger (Exo 23:21). Just as in a physical marriage when two become one, so too in a spiritual marriage — two do become one. The angel of the BeComingOne (who had the NAME in him) spiritually married Jesus Christ the man and they, who were two, became one. As Christians have their own angel (Mat 18:10), Christ also had his (Acts 12:8-11; Rev 1:1; 22:16), the very first-angel, the angel that carried the Word of God (GP 3). And as we will see later, in the type and antitype of the Bible, the spiritual are the antitype "males" while the physical are the antitype "females." So the antitype male (the angel of Christ) became one with the antitype female (Jesus the physical Israelite).

Jesus Christ's New Name

gp371» As a woman takes on the family name of her husband, in the fulfillment of this analogy Jesus also took on the NAME of God. The NAME of God is the BeComingOne (see GP 1). God or the BeComingOne is Jesus' *new name* (Rev 3:12, see Isa 62:2; Rev 14:1; Isa 65:15; GP1, "Name in Scripture" at ¶ gp72). Yet as a woman retains her personal name, so does Jesus retain his personal name, but his surname is now the BeComingOne (YHWH), the true God, for he went into the God. In a sense Jesus is now in the Family of YHWH — the BeComingOne.

gp372» The Spirit of the God and Jesus Christ are spiritually married. They are one, thus, share the honors of each other. That is why Jesus is called by the New Testament writers with the same titles as the BeComingOne was called in the Old Testament. Unlike the physical marriage — they are perfectly ONE. It is a perfect and complete relationship. What God does is perfect (Psa 18:30; Deut 32:4).. Two have become one as the commandment demands (Gen 2:24).

Notice how a perfect marriage should be:

- "So ought men to love their wives as their *own* bodies. He that loves his wife loves *himself*... let every one of you in particular so love his wife even as himself" (Eph 5:28,33).

gp373» Jesus Christ's human body is now God's body. "God is Spirit" (John 4:24). The angel of the BeComingOne (YHWH) is Spirit, for angels are spirits (Heb 1:7). Thomas called Christ, God (John 20:28). In fact, Jesus Christ the man *with* God (His Spirit) through their Spiritual marriage are ONE. Since they are one, the resurrected Jesus Christ is God (John 20:28; Titus 2:13; 2Pet 1:1; 1John 5:20; Jude 1:25; 1Tim 1:17; 4:10; see *The Trinity*, by Bickersteth, chap. 4).

Jesus Christ's Flesh

gp374» But notice *after* Jesus was resurrected and became one with his Spiritual mate, he appeared to his disciples from nowhere and:

- "They were terrified and affrighted, and supposed that they had seen a spirit. And he [Christ] said unto them, why are you troubled? And why do thoughts arise in your hearts? **Behold my hands and my feet, that it is myself** [Greek: 'I am myself']: **handle me, and see: for a spirit has not flesh and bones, as you see me have**. And when he had thus spoken, he showed them his hands and his feet ... And they gave him a piece of broiled fish, and of a honey comb. And he took it, and did eat before them."[Luke 24:37-43]

gp375» Scripture tells us of women actually taking hold of him after he ascended to God (Matt 28:9-10). Christ became one with God, thus one with Spirit, but here (Luke 24:37-43) scripture says the resurrected Christ was flesh and blood, he was like a human being. Is this a Biblical contradiction?

Two, Spirit and Flesh, Became One

gp376» No, for as God is spirit, so too the resurrected and ascended Christ as God, is spirit. But further, Christ is flesh and blood. God has Spiritually married and become one with mankind. And now they are one. The God is now in mankind and mankind is in the God through Jesus Christ (2Cor 6:16; John 10:38; 17:21; Rev 21:3). Two, spirit and flesh, have become one as the higher meaning of the commandment of Genesis demands.

Christ in the Image of God

The Image has Something to do with Two in One

gp377» We see that Christ fulfills the image of God, bodily (Col 1:15; 2:9; 2 Cor 4:4; Heb 1:3). What is the image of God? Since God is spirit and spirit is invisible (GP 3), the image or likeness of God is not necessarily the *appearance* of the man, but does include other aspects of the likeness. We see that "God created man in his image, in the image of God created He him; male and female created He them" (Gen 1:27). Notice that God created "him" in the image of God, but also God created "them" male and female. But look, "male and female created He them; and blessed them, and called *their* name Adam" (Gen 5:2). God created "him," meaning the male (Adam), in the image of God. But furthermore, God created *them* male and female and called *their* name Adam or man since the Hebrew word translated "Adam" is the same Hebrew word translated elsewhere as "man." So does this mean that male and female are in the image of God? Yes, because God's word says we can know the Godhead by his creation (Rom 1:19-20), and one of the most obvious aspects of the creation is the male and femaleness of it, and the reproduction aspect of it. Sex and reproduction penetrates the whole creation. So from the Bible we can ascertain that sex and other aspects of man are included in the likeness or the *image of God*:

- The male (Adam) was created in the image of God (Gen 1:26-27; 5:1) while the female is also the glory of man (1 Cor 11:7)
- Both male and female are called man, and thus, male and female are man (Adam) and are in the image of God (Gen 1:26-27; 5:1-2), but the female herself is in the reverse sexual image of the male
- After God created the first man, the man was alone (Gen 2:18)
- Woman came out of man (Gen 2:21-23), but in turn after the first man, man came out of woman (Gen 4:1; 1 Cor 11:12)
- Both the man and the women ("them") were to have rulership over the creation (Gen 1:26, 28)
- Both man and woman became one (Gen 2:24)
- Both were to be fruitful and multiply and have rulership over the earth (Gen 1:26)
- Both rested on the seventh day (Gen 2:1-3)

The male (Adam) was created in the image of God, but both male and female are called man. Thus, male and female are man (Adam) and are in the image of God. But as Paul indicated (1Cor 11:7) there is a double meaning here since the male himself is an image of God while the female herself is in the image or glory of man. And both are out of each other, but all things out of God (1Cor 11:12).

Male and Female are One

gp378» From the very beginning of creation God considered male and female as "man." God used the name "man" to include both male and female. In many languages today, "man" has a dual meaning of not only meaning male, but also mankind, which includes both sexes. The very act of sexual intercourse and marriage has the meaning of signifying two (male and female) becoming one (Gen 2:24; Mark 10:6-8). Male and female are two, yet in God's eyes they are one, they are "man" or "Adam."

Spirit and Flesh of Christ Become One

gp379» The antitypical male (Spirit of Christ) has joined with the antitypical female (the flesh of Christ) and they two have become one. Genesis 2:21-25 pictures the woman coming out of the man just as Jesus Christ the man came out of God (see GP 4). And Genesis 2:21-25 also pictures the woman coming back to the man to become one, just as Jesus the man was the first to go back and become one with the Father:

- "I have come out of the Father, and I have come into the kosmos, again I am leaving the kosmos and I am going toward the Father" (Greek, John 16:28, & see v. 5, 10, 17; and John 13:3; see Notes this Part).

Another Sense of the Image of God

gp380» There is still a higher meaning to the Image of God which we will leave until GP 8 to reveal. Since both male and female are in the image of God, the God also must in some sense be "male" and "female," and two in one. ("And God said, let us make man...." [Gen 1:26] Hint: there is a right and left side of God. [GP 8].)

Word Became Flesh

gp381» In GP 4 we explain one meaning of John 1:14: "and the WORD became flesh." The typical meaning of this verse is: "and the WORD [in] flesh became," for God came inside Jesus the man. But the Bible is dual (type and antitype) and this verse is of a dual significance. In Isaiah 52:5-6 the Bible shows us the BeComingOne is the one who spoke through the Bible, by the means of his angel (see GP 3). Now in GP 3 of these papers we manifested that the angel (a spiritual being) of the BeComingOne was the one who carried the words for the BeComingOne. He was the messenger for the BeComingOne. Hence the angel of the BeComingOne is the WORD. And in GP 5 we are showing you that the angel of the BeComingOne and Jesus Christ the man are now one. Therefore the antitypical meaning or the higher meaning of John 1:14 is that the WORD *became* flesh, or the angel of the BeComingOne became flesh. Or the angel of God took on the essence of the flesh. The BeComingOne's angel or WORD was infused with the physical Christ: "and the WORD became flesh." But since the angel had the NAME, then in a sense the BeComingOne became flesh.

gp382» Actually, this antitypical meaning of John 1:14 is what God intends us to understand. The book of John was written *after* Christ's resurrection when the angel of the BeComingOne and Jesus the man *had* already become ONE, thus, after the WORD had become flesh, that is, had become ONE with Jesus Christ the man. Read the section on John 1:1-18 later in GP 5 for greater detail.

New Creation: Two into One

gp383» Christ God has two essences: the physical and the Spiritual. This is the new creation (2Cor 5:17). Now the new creation described in 2 Cor 5:17 is speaking about Christians becoming new creations. But since we know that we will be changed into a body like Christ's (Phil 3:21; 1John 3:1-2), then what the Bible says about Christians is also true about Christ. Jesus the man and God were infused together as a new creation. Jesus Christ is the beginning of the creation of the true God (Rev 3:14). Thus, as a new creation, Jesus Christ is able to function as a spirit being (go through matter such as walls, John 20:19), yet he is also able to function as a physical being (eat, Luke 24:41-43; drink and eat, Acts 10:41).

Two Bodies in One

gp384» As there are two bodies in a physical marriage, so too in the spiritual marriage — "there is a fleshly body, and there is a spiritual body" (1Cor 15:44). "And as we have borne image of the earthly, we shall ALSO bear the image of the heavenly" (1Cor 15:49). "If there is a natural body, there is ALSO a spiritual body" (1Cor 15:44, NIV). The Bible does not say when humans are born of God they get rid of their physical essence.

New Soul

Saving of the Soul

gp385» We know from the "Body, Soul" paper [NM 6] in the *New Mind Papers* that "soul" in the Bible is a living physical body, that is, a physical body with the breath of life in it. And from that paper we know that souls can die. Thus the Bible speaks of the "saving of the soul" (1Pet 1:9; Heb 10:39; James 1:21; 5:20; Luke 21:19). The Bible speaks of the saving and resurrection of the physical body:

- "And if the Spirit of him who raised Jesus from the dead is living in you, he who raised Christ from the dead will also *give life to your MORTAL BODIES* through his Spirit, who lives in you" (Rom 8:11).

- "... the redemption [buying back] of our bodies" (Rom 8:23).

Using the example of Christ and Christians, the soul is saved ultimately by the dead physical body being resurrected from the dead and given the Spirit, and these two become one (GP 6). But the physical living body or soul is living because it has *breath* inside it (see "Body, Soul" paper). There is a dual meaning here. "Breath" in the Bible is translated from words in both Hebrew and Greek that can mean either *"breath"* or *"spirit"* (see "Body, Soul" paper). The old soul prefigured the new body or New Soul of Jesus Christ, the individual. When a soul dies, the "breath" and the "spirit" leave the body (John 19:30; Matt 27:50; Psa 146:4; cf. Gen 2:7; etc.). But a living physical body has breath and/or spirit in it. Following the analogy we see also that the new living body or the New Soul of Jesus Christ has the Flesh *and* the Spirit.

gp386» The Bible says that our old body will be transformed into a glorious body like Christ's (Phil 3:21; 1John 3:2). "If we have been united with him in his death, we will certainly also be united with him in his resurrection" (Rom 6:5). And the resurrected Christ has both spirit, and flesh and blood. He has two bodies or two essences in one like a marriage union. Did not the resurrected Christ say he was flesh and blood? Yes (Luke 24:37-43). And as God, he must also be spirit.

Angel of the Old Testament Prefigured the New Soul

gp387» As we've shown, in GP 3: God appeared through his angel looking like man *and* like flaming-fire. Flaming-fire is used in the Bible to indicate spirits or angels (see Heb 1:7; Psa 104:4; Ex 3:2). In Judges chapter 13 we've shown you in GP3 how the angel of the BeComingOne appeared as a man to Manoah, but then transformed himself into a flame and ascended into heaven. These manifestations of the angel of the BeComingOne to mankind were a foreshadow of the future Spiritual marriage of

God and man. These appearances prefigured the New Soul. From the beginning God was manifesting the future essence of God. Also sex and the laws given to man through Moses concerning marriage and sex have been manifesting God's plan to us, as we will continue to show you. Remember the BeComingOne's Name indicates that he is the BeComingOne, **He will be**. The angel of the BeComingOne of the Old Testament foreshadowed the predestinated future.

Beginning with Moses Christ was Manifested

gp388» "And beginning at Moses [the first 5 books of the Bible] and all the prophets, he [Jesus] expounded unto them in all the scriptures the things concerning himself" (Luke 24:27). This was the resurrected Christ speaking to two disciples. Jesus began at Moses to explain himself. Christ was at that time infused with His Spirit. As Christ began in the books of Moses to show some disciples His essence, so have we begun at the beginning showing you that the God manifested himself in the Old Testament through an angel. But now that angel, the archangel, *and* Jesus Christ the man have become ONE.

Spiritually Married

gp389» Parenthetically, even as the pleasure of becoming one sexually, so too the pleasure of becoming one or being one with the Spirit. The pleasure of the male and female becoming one physically and mentally, foreshadows the pleasure of the human body and Spiritual body becoming one in Spirit and body. This is one reason why in the Kingdom of God there will not be any marriage as we know it on earth (Luke 20:35). To be Spiritually in the kingdom of God you must be complete: you must be one; a new finished creation; you must be spiritually married. Physical marriage has pointed to the Spiritual marriage.

Christ: Second Adam

gp390» In analogy Paul called Christ the second Adam or the last Adam (1Cor 15:47, 45). Let's follow through on this by comparing the first Adam with the Second Adam:

- **First Adam**: Adam came from God (Gen 2:7); **Second Adam**: Christ came from God (Luke 1:35).

- **First Adam**: Man was in the image of God, male and female (Gen 1:26-27); **Second Adam**: The physical and Spiritual Christ is/will fulfill the image of God (Col 1:15), as Christ and the Church fulfills the male (husband) and female (wife) roles (Rev 21:2,9; Eph 5:22-32).

- **First Adam**: Adam started out alone until his wife was taken out of him (Gen 2:18, 21-23); **Second Adam**: Christ started out alone before his "wife" or church came into being from him (Acts 1:4-5, 8; 2:1, 4, 33).

- **First Adam**: Woman came out of Adam and is under his dominion (Gen 2:21-22; 3:16); **Second Adam**: Christ's wife the church comes out of Him and is under His dominion (John 1:13; Acts 2:33; NM papers; Eph 5:22-25).

- **First Adam**: Adam and Eve was to have rulership over the world (Gen 1:26, 28); **Second Adam**: Christ will rule the whole world with his "wife" (Rev 4:11; 5:10; Rev 21:2; etc.).

- **First Adam**: Adam and Eve became one (Gen 2:24); **Second Adam**: Christ's Spirit and Flesh became one (John 1:14; GP 5) as Christ's Spirit and the Church will become one (Eph 5:31-32).

- **First Adam**: Adam with his wife was to be fruitful and multiply (Gen 1:26); **Second Adam**: Christ with his "wife" would multiply and fill all (Eph 1:22-23).

- **First Adam**: Adam with his wife rested on the seventh day (Gen 2:1-3); **Second Adam**: Christ with his "wife" will rest on the 1000 year-seventh-day (Rev 20:3-5; NM papers).

Compare the above (A to H) with the previous section called, "Christ in the Image of God."

Christ the Man Became and is Becoming the God

gp391» Today, because Christ the man became one with the Spirit of God, Christ has become to us:

- "*the* Lord and *the* God" (John 20:28, see Greek).
- Christ as God is the "only God our Savior" (Jude 1:25; 1Tim 1:17; 1Cor 8:4).
- Christ is "*the* great God, our Savior" (Titus 2:13).
- Christ is "*the* true God" (1John 5:20).
- Christ is the "Living God" (1Tim 4:10).
- Christ has been given *all* the power of God (Matt 28:18), he is the Almighty God (Rev 1:8; 15:3).
- Christ thus has the power and wisdom of God (1Cor 1:24).
- Christ was given all things (Luke 10:22; John 3:35).
- But *now* all are not under Christ's power (Heb 2:8).
- But all will be put under Him (1Cor 15:25; Psa 110:1).
- He has "a NAME which is above *every* name" (Phil 2:9).

Christ's NAME is above every name because He is Christ, who has the very NAME of the God, the BeComingOne. The Spiritual being, the angel of the BeComingOne, that Jesus Christ the man was joined to and became ONE with, had the NAME of the God (YHWH) in him (GP 3). Thus, Jesus Christ is jointed to that NAME and is ONE in that NAME. In a sense, Jesus Christ is now Jesus Christ the God, or **Jesus Christ the BeComingOne** (YHWH).

Christ into the Glory of the Father

gp392» Notice, "and every tongue shall confess that the Lord Jesus Christ [went] *into* the glory of God the Father" (Phil 2:11). What Philippians 2:11 says when correctly translated is what Isaiah 9:6 and 22:21 prophesied about. In Isaiah 9:6 is pictured the Christ child being born, and thereafter receiving the rights of the government of God, and becoming the "duration *father*." In Isaiah 22:20-21 it pictures Eliakim (a typical representation of Christ) becoming "a *father* to the inhabitants of Jerusalem." Also in Jeremiah 3:19 the returning Christ God will be called by Israel, "my *father*." Christ in the glory of God is the Spiritual Father of the New Creation. Christ sitting on God's throne, at the right side of the true God, sends forth the Spiritual Seed, or Holy Spirit (Acts 2:24-33; 7:55-56; see "Seed Paper" [PR 1]).

gp393» Jesus Christ the man went into the God, "For in him dwells all the fullness of the godhead, bodily" (Col 2:9). And, "the light of knowledge of the glory of the God in the person of Jesus Christ" (2Cor 4:6). Note the following scriptures:

> gp394» "But Jesus answered them, saying, The time has come for the Son of man to be glorified ... Now is the Son of man glorified, and the God is glorified in him. And the God will glorify him [Christ] in Himself, and at once He will glorify him [Christ]." [John 12:23; 13:31-32]

Thus the glory of the God or the great appearance of the God is manifested in the person of Jesus Christ, and the fullness of the Godhead is (or will be) in him bodily. The great appearance or glory of God has been/will-be fulfilled in the resurrected Christ.

gp395» Christ the man thus went into the Godhead, he became ONE with the good God and the good Father, or God the Father incorporated Jesus the man into Himself. Christ the man was infused into the God, as a new creation, or as a New Soul.

Scriptures Now Make Sense

Better than Angels

gp396» Notice how scripture now makes sense when we know what was shown so far in these papers: "Being so much better than the angels, as he [Christ] has by inheritance obtained a more excellent name than they" (Heb 1:4). Jesus the man and the angel of the BeComingOne together as one have become ever so much better than angels. Both together are in a better state than they were before. The Spirit of God has a physical body; Jesus Christ the physical man has a Spiritual essence. This is much like a man and woman are in a better state when they are married, than when they are alone.

Under Christ, not Angels

gp397» "For if the word spoken by angels [the angel of the BeComingOne was the WORD] was steadfast, and every transgression and disobedience received a just recompense of reward. How shall we escape if we neglect so great salvation; which at the first began to be spoken by the Lord ... For unto angels he has not put in subjection the world to come" (Heb 2:2-3, 5). In the Old Testament, it was the angel(s) of the BeComingOne that ruled through the power that was predestinated to them and through the powerful words that were given them. This will become clearer as you read the rest of this book.

Jesus Christ the BeComingOne

gp398» The kingdom of God will not be under angels, but under the true God. The true God is the BeComingOne, YHWH (GP 1). The truest sense of the BeComingOne is the fullness of the Spiritual Body of Jesus Christ. All will eventually go into this true God (see GP 6, "All into Christ the BeComingOne"). We can call Jesus Christ, "*the* God," only if we know it is at the fullness of the Spiritual Body of Jesus Christ that Jesus Christ, in the truest sense, will be, "*the* God," the God all in all (see GP 6).

He was before All in Two Senses

gp399» Jesus Christ the BeComingOne calls himself "the beginning of the creation of God" (Rev 3:14). And, "he is before ALL things, and through him all things consist. And he is the head of the body: who is the beginning" (Col 1:17-18). Remember Jesus Christ is infused with God though the angel who had the NAME of God (YHWH) in him; thus, Christ shares the titles and honors of his Father because the angel was in his Father's NAME. Christ as the Spiritual wife of the angel of the BeComingOne shares his Spiritual husband's NAME, titles, and honors; as should a physical wife share the name, titles, and honors of her physical husband (1 Pet 3:7; Eph 5:28, 33, etc.).

gp400» Christ the **man** was born, he came in the flesh; he never existed before all things (present cosmos) except in the forethought of God (see GP 4). It was the angel or WORD of the BeComingOne who was before all things in the present or old creation. Christ the man was resurrected and created new with the angel of the Father, as a perfect marriage between Spirit and man. Christ is the first and is before all things in two senses:

- **(1)** Christ God is the beginning of the *new* creation of God. Christ the man is the first of the old creation to go back into God, therefore he is before all things as far as returning to God.

- **(2)** But also with the scriptures shown you previously, we know that the angel (WORD) of the BeComingOne was the first, the very beginning of the first creation of God, for all things came out of God (1Cor 8:6, see Greek), and the first to come out of the Father was the WORD (John 1:1; Psa 33:4; Heb 11:3).

Trinity, Godhead and the Law of Contradiction

Immortality and Death

gp401» According to the Bible God is immortal (1Tim 1:17). Thus, it follows from the Law of Contradiction[19] that God cannot be immortal (not capable of death) and yet at the same time be capable of death. Either God is immortal or he is not. He cannot be both mortal (capable of death) and immortal (not capable of death) at the same time. Furthermore, if at first, God was immortal, then at no time later can he die. If a so-called immortal person ever dies, it merely means, he was never immortal. If one denies this, he either denies the Law of Contradiction or denies the meaning of the word "immortal." To deny the meaning of "immortal" is to play a word game.

"With God Nothing Shall Be Impossible"

gp402» Now some will think that yes God is immortal and yes those who are immortal cannot die, but "with God nothing shall be impossible" (Luke 1:37, KJV). Thus, they reason, in so many words, God (or Jesus Christ) before his "incarnation" was immortal, but nevertheless died on the cross, for without this death no man could be saved. They reason that this contradiction is not contrary because "with God nothing shall be impossible." But this kind of "reasoning" makes a mockery out of reasoning. It is against the Law of Contradiction and against scripture

(They also use the argument that God is timeless, immortal, and immutable, and thus according to their theory, the fleshly body of the Son must have been "taken" because he could not literally be made flesh, for he was not mutable. See more against this argument in the *Trinity v. BeComingOne Comparative Tables* on the web site.)

Incorrect Translation

gp403» There is a problem with the above argument. They use Luke 1:37 of the Kings James Version (KJV), but this is a mistranslation of the Greek text. Luke 1:37 from the Greek language says: "for not shall be impossible with the God any word." The Greek word *rhema* (Strong's #4487) was not translated in Luke 1:37 in the KJV. The Greek word *rhema* means: "word, saying, any thing spoken." Thus in the very next verse, Luke 1:38, we find this same Greek word *rhema* translated as "word": "be it according to thy *word*" (Luke 1:38). What was being said in Luke 1:37, is that God's *word* that Mary would have the child Jesus even though she "know not a man" (Luke 1:34), was not impossible (Luke 1:37). Thus Mary believing the words answered the angel, "be it unto me according to thy *word* [Gk. *rhema*]" (Luke 1:38). The scripture that says in the KJV "with God all things are possible" (Matt 19:26; Mark 10:27; Luke 18:27) is in context merely saying that even the rich men can be saved, for such things are possible with God.

---

[19] See GP1 for definition of the law

God of Law, Not of Confusion

gp404» To say that God can go against the basis of reason, the Law of Contradiction, is mockery. God is a God of Law (Isa 33:22; etc.), not of confusion (1Cor 14:33). God is a God of His Word: "So shall my word be that goes forth out of my mouth: it shall not return unto me void, but it shall accomplish that which I please, and it shall prosper whereto I sent it" (Isa 55:11). "I have spoken, I will also bring it to pass; I have purposed, I will also do it" (Isa 46:11).

God's Word Not Impossible

gp405» Luke 1:37 is saying that all God's words are possible with God (see Greek text). Nothing God speaks or says is too hard for him for he created heaven and earth by his word (Psa 33:6). "Ah Lord GOD [YHWH] behold; you have made the heaven and the earth by your great power and stretched out arm, and there is not too difficult for you any *word*" (Jer 32:17). Notice in the KJV of Jer 32:17 there is again a mistranslation, "there is nothing too hard for thee," instead of "there is no word too hard for thee." It says in the Hebrew that no word (Heb. *dabar*) of God is too difficult for Him. Why? It is because God does not lie. Therefore any word he speaks is true. "The sum of your word is true," or "chief is your true word," or "truth is the head of your word," or "the head of your word is truth," or "your supreme word is true" (Psa 119:160, see Heb. and various translations). He who is the liar is Satan (John 8:44).

Truth Is

gp406» The truth is: *what is*, at one point in time. What is false is: *what is not*, at a certain point in time. One statement cannot be true and false <u>at the same time</u>. God cannot be immortal and yet be capable of death. God cannot be alive forever, and yet die. God cannot go back on his word (Isa 46:11). It is impossible for God to lie (Heb 6:17-18; 1John 5:18; etc.). Considering everything, it is impossible for God to go against the Law of Contradiction.

It Follows Thus:

gp407» From the above arguments it follows that:
- God did not die on the "cross" (tree "stake" or "post");
- God did not change from immortality to mortality in order to die on the cross (God cannot change what has gone out of his mouth); OR an immortal angel (note Luke 20:36) was not "transformed" from immortality to mortality in order to die on the cross;
- he who died on the cross was not God, <u>when</u> he died;
- he who died on the cross was a mortal, for he died;
- he who <u>died</u> on the cross could not have existed as God or angel (angels do not die, Luke 20:36) before his birth as a mortal, because those who are immortal cannot change from their state to mortality;
- he who was born (or thus came into an existence through a physical birth) and died (through the 'cross') was a man;
- that man was/is Jesus Christ the man who with a resurrection went into his Father (God) and became one with the God and now sits on the right side of the Power of the God (GP 4-8).

Jesus Christ as a mortal man *before* his resurrection was a man, "the man Christ Jesus" (1Tim 2:5). He was a go-between (mediator) between God and man (1Tim 2:5). He was a physical son of God. But he did not exist (the one who died) before his birth (GP 4).

Trinity Belief Impossible

What is the Trinity Belief?

gp408» From the above, especially when you understand the Law of Contradiction, you know that three uniquely different persons cannot exist as one person at the same time (Trinity theory). The Trinitarians have been changing and redefining their theory on God from the beginning of their theory. But what many of them are saying is this:

- There is *one God being* who created all and who is immortal and all-powerful (p. 87, *Systematic Theology*, by L. Berkhof; p 155-156, *The Trinity*, by Bickersteth);

- There are *three persons* (Father, Son, Holy Spirit) in this one God being; these are *not* three different metonymical names for the same essence in the one God being (p. 87, *Systematic Theology*; p. 156, 150ff, *The Trinity*);

- The whole essence of God belongs equally to each of the three persons (p. 88, *Systematic Theology*; p. 155, *The Trinity*).

gp409» From, *Logic and the Nature of God* (1983), by Stephen T. Davis, the trinity doctrine is stated:

- "The Christian doctrine of the Trinity is notoriously easier to state than explain. Augustine states it as follows:

  There are the Father, the Son, and the Holy Spirit, and each is God, and at the same time all are one God; and each of them is a full substance, and at the same time all are one substance. The Father is neither the Son nor the Holy Spirit; the Son is neither the Father nor the Holy Spirit; the Holy Spirit is neither the Father nor the Son. But the Father is the Father uniquely; the Son is the Son uniquely; and the Holy Spirit is the holy Spirit uniquely. All three have the same eternity, the same immutability, the same majesty, and the same power...." [p. 132]

gp410» Davis in his 1983 book further stated:

- "But is the doctrine of the Trinity coherent? Is there any good reason for a Christian to believe it? Let us say that the doctrine consists at heart of five statements:

- (1) The Father is God

- (2). The Son is God

- (3). The Holy Spirit is God

- (4). The Father is not the Son and the Son is not the Holy Spirit and the Holy Spirit is not the Father

- (5). There is one and only one God." [pp. 134-135]

What Mystery?

gp411» "Not surprisingly, Christian theologians almost with one voice have stressed that this doctrine is a great mystery, perhaps the greatest mystery in Christian theology" (p. 132). But some of them use scripture out of context to prove this. They quote Paul speaking about mystery:

- Without any doubt, the **mystery of our religion is great**: [NRS 1 Timothy 3:16]

and misquote Paul:

- That their hearts might be comforted, being knit together in love, and unto all riches of the full assurance of understanding, to the acknowledgment of the **mystery of God, and of the Father, and of Christ**. [KJV, Colossians 2:2]

gp412» Paul wasn't acknowledging any mystery, this last verse is better understood from the NRS version:

- I want their hearts to be encouraged and united in love, so that **they may have** all the riches of assured **understanding** and have the **knowledge of God's mystery, that is, Christ himself**, [NRS Colossians 2:2]

gp413» Paul was praying for others to understand the knowledge of God's mystery like Paul understood it. Paul did understand the mystery and in fact revealed it to the Church:

- **he has made known to us the mystery of his will**, according to his good pleasure that he set forth in Christ, [NRS, Ephesians 1:9]

- and how **the mystery was made known to me by revelation**, as I wrote above in a few words, 4 a reading of which will enable you to perceive my understanding of the mystery of Christ. [NRS, Ephesians 3:3-4]

- **This is a great mystery**, and I am applying it to Christ and the church. [NRS Ephesians 5:32]

- Pray also for me, so that when I speak, a message may be **given to me to make known with boldness the mystery of the gospel**, [NRS Ephesians 6:19]

- I became its servant according to God's commission that was given to me for you, to make the word of God fully known, 26 **the mystery** that has been hidden throughout the ages and generations but has **now been revealed to his saints**. [NRS, Colossians 1:25-26].

Therefore there is no mystery, for Paul was given the revelation to reveal it, and Paul did reveal it, as we will again, in more detail, reveal.

Trinitarian Belief against the Law of Contradiction

gp414» Thus, Trinitarians are saying that three uniquely different beings are a one, single, unique being at the very same time they are three. This is against the Law of Contradiction and against Biblical scripture as we will see. We can understand three in one, or even two in one, or even a million in one, but this "one," in its totality, cannot be exactly the same as *each* of the three, or *either* of the two, or *each* of the million.

One in Number, but Three in Person

gp415» Either there is only one (single/individual) God or there are three (as one, as a unit, in some kind of unity or oneness) at the same time, but both "the only one" and "the three persons" cannot exist as the only one (single/individual) at the same time. When the Trinitarians are speaking of *one* God, they are **not** using one as a synonym for "unity." To them the oneness of God is not the same as the unity of God. When they speak of the "only one" they mean singleness, numerically speaking, of God. Yet to them there are three persons in this *one* (numerically speaking) God. This is the first real contradiction. A drop of water can only appear as either ice, or water, or vapor at any one time: all three states of the same water drop cannot exist at the same moment.

Immortal Person Dies?

gp416» There is another real contradiction in their theory. In the Trinity theory they have an immortal being dying. Someone who is immortal cannot die. Someone with the potential to die is mortal. Anyone who says an immortal being can die either doesn't know the meaning of 'immortal' or is playing a word game. God's essence is not like the god of the Trinity as commonly taught today.

God Not the Trinity

gp417» One reason God is not a trinity is because the Trinity idea is against the Law of Contradiction. For other reasons (documented in this book) that God is not the Trinity, note the following:

- Jesus Christ the man was not God before his death and resurrection: he was the *son* of God.

- Jesus Christ the man did not exist before his birth. Jesus Christ was *foreknown* before his birth and death, but he did not exist before his birth, except in the mind and planning of the God (see Psa 139:16; Jer 1:4-5, NIV).

- But doesn't it seem to say in the Bible that Jesus Christ is God? Yes (see GP 5).

- Don't some titles of God in the Old Testament now appear on Jesus Christ? Yes (see GP 5).

- Doesn't the Bible seem to say that Jesus Christ is the Creator and God? Yes (see GP 5).

- BUT the Bible does not speak of Jesus Christ the **man**, *before* his resurrection and his going to his Father, as *the* God, or a God, or the Creator.

- When Jesus Christ was a man, before going to his Father, he spoke of his Father as the God of the Jews (John 8:54).

- He spoke of his Father as "my God" (John 20:17).

- He spoke of his Father or God as being greater than himself (John 14:28).

- And He prayed to his Father (John 17:1) as if his Father was a separate entity, which the Father was at one point in time.

In this book the problem of God and his Son has been solved. **Time** plays an important role in the answer.

But what about the Holy Spirit?

Fourth Person in the Godhead?

gp418» The Trinitarians argue:

- "First, we show that the Bible teaches that there is only one God. Second, we found that the Bible tells us that there are three persons who are called God. Hence, the inescapable conclusion: the three persons are the One God. Theologians have called this the Trinity"

(Of course, whether you know it or not, the theologians also deny that the three "persons" in the Trinity are in fact, persons. They use their own pseudo-word "hypostases" when they speak of the three *persons* in the Trinity, since they know that when we think of persons we think of distinct individuals, and three distinct individuals cannot be one in the sense the Trinitarians want to use "one." The Trinitarians wish to use "one" in a limiting sense that does not even coincide with the historical use and meaning of "one." (See "One in History" gp160)

The Trinitarians tell us that because three "persons" (Father, Son, Holy Spirit) are called God in the Bible that this is proof that they are God and are the three persons in the ONE God. And that this is the Trinity. But –

Four or More Persons in the "Trinity"?

gp419» Wait a moment. With the Trinitarians own logic we can prove that there are four or more "persons" in their "one" God. According to the Trinitarians own special logic the "Holy One" could be the *fourth* person in their "one" God:

- The **Holy One** is God (Psa 71:22; 78:41; Isa 29:23; 43:3; 48:17; 54:5; 55:5; 60:9; Hosea 11:9; Hab 1:12)
- The **Holy One** is YHWH (Isa 30:15; 48:17; 54:5; 55:5; 60:9)
- The **Holy One** is the Savior (Isa 43:3)
- The **Holy One** is the Redeemer (Isa 48:17; 54:5)
- The **Holy One** can be sinned against (Jer 51:5; Hab 1:12)
- The **Holy One** is (in a sense) Jesus (Mark 1:24; Luke 4:34)
- The **Holy One** is a person, a "he" (Isa 49:7; 54:5)

How about Five Persons?

gp420» We just identified a fourth person in the Godhead using the Trinitarians' own logic. How about a fifth person? The "Almighty" in the Bible did the same things the Holy Spirit did.

- The **Almighty** is God (Gen 35:11; 49:25; Rev 4:8)
- The **Almighty** is YHWH (Ruth 1:21)
- The **Almighty** is prayed to (Job 8:5; 21:15)
- The **Almighty** answers prayer (Job 31:35)
- The **Almighty** is beyond finding out (Job 11:7; 37:23)

- The **Almighty** gives spiritual understanding (Job 32:18)
- The **Almighty** does not sin (Job 34:10)
- The **Almighty** is the Father (2Cor 6:18)
- The **Almighty** is the Lord and God (Rev 11:17)
- The **Almighty** is the was, is, and will be (Rev 1:8; 4:8; 11:17)
- The **Almighty** is king (Rev 15:3)
- The **Almighty** is Jesus (Rev 1:8 cf. w/ 22:12-13, 20)
- The **Almighty** is a person, a "he" (Gen 43:14; Job 37:23; Eze 10:5)

So as the "Holy One" could be one of the "persons" in the Godhead, so could be the "Almighty" according to the logic that the Trinitarians used to put the Holy Spirit into the Godhead.

Metonymy and the Holy Spirit

gp421» The problem with the Trinitarian's logic is that the Holy Spirit, the Holy One, and the Almighty are merely words that describe different aspects of God and are being used in the Bible in a metonymical way. The phrase "Holy Spirit" or "Holy One" or "Almighty" are metonyms or words used in metonymy. Metonymy is a figure of speech. "*Metonymy* is a figure by which one name or noun is used instead of another, to which it stands in a certain relation" (*Figures of Speech Used in the Bible*, by E. W. Bullinger, p. 538). Or metonymy is the use of the name of one object or concept for that of another to which it is related, or of which it is a part, as "scepter" for "sovereignty," or "the bottle" for "strong drink" (*Random House Dict.*). Another example is the "White House" is used as metonym when we say, "the White House said today...." What we mean is "the President said today...." The White House is not a person or power, but is a name of an object closely related to the President. When we say "the White House said today," we are using language in a metonymical way (a figure of speech) to say "the President said today." When we say the "Holy Spirit dwells in us," (2Tim 1:14) we are using language in a metonymical way to say "God abides in us," (1John 4:12) or "Jesus Christ is in you" (2Cor 13:5; Col 1:27). The "Holy Spirit" is another name for God. God revealed his name of names to Moses in Exodus 3:13-15.

gp422» The Bible uses hundreds of different figures of speech as Bullinger manifested in his book, *Figures of Speech used in the Bible*. One figure of speech the Bible used was the "Holy Spirit" for God, or the "Holy One" for God. The "Holy Spirit" is God's spirit. God possesses spirit because he is made up of spirit, for God is spirit (John 4:24). His spirit is the "Holy Spirit" because he is holy. The phrase "Holy Spirit" is a metonym for God, not a name of a different person of the Godhead, but a name of a different aspect of God. The phrase "Holy One" is a metonym for God because God is Holy. The "Holy One" is not a separate person of the Godhead, but it is just another name for an aspect of God. The word "Almighty" is not a different person of the Godhead, but it is just another name for some aspect of God for God is all mighty. In fact, concerning the "Almighty" the Bible actually says that it was just another name for the God:

- "And I appeared unto Abraham, unto Isaac, and unto Jacob, by the name of God Almighty, but by my name JEHOVAH [YHWH] was I not known to them...." [Ex 6:3]

Father is God; Jesus Christ is God; Holy Spirit is God

gp423» God has many names as we show in chapter one of this book. The Bible used metonymy when referring to God. That is, the Bible used many different names and phrases for God. The Bible used the "Father" as a name for God. The Bible, starting with Christ's resurrection, used "Jesus Christ" as a name for God. The Bible used the "Holy Spirit" as a name for God. The Bible used the "Holy One" as a name for God. The Bible used the "Almighty" as a name for God. But God's most important Name is YHWH. This is why you baptize into the <u>Name</u> of the Father, Son, and Holy Spirit. The Name of the Father, Son, and Holy Spirit is YHWH (Jehovah, or Yehowah, or Yahweh, or). The Father, the Son, the Holy Spirit, the Holy One, and the Almighty are all just other names of YHWH.

Puzzle of the Godhead

gp424» Remember that Jesus did **not** say in Luke 10:22 that no one knew who the Father <u>and</u> who the Holy Spirit were, except the Son. No, Jesus said no one knew who the Father was except the Son, or no one knew who the Son was except the Father. The puzzle of the Godhead had nothing to do with the Holy Spirit, but only the nature of the relationship of the Father and the Son. The "Holy Spirit" is just as much God as the Son, because both the Father and the Son (after the son went to the Father) are Spirit. But the Holy Spirit is not a different person of the Godhead, just as the Holy One or the Almighty are not different persons of the Godhead. The Holy Spirit is a metonym that manifests one aspect of God. It is just another name for God. The name speaks about one aspect of God: He is *Holy* spirit, or He is spirit that is Holy. God has many names and they all teach us something about God. But the main Name for God is YHWH (Yehowah) as revealed to Moses in the original language of Exodus 3:14 ff.

Time and Change Play Major Parts in the Answer

gp425» The immutability theory blinds all who examine the scripture so that they cannot see through the paradoxes and are thus forced to hold on to an obviously contradictory theory, and are forced to call it a mystery even though Paul's writings indicate that the mystery of Christ was solved (Rom 16:25; Eph 1:9; 3:3-4, 9; 5:32; 6:19; Col 1:26-27; Paul's letters did not give *all* the details of the puzzle of the Father and the Son).

gp426» Knowing that time plays a major role, what we will see is this:

- At one time Jesus was a man (GP 4);

- At a later time Jesus was in the God (GP 5).

- At first only the Spirit of Jesus Christ existed (GP 3).

- Before Jesus Christ's physical birth, the flesh of Jesus only existed in the forethought of the God who had predestinated the Seed (through Adam & Eve and the patriarchs), the fleshly Jesus Christ, to come into existence at the chosen time (GP 4 & PR 1).

- Later, when the fleshly Jesus was born, the essence of Jesus Christ was in some way split between his Spirit and his flesh (GP 4).

- At the death of Jesus, his Spirit was given up, thus separating the Spirit from the physical body for three days (GP 4).

- Only after Jesus' resurrection did he go back into the God and became one with the Spirit, and at that time for the first time Jesus was called God and was God (GP 5).

- On earth Jesus was the *Son of God* before his resurrection; he never claimed to be God before his resurrection and his return to his God, only the *son* of God.

Notes for GP 5

John 1:1-18

gp427» Let's go over John 1:1-18 in detail because of the misunderstandings these verses have brought. First of all we must understand that the book of John was written AFTER Christ the man was resurrected, and *after* he became one with God through God's Spirit. They did not go around calling Jesus, "Christ," before he was resurrected (GP 4). But those who wrote about him *after* he went to the Right Hand of the God called him "Christ" (GP 5). Knowing this let's begin.

gp428» We will now give you a literal translation word for word. Then we will explain after each verse(s) about the translation, and point out other scriptures that reiterate the same information.

Translation and Notes

- In [the] beginning was [imperfect tense = imp.] the word, and the word was [imp.] towards the God, and God was [imp.] the word. This [God or the word] was [imp.] in [the] beginning towards the God (John 1:1-2).

gp429» *Notes on Meaning:* These verses say God was the WORD and was in the beginning, as does Psalm 119:160, "your word true the beginning," and Genesis 1:1, "in the beginning God." But notice the WORD was towards the God (cf. Rev 12:5, Greek text). This is movement *towards* the God, the finished essence of God. Notice that in someway, "God was the WORD." The angel of the God [angels are called god(s). See GP 3] in the beginning was the spokesman for the God.

gp430» The "Word" came through the angel of the BeComingOne as Isaiah 52:5-6 indicates and as this book indicates (GP 3). Angels are spiritual messengers. God's angel carried God's message. Thus, it is the angel of the BeComingOne who was the agent and spokesman of the God, and who was in the beginning, and was the beginning, and was the WORD of God (see "Image of God"). But Jesus Christ became the *new BEGINNING* of the new creation of God (Rev 3:14). John 1:1 speaks about the "beginning." What beginning? The following verses indicate that the "beginning" John was talking about was the *new* beginning of Jesus Christ (Compare "beginning" in: John 1:1; 15:27; 1John 1:1; 2:7; 2John 5,6; note Luke 1:1-3).

- All things through him [the WORD] came [aorist] into existence, and apart from him came into existence not even one [thing] which has come into existence (John 1:3).

gp431» *Notes on Meaning:* Genesis 1:3, 6, 9; Rev 21:5 and so on show us God creates through "verbal" (the "WORD") commands. The pre-creation Power creates from himself, everything, for the BeComingOne is everything and everywhere; for he is spirit, and his spirit is everywhere and everything (John 4:24; Psa 139:7-8; 1Kings 8:27; Jer 23:24). Even the visible is from the invisible (his spirit), or a manifestation of his spiritual substance (Heb 11:3). The pre-creation Power, or Life, or Being created from his substance, or from his spirit a new system of things — the present cosmos. And this pre-creation Power predestinated all his power to the BeComingOne (Jer 32:17, 27), who was represented by the angel (Exo 23:21) who was the spokesman of the completed God Being. This BeComingOne (YHWH) is moving towards the completed God, or the BeComingOne who has become (John 1:1-2).

- In him was life, and the life was the light of the men (John 1:4).

gp432» *Notes on Meaning*: Jesus the man said he was "the light of the world," and he qualified this by saying this light was "the light of life" (John 8:12). But Jesus the *man* was not "the light of life," but the WORD or God *in*side him spoke the words and did the power that Christ the man spoke and worked (John 12:49; 14:10).

gp433» The BeComingOne, or the WORD of the Father, who was inside Christ the man, was the "light of life," or the way of life as John 8:12 indicates, "I am the light of the world: he that follows me shall not walk in darkness, but shall have the light of life." The WORD, or the BeComingOne was not only the *way*, or the *light* of life, but he was *life* as John 1:4 John 5:26 indicate.

- And the light [the WORD] in the darkness appears, and the darkness comprehended it not (John 1:5).

gp434» *Notes on Meaning*: The words, "light," and "darkness," are contrasted throughout the Bible with "light" being synonymous with God, or his ways (1 John 1:5; etc), and "darkness" being synonymous with Satan, or Satan's ways (1 Pet 2:9; Col 1:13; Eph 6:12; Rom 13:12; etc). Thus, John 1:5 says God (the light) appeared in the darkness (the world's present system), but those of the darkness comprehended it not. See GP 7 for more understanding on this.

- There was a man sent forth [as a messenger, or agent] from God, his name John. He came for a witness that he might testify [give evidence, to prove] about the light that all might believe through him. He was not the light, but [he was sent so] that he might testify about the light (John 1:6-8).

gp435» *Notes on Meaning*: Now this "John" was the one promised to go forth as a messenger for God. This messenger was to come before God came to earth (Mal 3:1; 4:5). John came "in the spirit and power of Elijah ... to make ready a people prepared for the Lord" (Luke 1:17, 13-17). John was the one prophesied of in Malachi 3:1 and 4:5 as Luke 1:17, 76 and Matthew 11:12-14 indicate. But John was only a typical one to come in the spirit of Elijah to testify of the typical coming of the Lord.

gp436» Because John testified of Christ's first or typical coming, and because the Bible is dual, and because the Bible said John had come in Elijah's spirit, and because John did not fulfill to the fullest extent the prophecy about Elijah; then this means John was a typical representation of the Elijah who is to come before the Lord.

gp437» But an antitypical "Elijah" or "John" shall come before the antitypical coming (2nd physical coming or manifestation) of God to announce His coming. This person will be in the spirit of Elijah, not the Old Testament Elijah himself, but doing in an antitypical way what the Old Testament Elijah did.

- [this light] was the true light which lightens every man coming into the cosmos (John 1:9).

gp438» *Notes on Meaning:* This verse antitypically prophesies of ALL mankind being enlightened by the true light (see "All Saved" paper [NM 13]). This verse typically merely says the sun (the light) shines on every man born.

- In the cosmos was [the light], and the cosmos through him came into existence, and the cosmos of him knew not. Before his own he came, and his own received him not (John 1:10-11).

gp439» *Notes on Meaning:* The Light, or the WORD, or the God (all these names are metonymical descriptive words of the same power) came into the cosmos, or the present order of things, but even though the cosmos came into being through him, and even though he came to his own people, they did not accept him. The Light, or the WORD, or the God was *in*side Christ the man before he died (see GP 4). People of Christ the man's own nation did not receive him, but killed him. After Christ the man was resurrected and became one with God, this Christ appeared to his own disciples and they were afraid of him (Luke 24:36-37, 41 "while they yet believed not"). Only when his disciples received the Spirit on the day of Pentecost did they truly believe. In effect they rejected the "light" inside Christ. As we have seen in this book all mankind are or will belong to the Light. The Light came to His future own and they rejected Him. See *New Mind Papers* for a better understanding on true belief.

- But as many as received him he gave to them ability [or energy, or power] to be children of God [that is] to those that believe into the name of his (John 1:12).

gp440» *Notes on Meaning:* Most of the cosmos or world did not accept the WORD, but a few did, because they were given the power of the Spirit to be children of God, and these believed or will believe into his NAME. God in a sense is the WORD since He gives His full power to His WORD. Thus, those who accepted the WORD of the Light believed into the NAME of God, and became children of God. When the Bible speaks of God's NAME, it means YHWH — the BeComingOne. The angel of the BeComingOne had the NAME, Christ was given that NAME, it is Christ's new NAME (GP 1, 3-5).

- (these who are children of God are those) who not out of bloods, nor out of the will of flesh, nor out of the will of man, but out of God were begotten (John 1:13).

gp441» *Notes on Translation:* The Greek word translated "born" in the KJV is a Greek word of dual meaning, with a meaning of either: begotten or born. See "Begotten, Born Paper" [NM 5].

gp442» *Notes on Meaning:* Those who are children of God are children of God because from God (not man, not flesh) they are begotten. Since God is Spirit (John 4:24), then the children of God are begotten from God's Spirit (1 Pet 1:23 with Rom 8:14, 16; "Baptism Paper" [NM 4]). They become children of God not through their own will, but the predestinated will of God (see "Predestinated Paper" [NM 8]).

- And the word [the angel of the Lord] became* [in] flesh, and he lived* among us, (and we discerned* the great appearance of him, an appearance a *one-of-a-kind* from father) completely full of grace and truth (John 1:14).

gp443» *Notes on Translation:* The "*" after the verbs indicate that it is translated from an aorist verb, a verb of action, not time.

gp444» *Notes on Meaning:* Now this verse is dual as is the meaning of "light" [light = God's Spirit] or "John" [John = Elijah]. The WORD, the angel of the Lord, became *in* flesh as we showed in GP 4 by being *begotten* inside Christ the man. And because of this he by being inside Jesus lived among mankind. The great appearance ("glory") of the WORD in the flesh was *as* the one-of-a-kind from the Father. Jesus was actually the only physically begotten son *from* the Father through a miracle (see GP 4). Since God was in a sense the WORD, and God is spirit, and because spirit can not be seen; then the WORD's glory, or great appearance was *in* Jesus the man.

gp445» But antitypically, the WORD became flesh, or the angel of the Lord did become flesh, or did incorporate flesh (Christ the man) into his essence (see GP 5). And he, as flesh (also spirit), lived among man *after* the resurrection of Christ to God for a short time. And this glory, or great appearance was like the only-BORN of the Father (John 1:18, see some Greed texts). Christ the BeComingOne is the only-BORN son of God until He physically returns again, then 144,000 will also be born of God (Rev 14:1-5; 1Cor 15:23). Later, at the end of creation, the third unit or the rest of mankind will be born of God (see the "All Saved Paper" [NM 13]).

- John testified about him, and cried, saying, this was he of whom I spoke, he who comes after me he has preference of me, for before [in place or time] me he was. For out of the fullness of him we all receive, and grace upon grace (John 1:15-16).

gp446» *Notes on Meaning:* Christ the man was sinless. Thus, he was before John in *place* or position. The WORD inside Jesus the man did Christ's works (John 14:10). And it was because of this, and by this, that Jesus the man was given the fullness of grace (John 1:14, 16) without measure (John 3:34). Not only was Christ the man given the fullness of the Spirit (grace), but after he was resurrected he was given the power of all the grace (Matt 28:18) to give as God had willed (Acts 2:33; John 5:30) before the cosmos began (Eph 1:4-6).

gp447» In another sense Christ (with God in him) was before John in *time*, because the angel of the Father in Christ was before John in time. See GP 3 and GP 4.

- For the law through Moses was given: the grace and the truth through Jesus Christ came (comes/will come) (John 1:17).

gp448» *Notes on Translation:* The Greek word translated into "came" is an aorist word that is a verb of *action* only, not a verb of time.

gp449» *Notes on Meaning:* Jesus Christ the man came with truth and grace because he had it *in*side of him since the WORD was inside him. But Jesus Christ resurrected into the Godhead still comes with grace and truth since from him comes the Spirit of God (Acts 2:33). It is through this grace that comes from the Spirit that man is now being freed or saved (Rom 5:10, 15, 21).

- God, no one has seen at anytime; the one-of-a-kind son who is into the bosom of the father, he revealed [him] (John 1:18).

gp450» *Notes on Meaning:* In GP 2 we showed you that God the Father was the BeComingOne of the Old Testament. Now verse 18 says no one has seen this God, but Christ who went into the Father reveals, or revealed him. Yet we showed you in GP 2 that Moses and others had seen God in visions, and others of God can see God, Spiritually, as John 6:46 and John 14:7 indicate. The reason no one could see God was because God was spirit (John 4:24), and spirit is invisible (Heb 11:3). Hence, the Bible qualifies John 1:18 by saying those of God can "see" God, Spiritually speaking, but not physically speaking. Also we must remember that God is YHWH — the BeComingOne. He exists in his truest self at the end of creation, thus, of course, up to that time no one will have seen Him in the truest sense.

> Christ literally did go *into* the bosom of God as John 1:18 says. And Jesus Christ as God, reveals God in himself, or through himself, for he himself is in the God, thus can be called God or even called the BeComingOne, for he has the NAME. But he is God that is moving towards the truest sense of God — the fulfilled God.

Symbolic Meaning of the Sun and Moon

gp451» God at the beginning manifested the fact that the stars, sun, and moon were for signs (symbols) as well as for telling the days and seasons (see Gen 1:14). Further in Romans 1:19-20 it manifests to us that all of God's creation shows us about His essence and thus His plan. His Bible tells us the physical is symbolic of the Spiritual (Heb 10:1; see "Duality of the Bible" [See Intro]). But God cautions us to look to the higher meaning — the Spiritual— and not to the physical symbols (Col 3:2).

gp452» The sun and moon are symbolic of something. The problem is that some look to the physical symbols themselves, instead of the *meaning* of those symbols. This is similar to making a big commotion out of words themselves instead of their meanings. Words are merely symbols of meaning, just as the sun and moon are symbolic of something. What is the Biblical interpretation of the meanings of the sun and moon in God's plan?

Sun

gp453» First of all the sun is merely a star. And the Bible interprets stars as being angels (Rev 1:20). And further the Bible tells us angels are spiritual beings (Heb 1:7). So the sun is symbolic of a spiritual being. But which spiritual being? The sun symbolizes the angel of the BeComingOne or the resurrected Christ the BeComingOne because he now encompasses the angel. By comparing the following verses this is shown:

- Psalm 19:4-5 equates the sun with the bridegroom coming out of his chamber. Who is *the* Biblical bridegroom? By comparing the parable of the marriage feast (Matt 22:1-13) and the parable of the ten virgins (Matt 25:1-12), with Revelation 19:7-9, we know *the* bridegroom is Christ the BeComingOne at his return. Thus, since Psalm 19:4-5 equates the sun to the bridegroom, and since the Bible equates *the* bridegroom to Christ the BeComingOne, then the sun is symbolic of Christ the BeComingOne.

- Malachi 4:2 calls the coming Christ the BeComingOne, the "*sun* of righteousness."

- Christ the BeComingOne calls himself the bright and morning star (Rev 22:16).

- Peter in context tells us Christ the BeComingOne is the day star (2Pet 1:19).

- The book of Revelation tells us Christ the BeComingOne looks like "the sun shines in his strength" (Rev 1:16).

- Deuteronomy 33:14 tells us "the precious fruits [are] brought forth by the sun." Who are the world's precious fruits? They are the Spiritual "first-fruits" (Rev 14:4; 1Cor 15:23). Who brings forth the fruits of the earth? It is God/Christ (Psa 104:30; Rev 14:4). The antitypical meaning of precious fruit is those born of God. The antitypical of the sun is Christ the BeComingOne.

Moon

gp454» What is the moon symbolic of? It is symbolic of Christ the man. As Christ the man was a manifestation of the angel of the BeComingOne in himself (John 14:10; 12:46, 47, 49; 1Tim 3:16; see GP 4), so too is the moon a manifestation of the sun's light. Remember stars or burning heavenly bodies are symbolic of spirits or angels. Now the moon has no light of its self, but is a reflection of the light from the sun. One can say the moon manifests or reveals the light of the sun. The moon manifests a sphere (the sun), as did Christ the man reflect or manifest the true light (of the Father through the Spirit) in himself. From GP 2 we saw that Jesus Christ's father was the BeComingOne (YHWH) of the Old Testament. From the New Testament we see that the God is symbolically or typically represented by light, "God is light" — 1 Jn 1:5. The light of the Sun and the moon represent God — His good Spirit.

gp455» Notice some of the scriptures that indicate how the moon represents symbolically or typically Jesus Christ the man:

- **(1)** Deuteronomy 33:14 tells us the moon (Christ the man) put forth precious things. What precious things did the antitypical moon put forth? They were the

- **(2)** Genesis 3:15 tells us the serpent (Satan) would bruise the heel of the woman's seed, but that this seed would bruise the serpent's head. Now Romans 16:20 tells us this seed of Eve who is to bruise the serpent's head is Christ the BeComingOne. And Revelation shows us that at his coming he will bruise Satan's head, which is the Beast, Satan's kingdom, with its seven *heads* and the power of the Beast which is the dragon (Satan) (Rev 19:20; 20:10; 13:2; and Psalm 91:13; see "Seed Paper" [PR 1] and Beast-System Paper" [PR 2 & see PR 3]).

- **(3)** But Genesis 3:15 said Satan would bruise the heel of the seed. And since Christ is the seed (Gal 3:16), then Satan has bruised Christ. Now we know Satan is not going to bruise Christ the BeComingOne, but Christ the man was bruised on the cross. The Bible said that Satan put the idea into Judas to betray Christ (Luke 22:3-4; John 13:2).

- **(4)** Now the Bible calls God's Church his body (1Cor 12:12). Christ is the head of the body or his Church (Eph 1:22; 4:15). In other words, in symbolism, all of Christ's body is the Church, but the head of this body is Christ. Further, the Bible calls the Church a wife (Eph 5:22-25; Rev 19:7). Christ the BeComingOne is the head of the Church (his body) as a husband is the head of his wife. Thus, Christ's body (Church) is represented by a woman (wife), and Christ is the head of that woman.

- **(5)** Satan bruised Christ the seed's heel — Christ the man. But Christ's body in Biblical symbolism is a woman (his wife; the Church). Notice Revelation 12:1 where it pictures a woman (the Church; Christ's body) clothed with the sun (the Spirit of God) and the **moon** under her feet (at *her heel*). The **moon** is at the *heels* of the body of Christ (the woman; the Church). It was the heel of the seed that Satan was to bruise. It is the MOON that is at the heels of Christ's body, and it is Christ who was the seed that was promised to come. And it was Christ the man who was bruised on the cross.

Thus, the moon under the woman (Christ's body, Rev 12:1) is symbolic of Christ the man. And remember also that Christ the man died on the Passover, and that on the Passover the moon is full. Christ the man's time was fulfilled on the Passover also.

Glory of God

gp456» What is the "Glory" of God. The word "glory" is translated from the Hebrew word *kabod* (# 3519) or the Greek word *doxa* (#1391). Both of these words had a wide application literally and figuratively in both languages, and have approximately the same meaning as the English word "glory." Thus the glory of God is:

- the great splendor of God
- the great magnificence of God
- the great prosperity of God
- the great honorableness of God
- the great exultation of God
- the great fame of God
- the great grandeur of God
- the great brilliance of God

- the great showing of God
- the great state of God
- the great triumph of God
- the great majesty of God
- the great distinction or honor of God

Great Age and Glory

gp457» The Glory of God will endure for *olam* (Psa 104:31). The Glory of God will be in the Church and in Christ in the great age (Eph 3:21, "age of ages"). The Glory of God in the Church in the great age is the same glory as Christ's agelong glory (2Tim 2:10, see "Age Paper" [NM 7]). This age is the endless age of the Kingdom with its glory (Dan 7:14; 2:44; Luke 1:33, see "Age Paper"). The "Glory of God" and the "Kingdom of God" are different names for the same great age of glory and rulership of harmony. An examination of the scriptures concerning the Glory of God as compared with the Kingdom of God shows the similar qualities and thus points to their agreement and sameness.

gp458» As we learned in this book Jesus Christ went into the BeComingOne [YHWH — Jehovah or Yehowah] and now is in the NAME of the BeComingOne with the BeComingOne's titles and powers. Thus we see that what the BeComingOne or Jehovah was said to be in the Old Testament is what Jesus Christ is said to be in the New Testament. Remember this when you compare the following verses:

- Jehovah is king of glory (Psa 24:10)
- Christ is king of glory on the throne (Matt 19:28; 25:31; Rev 5:13; 2Pet 1:11; Rev 12:10; Rev 5:12)
- Jehovah is king for *olam* (Psa 10:16; 29:10; Jer 10:10; Matt 6:13 ["into the ages"])
- Christ is king for *aion*, an *aionios* kingdom (2Pet 1:11; Luke 1:33; Dan 7:13-14)
- This *olam*, this *aion* has no end (Dan 7:14; Luke 1:33; see "Age Paper" [NM 7])
- Christ's Glory is his Father's, who gave ALL to him (Psa 110:1; John 13:31-32)
- "Jesus Christ, Lord, into the glory of God the Father" (Phil 2:11; Matt 16:27; 24:30-31; 25:31)
- "Now is the Son of man glorified, and God is glorified in him [JC]. If God be glorified in him [JC], God shall also glorify him [Christ] in himself [God], and shall straightway glorify him [Christ]." (see Greek, John 13:31-32)
- "to the only wise God be glory *through* Jesus Christ" (Rom 16:27)
- "All things that the Father has are mine" (John 3:35; Luke 10:22; Matt 28:18; John 16:15)
- All nations and peoples are gathered to "see" the GLORY of God (Isa 66:18-19; Psa 97:6; Isa 40:5)
- This is the same gathering of the nations at Christ's coming with his Kingdom to see Christ and be judged (Matt 25:31-32ff; Matt 16:27; Mark 8:38; Matt 24:30-31; Mark 13:26-27; Rev 1:7)
- "EVERY ONE [all, the whole] who is called by my NAME and to my glory, I have created him [each of the all who is in His NAME], I have formed him, yea I have made him." (Isa 43:7, Hebrew text)

gp459» The fact is that all will *see* (this points to Spiritual sight) the Glory of God (Isa 40:5; Psa 97:6; etc.), and that all will be in God's NAME and in God's Glory (Jer 3:17; 4:2; Zeph 3:9, see Hebrew text; Eph 3:15; Phil 2:11). As shown in other papers ALL will also be in God's Kingdom, for ALL will be saved ("All Into Christ," "All Saved," "Does All Mean All" papers).

gp460» Further study by you of the "Glory of God" and the "Kingdom of God" and synonyms for these terms will give you a better understanding that the Glory of God is the Kingdom of God.

Review of GP 5

gp461» We have seen in this part that after Jesus Christ the man's death and his burial for three days and three nights, he was resurrected and became ONE with the Spirit or Angel of the BeComingOne: two became one. The Spiritual marriage of mankind back to God *began* when Jesus Christ the man went into God. Since the beginning of creation, when all went *out of* God, God and man were separate. But through Jesus Christ the man, mankind is beginning to go back into God, or into the BeComingOne (the YHWH). Through the angel with the NAME, the BeComingOne incorporated Jesus Christ the man into Himself: the Spiritual WORD became flesh. The two, the man Jesus Christ and the Angel of the BeComingOne ("Lord" in the New Testament text), as ONE are called: Jesus Christ, God, or in another sense he is/will-be Jesus Christ the God. Jesus Christ the man has become Jesus Christ *the* God, in one sense, because ALL will eventually go into Jesus Christ by the End (see GP 6). But as of now we do not see ALL in Jesus Christ the God (see Heb 2:8). In two senses Jesus Christ is "the beginning of the creation of the [true] God" (Rev 3:14): the Spirit of Jesus was the First, the beginning of the "old" creation of God; but Jesus Christ the man and his Spirit as ONE is the beginning of the "New" creation.

General Review

In GP 1 we started our search: who or what is God? From the Bible we learned about the apparent paradoxes of God: "I make peace, and create evil: I the LORD do all these things" (Isa 45:7). God who is Love (1John 4:8) has somehow and for some reason created evil; He has even killed (Deut 32:39). But how can God be Love and also a killer?

We next learned that there are two basic laws and one basic fact we must understand in order to rightly perceive the true nature of God: the Law of Contradiction and the Law of Knowledge plus the fact that the God cannot lie.

We then went on and explained the Law of Contradiction.

We further showed the many attributes and titles of God and put forth that "time" is very important in our understanding of the paradoxes of God.

We also showed you the very NAME of the true God: YHWH, or Jehovah, or Yehowah, or He (who) will-be, or the BeComingOne, or the One who was, who is, and who is coming. God's NAME and its meaning is the real secret in revealing the answer to the Paradoxes of God. God's NAME is an *imperfect* (incomplete) verb and not as would be expected a *perfect* (complete) verb or a noun. Names are very important in the Bible and many times describe some facet of a person. The true NAME of the true God is important for it is the secret in explaining the apparently unexplainable scriptures about God.

In GP 1 we also looked into the meaning of "with God all things are possible," the *"one* Yehowah," the so-called unchangeableness of God, and other matters concerning the God. What GP 1 does is set the stage in our search for who or what is God.

In GP 2 we learned that Jesus Christ's Father was the BeComingOne (YHWH) of the Old Testament: He was the Jews' God.

In GP 3 we learned that the angel of the BeComingOne and the BeComingOne of the Old Testament were closely connected. Since angels are messengers, this means the angel of the BeComingOne is a messenger of the BeComingOne or this angel is the WORD of the BeComingOne. Therefore, the words that the angel of the BeComingOne spoke belonged to the Great BeComingOne Power — the true God. This angel stood in the NAME of the true God (Exo 23:20-21); he represented the great NAME. This angel was in a sense the very WORD of God. The Word (logos) of God before Christ's resurrection was a spirit, the chief-spirit, the chief-angel, the angel of the BeComingOne. The age before Jesus Christ was subjected to angels, even the commandments given on Mount Sinai were from an angel (Acts 7:38).

We have shown **in GP 4** that *before* Jesus Christ was resurrected, he was a human being because he was born from a woman. Thus, Christ before his death and resurrection was a man; he was Jesus Christ the man. He was called Son of man because he was born of mankind through the means of Mary his mother. Jesus the man was not just any human being. Christ was a Son of God, both physically (through the Holy Spirit's union with Mary) and Spiritually (through the medium of God's Spirit inside of him). Christ was a mediator between man and God; he was the Son of God and the Son of man. He is the "one *mediator* between God and men" (1Tim 2:5). Jesus Christ the man actually had the Spirit or Angel of the BeComingOne (YHWH) inside him leading him in the right way. It was because of this Spirit that Christ the man was sinless. God was not Jesus Christ the man, but God (through the power of His Spirit) was inside of Christ the man. When Jesus Christ the man died, his Spirit was then separated from him (Luke 23:46). The Spirit or angel of God did not die *as* Christ the man or *with* Christ the man, for Spirit cannot die. The angel of the BeComingOne separated himself from Christ the man when Christ died.

To say it in slightly a different way, in GP 4 we have shown that Jesus Christ before he was resurrected was a man with the Spirit or angel of the BeComingOne inside him leading him in the way of love. Jesus Christ the man was born from woman and by a miracle of God. Thus, Christ the man was from mankind (through Mary) and from God because of the miraculous conception by the power of God. Jesus Christ the man was a son of man, and a son of the God. He is the "one *mediator* between God and men" (1Tim 2:5). Christ the man wasn't God, but God's WORD and power was inside of him. The angel of the BeComingOne was inside Jesus Christ the man. When Christ died the angel of the BeComingOne separated from Christ the man's body. Thus, Christ the man died, but his angel inside of him stayed alive, for the angel (spirit) separated himself from Christ the man when Christ died (Luke 23:46).

In GP 5, we have seen that after Jesus Christ the man's death and his burial for three days, he was resurrected and became ONE with the Spirit or Angel of the BeComingOne: **two became one**. The Spiritual marriage of mankind back to God *began* when Jesus Christ the man went into the BeComingOne, the God. Since the beginning of creation when all went *out of* God, God and man were separate. But through Jesus Christ the man, mankind is beginning to go back into God, or into the BeComingOne (YHWH). Through the angel with the NAME, the BeComingOne incorporated Jesus Christ the man into Himself: the Spiritual WORD became flesh. The two, the man Jesus Christ and the Angel of the BeComingOne

("LORD"), as ONE are called: Jesus Christ, God, or in another sense he is/will be Jesus Christ the BeComingOne. Jesus Christ the man has become Jesus Christ *the* God, in one sense, because ALL will eventually go into the Spiritual Body of Jesus Christ by the End (see GP 6). But as of now we do not see ALL in Jesus Christ the God (see Heb 2:8). In two senses Jesus Christ is "the beginning of the creation of the [true] God" (Rev 3:14): the Spirit of Jesus was the First, the beginning of the "old" creation of God; but Jesus Christ the man and his Spirit as ONE is the beginning of the "New" creation.

GP 6: All into Christ

Great Mystery
All Back into God
Angels and Spirits
An Angel for Everyone
BeComingOne Himself the Elohim
Great Cycle
New Body, New Soul

Mankind To Be Like Christ

gp462» "Who will transform our lowly body that it may be conformed to His [Christ's] glorious body, according to the working by which He [Christ] is able even to subdue ALL things to Himself" (Phil 3:21, NKJV — emphasis added). We have just explained to you Christ's body of glory or New Soul. His glorious body is his resurrected body that was joined to the angel of the BeComingOne (YHWH). Thus his body of glory is the new creation: two (the physical and spiritual) are one. But notice carefully that through the power given to Christ, Christians' ("our" — Phil 3:21) bodies will be created like Christ's AND with this same power all will be subdued to Christ. We need to know what it means "to subdue all things to" Christ.

Christ Now Has All The Power

gp463» Jesus Christ was given ALL the power of his Father (John 3:35). All are subjected to Christ (Matt 28:18; 1Pet 3:22) because God gave His NAME and power to Christ (Phil 2:9-11) by infusing Jesus the man into the God through the Spirit of the God (GP 5). But all are not yet under Christ (Heb 2:8). Yet as we see from Phil 3:21, Christ does have the power to subdue all to himself. And as Romans 8:32 indicates, God with Christ gave *us*, meaning Real Christians, all things (note also 1Cor 3:21). Furthermore, not only will Christians receive all things with Christ, but all people ever born will receive all things with Christ. Let's look at the Biblical evidence.

All Saved

gp464» "And the angel said to them, Do not fear. Lo, I bring you good news of great joy, which shall be to *all* people ... and *all* flesh shall see the salvation of God" (Luke 2:10; 3:6; see "All Saved," and "Does All Mean All" papers). Somehow most have overlooked scriptures concerning *all* of mankind inheriting peace and immortal life like Jesus Christ. Somehow mankind has felt a need to damn others. But while damning others, they project themselves as being superior to the ones they damned.

Jesus Christ's Commission to Save

gp465» Jesus Christ was given a commission to be Savior of the whole world, not just some elect group. Let's see where the Bible says through Jesus Christ that *all* will be saved and go into the God. Jesus Christ the BeComingOne is Savior of the world; he has come to free the world from its madness (1John 4:14; Luke 9:56). God will come to save the world from destroying itself at His physical return to earth (Matt 24:22). Thus, at that time He will have saved the world from destroying itself; and from that point on will begin to set the ground to save the world Spiritually as other scriptures indicate.

Great Mystery – Christ Fulfills All

gp466» In the Book of Ephesians we see that God had revealed to Paul a great mystery,

- "how that by revelation he [God] made known unto me the mystery; (as I wrote afore in a few words, Whereby, when you read, you may understand my knowledge in the mystery of Christ)" (Eph 3:3-4).

All in Heaven and Earth

gp467» What did Paul write about before in a few words that he calls the mystery of Christ? We merely look back from chapter 3 to chapter 1 to see the answer:

- "Wherein he [God] has abounded toward us in all wisdom and prudence; Having made known us the MYSTERY OF HIS WILL, according to his good pleasure which he has purposed in himself: That in the dispensation of the fullness of times he might *gather together in one ALL THINGS* in Christ, both which are in heaven, and which are on earth in him" (Eph 1:8-10).

["Heaven" represents the Spiritual reality as the "earth" represents the physical reality (cf "heaven" and "earth" in Isa 55:8-9; 1Cor 15:44-49; Phil 3:18-19; Col 3:1-2).]

gp468» Thus the answer to the great mystery is that *all* things will be gathered into Jesus Christ by the "fullness of the times." Paul reiterates this in Colossians:

- "and having made peace through the blood of his cross, by him to reconcile *ALL THINGS* unto himself; by him, I say, whether they be things in the earth [physical], or things in heaven [spiritual]" (Col 1:20).

gp469» And again in another book, Philippians, Paul states the answer to the mystery:

- "according to the working whereby he is able even to subdue *all things* unto himself" (Phil 3:21).

All into the Church

gp470» But what does it mean to reconcile all to himself — to Christ the BeComingOne?:

- "This is a *great mystery*: but I speak *into* Christ and *into* the Church" (Eph 5:32).

gp471» This mystery has something to do with reconciling all to Christ the BeComingOne. Now Paul says that this "great mystery" is something about "into Christ and into the Church." Reconciling all into Christ, into the Church, what does that mean? Will all be reconciled to Christ the BeComingOne through the medium of the Church?

Christ's Spiritual "Wife" – the Church

gp472» Notice in Ephesians 5:32 Paul said, "this is a great mystery." He had just finished writing about a subject, and concerning that subject he said: "this is a great mystery." What was he writing about before he made that statement? Read Ephesians 5:22-31 and you will see what he was writing about. He was comparing Christ as the head of the Church with man as the head of his wife. He was comparing and equating in a symbolic way the Church as a wife and Christ as the husband. Thus, in a sense women are symbolic of a church. Hence, in Ephesians 5:22-33 we can transpose Church for wife and Christ for husband and we will get the antitypical or higher meaning for these verses. Let's do that:

- "So ought men [Christ] to love his wife [Church] as his own body. He [Christ] that loves his wife [Church] loves himself. For no man ever yet hated his own flesh; but nourishes and cherishes it, even as the Lord the Church: For we are members of his body [Christ's Church], of his flesh, and his bones. For this cause shall a man [Christ] leave his father and mother, and shall be joined unto his wife [Church], and they two shall be one flesh. This is a great mystery: but I speak *into* Christ and into the Church" (Eph 5:28-32; see 1Cor 12:12 and Eph 1:22-23; Col 1:18; 2:19; Eph 4:15).

Great Mystery is Going into Christ

gp473» The word Paul used that was translated into "mystery" is a word that actually means *revealed* mystery.

> **03521** μυστήριον, ου, τό *mystery, secret;* (1) as a relig. t.t. in the cults of the Graeco-Roman world, a relig. *secret* confided only to the initiated, *secret rite,* not used in the NT; (2) in the NT; (a) as what can be known only through revelation mediated fr. God *what was not known before* (MT 13.11); (b) as a supreme redemptive revelation of God through the Gospel of Christ *mystery* (RO 16.25; EP 3.9); (c) as the hidden mng. of a symbol w. metaph. significance *mystery* (EP 5.32).

It is going into Christ, his body, which is the Church. Going into Christ is like going into the Church. Thus, when Paul speaks about the mystery that was revealed to him (Eph 3:3-4; 1:9) and says it is gathering "together in *one all things* in Christ [his body], both which are in heaven [the spiritual] and which are on earth [the physical] in him," we know when Paul says this, he is saying all will come into Christ's Spiritual Body, which is the Church.

All Back Into God through Jesus

gp474» All will be gathered into Christ, his body, his Church:

- "therefore any man be in Christ, he is a new creation: old things are passed away; behold, all things are become new. And *all* things are out of the God, who has reconciled us to himself by Jesus Christ, and has given to us the ministry of reconciliation; to wit, that God was in Christ, reconciling the world unto himself, not imputing their trespasses unto them; and has committed unto us the word of reconciliation. Now then we are ambassadors for Christ, as though God did beseech you by us: we ask you in Christ's behalf, be reconciled to God. For He [God] has made him [Christ] to be sin for us, who knew no sin; that we might be made the righteousness of God in him" (2Cor 5:17-21, see Greek text).

God is reconciling the world back to Himself through Christ. The Church is supposed to be teaching the world this. When one is reconciliated to Christ he becomes a new creation.

gp475» What does it mean reconciling the world back to God: "behold, the man is become as one *out of* us" (Gen 3:22). This is a correct translation from the Hebrew. Man after breaking God's law went out of the way of God. Today, through Christ the BeComingOne, the process of reconciliation is bringing the whole world back to God. How is this being done?

gp476» Notice that Christ was made sin for us so that Christ could make us the righteousness of God by us coming to God through him (2Cor 5:21). Read Isaiah 53:10-12 which shows that God allowed Christ the man to be killed for our transgressions, and that Christ the man "made intercession for the transgressors" (Isa 53:12). Compare Isaiah 53:1-12 with 2 Corinthians 5:19-21. To be an intercessor for something is to go between something — it is to be a mediator. Christ the man was a mediator!

- "For there is one God, and one mediator between God and men, the *man* Christ Jesus; Who gave himself [his life] a ransom for *all* to be testified in due time." [1 Tim 2:5-6].

gp477» How is God reconciling or harmonizing the world through Christ? God is reconciling the world through Christ by having Christ the man die for our sin as a ransom for ALL. Then Christ the man was reconciliated to God; he actually became God as we have shown previously in this book. He went into the NAME. Christ the man went between man and God, so as to bring God and man back together through Christ's death, a death he did not deserve, for he was blameless.

gp478» "And I, if I be lifted up from the earth, will draw *all* men unto me. This he said, signifying what death he should die" (John 12:32-33). In Christ's own words he said if he was lifted up, he would draw all to himself, he would reconciliate all to God as we've shown you. "For out of him, and through him, and into him, all things" (see Greek text, Rom 11:36). All of us came out of God, all because of the mediator, Christ the man, will return to God. At the fullness of the time all will be in Christ (Eph 1:10). It is the fullness of Jesus Christ that fills all in all:

- And He [God] put all under his feet, and gave him [Jesus] to be head over all to the church, which is his body, the fullness of him who fills all in all (Eph 1:22-23).

All things will be put back under the power of God and his system of love so "that may be the God, all things in all" (1 Cor 15:28). When *all* is the God (YHWH) then comes true the word: "I am the BeComingOne [YHWH], and there is none else" (Isa 45:5, 6, 21, 22).

NAME and the *All*

gp479» *All Power*. The true God gave all (including *all* power) to the Son, Jesus Christ (John 3:35; Luke 10:22; Matt 28:18; John 17:2). Since everything belongs to the true God (Deut 10:14), then He can, in some way, give ALL to Jesus Christ after He sets him at His right side of power (Psa 110:1). All will be subjected to Jesus Christ (Heb 2:8; 1Pet 3:22; Phil 2:9-11), because Christ was given *all* the power (Matt 28:18) by being set at God's right hand. That is why Christ is now called the Almighty (Rev 1:8 with 1:17-18).

gp480» *All Spirit*. When Christians are in Christ, they are one with Him, they are one with His Body, they are one with His Church, and they are one with His Spirit (1Cor 8:6; 1Cor 12:4, 11-13). Real Christians are in Christ as Christ is in the true God and as God is in Christ (John 17:22; see 1Cor 12). Thus, as Christ was given ALL, so too are Christians given ALL (Rom 8:32; 1Cor 3:21).

gp481» *All Glory*. The God does not give His glory to others (Isa 42:8; 48:11) because first He brings the others back into Himself, and by so doing gives them some share in *His* glory. Thus when all are back in God, or are in His NAME, then comes true the saying, "I am the BeComingOne [YHWH], and there is none else" (Isa 45:5, 6, 21, 22). As the God gave His glory to Christ (by bringing Christ into His glory), so Christ gives the glory to Christians (John 17:22) by bringing them into his glory.

gp482» *All Name = All BeComingOne.* God's NAME was in the angel who was made one with Christ the man. Thus, Christ the man was given God's NAME through the angel. When Christians are baptized into the NAME of God, they are given the NAME of God (Matt 28:19; Acts 8:16). But ALL will go into the NAME (Jer 3:17; 4:2). All people will be called by God's NAME (Zeph 3:9, see Hebrew text; Eph 3:15). All will be in the NAME, for all will be the BeComingOne. All will be that great Power. There will be nothing but the BeComingOne (Isa 45:5, 6, 21, 22), God, all in all (1Cor 15:28). The NAME of God is for the *new age* — the time of *olam* (Psa 135:13; 102:12; see "Age Paper" [NM 7]).

gp483» *When All.* Jesus Christ will fulfill all things (Eph 4:10; 1:22-23). When Jesus Christ fulfills all things is when God will be all in all (1Cor 15:28). This will be when all will be the BeComingOne, or when God's Spirit will fill all (Psa 139:7-8; 1Kings 8:27; Jer 23:24; Job 34:14-15; Acts 17:28; etc.). This is when the BeComingOne, will be. This gift of the true God (YHWH) to ALL, is given when all receive God's NAME. Everyone will be born of God by the true end of creation, at the creation of the new heaven and earth. See the "Thousand Years and Beyond" paper [NM 15] and other papers on the end of creation.

Angels and Spirits

gp484» Let's go into the details about "our body" being made like unto Christ the BeComingOne's (note Phil 3:21). As Jesus has his angel, so does each of us have our angel. As Jesus Christ the man was infused with his angel after his resurrection, so too will each of us be infused with our own angel after our resurrection from the dead to the real life. Before we can go into this subject we must remember that the Bible is dual as the creation is dual. There is a type for the antitype, or the shadow for the real. As Romans 1:19-20 indicates, the physical first creation by God is representative and has meaning in the spiritual or invisible dimension. The Bible is one part of that creation, as is marriage, as is sex difference, as is ....

gp485» As we've shown you in GP 5, male and female, and even marriage are representative of Spiritual truth. Even the sun and moon have a meaning in God's plan. The moon represents Christ the man. The light of the sun represents the truth of God as represented by the angel of God or now by the resurrected Christ, who carries the Truth or Light of God (see notes for GP 5).

Stars and Angels

gp486» "And God said, Let there be lights in the firmament of the heaven to divide the day from the night; and let them be for *signs*, and for seasons, and for days, and years" (Gen 1:14). The stars are for signs. What kind of sign?

gp487» What does the word translated "sign" mean. Both in the Hebrew and the Greek, it means — sign. We can look to our dictionary. A good dictionary tells us basically a "sign" represents something else. As a word is a sign of a meaning or a sign for a thing, so too are stars: they are a sign or symbol for something else. The Bible defines its signs or symbols. And in Revelation 1:20 it defines stars as being symbolic of angels. And from other scriptures we know that angels are spiritual beings (Heb 1:7). Angels are classified into two groups, God's and Satan's. As the Bible shows, at the end of the age of Satan, one-third of the angels (stars) will have gone over to Satan's side, thus two-thirds of the created angels are God's angels or God's Spirits since angels are

Spirits (Rev 12:4, 7-9). Jesus told us in Luke 24:39 that spirits do not have bodies of flesh and blood, so angels do not have physical bodies.

gp488» God is the Father of spirits (Heb 12:9), or Father of the angels, for angels are spirits. God created these Spirits, therefore he is their "father." The angel of the BeComingOne's father was God the Father — the BeComingOne (YHWH). The BeComingOne is the Father through His *power* of predestination. One-third of these angels or spirits will have been under Satan, after God "allowed" them to separate themselves from his Spirit for a higher purpose; Two-thirds of the rest of the Spirits are God's, for they follow in the true God's way (gp627).

Our Own Angel

gp489» Everyone that becomes a "son of God" must be begotten of the Spirit (Rom 8:9-10, 16). What is this Spirit? What does it mean to be begotten of God's Spirit? Notice that those begotten of the Spirit are led by it (Rom 8:14). The Spirit in them, leads them.

gp490» Notice that "these little ones" have in heaven "their angels" (Matt 18:10). The Greek word translated "their" means "of one's self." These "little ones" are Spiritual children of God (1 John 2:12-13). And these little ones have angels of their own self. Or, thus, since angels are spirits (Heb 1:7), Christians have their own angels or Spirits.

gp491» What do these angels or Spirits do? "For he shall give his angels charge over you, *to keep you in all your ways*" (Psa 91:11). In other words, angels lead them, as the Spirit leads the little ones or sons of God (Rom 8:14). Psalms 91:11 was used in a physical sense concerning Christ (Matt 4:6). But the Bible is dual and speaks in a dual sense, the physical sense and the Spiritual sense. We are to look to the higher sense — the Spiritual (Col 3:1-2). Not only do angels help out physically, but they help out Spiritually. And since Christ is our example, and the forerunner, then what applies to him applies to all others (cf Col 1:18; Rom 8:17; John 14:6).

gp492» Each son of God has his own angel (Matt 18:10). And these angels lead them in the way (Psa 91:11), as the angel of the BeComingOne led Christ (John 14:10, GP 3 & 4), who is our example. Thus, the Spirit of God that leads Christians (Rom 8:14) is an angel of God that is in them. One of God's own Spirits leads each one of them. These Spirits or angels are for the elect humans who are the sons of God (1Pet 1:1-2). These angels or Spirits serve the elect, they are ministers or servants "for them who shall be heirs of salvation" (Heb 1:14). These angels are the "elect angels" (1Tim 5:21).

Two into One

gp493» Christians at their resurrection, like Christ the man, will be Spiritually married to their own Spirit or angel: "to the general assembly and church of the first-born, which are written in heaven [in the Book of Life], and to God the Judge of all, and to the spirits [angels] of just men made complete" (Heb 12:23). The Christians are complete when they are infused with their Spirit.

gp494» Notice what the Bible calls Christ's "completion" with his Spirit: "Though he were a Son, yet learned he obedience by the things he suffered; and being made *complete*, he became the author of aeonian salvation unto all them that obey him" (Heb 5:8-9). And, "that they may be one, even as we are one: I in them, and you in me, that they may be *complete* in one" (John 17:22-23). Jesus Christ is asking in prayer that others ("they") be made complete like he and his Father.

Engaged - Married Metaphor

gp495» The Church is the wife of Christ (Rev 19:7; 21:2,9-10; Eph 5:22-32). But the Church is to be presented to Christ as a chaste virgin (2Cor 11:2). The Church is the five virgins with oil and the bridegroom is Christ (Mat 25:1-13). According to this Spiritual metaphor, before the marriage at Christ's coming, the Church, the betrothed wife of Christ, has not been made <u>one</u> with her future husband, for she is a Spiritual virgin. She enjoys Spiritual interaction (social intercourse) with her future husband, but not Spiritual intercourse (sexual intercourse) with her husband: she is not <u>one</u> with her future husband in the sense that married couples are one.

Begotten - Born Metaphor

gp496» There is a dual meaning here. A Spiritual *begotten* Christian is a typical completed person, but a resurrected Christian (*born* of God) is an antitypical completed person. Those born of God are made complete with their angel or Spirit (see "Begotten, Born Paper" [NM 5] to understand being begotten or born of God; see the "Duality of the Bible" [See Intro] to understand our use of "typical" and "antitypical").

An Angel for Everyone

Stars and Angels

gp497» Not only do the elect have angels but all human beings ever conceived have angels, for all will be born of God eventually by the end of God's Spiritual creation (see "All Saved Paper" [NM 13]). Therefore each person has an angel. This may be how some get their theory that each man born has his own star. We'll now show you *where* they got this belief. Believe it or not they are right, each has his own star. But stars are merely symbolic of angels. Each has his own angel that each will be Spiritually married to. The angels are antitypical males as was the angel of the BeComingOne; mankind are antitypical females. Both the angels and mankind will be spiritually married. Those who think only of the physical while ignoring the spiritual reality are wrong, for they look to the typical creation (stars) instead of to the antitypical meaning (angels). But we are to look to the higher meaning, the antitype.

gp498» From the very beginning God has been saying what we have put forth herein. Notice one of the first promises to Abraham: "And he brought him forth abroad, and said, Look now toward heaven, and count the *stars*, if you be able to number them: and he said unto him, *so shall your seed be*" (Gen 15:5). Abraham's seed will be numbered as much as the number of stars (Gen 22:17). Further, "and lest you lift up your eyes unto heaven, and when you see the sun, and the moon, and the stars, even all the hosts of heaven, and should be driven to worship them, and serve them, **Which the BeComingOne your God has divided unto all nations under the whole heaven**" (Deut 4:19). Moses is shown in the Bible reminding God of this promise (Ex 32:13). Now remember stars are symbolic of angels. *God in the Spiritual meaning of these verses was saying all people were appointed or given a Spirit or angel.*

gp499» God said *if* they could number the stars, then that number would be how many of Abraham's seed who would be born. In the higher or antitypical meaning of this scripture, an equal number of persons will be born as there are angels (stars). But we know that all who go *into* Christ, or thus are begotten of the Spirit, do become heirs to the promises given to Abraham (Gal 3:16,29). Since it can be proven that all will go into Christ eventually, then all ever conceived will be made complete with their own angel or Spirit and they will become like Christ.

gp500» Now God says he *has* numbered the stars, and further, has given them names (Psa 147:4). Thus, even though *we* cannot count the stars, they are countable. And as many as there are stars, so too, will they receive the promises of Abraham. But the higher meaning of stars is angels. And we are to look to the higher meaning (Col 3:1-2).

gp501» Hence, throughout all the creation, there will be born as many human beings as there are angels (stars). And the higher meaning of Psalms 147:4 is that God has numbered the angels, and named them. God has created stars to represent angels. Furthermore, he knew from the beginning that there would be conceived one man per angel (star). God is in FULL control of the creation.

gp502» Notice in Daniel 12:3, "and they that be wise shall shine as the brightness of the firmament; and they that turn many to righteousness **as the stars** to the age and onward."

gp503» And in Revelation 21:17, "and he measured the wall thereof, a hundred and forty and four cubits, according to the measure of man, that is, angel." **The measure of man, or the number of man is equal to the angels.**

"You Are Gods"?

gp504» Then what does this all mean? What is the God doing? What is the God creating here on earth? "You are Gods" (John 10:34). The whole purpose is to create ALL of mankind into what the Bible calls, Gods. The actual NAME of God is the "BeComingOne" (see GP 1). God is becoming: He will be. God is not only becoming, He is the Gods (Hebrew text, Deut 4:35, 39; 7:9; 1Kings 18:39; etc.). The true translation from the Hebrew of the English translation, "LORD God," is the "YHWH Gods" or "he (who) will be Gods." Most of the places in the Old Testament of the Bible (King James Version) where it has "God" is actually an incorrect translation. It should read Gods since the Hebrew word is *elohim*, which is the plural of *el*. "El" means God, therefore *elohim* means Gods. The true NAME of God is the "BeComingOne" (see GP 1). In the Old Testament the "BeComingOne" (YHWH) was described as the "BeComing Gods" (*Yehowah Elohim*) or the "BeComingOne himself [is] the Gods" (Deut 4:35). The true essence of God is that he is many in one. The BeComingOne, the God who will be, is *many in one*. The BeComingOne (YHWH) is ONE, means He is in unity (see GP 1).

BeComingOne Himself the Gods (Elohim)

gp505» This heading is a literal quote from the Hebrew text (Deut 4:35, 39; 1Kings 18:39). Other scriptures say the same thing (Deut 7:9; Josh 22:34; 1Ki 8:60; 18:24; 2Ki 19:15; 1Ch 17:26; 2Ch 33:13; Ezra 1:3; Neh 9:7; Isa 37:16; 45:18). What does this mean? It has everything to do with everyone in some sense becoming God-like. Notice the following scriptures about people being Gods or children of God:

- "The Jews answered him, saying, We are not stoning you for a good work, but for blasphemy, and because you, being a man, make yourself God. Jesus answered them, Is it not written in your Law? 'I said, you are gods.' If *He called them gods* to whom the word of God came, and scriptures cannot be broken.

- I have said, You are gods; and all of *you are children of the Most High*.

- See what love the Father has given to us, that *we should be called the children of God*. For this reason, the world does not know us, because it did not know Him. Beloved, now *we are children of God*.

- For as many as are led by the Spirit of God, these are the *sons of God*.

- For our citizenship is in heaven, from which we also are looking for the Lord Jesus Christ as Savior, who will completely transform our body of humiliation, for it to be *made like His glorious body.*
- *you might be partakers of divine* [Greek "godly"] *nature."*

[John 10:33-35; Psa 82:6; 1 John 3:1-2; Rom 8:14; Phil 3:20-21; 2Pet 1:4: see Great Cycle in GP 6]

We see scriptures that say the BeComingOne himself [is] the Gods (Deut 4:35), and we see that people will somehow be Gods (John 10:33), or at least offspring of God. If you are an offspring of a man, are you not a man? If you are an offspring of God, are you not somehow God? But what does this mean?

From One to Many

gp506» The Bible uses the name "Israel" to describe a whole nation. Israel was originally the name of one person. From a man named Israel came a nation of people called Israel. As with "Israel" so too with God. From one God-being (Christ) a whole nation of God-persons will become, they will come into existence and the totality of them will be the Spiritual Body of Jesus Christ. Jesus Christ was the first to go into God. ALL will become like Jesus the man became. Jesus Christ went into God and now is ONE with the God as we have shown in GP 5. After the 1000 years ALL will have followed in Jesus Christ the man's footsteps: All will go into God. All will be God all in all.

Great Cycle

All out of the Father; All Back into the Father

gp507» In the beginning all went out of the Father. But by the end of creation all will be brought back into the Father, the great God. The Great Cycle is the cycle of ALL coming out of the intelligent pre-creation Power (Father) at the beginning of creation, and the returning of the ALL, through Jesus Christ's Spiritual Body, to this great Power by the end of creation. (The creation is still going on.) For *out of* the One God, the Father, came all things (1 Corinthians 8:6; see Rom 11:36; 1Cor 11:12; 2Cor 5:18). All things will return to the Great God, the Father of ALL, *through* Jesus Christ. "Now all things out of the God, who has reconciled us to himself [Father] through Jesus Christ" (2Cor 5:18). Jesus Christ is the mediator between God and mankind (1Tim 2:5-6). It is through Jesus Christ that all will come back into the Father so that God will again be all in all (everything) (1Cor 15:24-28). The Great God is using Jesus Christ to make all things new:

- "[Jesus Christ] **who is the image of the invisible God** [if Jesus is the "image" of the God, he is not, in the truest sense, the God], **firstborn of all creation** [first born from the dead, the first or beginning of the new creation (Col 1:18; Rev 3:14; James 1:18; 1Cor 15:23)] ; 16 **because in him being created** [*aorist* verb, a verb without a time element] **all things, the things in the heavens and the things upon the earth, the visible and the invisible, whether thrones, or lordships, or principalities, or authorities: all things have been created through him and into him. 17 And he is before all** [the Spirit or angel of Jesus was before all things in the creation (GP 3); after the resurrection, Jesus was first in the new creation (GP 5)], **and all things subsist together in him. 18 And he is the head of the body, the assembly** [Church]; **who is (the) beginning, firstborn from among the dead, that he might have the first place in all things:** [in the creation] 19 **for it pleased** [the Father;

pre-creation Power who predestinated all] **that in him** [Jesus Christ] **all the fulness was to dwell**" (Col 1:15-19)

When all are in Jesus Christ, then at that very time will all be back into the Father, so that, God will be all in all (1Cor 15:28). Jesus, "**the son will be subjected to** [the One who gave the] **the subjection to him of all things, in order that, the God, all things in all**" (1Cor 15:28). The One who subjected all to Christ was the Father, YHWH, the BeComingOne. The Father is the source of all. During the creation he has given himself the Name, BeComingOne, to signify that He is becoming something other than what He was before the beginning of the creation.

gp508» ALL went out of the pre-creation Power to learn good and evil so by the end ALL will understand, know, and appreciate the coming utopia (GP 7). The true God is the BeComingOne (YHWH). The BeComingOne is ALL that will be in the Great Power by the end of creation. The BeComingOne is the goal of creation. When the Great Cycle is complete, when ALL are back in the God Power, then the BeComingOne *will be* in the truest sense and the Great Cycle will be complete. ALL will be back in the Power, but in a different manifestation than before the beginning of creation.

gp509» What the Power will have done by this Great Cycle is create from His pre-creation essence many new individuals with the ability to be joyful and happy without end in the coming Utopia (Kingdom of God or Heaven). The most obvious process in the creation is reproduction — the sexes coming together and creating new life. What the pre-creation Power is doing is reproducing Himself, with the help of the physical dimension, into new individuals with the ability to enjoy life for an endless age. We may never be able to know or understand what was before the beginning of creation or the essence of the God Power before creation. Since there is an analogy of the male and female representing the spiritual and the physical dimension (see "Image of God," GP 5 GP 8), then from Genesis 2:18 — "not good that the man should be alone," we may surmise that the pre-creation Power may have in some way been "alone." Thus, the pre-creation Power is reproducing Himself in some way so as not to be alone.

New Body, New Soul for All

gp510» Now we have shown in GP 5 that the resurrected body or New Soul will be both spirit and flesh. Jesus Christ the BeComingOne has a fleshly body. He was resurrected as a young man (Mark 16:5). Since we will be like Jesus (Phil 3:21), we too will have a body like Christ.

Sexuality

gp511» But what about our sexual organs? will someone resurrected have sexual organs? The answer is yes. Now we'll show you why the answer is yes.

gp512» In Deuteronomy 23:1 it speaks: "he that is wounded in the testes, or has his penis cut off, shall not enter into the congregation of the BeComingOne." It says those without genitals will not enter into the congregation of the BeComingOne. But in Isaiah 56:3-7 it indicates that eunuchs (castrated men) can be in the Church and will be in the kingdom of God. By putting Deuteronomy 23:1 and Isaiah 56:3-7 together, and knowing that the Bible does not contradict itself in its higher meaning, we know those who are eunuchs *now*, when resurrected *later* will have their genitals. God tells us to look to the higher, heavenly, or Spiritual meanings (Phil 3:19; Col 3:2; John 4:24; 6:63). Thus the "congregation of the BeComingOne" of Deuteronomy 23:1 is the antitypical congregation of God, which is the kingdom of God, or those born of God. Those born of God will have their genitals. Yet those who are eunuchs now, can be in the Church and will be in the kingdom of God, or will be born of God. But these eunuchs will be born of God with genitals. The same with women. Women when born of God will have female genitals.

gp513» Some people take Galatians 3:28 out of context and say men and women will be the *same* when born of God. These people say there will not be sexual differences in the kingdom of God. But the higher sense of Deuteronomy 23:1 says those in the kingdom will have genitals. Galatians 3:28 is speaking about everyone being of the one seed of Abraham's when in Jesus Christ. It is not saying that everyone in Christ is a non-sexual being, but this verse in context is saying that everyone in Jesus Christ is one, because they are of the *one* seed of Abraham's (V. 29, 16).

gp514» Hebrews 4:3 says "the works were finished from the foundation of the world." And "at the beginning made them *male* and *female*" (Matt 19:4). God isn't suddenly going to take the sex differences away. One will be either male or female in appearance when born of God. If one was born male on earth, he will be born male in the kingdom of God. If one was born female on earth, she will be born female in the kingdom of God.

Two Into One

gp515» Remember there are two essences or bodies to each one who is born of God. The spiritual body or essence and the physical body or essence. The physical body is resurrected and infused with a spiritual body. If one had a male body when on earth, this male body will be resurrected and infused with a spiritual body for a new creation. If one had a female body when on earth, this female body will be resurrected and infused with a spiritual body for a new creation.

No Deformities

gp516» In Leviticus 21:16-24 it projects to us that no one who will go into the antitypical sanctuary, or into the holy of holies, or be born of God shall have a physical blemish of any kind. There will be no lame, blind, and so forth among those born of God.

Resurrected Young

gp517» Job 33:25 shows us that those resurrected will have flesh "*fresher* than a child's, he shall return to the days of his youth." Those born of God will be born youngish with skin fresher than a baby. Christ was resurrected looking like a young man (Mark 16:5).

Spiritual Element

gp518» The physical form of those born of God will be perfect. But further since those born of God will have a spiritual essence, they will reap all the benefits of the spiritual dimension. Because of this spiritual dimension, those born of God will be like the angel of the BeComingOne, they will never be faint or weary (Isa 40:28).

Memory of Both the Spirit and the Body

gp519» We are born and die in the physical world. During our life we have a spirit(s) that lives in us. But we do not have full access to his mind, and he does not have full access to our mind. The "other-mind" has some influence over us in this old age, depending on the measure of power given him, and depending on our physical condition. If we have the New Mind he influences us somewhat, depending on the measure of power given to him, and depending on our physical condition. But when we are made one with our own Spirit we will have great influence over him, and he will have great influence over us. This "marriage" of our Spiritual mind to our physical mind will be similar to the intercourse between the left and right sides of our brain; our left and right brains in some ways function differently and independently, but at the same time work together for speech, movement, and behavior. The Spirit we will receive has lived since the beginning of creation and will have memory of a vast period of time, but without any direct memory of physical pain and pleasure.[20] Contrariwise, each of our minds will have the memory of our relatively short live span, but with memory of physical pleasure and pain. When joined both natures will bring together each other's memory. Our future Spirit will have the memory of what we saw, and we will have the memory of what they saw in their life span. If the spiritual world can see our world, then we will be able to see the entire history of the world through the memory of our future Spirit.

Pleasures of Both the Physical and Spiritual Dimensions

gp520» Those born of God will have the "infinite-like" dimension (the spiritual) as well as the finite (the physical). Their bodies will encompass both qualities. They can at the command of their mind change their form into the spiritual essence and travel throughout the earth or universe in an instant if need be. There will be no need for planes, or cars, or any other form of transportation for those born of God. They will enjoy the pleasure of both the physical and spiritual dimensions, as Christ did after he was resurrected and became one with his Spirit. (Gp5 & GP7)

gp521» *In GP 6* we learned how the rest of mankind will follow in Christ the man's footsteps. All of mankind each has their own angel which each will eventually be infused with. As Christ the man Spiritually married his angel, so too will each of mankind Spiritually marry his own angel so that two will become ONE. Since the beginning of creation mankind has been out of God. But through the power of Christ and God all will come back into God so "may be the God, all things in all" (1Cor 15:28).

---

[20] This is reversed in the case of those born during the millennium. See GP7, under "Two-Thirds ..."

GP 7: The Real Reason Why

Law of Knowledge
God has Created Evil? (Isa 45:7)
Why Physical and Spiritual Dimension?
Not New Knowledge
Law of Knowledge Table
More Details on the Law of Knowledge

gp522» Why is there evil in this life? Why are there diseases? Why do children get sick? Why are there natural catastrophes? Why is there war? Why is there death? Why is there hunger? Why is the world the way it is? Why are there male *and* female? Why does God have two becoming one? Why are there good *and* evil? Why has God allowed evil? Why has God split up the creation into the physical and spiritual. Why didn't God just create all his spiritual messengers ("angels") with physical bodies? Why is there a spiritual reality and why is there a physical reality? Why didn't God just make everything complete and perfect at the beginning? Or why has the BeComingOne (YHWH) created evil?:

- "forming light and creating darkness, making peace and creating evil; I, the BeComingOne [YHWH], do all these things" (Isa 45:7, see Hebrew text).

Why evil? If God is all-powerful, why did he allow ("create") the age of confusion, tears, and evil?

To Know Good and Evil?

gp523» "And the LORD said, Behold, the man is become as one *from* us, to know good and evil" (Gen 3:22, see Hebrew; see Greek also). This comment was made right after mankind had broken God's first commandment by the influence of the serpent (see The "Other Mind" paper [NM 20-22] for more details). Thus scripture says that man was getting to know good and evil from the plurality ("us") of God (LORD or YHWH). From the "us" of God man is learning good *and* evil. There was/is a plurality to God as we are manifesting in this book.

gp524» In the middle of the garden of Eden was "the tree of KNOWLEDGE of good and evil" (Gen 2:17). It was a tree of good and evil, not just a tree of good or not just a tree of evil. It was not just an ordinary tree, but a tree of *knowledge*. After mankind took from the forbidden fruit from the tree of knowledge of good and evil, God said man was getting to KNOW good and evil (Gen 3:22). God then took away the tree of life and placed the cherubs to guard the way to the tree of life (Gen 3:23-24). The Hebrew word translated "*from* us" in Genesis 3:22 can also be translated "*out of* us" or even "*of* us" as it is translated in most English Bibles. Because of Adam and Eve's behavior mankind did at this time go "out of" the God, but also, since the God knows all, including good and evil, then mankind was becoming like ONE *of* the God (of the "us" [His hidden plurality]) by learning good and evil. "One" here can be translated "whole" since in history the word one was more likely to mean "whole" or "unity" rather than just the number one (See this book under "One Yehowah"). Consequently, as events manifested, man was mostly left under the influence of the evil spirit of Satan, who was symbolized by the serpent of Genesis (see "Other Mind" paper [NM 20-22]). In the New Testament Paul said we were and are under the influence of the devil/Satan/evil powers and so forth (Eph 6:12).

gp525» We know from earlier chapters that the true God is ALL MIGHTY. Thus, He has the power to stop the evil, if this is what He wishes. But God has allowed this kind of world because He knows man *must* endure in evil in order to be happy. What are we saying?

Why Know Evil

gp526» Man went out of the Garden to know good *and* evil. Why know good *and* evil? Why know evil? Why live evil to know it? The main difference between a man and any other animal is his higher power to reason and know. So far, it is true he has misused this power, but, nevertheless, greater knowledge is what makes man greater than most other creatures of God. But why know evil at all? Why not just know good? Why good <u>and</u> evil? Before we answer this we must know how one knows evil.

Experience Teaches

gp527» In order to know something, to truly know something, you must live it. It takes experience with something to know it. It takes experience with evil to know evil. Our very life today teaches us that. How can you know pain if you had never felt it? How can anyone explain pain to you if you have never felt pain? Just stop and think for a moment. Try to imagine that you have never felt pain. If someone showed you someone else in pain, would you know what it was to be in pain, if you had never *felt* it? As you looked, you would see this person with an expression on his face like he was in pain. But how can you know pain through the face of a person in pain? Remember you have never *felt* pain. Any outward sign of a person in pain is just that, a sign or symbol of pain. Just because you see someone in pain, it doesn't mean you *know* pain for remember you have never *felt* pain, or *experienced* pain. You must *feel* pain to know it.

gp528» The same applies with evil. To truly know evil, one must live it. How would you explain misery to one who never felt or lived misery? How would you explain the pain of losing a loved one to someone who has never felt such a feeling? Now on this latter example, you could compare it with some other form of misery or pain. But, what if the person who you were trying to explain this grief to, had never felt any grief, misery, or pain? You could never compare your grief of losing a loved one with anything that would allow that person to know of your misery. To obtain the knowledge of knowing evil, then, you must *live* it and *feel* it. To obtain the characteristic of knowing evil we must live in such a world as we now live in.

Know Evil To Know Good?

gp529» But this is only a part of the overall picture. We must know evil to know good! Evil and good are inseparable! We must suffer evil to know good. Again, does that shock you? But why should it? Every day you live, you prove the principle that you cannot know good without real knowledge of evil. Every day that you obtain knowledge, you live this principle, and prove this principle. You cannot know good unless you know evil. You cannot separate the knowledge of good and evil. The very Law of Knowledge tells us that. What is that law?

Law of Knowledge

gp530» As mentioned in the first chapter (GP 1), there are three things you must know in order to understand who or what is God. You must know that the God cannot lie. You must know the Law of Contradiction. And you must know the Law of Knowledge. The Law of Knowledge is obvious, almost too obvious. Yet with the cognition of it you will come to understand why God has allowed misery to go on and on.

The Law of Knowledge can be stated:

gp531»

- ***Generally.*** Knowledge of *A* is dependent upon knowledge of *non-A*. Or to know *A* you must also know *non-A*. Or the knowledge of *A* presupposes knowledge of *non-A*. Or you know what is *A* because you know what is *non-A*. In order to "know" *A* you must compare *A* with *non-A*. Correlatively, the knowledge of *A* is proportional to the knowledge of *non-A*; or the more you know about *non-A* the more you understand the uniqueness of *A*; or the extent of your knowledge of *A* is dependent on the extent of your knowledge of *non-A*; or the more you compare *A* with *non-A* the more you know *A* (For greater detail, see notes in GP 7).

gp532»

- ***Opposite qualities.*** Particularly, in the case of opposite qualities (light and darkness, etc.) you must know *both* qualities to know either: you must compare each with the other to know either. Thus, in the case of opposite qualities: to know light ("A") you must compare "light" with non-light (non-"A"); "darkness" (the opposite of light) is included in what is non-light (non-"A"); and it is with the knowledge of "darkness" *and* the knowledge of "light" that we are able to know either "light" or "darkness;" but to *know* light ("A") you must compare light with "darkness" (opposite of "A" or opp-"A") and vice versa — you must know *both* qualities to know either (For greater detail, see notes).

gp533» It follows then that since good and evil are opposite qualities, then to know good you must know evil, but also to know evil, you must know good. But in order to "know" either quality you must *compare* both qualities with each other.

In the rest of this paper we will deal with opposite qualities, but see the Notes for this section to understand the Law of Knowledge in a more detailed way.

Knowledge of Opposite Qualities

Blind: Light <u>and</u> Darkness

gp534» To amplify on this law we will use the example of a blind person. We want you to try to empathize with a person that was totally blind from birth. Try to put yourself in such a person's mind. Close your eyes and imagine yourself as being blind. Now such a person has never seen light. Light is the quality that allows one's eyes to see objects. Without light no one would see even if they had perfect eyes. Light is the quality that the totally blind person cannot perceive or comprehend.

gp535» If you had never seen light, how would someone explain light to you? What choice adjectives would describe light to someone who has never seen light? To explain anything to someone who has never seen it, you have to use comparison, and say it is like this or like that. But there is no comparative quality in the universe that compares with light. It would be impossible for someone to explain light to you, let alone sight, if you had never seen light.

Knowledge of Each Presupposes Knowledge of Both

gp536» Yet at the same time one truly doesn't know what *darkness* is until one has seen light. The very definition of dark is: "without light." Darkness means without light as light means "without darkness." Each definition is dependent on its opposite quality. A definition of something is a statement of the knowledge of that thing. To know light or darkness by their very definition presupposes knowledge of each other. A blind person in order to know what darkness is, would have to see light. He knows darkness only if he sees light, for it is only then that he will understand what people were talking about when they spoke of darkness. The only reason that you can close your eyes, and call the result darkness, is because you have *seen* light. One cannot know darkness or light unless one has seen both and compared both qualities with each other.

gp537» Thus, specifically in the case of opposite qualities, your knowledge of light ("A") is dependent upon your knowledge of darkness (opposite-"A"), and vice versa. Because they are opposite qualities, you must know both to know either quality, but in order to know either quality, you must compare each with the other.

gp538» Furthermore, remembering that a blind person is blind because he cannot see light, it also follows that if there was only white light we would also be blind because we would not see or recognize any object, since in order to see anything, we need different shades of light and darkness, or more correctly since most of us see in color, in order to see anything, we need different shades of light and darkness and different hues of color.

Sound and Silence

gp539» The same applies for sound and silence. If you had never heard sound, how would you know what silence was like? Silence and sound are opposite qualities as light and darkness are opposite qualities. You must know both to know either, and you must compare each with the other to know either. Since these two qualities are interrelated, one has to know both to know one. The very basic definition of sound ("without silence") and silence ("without sound") need the opposite quality to define it. To know sound or silence by their very basic definition presupposes knowledge of each other.

Hot and Cold, Good and Evil

gp540» The same can be said about hot and cold. "Hot" and "cold" are relative opposite qualities. One knows something is cold only so far as he has something hot to compare it with. You can place your hand into a container of water that is 90 degrees and it will feel warm to you. But if you place your hand into a container that is 110 degrees and keep it there for a while, and then place it again into the container of water of 90 degrees, the 90 degree water will then feel cool while before it felt warm. Your knowledge of hot or cold is obtained through contrast and comparison of both qualities. Knowledge of hot or cold presupposes knowledge of the other quality. The water of 90 degrees can be compared to a town with 50 murders per year, while the water of 110 degrees may be the same town, but with 500 murders per year. When the town had 50 murders a year, you felt it was bad, but when it became 500 murders a year, you could look back at the 50 murders per year as "the good old days." Here is an example of relative evil. An example could also be given about relative good. So there is relativity to good and evil. But to have real knowledge of either (good or evil) you must have knowledge of both, you must compare one with the other because both are *comparative* qualities. You understand good by comparing it to evil; you understand evil by comparing it to good.

Life and Death

gp541» Further, one doesn't know what life is until he has seen death. To have knowledge of life you must have knowledge of death. One is very aware of life only if one has seen or become aware of death. Adam and Eve didn't know death and that is one reason why they chose death in the garden of Eden. Adam had never seen or felt the pain of losing a loved one. All he saw around him was life. This is very difficult for us to perceive today, for around us are the dying and the dead. It is difficult for us to put ourselves into Adam's position.

Right and Left & More Examples

gp542» The right side has no meaning unless there be a left side. You do not know what the meaning of right is until you know about left; you do not know what left is until you know what about right. You need knowledge about both to know either. You do not know something is "high" unless you know there is something "lower." You do not know something is "low" unless you know something is "higher." You do not know a "plus" quality until you know its "minus" quality. You do not know a "minus" quality unless you know its "plus" quality. You do not know light if you do not know darkness. But you can know light if you know darkness. You do not know or realize harmony, if you have never known confusion. Think on what is being said. If you had always lived in an environment where there was no confusion, where there was harmony, would you realize the goodness of that harmonic environment? Would harmony mean anything to you in such a harmonic environment? Can you really *appreciate* harmony if you have never lived in confusion?

gp543» If you had good vision for forty years, and then lost your sight, you would truly know the value of sight, as does a blind person who miraculously gains his sight. But how does someone after he loses his sight, come to *appreciate* the sight he once had?

Appreciation

gp544» What does it mean to appreciate something? Webster's Dictionary says that to appreciate something one must: "recognize it gratefully; estimate its worth; estimate it rightly; be fully aware of it; and notice it with discrimination." Thus, when one comes to appreciate something (especially if it is good), one in fact comes to know that thing. To appreciate something is to know it; to know something is to appreciate it.

gp545» When one loses a loved one, one by the loss of the loved one knows the worth of the loved one. The same with good. One comes to know the worth of good only after he has lived in evil.

gp546» How can we know joy, until we have lived sorrow? How can you really become happy unless you have been sad. How can we know good until we know evil? Opposite qualities need to be compared to each other to know either.

God Has Created Evil? ...

gp547» God (YHWH), through his predestination power, before the world began[21] *created* evil (Isa 45:7) so we can know good, to know good's worth, to appreciate good, and to enjoy good. The reason we must suffer the effects of evil is so we can know, to truly know good. To know what is good we must have something to compare good with. God has given man a time for good and a time for evil (Eccl 3:1-8), so as to know each. Thus in this way mankind comes to realize the value of good and harmony. God has given us joy to balance against adversity, so as to know joy (Eccl 7:14). To be able to know goodness, one must know evil. "For in much wisdom is much grief: and he that increases knowledge increases sorrow" (Eccl 1:18). "Sorrow is better than laughter: for by the sadness of the face the heart is made to be good" (Eccl 7:3). When man sinned they went out of God "to *know* good <u>and</u> evil" (Gen 3:22).

Should We Then Seek Evil?

gp548» Then does this mean we should seek evil? No! Once we come to realize how bad evil is, then evil has served its purpose as the comparative quality to good. But we will not know we live in evil until we see the good. In good is where the happiness lives, not in evil. We in this age are mainly learning evil; we are blind and live in the darkness. There are moments of joy and happiness in this world which allow us to partially perceive just how bad evil is, and at the same time allow us to perceive how precious good is.

Light Brings True Knowledge

gp549» The best and only way to truly perceive good is only with God's Spirit — the New Mind. Through God's Spirit man begins to renew his knowledge and mind to the ways of good (Col 3:10; Rom 12:2). Before man receives God's Spirit, man is like a blind man: he lives in darkness, yet comprehends it not, for the blind do not know light. "And the light shines in the darkness; and the darkness comprehended it not" (John 1:5). Why? Because this world is Spiritually blind, this world or this age cannot perceive their sad state of affairs. This age and most people in it, do not and cannot know how bad this age really is until they receive God's Spirit — the New Mind, which is the Spirit of truth (John 14:17). This age only partially perceives how bad this age is, and this only because there is some joy in this age to compare with the average state of affairs. But those who have received God's Spirit know eversomuch more just how bad this age is (Rev 12:11).

Two Forces

gp550» There are two spiritual forces or extra-physical mental forces in the world today: God's Spirit and the enemy spirit, which we call euphemistically, the other-mind or the Enemy's spirit. God's Spirit is ("A") and the other-mind's spirit is (opposite-"A"). Your knowledge of God's way ("A") is dependent upon your knowledge of the other-mind's way (opposite-"A"); To know the way of God ("A") you must compare it with the way of the Enemy (opposite-"A"). Mankind will only have the knowledge of good and evil after they live under the bondage of the other-mind's rule and under the harmony of God's rule. That is why all, who are eventually born of God,

---

[21] Which was before time, before good, before evil, before law, and before sin

will and **must** live under the other-mind's spiritual law of confusion *and* under God's Spiritual law of harmony.

Sow in Tears, Reap in Joy

gp551» All must suffer evil. So that "they that sow in tears shall reap in joy" (Psa 126:5). The tears come first for man, the joy is the dessert of the creation. We learn unhappiness or the knowledge of sin through the other-mind's way. And it is through this knowledge of sin that we are able to truly know good, for then we have something to compare with God's way and his law of harmony.

Light = Good; Darkness = Evil

It is through God's Spirit and his law in our mind that we see good (the light). And it is because of our former blindness (Spiritually speaking) concerning the good (light) that we are able to comprehend the worth of good. Mankind is like a blind person who has lived in darkness (the other-mind's way) yet really didn't know how bad it was until he gained (or will gain) his sight (through God's Spirit) and was made able to comprehend the light (good), then all became understandable to him.

Time to Love; Time to Hate

gp552» Since the knowledge of God depends upon the knowledge of Satan, then man must have a period under the way of Satan and a period under the way of God in order to understand the goodness and worth of God and His way. "A time to love and a time to hate; a time of war and a time of peace" (Eccl 3:8). "Better is the end of a thing than the beginning thereof" (Eccl 7:8).

Mankind in School

gp553» We are going through a spiritual creation. Mankind is in school. Man is going through a process of discriminating between plus and minus qualities. Mankind is learning to discriminate between good and evil, by living each. Man is living each for it is impossible to teach it through words. How can you know pain through words? How can you teach a blind person what light is by words? No, man must *feel* pain to know pain, and the blind must *see* light to know light. But further, the blind must see light to know darkness, for our very definition of light ("without darkness") and our basic definition of darkness ("without light") projects to us that opposite qualities need each other to *know* either one of the qualities. A totally blind person even though he lives in darkness, doesn't know darkness until he sees light. We only know darkness because we have seen light. To know what is darkness one must have something to compare it with.

- "Except they give a distinction in the sounds, how shall it be known what is piped or harped?" (1 Cor 14:7)

Except that there be a period of time to distinguish between good and evil, how else would mankind learn or understand what is good? We know there is a right only because we know there is a left. We know something is "up" only because we see something below it in position. If everything were of the same height, there would be no "up" or "down."

Harmony Means Nothing without Disharmony

gp554» The same principle, or law of knowledge, holds true for pain and non-pain, or sound and silence, or right and left, or up and down, or big and small, or for that matter clean air and smog. But, what is important for us in this paper is that this principle holds true for good *and* for evil. If you only had lived in an environment of harmony, how would you know it was a good environment? You would have nothing to compare it with. You would be like a person who lived all his life at the top of a hundred story building in a room without any window or way to go downstairs. Even though you have 99 levels below you, you do not know you are at the top, for you do not know there is a down.

Time & Why Did God Do This?

Why did not God just put the knowledge of good and evil in our minds at the beginning and forget the 6000 years of evil?

What is Time?

gp555» The answer to this has to do with the knowledge of *TIME*. "Time" is used in different ways: (1) time is used as if it were *chronology* or *history*, or time is thought of as the passage of sequential events, "the passage of time;" (2) time is used as the *method* of reckoning and measuring events, "time can be reckoned by new moons or seasonal cycles (year) or clocks;" (3) similar to number 2 above, time is used as an *era*, instead of saying the age of communism, one may say the time of communism; (4) time is used as the fourth dimension in mathematical formulas; etc. **When we speak of time, we mean chronology or history; when we speak of <u>before</u> time we mean before history, or before our cosmos.**

Time and Language

gp556» Without time it would be impossible to communicate. Our speech is based on words laid out sequentially in sentences. One word follows another word. Sentences are words one after another spoken in the continuum of time. Words themselves are letters, one letter following another. We could not talk or communicate to each other without time, for all words would blur into one another. We think sequentially. We live in a world of sequential events. In fact we could not know a real contradiction without time, and thus not know anything without time (see GP 1, "Law of Contradiction").

Life, Death and Time

gp557» Without time there could be no life. Death is the opposite to time because it stops the history of each person. Life can only take place in time. We become aware of time because we have historical records which pictures a continuum of events. We become more aware of time because of death which stops time for each individual. Death gives us something to compare time to. Without death we would be less aware of life or time. Death stops time. Life is organized movement within time. It would have been impossible for the God to teach us good and evil without time. We need a period of time with evil in order for us to know the good. See the Chronology Papers for more information on "time."

gp558» Even though we do not enjoy our existence or time in such a world as it is today, we must live in it in order to have *knowledge* of good. If you have never lived sorrow, how would you know what joy is? "Better is the end of a thing than the beginning" (Eccl 7:8). If it is true that mankind will be given immortal life, then this seventy or so years of sorrow on earth will seem little after millions of years of joy. These seventy years seem like a long time, but it is worth it to have the knowledge of good through living in a time period of evil. "Now no discipline for the present seems to be joyous, but grievous: nevertheless afterward it yields peaceable fruit of righteousness unto them which are exercised thereby" (Heb 12:11; see Deut 8:16).

gp559» Mankind has gone out of God to *know* through evil the worth and the fact of good. Man is learning by experience, which is the hard way to learn, but yet the best way to learn. In fact it is the only way that we could have learned.

gp560» Now we know WHY we have the confusion of this age. Today, the true God is not causing the madness of this age. It is Satan, that other-mind, that is now presently in control of this age, and it is the other-mind that is causing the confusion of this age. The BeComingOne in a sense did indeed created evil (Isa 45:7) by predestinating everything good and evil before the cosmos, before good (as we know it), before evil (as we know it), before law (as we know it), before sin (as we know it). And, this is very important, we know that the creation as a whole is not complete until the Spiritual or antitypical "days" are over. There was no way to create the knowledge of good, the knowledge of pleasure, or the knowledge of paradise without a period of time for the creation to learn good and evil and other important knowledge. Only when the entire creation is finished, will God be ONE, and then there will be good in its most perfect sense.

Why Physical and Spiritual Dimensions?

gp561» But why has God created from *two* parts (angel and man) the one New Soul? Why the split creation? Why spiritualkind and physicalkind? Let's look at sex differences for an answer. Why sex? As Romans 1:19-20 and other scripture show, God created the physical world to point to the Spiritual. Adam and Eve were the physical image of the spiritual God (Gen 1:26-27). The sexes come together in complementary ways, both physically and mentally? They fulfill each other. In a relationship a male and female bring a slightly different view point to that relationship. The sexes were meant to complement each other, not only physically, but also mentally. It wasn't good for man to be alone, thus God created a mate fit for him (Gen 2:18). Woman is what man lacks, and man is what woman lacks. Only together are they one (Gen 2:24). They were made for each other. They are complementary to each other. From the example of the sexes we learn why God has split the future one New Soul by first making spirits and mankind as separate entities in the first creation, and later joining them together into the New Soul for the New Creation.

gp562» One needs to live in an incomplete state in order to appreciate a perfect state. For example, if each sex had from birth a continuous state of physical and mental fulfillment, why would contact with the opposite sex be appreciated? Not only would males and females not appreciate that union, but they wouldn't get any pleasure from the union. God has created pleasure between the sexes by making them two. The pleasure is in the coming together mentally and physically. But if all were born unisexual, with the qualities of both sexes in them, a whole dimension of pleasure and good would never have been possible. Because they were apart, the act of being together physically and mentally is good and pleasurable. But if they had always been one, this dimension of pleasure would never have been possible. This same principle also applies to the physical and spiritual beings. Because the spiritual and physical beings were apart, when they are joined their very bodies and very minds will have innate pleasure. This is one reason God has created the spirit half and the physical half apart from each other and later joins them into one.

Another Reason: One-Third / Two Thirds

gp563» There is another reason for the split creation. Remember that one-third of the angels are of Satan, and that two-thirds are of God (Rev 12:4). Now being of God is to be sinless, for those of God do not sin. Sin is behavior that is harmful. Now the Law of Knowledge tells us: one must live good *and* evil to know either good or evil. After man has lived evil he will be "begotten" of his own Godly Spirit or "engaged" to be "married" to his own God-Angel. At that time he begins to know and live the good, while at the same time is able to perceive Spiritually the evil he was living in before. For example, mankind is like a blind man (Spiritually) who has never seen light (the good). But when this blind man (mankind) sees the light (the good), then he knows what darkness was and is. Man sees the light (good) through the medium of God's Spirit which allows man to perceive things Spiritually.

Complementary Knowledge

Man from Satan's Age

gp564» It is one of God's angels who dwells or will live in mankind's mind, and this spirit complements the learned evil in man's mind who lived in the age of Satan. When they are joined in the Spiritual new creation as one (spirit and man), each brings an element to this Spiritual marriage. As a male and female bring elements that the other does not have to their union, so do the Spiritual angels and physical mankind bring different elements to their union. God's angels, who are the antitypical males of the creation, bring the "knowledge" or experience and ways of God to mankind. And mankind, who lived in Satan's age, are the antitypical females of the creation, and they bring the "knowledge" or experience and ways of Satan's influence to God's angels. Thus as one, they complement each other, and this makes it possible for each other to know and appreciate more fully the way of God. As one, they are in God, thus, do not go against the way of happiness any more. But in their minds they have stored in their memory, the way of Satan. Thereby they are able to compare it with their God-life. They have a built-in comparison to always remind them of the other way, thus, giving them appreciation of the ways of love. And since when one appreciates something good, he in essence has pleasure in it, then, because of their time of evil on earth they will be able to live in the New Age with great joy and pleasure. We who have lived and suffered in Satan's age will have great joy in the ways of God because in our memories we will have the way of Satan to always compare to the new great life. Because we have lived the ways of Satan and know its worthlessness, we are able to comprehend and appreciate God's way much more than if we had never lived evil.

"Ought not Christ to have suffered these things"

gp565» Remember if we had never suffered, we could not enjoy harmony and the good. For in order to have joy, one must know sorrow. Man has to suffer as did Christ: "Ought not Christ to have suffered these things, and to enter into his glory" (Luke 24:26). The angel of God, that is, the angel of the BeComingOne, incorporated Christ into his essence so the angel too could know suffering and death, something that the good angel could not know in the sense of the knowledge of someone who has experienced or suffered under the confusion of this evil age. In the book of Revelation God says, "and I became dead, and behold, I am living into the ages of the ages" (Rev 1:18). God, the BeComingOne, through Jesus Christ has actually incorporated physical death into

Himself. In this way, God complemented Himself with Christ the man who suffered by the evil age he lived in. The true God knows all things, but remember, God before Christ never lived evil. Also remember that the true God, the BeComingOne, is only manifested at the total fulfilling of the Spiritual Body of Jesus Christ which is fulfilled in the future; there is a difference in "away" knowledge and the knowledge of experiencing. We can know *about* pain, but to suffer pain is *real* knowledge of it.

Man from God's Age

gp566» But what about the spiritual beings of the Enemy? And what about those born of mankind under God's kingdom? God did say that *all* in heaven and earth would be one in Christ (Eph 1:10). That means the Enemy and his angels will also be in Christ the God. After all we were at one time all the enemies of God, but He reconciled us (Rom 5:10). Is God biased or partial? He asked us to love and forgive our enemies (Luke 6:27-37). He won't forgive His enemies?

gp567» Now those of mankind physically born under Satan's kingdom experience evil because they have lived in evil before they come into God's kingdom. But those physically born under God's kingdom will not experience evil because they never will have lived in evil. How can those born under God's kingdom obtain the experience of evil and thus be able to obtain the knowledge of good? One must simply reverse what we have put forth so far. Those born in God's kingdom will be joined to a former-enemy spirit: good thus complements the evil and allows both to understand good.

gp568» If God is to draw *all* to him, as explained before in these papers, the Power/God must change Satan and his spiritual power of evil to good. But when? After Satan's 1000 year judgment (Rev 20:1-3), then he will be loosed to Spiritual atonement for the short period after the millennium. The period after the millennium is a Great Day of Atonement, or union with God (see "Thousand Years and Beyond" paper [NM 15]).

Young Ones

gp569» So the angels who once belonged to Satan's power will be joined in the Great Day of Atonement to those born after the beginning of God's Government on earth, and those angels will also be joined to the young ones who died in early childhood or possibly through abortion during Satan's age. And after the 1000 year refinement period for Satan's angels, they in totality will be changed from evil to good, and will be begotten or joined to those of mankind born during God's millennium or those young ones who died during Satan's age. In other words, Satan and his angels because of their changed nature will then be at that time God's angels. Thus, after the millennium those of mankind born during the millennium will have a repentant or changed spirit in their minds that will at that time have the qualities of God's Spirit. But there is one exception. Satan's angels lived evil, thus in their spiritual minds they will have the experience of evil. With this experience of evil, Satan's repentant angels will complement mankind born in God's kingdom who didn't known evil. Do you see?

Two-Thirds and One-Third of Mankind

gp570» About two-thirds of mankind will be born under Satan's kingdom, and will have learned evil with Satan's angels or messengers of evil. Then at or before the end of the spiritual creation these two-thirds of mankind will be joined to the two-thirds of God's angels. Another approximately one-third of mankind will not have lived under the evil of Satan's age, for they were born in God's age or kingdom, or they died in Satan's kingdom as young ones with none or very little knowledge of evil. This one-third of mankind will be joined with the repentant angels of Satan, who at that time will have become God's angels. Thus one-third of the total number of angels, who belonged to Satan's way during Satan's age, will be joined to the one-third of the total number of mankind, who knew no or little evil, and will complement each other's former experience in order to form the knowledge of good and evil. Then *all* will become somewhat equal in their knowledge of good and evil. Typically, this equality was foreshadowed by equalizing designs of the Jubilee and other examples (Lev 25:15-16; Ex 16:18; 2Cor 8:14-15). Everyone will be more or less equal in knowledge and ability when the creation is finished, except that each will be unique individuals with individual experiences.

Reincarnation?

gp571» Each person in the present age of confusion has at least one angel or messenger of evil inside their mind feeding negative and confusing thoughts. When a human being dies in this age, their messenger of evil is released and *may* be allowed to enter another person's mind, and in most cases this is an infant who has just been born. Remember that two thirds of mankind live in evil, but only one third of the angels live in evil. Thus, the evil angels on average live in two humans during the first 6000 years. As each person dies, the evil angel may enter another person. As we can see this is a form of reincarnation. But it is the evil spirit that is reincarnated. You and I, that is, our physical bodies, are not reincarnated. It is the evil spirit in us that is reincarnated. The idea of reincarnation comes from the evil spirit that lives in man's mind. He is projecting his own experience to us through his thoughts that he feeds us from time to time. It is through the evil spirits that evil is spread throughout the ages. It is also through this evil that the evil spirits come to know evil. It is this experience with evil which helps to create the real knowledge of good and evil, for evil is the comparative quality that helps to create good.

Mankind From The 1000 Years

gp572» Soon a 1000 year utopia will be created on the earth. Those born in this age will not see nor learn evil. Because they will not know evil, they will not know good, in its truest sense. They will not appreciate the good in the 1000 year age. Real Christians who before their resurrection lived and learned evil in Satan's age, will be amazed how mankind during the 1000 years will not really grasp the greatness of the 1000 years. These Christians will then understand why the God had to create evil through the age and way of Satan.

Not New Knowledge

gp573» The idea that good and evil are inseparable to the knowledge of either in not a new idea. In C.K. Barrett's *The New Testament Background* (1961, Harper Torchbooks, he has a fragment from the Stoic writer Chrysippus (about 280-205 B.C.), we read:

gp574»
- "There can be nothing more inept than the people who suppose that good could have existed without the existence of evil. Good and evil being antithetical, both must needs subsist in opposition, each serving, as it were, by its contrary pressure as a prop to the other. No contrary, in fact can exist, without its correlative contrary. How could there be any meaning in 'justice,' unless there

were such things as wrongs? What *is* justice but the prevention of injustice? What could anyone understand by 'courage,' but the antithesis of cowardice? Or by 'continence,' but for that of self-indulgence? What room for prudence, unless there was imprudence? Why do not such men in their folly go on to ask that there should be such a thing as truth, and not such a thing as falsehood? The same may be said of good and evil, felicity and inconvenience, pleasure and pain. There things are tied, Plato puts it, each to the other, by their heads: if you take away one, you take away the other." [*Chrysippus, Fragment* 1169. On the problem of evil. Barrett, p. 64]

Law of Knowledge	
(Pertaining to Opposite Qualities)	
Both sides complement the other and give meaning to each other; you must know both qualities to know either: you must compare each with the other to know either	
One Side	**Opposite Side**
love	hate
light	darkness
right	left
front	back
up	down
affection	contempt
good	evil
grace	ungracefulness
peace	war
kind	unkind
helpful	troublemaker
forgiving	unforgiving
thankful	unthankful
reconciliatory	revengeful
lawful	lawless
hope	hopeless
truthful	liar
fairness (impartial)	unfairness (partiality)
brave	coward
temperance	overindulgence
honorable	dishonorable

Law of Knowledge	
(Pertaining to Opposite Qualities)	
Both sides complement the other and give meaning to each other; ***you must know both qualities to know either: you must compare each with the other to know either***	
unpretentious	pretentious
elegant	crude
patient	impatient
sympathetic	unsympathetic

More Details on the General Law of Knowledge

Specifically, Knowledge of Non-Opposite Qualities

gp575» In this chapter we mostly talked about so-called opposite qualities such as light and darkness or good and evil. But the Law of Knowledge not only explains knowledge of opposite qualities, but also knowledge of everything capable of being known. The General Law of Knowledge Is:

gp576» Generally. Knowledge of *A* is dependent upon knowledge of *non-A*. Or to know *A* you must also know *non-A*. Or the knowledge of *A* presupposes knowledge of *non-A*. Or you know what is *A* because you know what is *non-A*. In order to "know" *A* you must compare *A* with *non-A*. Correlatively, the knowledge of *A* is proportional to the knowledge of *non-A*; or the more you know about *non-A* the more you understand the uniqueness of *A*; or the extent of your knowledge of *A* is dependent on the extent of your knowledge of *non-A*; or the more you compare *A* with *non-A* the more you know *A*.

Basic Definition of the Law of Knowledge can <u>also</u> be stated as:

Knowledge of A is equal to and dependent on the knowledge of non-A.
   Where **A** can be any particular object, technique or belief;
   n**on-A** is anything but that particular object, technique or belief.
It follows —
   The depth of one's knowledge of **A** (and it truthfulness) is contingent upon the depth of one's knowledge of **non-A**; particularly, in the case of opposite qualities (light and darkness), you must know both qualities to know either; you must compare each with the other to know either.
In other words —
   ▪ To know **A** you must also know something to everything about **non-A**;
   ▪ The knowledge of **A** presupposes at least some knowledge of **non-A**;
   ▪ In order to know **A** you must compare **A** with **non-A**;
   ▪ the knowledge of **A** (and its truthfulness) is proportional to the knowledge of
non-A.

True Knowledge through the law of knowledge:

The continuum from incorrect knowledge —> to absolute true knowledge
   ▪ The less one knows about **non-A**, the less one knows about the truthfulness of **A** and the more likely one's knowledge is incorrect.
   ▪ The more one knows about **non-A**, the more certain one knows the truthfulness of **A**.
   ▪ If one knows all that is **non-A**, one knows absolutely the truthfulness of **A**.
      (An omniscient being would know the full truth; less than omniscient beings would not know the full truth.)

How Children Learn

gp577» One way to understand the Law of Knowledge is to understand how a child learns. Children's simple generalizations reflect lack of differentiation. That is, a child's wrong generalization about *A* (cow) reflects lack of knowledge of the difference between a cow and all that is not a cow (*non-A*) such as other four legged animals.

gp578» A child when he is first learning about four legged animals sometimes may mix up a cow and a horse, or a cow and a deer, or even a cow and a dog. This is because the child does not know what a cow is not. When parents first begin telling their child what a cow is, they point to a cow and say, "that is a cow." The child with the aid of other knowledge in his memory and his senses "sees" this living animal with four legs. Depending on how many other four legged animals are pointed out to him, he may mix the cow up with any or all other four legged animals.

gp579» After a cow is pointed out to him he may call a horse a cow, after all, to the child a horse is a four legged living animal (not a two legged animal or a toy animal or stuffed animal) just like the one pointed out earlier by his parents. But the child is wrong. This four legged animal is a horse, not a cow. The child fails to differentiate between a cow and a horse. How does the parent correct the child? The parent says, "no, it is not a cow, it is a horse." The parent is telling the child what a cow is not. The parent by telling the child what is not a cow is helping the child to learn what is a cow. Normally, after the child learns that a horse is not a cow, he doesn't call a horse a cow again. But the child may call a deer or other four legged animals a cow. When the child does this he is again corrected, "no, it is not a cow, it is a deer." The child has learned something else is not a cow (*A*); he has learned one more of the *non-A's* (all else besides cows). The more the child learns about other four legged animals not being cows, the better he is able to understand what a cow is. A cow is a four legged animal of a certain size (a cow is not a dog because for one thing a cow is bigger than a dog, etc.), but it is not any other four legged animal: it is not a dog, it is not a horse, it is not a deer, it is not an elephant, it is not a bear, etc.

gp580» But further the child from other knowledge knows a living cow is not a mountain, it is not dead (not a dead toy, not a dead stuffed animal, etc.), it is not a rock, it is not the sky, it is not a two legged animal, it is not an ant, it is not a fish, it is not fog, it is not a color, it is not a quality like "good," it is not a plant, it is not water, etc. The child knows more what a cow is, by the more he knows what a cow is not. Thus, the knowledge of a cow (*A*) is dependent on the knowledge of what a cow is not (*non-A*); or the child knows more about what is a cow (*A*), by the more he knows what is a cow is not (*non-A*).

The Color Green

gp581» Let's take another example, the color green. The more we know what the color green is *not* the more we know the uniqueness of the color green. The only way to point green out is to show what green is *not*. Since most of us know what the color green is (because we know what green is not), we will again try to understand how a child learns about the color green.

GREEN a color is "A"

gp582» The knowledge of GREEN (A) is dependent upon the knowledge of all that is not green (non-A).

- First "green" is a subdivision of color. Before a child can learn what the color "green" is, he must know what is color. In order for a child to understand "color" his parents tell him, "that thing is the *color* red, that thing is the *color* blue, that thing is the *color* orange, that thing is the *color* green, that thing is the *color* ...." Along the line of learning "color" the child comes to understand (through comparison) what "color" is *not*: the color blue on a wall is not the wall, it is not the *material* that makes up the wall such as wall board, or wood studs, or nails, etc., but the quality on the wall that we call "color" is the *color* of the wall. A child learns what color is by understanding what color is not. So before a parent can make a child understand what the "color" green is, the child has to understand what "color" is, by understanding what "color" is not.

Now assuming that the child knows what "color" is we will continue:

- We know GREEN by knowing what is *not* green (non-A). Thus the child comes to know GREEN by knowing what is not green.

What the color green is not (non-A)

gp583» **Green Is Not:**

- *More generally green is not*: a tree, a bush, a rock, an animal, a fish, a man, the universe, the sun, the moon, our parents, a car, a road, atoms, space, form or shape, relative position in space, time, a dimension, or any other thing or quality except for a quality we call "color."

- *More specifically green is not*: red, blue, orange, purple, or any other color, but the color we call green.

To summarize, *GREEN* is A; *GREEN* is not non-A. We know *GREEN* (A) because we know what *GREEN* is not (it is not non-A).

Review of GP 7

gp584» In this part we learned the reason evil was created (Isa 45:7) by the God. It was "allowed" because man needs a time of evil in order to have something to compare with the coming utopia that God will soon create. If God just put mankind into the coming utopia without a time of evil, man would not comprehend the worth of the utopia, and thus, man would not be able to enjoy the utopia. We showed in GP 7 that the very Law of Knowledge tells us man must have a period of evil in order to understand and enjoy the good. In order to know the good, we must know evil because good and evil are opposite qualities that need to be compared against each other in order to know either. Also in this part we learned the reason God created the creation in two: the spiritual part and the physical part. It was done this way basically so that both the spiritual dimension and the physical dimension can comprehend the knowledge of good and evil and thus be able to enjoy the coming utopia.

General Review

gp585» In GP 1 we started our search: who or what is God? From the Bible we learned about the apparent paradoxes of God: "I make peace, and create evil: I the Lord do all these things" (Isa 45:7). God who is Love (1John 4:8) has somehow and for some reason created evil; He has even killed (Deut 32:39). But how can God be Love and also a killer?

We next learned that there are two basic laws and one basic fact we must understand in order to rightly perceive the true nature of God: the Law of Contradiction and the Law of Knowledge plus the fact that the God cannot lie.

We then went on and explained the Law of Contradiction.

We further showed the many attributes and titles of God and put forth that "time" is very important in our understanding of the paradoxes of God.

We also showed you the very Name of the true God: YHWH, or Jehovah, or Yehowah, or He (who) will-be, or the BeComingOne, or the One who was, who is, and who is coming. God's Name and its meaning is the real secret in revealing the answer to the Paradoxes of God. God's Name is an *imperfect* (incomplete) verb and not as would be expected a *perfect* (complete) verb or a noun. Names are very important in the Bible and many times describe some facet of a person. The true Name of the true God is important for it is the secret in explaining the apparently unexplainable scriptures about God.

In GP 1 we also looked into the meaning of "with God all things are possible," the "*one* Yehowah," the so-called unchangeableness of God, and other matters concerning the God. What GP 1 does is set the stage in our search for who or what is God.

In GP 2 we learned that Jesus Christ's Father was the BeComingOne (YHWH) of the Old Testament: He was the Jews' God.

In GP 3 we learned that the angel of the BeComingOne and the BeComingOne of the Old Testament were closely connected. Since angels are messengers, this means the angel of the BeComingOne is a messenger of the BeComingOne or this angel is the Word of the BeComingOne. Therefore, the words that the angel of the BeComingOne spoke belonged to the Great BeComingOne Power — the true God. This angel stood in the Name of the true God (Exo 23:20-21); he represented the great Name. This angel was in a sense the very Word of God. The Word (logos) of God before Christ's resurrection was a spirit, the chief-spirit, the chief-angel, the angel of the BeComingOne. The age before Jesus Christ was subjected to angels, even the commandments given on Mount Sinai were from an angel (Acts 7:38).

We have shown ***in GP 4*** that *before* Jesus Christ was resurrected, he was a human being because he was born from a woman. Thus, Christ before his death and resurrection was a man; he was Jesus Christ the man. He was called Son of man because he was born of mankind through the means of Mary his mother. Jesus the man was not just any human being. Christ was a Son of God, both physically (through the Holy Spirit's union with Mary) and Spiritually (through the medium of God's Spirit inside of him). Christ was a mediator between man and God; he was the Son of God and the Son of man. He is the "one *mediator* between God and men" (1Tim 2:5). Jesus Christ the man actually had the Spirit or Angel of the BeComingOne (YHWH) inside him leading him in the right way. It was because of this Spirit that Christ the man was sinless. God was not Jesus Christ the man, but God (through the power of His Spirit) was inside of Christ the man. When Jesus Christ the man died, his Spirit was then separated from him (Luke 23:46). The Spirit or angel of God did not die *as* Christ the man or *with* Christ the man, for Spirit cannot die. The angel of the BeComingOne separated himself from Christ the man when Christ died.

To say it in slightly a different way, in GP 4 we have shown that Jesus Christ before he was resurrected was a man with the Spirit or angel of the BeComingOne inside him leading him in the way of love. Jesus Christ the man was born from woman and by a miracle of God. Thus, Christ the man was from mankind (through Mary) and from God because of the miraculous conception by the power of God. Jesus Christ the man was a son of man, and a son of the God. He is the "one *mediator* between God and men" (1 Tim 2:5). Christ the man wasn't God, but God's WORD and power were inside of him. The angel of the BeComingOne was inside Jesus Christ the man. When Christ died the angel of the BeComingOne separated from Christ the man's body. Thus, Christ the man died, but his angel inside of him stayed alive, for the angel (spirit) separated himself from Christ the man when Christ died (Luke 23:46).

In GP 5, we have seen that after Jesus Christ the man's death and his burial for three days, he was resurrected and became ONE with the Spirit or Angel of the BeComingOne: **two became one**. The Spiritual marriage of mankind back to God *began* when Jesus Christ the man went into the BeComingOne, the God. Since the beginning of creation when all went *out of* God, God and man were separate. But through Jesus Christ the man, mankind is beginning to go back into God, or into the BeComingOne (YHWH). Through the angel with the NAME, the BeComingOne incorporated Jesus Christ the man into Himself: the Spiritual WORD became flesh. The two, the man Jesus Christ and the Angel of the BeComingOne ("LORD"), as ONE are called: Jesus Christ, God, or in another sense he is/will be Jesus Christ the BeComingOne. Jesus Christ the man has become Jesus Christ *the* God, in one sense, because ALL will eventually go into the Spiritual Body of Jesus Christ by the End (see GP 6). But as of now we do not see ALL in Jesus Christ the God (see Heb 2:8). In two senses Jesus Christ is "the beginning of the creation of the [true] God" (Rev 3:14): the Spirit of Jesus was the First, the beginning of the "old" creation of God; but Jesus Christ the man and his Spirit as ONE is the beginning of the "New" creation.

In GP 6 we learned how the rest of mankind will follow in Christ the man's footsteps. All of mankind each has their own angel which each will eventually be infused with. As Christ the man Spiritually married his angel, so too will each of mankind Spiritually marry his own angel so that two will become ONE. Since the beginning of creation mankind has been out of God. But through the power of Christ and God all will come back into God so "may be the God, all things in all" (1Cor 15:28).

In GP 7 we learned the reason why God created evil (Isa 45:7) in this age. We saw that in order to understand the good and to enjoy the coming utopia, mankind and angelkind must have a time of evil. Good and evil are opposite qualities that need to be compared against each other in order to understand either. A person who grew up with all the good things that the earth has to offer doesn't know the worth of these things until he actually loses them. After he loses the good things he then begins to understand the worth of the good things. If God just automatically at first put the creation into an everlasting utopia, the creation itself would not have the understanding of the worth or value of the utopia. In fact as we learned in GP 7 mankind would not have any understanding of good, if they never had learned evil. But by God putting the creation through an evil period God is actually teaching the creation the value of good and the evil of evil. The creation now is actually learning about good and evil. It is through the evil spirits in the minds of mankind that evil is spread on earth. It will be through the good spirits that mankind will live in good.

GP 8: Right & Left Hand of God

Jesus Christ on Right Side of God
Jesus Christ is the BeComingOne
Cherubs
God's Left Side?
Who is Left Side of God?
Image of God
Christ Fulfills the Image
Cherubs Protecting the Garden
God of the New Testament
Scriptures on Satan
Table on Right & Left Side

gp586» "But he, being full of the Holy Spirit, looked up steadfastly into heaven, and saw the glory of God, and Jesus standing on the right hand of God" (Acts 7:55, KJV) or **"right hand of the power of God"** (Luke 22:69; Mat 26:64; Mark 14:62; see Psa 110:1; Heb 1:3). If Christ the man became God, then why does the Bible say he is on or at the right side or *right hand* of the power of God. Surely this means there is a God besides Christ, and Christ is on his right side? (Remember we are speaking of the resurrected Christ who went into the Father. See GP5.) What does it mean to be on the right side of God? To these questions we'll add: What is the mercy seat, with those two cherubs on each side, one on the left, and one on the right? The angel of the BeComingOne (YHWH) usually appeared between these two cherubs (Exo 25:22; Lev 16:2).

Paul and the Cherubs

gp587» What did Paul have to say about the mercy seat and the cherubs?

- "And over it the cherubs of glory overshadowing the mercy seat; of which we cannot speak particularly" (Heb 9:5).

Paul could not speak particularly on that subject at that time. Does this mean he did not know the symbolic meaning of it? This is a possibility, yet, also, he may have had doctrine on it, but God did not see fit for it to be placed in the Bible. Thus, no one really knows the symbolic meaning of the cherubim and mercy seat?

Knowledge Not to Stay Hidden

gp588» But,

- "fear them not therefore: for there is nothing covered, that shall not be revealed; and hid, that shall not be known. What I tell you in darkness, that speak you in light: and what you hear in the ear, preach you upon the house tops" (Matt 10:26-27).

- "For there is nothing hid, which shall not be manifested; neither was any thing kept secret, but that it should come abroad. If any man have [Spiritual] ears to hear, let him hear" (Mark 4:22-23).

- "Behold, the former things are come to pass, and new things do I declare: before they spring forth I tell you of them [through his Spiritual power, 1Cor 2:10]" (Isa 42:9).

- "Surely the BeComingOne will do *nothing* ["no word"], unless he reveals his secret unto his servants the prophets" (Amos 3:7).
- "But you, O Daniel, shut up the words, and seal the book, even to the time of the end: many shall run to and fro, and *knowledge shall be increased*" (Dan 12:4).

Knowledge *shall* be increased, not reiteration of old knowledge.

Christ on the Right Side of The God

gp589» Jesus Christ being on the right hand side of the power of the God has something to do with the mercy seat and cherubs. Let's correct something first before we go on. In the Greek text of the Bible, it doesn't say "on" or "by" or "at" the right hand of the God as translated in the King James Version. It says in Greek:

- "*Out of*" (Acts 7:55, 56; 2:25, 34; Heb 1:13; Matt 26:64; Mark 14:62);
- "*In*" (1 Pet 3:22; Col 3:1; Heb 1:3; Rom 8:34);
- "*To the*" (Acts 5:31) right hand of the God

The majority of these scriptures say that Christ is now out of, or in, or to the right hand of *the* God (see Greek text). Furthermore the "right hand" can be correctly translated "right side." "This one [Christ], Prince and Savior, the God exalted to the right side of Him" (Acts 5:31). Jesus Christ was made the right side of *the* of the power of the God, and as the right side, Christ is God, but not all *the* God in His truest sense. Christ was given all the power of the *right* side of the God, but not all the power has been taken (from the left side) by Jesus Christ yet (Heb 2:8). At the End is when all power is taken by the God so at that time all will be in the God, God all in all (1Cor 15:24-28).

First and Last

gp590» The NAME of God (YHWH) was explained in GP 1, and it means the *BeComingOne*, or *He-(who)-will-be*.

- I the BeComingOne, the **first**, and with the **last ones**; I *am* he (Isa 41:4; 44:6; 48:12; see Hebrew text).

What does this mean? The BeComingOne is the first and with the last ones?

First

gp591» The great God, the great He-will-be ONE (YHWH), is now somehow not yet complete:

- "I the BeComingOne, the first" (Isa 41:4).
- "Before me there was no God [*el*] *formed*, neither shall there be after me" (Isa 43:10).

Not only does the God say in Isaiah 43:10 that no God was formed before him, but "neither shall there be *after* me," or "neither shall there be formed a God after me." Remember that Christ now has the very NAME, and he is the only God (1Tim 1:17), because he is the only one now truly in the God or the only one born of God (John 1:18; some Greek texts). Jesus the man became God when the first-angel of the BeComingOne (who had the NAME) and Jesus Christ the man became one or were both formed as one (GP 5). He was the first and there will be no other God formed after him. Not only is the BeComingOne the first, but he is the last, "I am the first, and I am the last" (Isa 44:6). Or as the Hebrew reads, "I the BeComingOne [YHWH] the first and with the last ones" (Isa 41:4).

First or Beginning of the Creation of the God

gp592» It was the resurrected Jesus Christ who was given through the spiritual marriage the NAME and titles of the BeComingOne (see GP 5). It is through this Christ with the NAME that ALL will be saved, and the Spiritual Body of Christ will be filled so that ALL will be in Christ (see GP 5 and 6). *It is this Christ who was the **first**, the **alpha**, the **beginning**, "the **beginning** of the creation of the God"* (Rev 3:14; see John 6:62, Greek text; Acts 26:23; etc.).

Last and with the Last Ones

gp593» Jesus the man was the *first* one to go back into the God (see GP 5). He is the beginning of the new creation. But not only is he the beginning, but he is the last, the end, and with the last oneS (Rev 1:11, 8; Isa 41:4, remember Christ now has the power and the NAME).

Christ is the BeComingOne

All Not Yet Under Him

gp594» But not only is this Christ the first and the last he has been given ALL the power; thus, this Christ is or will be the Almighty (Jude 1:25; Rev 1:8; 19:6; John 3:35; Matt 28:18; 1Pet 3:21-22; Heb 2:8, etc.). This Christ is the first, the last, the almighty, and He is: "Lord God Almighty, *which was, and is, and is to come*" (Rev 4:8; 1:8). In other words, this Christ is the very YHWH; he has the NAME; He is Yehowah; he is the BeComingOne. "*But now we see not yet ALL things under him*" (Heb 2:8) because he is waiting for all his enemies to put under his control (Psa 110:1; GP 6). In the highest sense, the Spiritual sense, the Biblical words are meant in their literal sense except if they are clearly figures of speech (see "Duality of the Bible" [see Intro]). "All" being under him, not only includes all that is good, but all that is evil. All will be saved; all will be in the NAME (see "All Saved," "Does All Mean All," and "All Into Christ" papers; Jer 3:17) through the two coming resurrections to life.

Not Yet Complete

gp595» We know that the two resurrections when mankind will be born of God have not happened yet. We also know that this Christ has "the fullness of the Godhead, bodily" (Col 2:9). After these two resurrections, then all will be in the Spiritual Body of Christ. But as of now the fullness is not manifested in this Christ (Heb 2:8). Therefore the God cannot be totally formed yet; He cannot be totally complete yet. For one thing, His NAME indicates He is incomplete: the BeComingOne (see GP 1). Jesus Christ who is now in the God, and in His NAME, cannot be totally complete yet, because after he is totally formed no others will be formed (Isa 43:10). Yet the Bible indicates other offspring of God will be formed. ALL will go into the true God. Thus in order for other offspring of the God to be formed, Christ God must be "formed" *again*. The individual and the Spiritual Body of Christ are not a finished creation; he is not the completed God: He is Becoming. Between now and Christ's total completion other sons and daughters will be born, for God says: "I am the last; apart from me there is no Gods [*elohim*]" (Isa 44:6, see Hebrew text).

Other Offspring in the BeComingOne

gp596» We know there will be formed other offspring of the God besides Christ (GP 6). We know the Bible calls men "Gods" (John 10:34-35), and that mankind will be born of God (see "Begotten, Born Paper" [NM 5]). Remember scripture cannot be broken (John 10:35). Thus, mankind will become sons or daughters of God (in a sense a part of the God's family, nation, or Name):

- Mankind will go into in the NAME of the God.(Jer 3:17; 4:2; GP1, under "Great Significance of the Name")

gp597» As scripture shows *all* the offspring of the God now in the process of being created, are being created by and through the Godhead, Christ the God (Col 1:16-20). Thus none will be created *apart from* God as Isaiah 44:6 manifests. "Before me there was no God formed [he was the first], neither shall there be after me [he will be the last formed]" (Isa 43:10). It is between God's first formation and God's last formation that the rest of the offspring of the God will be created.

Christ the Individual and the Spiritual Body of Christ

gp598» Yet this should be qualified. The BeComingOne, Christ the individual, will be the last formed, but he will not be lastly formed *alone*. "I the BeComingOne, the first, and *with the last ones*; I am he" (Isa 41:4). At the moment of the creation of the totally NEW heaven and earth billions of mankind and angelkind will be fused into the Godkind (GP 6), and at that moment the BeComingOne (Christ) also will be lastly formed with the last ones of creation. Thus all formed at that time are the last ones formed. But there is more to Christ than the individual Christ. Paul's letters in the Bible spoke of the Body of Christ, and we are members of his Body (1Cor 12:12 ff). Christ, the individual and Christ's Spiritual body, will in some way be the last formed "Gods."

Many in ONE Body

gp599» Remember, from GP 1, that God's true NAME is YHWH, the BeComingOne. This NAME was used interchangeably with *elohim* or Gods. The God's NAME is *BeComingOne of Gods*, or *BeComing Gods* or *He (who) will be Gods*. There can be and is plurality in the ONE true God (see GP 1). There can be and are more than a single individual in the BeComingOne. **A definition of the BeComingOne: "The BeComingOne [YHWH] you yourself the Gods"** (2Sam 7:28, Hebrew text). Remember here that Christ's Body has many members (1Cor 12:12). Remember he called them Gods and scripture cannot be broken (John 10:34-35; Psa 82:6). Jesus our God told us this, not the preacher down the road. This was said to the congregation or church of the God (Psa 82:1). Also remember that the church of God is the Body of Christ, which will fill all (Eph 1:22-23).

Besides those of the second resurrection what aspect is missing from Christ, the individual and the Spiritual Body of Christ, that will be in the completed God when God is all in all?

Cherubs

In The Tabernacle

gp600» Now the mercy seat and the cherubs are in the tabernacle (Heb 9:1-5). Behind the first veil was the candlesticks, etc (Heb 9:2). The room behind the first veil as a whole is called the sanctuary or holy place. All the things in the sanctuary have to do with those in the Church of God who lived in the age of Satan and received the new

Spirit in the age of Satan. For example, the candlestick in the sanctuary is symbolic of the Church itself (Rev 1:20), and the altar of incense is symbolic of Christian's prayer (Rev 8:3-4).

Most Holies

gp601» But behind the second veil is the room called the holy of holies, or the most holy place (Heb 9:3). And it was in this room where the mercy seat and cherubs sat. What was this room symbolic of? The things of the sanctuary or holy place had to do with the Church, that is, those in the Church who receive the Spirit before the end of Satan's age (NM16). But what about the most holy place? The "holy of holies" means that this place was set apart much more than the sanctuary or holy place. In other words, the "holy of holies" was more holy or set apart than the holy place or what the holy place represented. When Christ died the veil that separated the holy of holies was ripped in half signifying that it was time for man to enter the most holy place (Matt 27:51; Heb 6:19; 9:3; 10:20). But what was the "holy of holies" or "most holy place" symbolic of?

Sanctuary a Type of the Real

gp602» Scripture shows us that the tabernacle is a *type* or pattern of God's plan (cf Heb 8:5; 10:1; 9:22-24; Rom 1:20; NM16). "For Christ did not enter a man-made sanctuary that was only a copy of the true one; he entered heaven itself" (Heb 9:24, NIV). Christ didn't go into a physical sanctuary or holy place, he went into heaven or the Spiritual essence itself. Now up to this verse in Hebrews chapter 9, it had been talking about Christ's sacrifice of himself for the sins of mankind, and how this was a much better sacrifice than the sacrifice of animals as physical Israel used to do.

High Priest a Type of the Real

gp603» Physical Israel used to have a high priest who offered once a year: "the high priest entered into the holy place [most holies — cf. Lev 16:2, 29; Heb 9:7] every year with blood of others" (Heb 9:25). But unlike these high priests of Israel, Christ has offered himself *once* for the sins of all mankind (Heb 9:26, 15; 1Tim 2:6). Christ is the antitypical high priest (Heb 3:1; 7:21; 10:21). Christ is the heavenly high priest. After his sacrifice he entered into heaven or the Spiritual dimension, for any time "heaven" is used we know that it is speaking of the Spiritual dimension (compare the usage of "heaven" in Isaiah 55:8-9; 1Cor 15:44-49; Phil 3:18-19; Col 3:1-2). Christ the man after his physical sacrifice entered himself into the Spiritual, he became God as explained previously. **The most holy place or holy of holies is symbolic of Jesus Christ the BeComingOne.** Going into the most holy place is symbolic of Him being *born* of God (see "Begotten, Born Paper" [NM 5]).

Christ: Right Cherub

gp604» Christ fulfilled the prophecy of Psalms 110:1:

- "The BeComingOne said unto my Lord (Jesus), You site at my right hand..."

- "This one, after he had offered one sacrifice for sins into the perpetuity, sat down in the **right** side of the God" (Heb 10:12).

Christ went into the antitypical most holy place and sat down in the right hand side of God. Now the typical most holy place had two cherubs in it, and *between* these cherubs in the old days the BeComingOne used to appear (Ex 25:22; Lev 16:2). But it was the *angel* of the BeComingOne who appeared on the mercy seat in a cloud between the two cherubs with one cherub on his right, and one cherub on his left (Exo 25:22; Lev 16:2; the angel went with Israel in the OT: Exo 23:20ff; Acts 7:30, 38; Heb 2:2, 5; see GP 3).

- "The angel the one speaking to him [Moses] in the Mount Sinai" (Acts 7:38, Greek text).

This angel was the one that spoke to Moses in the bush and with the fathers of Israel, and this angel is the one who gave the commandments to Moses in Mount Sinai (Acts 7:30,35,38). This angel is the angel with God's Name in him (Ex 23:20-21). This angel represented the God who is becoming, for he was the angel who spoke between the cherubs, and the cherubs represent the BeComingOne (2Kings 19:15; Psa 80:1). As quoted previously Christ is *out of* and *in* the right side of God. Or as other scriptures show, Christ is *the* right side of the power of the God. Thus, when Christ went into the Most Holies He sat down in the place of the cherub on the *right* side of the BeComingOne, the true God. The Spirit of Christ is now the real right cherub, that is, he is the right side (hand) of the power of the God. He is the (Right) arm of God (Ex 6:6; Deut 9:29; Psa 44:3; 77:15; 98:1; Isa 40:10; 51:9-10). He is the right side waiting for all to come under his becoming one power (Psa 110:1).

Two Cherubs: One with Mercy Seat

gp605» Notice how the two cherubs were constructed at first,

- "One cherub on the one end, and one cherub on the other end; *of one piece* with the mercy seat he made the cherubs on its two ends" (Ex 37:8, RSV).

The two cherubs were of one piece with the mercy seat. Hence, the two cherubs and the mercy seat were of one piece physically. As God's festivals, described in the Old Testament, are foreshadows of what is to come (Col 2:16-17), so too are the two cherubs. These two cherubs represent different qualities of the finished God. We have just seen how Christ is in the place of the right cherub. Now we see that *physically* the two cherubs and the mercy seat were of *one* piece. Thus, since we know the Bible is type and antitype, whatever the physical or typical is like, is what the Spiritual or antitypical *will be* like. Whatever the cherubs and mercy seat represent Spiritually, eventually we know they will be of one.

Christ The Man: Mercy Seat

gp606» Notice that Jesus the man, the one who died, is the mercy seat, "the redemption that is in *Christ Jesus. Who God has set forth to be a mercy seat* through faith in his blood" (Rom 3:24, 25). [The word translated into "mercy seat" in Hebrews 9:5 is the same Greek word translated in the King James Version as "propitiation" in Romans 3:25.] So of the symbolic items in the holy of holies, Christ now fulfills the mercy seat *and* the right cherub.

Cherubs Face Each Other

gp607» Notice further that the faces of the cherubs are toward each other and both are facing toward the middle of the mercy seat (Ex 37:9). It was between these cherubs on the mercy seat that the angel of the BeComingOne appeared (Ex 25:22; Lev 16:2). The angel of the BeComingOne represented the goal of creation, the completed God. He had God's NAME in him (Exo 23:21). The two cherubs thus faced toward the goal, the BeComingOne. But since the *angel* of the BeComingOne was not the true complete God, but a Spiritual messenger for Him, then actually the *angel* prefigured the true God — The BeComingOne who will become.

Left Side of God?

gp608» Christ after his resurrection became one with the right cherub. Christ the man is also the true mercy seat as we just showed you. He is the one who covers all sin. Thus the only part that remains to be incorporated into the Godhead is the left cherub. So far the God is only completed in the sense that Christ, the individual, has the new body, both the physical and the Spiritual essence (typical sense of Col 2:9). But the Spiritual Body of Christ will incorporate those of the next two resurrections so that "in him [Christ] dwells all the fullness of the Godhead, Bodily" (Col 2:9; see Eph 1:22-23, 10; Col 1:19; see "All Saved" paper [NM 13]; etc.).

Left Cherub?

gp609» What about the left side of God? What about the left cherub? Who is it, or what is it? There are only two cherubs, one on the right, and one on the left of the mercy seat. If we can ascertain what is the left side of God, then we will know the secret of the cherubs and how God will be completed.

Three Things to Understand

gp610» We must understand three things:

- **(1) God is the BeComingOne:** From GP 6 we learn that the true God will bring ALL back into Himself through Christ, so that "God will be ALL in ALL." In other words, God is the BeComingOne (Elijah = "God is the BeComingOne").

- **(2) Law of Contradiction:** Remember, from GP 1, that the true God not only is good, but He somehow kills and He somehow destroys. But we know from the Law of Contradiction that for the God to be love, to be good, He cannot *at the same time* when He is good also be evil or kill or destroy. A Christian can be "good" now, but in past could have done evil or even killed. We can in the English language call this Christian a killer, for in the past he has killed. A person in prison who has killed is called a "killer" even though he may never kill again, for he may have repented of his past behavior.

- **(3) Law of Knowledge:** And remember from GP 7 that because of the very Law of Knowledge, those who know good must also know evil. From the first chapter we know that the God knows *all* things. In order for the true God to know ALL things (that includes evil), then the God Himself must know evil. GP 7 clearly slows that one can only know evil by knowing good AND evil. The only way to learn good or evil is to live in both.

Missing Part of the God are the Last Ones

gp611» In order for the true God (YHWH), who is good, to be somehow a killer (Deut 32:39), He must somehow incorporate such evil into Himself before the End of Creation. Since we know that the "all" that will go into the Spiritual Body of Christ, means all (see "Does All Mean All" paper [NM 14]), then this "all" *must* include those who have been evil. The missing parts of the completed God — the true God, YHWH — are the evil ones. Not only is YHWH the first He is also "with the last ones" (Isa 41:4). The "last ones" can mean either the last ones in time or the last ones in position. To the good God sinners are definitely the last in position or rank, and most who have sinned will be completed last in time. They are the third unit and last in time to go into the God (see "All Saved" paper [NM 13]). The missing part of the God is the evil ones, or last ones, going into the God.

Hence, the *left* side of God, when incorporated into the God will be <u>repentant</u> "sin"[22] infused into the God. Notice that "death" in one sense has already been incorporated into God. "I am He who lives, and *I became dead*; and, behold, I am alive into the ages of ages" (Rev 1:18, Greek text). Christ the man, who physically died was physically resurrected, was then incorporated into the God (Parts 4 & 5). In this sense death and the knowledge of death came into God because Christ the man went into the God.

One Side Good; One Side Evil

Right and Left Side

gp612» Notice that the right side in the Bible is the good side (Matt 25:32-34, 41; Isa 41:10; 48:13; 62:8; Psa 78:54; 80:15; 89:13; 91:7; 98:1; etc.). Christ as the right side of God, is the right side of the totally completed God; he is the good side of God. Christ has not sinned. The left side then must be the evil side. Scripture projects that spiritually speaking the left side is the evil side (Matt 25:32-34, 41).

Who is the Left Side of The God?

Left Cherub

gp613» Who or what is the left side of the God or the left cherub? "You art the *anointed cherub* that covers" (Ezek 28:14). This *cherub* was the antitype of the King of Tyrus (Exek 28:12), who was in the garden of eden (v. 13), but who became corrupt and puffed-up (Ezek 28:17), and because of this will be sent down to a fire destruction (Ezek 28:18). This describes an evil cherub, not a good one. Since there are only two cherubs in the most holy place, and Christ now fulfills the good right cherub, and because the right side is good in Biblical symbolism, then this cherub described in Ezekiel 28:14 is the left cherub, and is the evil side. If one reads all the 28th chapter of Ezekiel in its higher sense, he knows the cherub described here is Satan (see "Other Mind" paper [NM 21]). God has an evil side since God created evil by predestinating evil (Isa 45:7; see GP 1). Thus, *Satan is the left cherub or the left side of God*, for everything in the most holy place foreshadowed the true God, the BeComingOne. The two cherubs are in the place called the most holy place, thus the two cherubs somehow represent the BeComingOne, the Will-be-One, the Most Holy. In fact the Bible says that the BeComingOne dwells [as] <u>the</u> cherubs (2Kings 19:15 & 1Ki 18:39 [Heb.]), not "sits on the" cherubs (cf. phrase usage in 1Ki 1:48; 3:6; 8:25). But also in the Old Testament the BeComingOne also spoke to Moses *between* the two cherubs in a cloud (Ex 25:22; Num 7:89; Lev 16:2). The one who spoke to Moses was an angel (GP3), so this angel was an angel or messenger of the BeComingOne; he spoke for the future One who would fulfill both cherubs and the mercy seat.

---

[22] Past "sin," not one still sinning

Right and left Side Join to Create Knowledge

Right and Left Hemispheres of the Brain

gp614» The greatest evil (left side) will be fused with the greatest good (right side) so that "the God all things in all" (1Cor 15:28). In such an infusion of two qualities, the good and evil will contrast each other, and thereby make it possible for all to know good and evil. Genesis 3:22 can also be translated from the Hebrew:

- "the man has become like ONE of us, to know good and evil."

The BeComingOne here speaks of the *one* of *us*. And it is the *one* or *unity* of the BeComingOne who is the "us" that will bring the knowledge of good and evil. The right and left side of God are similar to the right and left hemispheres of the brain. Both sides process information in different ways, but both together create our thoughts and knowledge.

Mercy Seat and Cherubs Prefigured God

gp615» The mercy seat and the cherubs prefigured the coming true God. They were of *one* piece, thus pointed, in its higher meaning, to the *oneness* of the Right *and* Left side of the God. It is the *oneness* of the Right and Left side of the God that will produce the knowledge of good and evil. Further when the former Enemy is infused into the Godhead, then the two antitypical cherubs and the mercy seat will be one piece like the physical cherubs and mercy seat. The angel of the BeComingOne was represented by the right cherub; Christ the man, the Lamb of God, was represented by the mercy seat; and the former Enemy was/is represented by the left cherub. The angel of the BeComingOne and Christ the man have become one (GP5). But repentant evil, the left side of the God, has yet to somehow be joined to God (see Heb 2:8).

Image of God

Male & Female are One

gp616» From GP 5 we see that from the very beginning of creation God considered male and female as man ("Adam") and as one. God used the name "man" to include both male and female. In many languages today, "man" has a dual meaning of not only meaning male, but also mankind, which includes both sexes. The very act of sexual intercourse and marriage has the meaning of signifying two (male and female) becoming one (Gen 2:24; Mark 10:6-8). Male and female are two, yet in God's eyes they are one, they are "man" or "Adam."

Two in One

gp617» From GP 5 we see that man is in the image of God, and that "man" consists of *both* male and female. Thus, the very image of God must in some way consist of two in one. There are and were more than one entity in the God. That is why the Bible says in the Hebrew text:

- "In the beginning *GodS* created the Heavens and the Earth" (Gen 1:1). "And *Gods* said, Let *us* make man in *our* image, after *our* likeness" (Gen 1:26). "So *Gods* created man in his image, in the image of *Gods*" (Gen 1:27). [*Gods = elohim*] Also note the "creators" of Eccl 12:1, the "makers" of Psa 149:2, the "us" of Gen 3:22, and the "us" of Gen 11:7, the "themselves" of the Hebrew of Gen 35:7 : "for there *the* Gods [elohim] revealed themselves."

Two Opposite yet Complementary Qualities

gp618» Adam is the name of man. From the beginning Adam was two physical sexual opposites, male and female, who became one through intercourse and consequently had a child with half the qualities (genes) of each of his parents. BeComingOne is the NAME of the true God. From the beginning the BeComingOne was two opposite spirits, one good and one evil (see GP 7, 8, 9), who through interaction and the Power of the God will become ONE after the 7000 years so that the knowledge of good and evil will be in totality (Gen 3:22). The evil god rules now, but the good God will rule over evil in the New Age and beyond – the fruit of knowing good and evil will create happiness for all. (Study GP7) See Happiness and Knowledge.

From an Imperfect One

gp619» Since the very beginning, when Satan manifested himself as evil, the true God and the other god (Satan) were not one in the truest sense, much like the male and female were never one in the truest sense:

- Male and female were one in a *typical* sense, through physical intercourse. In another sense male and female become one — they have a child with the combined elements or traits of each other. Both male and female complement each other: you cannot have one or the other without each other (1Cor 11:11-12).

- The right and left side of God were one also in a *typical* sense, because both sides were/are/will be the BeComingOne. They were one in the typical sense in that they spiritually "worked" together in creating the knowledge of good and evil and even the universe (Gen 1:1, Hebrew Text). Both good and evil complement each other: you cannot have one or the other without each other (GP 7).

Male and female as two were in the *physical* image of the right and left sides of the God. Since the beginning until now, the right and left side of God were not one in the truest sense, and neither were the male and female one in the truest sense. Both man's oneness and God's oneness pointed towards the oneness of the physical perfect harmony in the Spiritual Body of Jesus Christ.

Christ Fulfills Image of God

Different Senses to the Fulfillment

gp620» When God appeared in the Old Testament times, he always appeared in visions or dreams as an angel. But when God shall appear again he will be in the form of Christ's body, for Christ fulfills the image of God, bodily (Col 1:15; 2:9; 2 Cor 4:4; Heb 1:3). There are different senses to this fulfillment:

- Physically now Jesus is in the image of God (GP 5), but Christ the individual will also fulfill all aspects of the image of God by fulfilling both cherubs and the mercy seat: He becomes the cherubs and the mercy seat.

- Jesus Christ's Spiritual Body which is the Church fulfills the image of God *when* the Church is totally fulfilled: when *all* go into the God.

Fulfilled within Three Days

gp621» When he walked on earth before his death Jesus in a sense fulfilled the image in the holy of holies because the physical Jesus was the Mercy Seat, the Spirit of God in him was the Right Side of God; the spirit of Satan in him (tempted him, Luke 4:2) was the Left Side of God. When Jesus Christ predicted that he would raise from the dead in three days, he was predicting when he would again and perfectly fulfill the Mercy Seat and both sides of God. Notice the time aspect to Jesus' prophecy:

- John 2:19 Jesus answered and said unto them, Destroy this temple, and **in three days I will raise it up**. 20 Then said the Jews, Forty and six years was this temple in building, and wilt thou rear it up in three days? 21 But he spake of the temple of his body.

Remember the Power of Christ came from the Spirit of his Father, his Father did the works (GP 4). So it is the Power of the Father that will raise Jesus up in all his aspects in three days. And Remember that there is a type and antitype to scripture. So there are 24 hour physical days and there are three 1000-year spiritual days, since a day to God is like a thousand years (2Pet 3:8; Psa 90:4; see NM).

Fulfillment of the Image of God in Three Orders in Three Days

gp622» Christ is different from all others, he, or his Spiritual Body, fulfills all things (Eph 1:23; 1Cor 15:28):

- **Christ the Individual – First Order of two becoming one:** three 24 hour days after Christ's death and burial, the angel of the right side of the power of God was united with Christ our mercy seat (Rom 3:25) as the beginning of the new creation (Rev 3:14; Col 1:15,18). In the case of Christ the individual, there were two becoming one: the physical being infused with the Spiritual (GP 6).

- **Christ's Spiritual Body – Second Order of two becoming one:** two 1000 year-days (Hosea 6:2) after Christ's death and resurrection, in the beginning of the seventh spiritual day, will occur the infusion of the physical Christians into the Spiritual Body of Christ through a Spiritual "marriage" of each Christian to their own Spirit or angel of Christ. Again, two (physical and spiritual) are becoming one, as well as the good and evil are joined to create the knowledge of good and evil (NM16, "Pentecost").

- **Both Christ the Individual and Spiritual Body – Third Order of two becoming one:** three 1000 year-days after Christ's death and resurrection, in the beginning of the eighth spiritual day, the repented spirits of Satan will be brought into the Spiritual Body of Christ so that God will be all in all (GP 7). The *individual* Christ will be infused with his repentant spirit as explained in GP 8, and the rest of mankind and angel kind will be joined so that God will be all in all when all go into the Spiritual Body of Christ, and at the same time will occur the joining of good and evil to create the knowledge of good and evil (GP 6 & GP 7).

Evil: Who Is To Blame?

gp623» At the end of creation the evil force will be fused with the good force thus giving the result of the true knowledge of good and evil. Now since the "works were finished from the foundation of the world" (Heb 4:3), or as good as finished, for all that was planned will happen; then the angel of the BeComingOne as the representative or messenger of the completed God could say before his true completion, "I kill, and I make alive; I wound, and I heal" (Deut 32:39). In a sense God does kill and wound, for a part or one side of the totally finished God is the power of this kind of work; and that part or side was/is Satan — who after he is changed will be the future left side of God. But now the right side of God, he himself, is not doing any evil. It is Satan, the left side of the power of the God (who will in the future become one with God) who is now leading the madness. Thus, as of now, Christ is in himself *not* to blame for today's madness. Satan is doing it. Satan is to blame, but not God, if one wants to find fault. For example compare the following parallel verses in two different books of the Bible:

- "And again the **anger of the LORD** was kindled against Israel, an he moved David against them to say, Go, number Israel and Judah." [2Sam 24:1]
- "**Satan** stood up against Israel, and provoked David to number Israel." [1Chron 21:1]

The *anger of the BeComingOne* that provoked David was Satan (the left side of God), not the good right side of God.

But remember all things have been predestinated to happen as they will happen (see "Predestination Paper" [NM 8]) before the cosmos, and consequently before sin (as we know it). Our God is the BeComingOne, who is good in totality when He becomes One (Deut 6:4; Matt 19:17). The evil that was predestinated was predestinated before sin. Therefore, predestination is outside sin, even before sin. One cannot find fault for the creator's predestination.

Blame to All

gp624» In the true God, the completed God, or that is, God in its truest sense, there will be no one who can stand up and say he is better than any other, for all will have contributed to the madness, and soon to come, all will contribute to the harmony. Thus, at the end no one can stand up and accuse another, for all will have killed, and all will have healed in a sense. The BeComingOne said, "I kill, I make alive" (Deut 32:39). At the End there is nothing, but the BeComingOne, "I the BeComingOne [YHWH] and none else" (Isa 45:18, 5, 22). The truest sense of the NAME, the BeComingOne, comes true only at the End (1Cor 15:24-28; etc.). At that time God — the BeComingOne — will be all in all, or that is, God will be everything, or everything will be the God: "I the BeComingOne [YHWH] and none else" (Isa 45:18, 5, 22).

Repentant Evil plus Good are One in Harmony

gp625» As we saw in GP 7 the two-thirds of mankind who will have lived under Satan, along with Satan and his angels, are the killers and destroyers. But the others of mankind along with God's angels are the healers. One killer will be fused with one healer to make ONE completed person. Or more technically, the one-half (one-third of the angels, two-thirds of mankind) of the completed Godship who had been destroyers will be fused with the one-half (one-third mankind, two-thirds of the angels) that had been the healers by the End of Creation. And thus the same with Christ the individual. He is the healer, the right half of the completed God (Angel of God, 1/3) with the mercy seat (Jesus Christ, 1/3), who is to be infused with the converted former destroyer (Satan, 1/3), the left side of God, by the end of the spiritual creation, so that 1/3 + 1/3 + 1/3 = ONE.

Cherubs Protecting the Garden

Why the Contrast Between the God of the Old Testament and the God of the New Testament

gp626» In Genesis 3:24 it says that the BeComingOne (YHWH) put the cherubs in the garden to guard the way to the tree of life. Now that we know what the true meaning of the cherubs is, we can now know what Genesis 3:24 says.

- So He drove the man out; and at the east of the garden of Eden He stationed the cherubs [right & left] and the flaming sword which turned every direction to guard the way to the tree of life. (Gen 3:24)

What this verse is really saying in context with what we now know about the cherubs is this:

- Mankind finds it difficult to get to paradise because the left cherub keeps misleading and contradicting the right cherub.

gp627» When two people (one who is a liar and one who is not) tell you two different things, how do you tell who is telling the truth, if you do not have any experience with either person? You must get to know each for a while until by experience you are able to ascertain who is the liar. Both cherubs guarded the garden. One was a liar, the greatest liar; one was the truth teller. Since the left cherub misled through the other-mind (see "Other Mind" paper [NM 21]), and since God did not give many the New Mind, mankind as a whole was misled (Rev 12:9). It was only after Satan's spirit was cast out by the death of Jesus that the way to life was/is/will be made clear to ALL (John 12:31-33; Heb 2:14-15).

Satan Cast out of Man

gp628» Christians in the old age had the "other-mind" tempting them (NM20). Formerly, Christ had an "other-mind" tempting him (Mark 1:13) and that was Satan or a spirit of Satan (NM 21). Christ of course had the pure mind of the angel of God inside him when he was a man, but he also had the other-mind inside his mind that was testing and trying to confuse him (note Mark 1:13; Heb 2:18). It was this other-mind of Satan that was cast out of Jesus at his death (John 12:31-33; Heb 2:14-15), and this was the beginning of Satan's power being put out of mankind.

God of the New Testament

gp629» The New Testament was written after Christ sat at the right side of the power of the God. Thus, the God of the New Testament times, Christ the BeComingOne, is pictured as the Right Side of the true God — the good God of the *Gods* of the BeComingOne (YHWH). Remember the BeComingOne is of the *Gods* or is the *Gods* (Deut 4:35, 39). The BeComingOne is the good God and in a sense also the bad god, since *all* power comes from the BeComingOne. The bad god is Satan (2Cor 4:4; 11:14). When Christ died Satan was put out of him, and in a sense, out of the BeComingOne (note John 12:31-32; Heb 2:14). This is one reason in the New Testament that the word God is written in the singular case and the not in the plural case as in the Old Testament. In the Old Testament the BeComingOne was of *Gods*. An examination of the Hebrew Old Testament shows us that it wasn't just a singular "BeComingOne" who did things, but it was the "Lord God" or "YHWH Elohim" or the "He (who) will be Gods" that did things in the Old Testament. Jesus Christ is now the BeComingOne, but He is *not* now of gods in the Old Testament sense because the evil god was cast out. Christ has nothing to do with evil, for He is the only good God — the true God. The BeComingOne will be of *Gods* in a different sense because of the next two resurrections to life.

Two in One and the Duality of *Elohim*

"In the beginning **God** created the heavens and the earth." When you see "God" in most English translations of the Old Testament it is translated from its plural/dual form (*elohim*). The Hebrew meaning for *elohim* is "powers" in the plural or dual depending on context. See Gesenius §87(a) &88(a)(e) to see how the plural and dual forms work. Also study GP8.

Many think that Hebrew *elohim* ("God" with the capital G) in the Old Testament of most English Bibles is speaking of the true *one* God, as they understand Him. So they think of Him in a singular way, not a plural or dual way. (Of course the three in one Trinity god confuses all of this.) Because of this they say the plural *elohim* is a *"pluralis excellentiae."* (Gesentius' Heb. Gram. § 132*g,h*) But this is mistake.

> **First** the word is NOT in a singular form in the Hebrew language. It is in a plural/dual form by the addition of "im" as its suffix. There is nothing special about this that it should be given a special name – *pluralis excellentiae*.

> **Second** because of other biblical scriptures we know there are **two** spiritual gods: one being the True God and one being Satan. And each god has it own kingdom: Kingdom of God and a kingdom of Satan.

> **Third** we know that mankind was made in the **image** of God (*elohim*). (Gen 1:26-27) Therefore from mankind being in the "image" or likeness of God, we can ascertain what the real essence of God must be.

Literally, "And said (the) Gods, Let **US** make man in **Our** image and according to **Our** likeness... And (the) Gods created the man in His image and in the image of Gods He created him [Adam]; He created them – male and female." (Gen 1:26-27) Both of them, male and female, were made corresponding and complementary to one another as well as opposite to one another [Gen 2:18, 20, Heb.], yet – these **two were one** [Gen 2:24]. Both together are called Adam or mankind [Gen 5:1-2] *and* they both were made in the image of *Elohim* [Gen 1:27]. There is a *two in one* aspect to mankind, and since they are in the image of God, there MUST be a *two in one* aspect to the essence of God. This is why when speaking about God, the Bible uses the plural/dual for the word God. Study GP6 - GP9 & Ex. 25:17-22.

Following this logic, what is the *two in one* aspect of the real God?

Notice in the Holy of holies (Ex 25:17-22ff) where the *Becoming-One* appeared during Moses' time, there were two Cherubs representing two angels. The two cherubs/angels were made from ONE piece with the mercy seat. The faces of the cherubs faced toward each other and toward the center of the mercy seat as the faces of male and female face each other in sexual intercourse. We show in the *God Papers* that the two cherubs represent two spirits or gods who were different in behavior: one was good; one was evil. The two behaviors were different, but complemented each other, for without the two no one could know about good and evil. If you never learn about good and evil, you would never know what good was or feel pleasure or know how wonderful life was or any of the other aspects of knowing good and evil. (See GP7; NM19-21) The construction of the two cherubs and the mercy seat were made of one piece thus foretelling the coming together of what the two cherubs and the mercy seat represented because Moses' tabernacle and its Holy of Holies were a pattern of what was in the heavenlies. (Ex 25:8-9; Heb 8:5; 9:24) Read all of the *God Papers* for fuller details and see *Male & Female* revised version book.

Way to the Tree of Life

One scripture says that the two cherubs and its flaming sword were put in place to hid the way to the tree of life:

Gen 3:24 So he drove out the man; and he placed at the east of the garden of Eden Cherubs,[23] and a flaming sword which turned every way, to guard the way of the tree of life.

But it was through Christ (our Messiah, our King of kings, the Right Cherub and Mercy Seat), who defeated the left cherub and its dysfunction, and made the path to the Tree of life possible through His Spirit and Truth. He took away the flaming sword that guarded the way to the Tree of Life.

Remember Moses wrote the first five books of the Bible which included the books of Genesis and Exodus. He used the plural/dual (*elohim*) Hebrew word for God instead of the singular Hebrew word (*el* or *eloh*) for God because he was inspired to write that and because he was told that the Holy of holy was the physical representation of the True God – it was the pattern of the Heavenly/Spiritual essence. (Ex 25:17-22)

Scriptures on Satan

gp630» The scriptures concerning Satan and his angels can be found throughout the Bible. Most of these scriptures speak in a typical way or physical way about Egypt, or Babylon, or the Pharaoh, or the evil one(s), or Elam, or Edom, or the prince of Tyrus, or the king of Tyrus (Ezek 28:12), or the king of Assyria (Isa 10:12), or king of Babylon (Isa 14), or Lucifer (Isa 14), or Leviathan (king of the children of pride — Job 41), and so forth. But these verses point to the antitype or to the spiritual or higher meaning. For example, the scriptures of the physical Pharaoh point to the spiritual evil Pharaoh. God through the Bible is speaking to us in a spiritual language (see "Duality of the Bible" [See Intro]).

gp631» See the "Last War and God's Wrath" paper [PR 5], the "Other Mind" paper [NM 21], and other papers such as the "Thousand Years and Beyond" paper [NM 15] to help you understand the higher meaning of scripture concerning Satan, his angels, and their fate.

Satan Does Not Understand Now

gp632» But why doesn't Satan understand his future now? He does not understand now nor does he wish to understand, the same way as those without God's Spirit do not understand now nor do they wish to understand. These are the ones with physical ears that can only hear physically. Only those of the Spiritual ears, hear Spiritually. Jesus said, "every one of the truth hears my voice" (John 18:37). And those of the Truth, have the Spirit of Truth (John 16:13).

gp633» This is why Satan and those belonging to Satan cannot understand that Satan and his angels are also to become one with God:

- "But we speak the wisdom of God in a mystery, even the hidden wisdom, which God ordained before the world unto our glory: which *none* of the princes of this world [the spirits of Satan are the power behind the physical princes] knew: for had they known it, they would not have crucified the Lord of glory. But as it is written, Eye has not seen, nor ear heard, neither have entered into the heart of man, the things which God has prepared for them that love him. But God has revealed them unto us by his Spirit: for the Spirit searches all things, yes, the deep things of God" (1 Cor 2:7-10).

---

[23] *Cherubim*, See Holy of holies & GP8

Satan in Darkness

gp634» "And angels who had not kept their own original state, but had abandoned their beginning, for [the] judgment of [the] great day; chained perpetually[24] under gloomy darkness, he keeps [them]. (Jude 1:6) This "day" begins when Christ returns and continues for an antitypical Sabbath, the seventh 1000 year Spiritual day. Thus, during the millennium of joy for God's Kingdom, it will be the millennium of judgment for Satan's kingdom. (Satan did not keep the physical seventh day for 6000 years, so his punishment is for him to keep quiet during the seventh 1000 year period [Lev 26:34-35].) But *after* Satan's judgment (they are in perpetual chains during that time — Rev 20:2, 7) he will be atoned to the true God (see "Thousand Years and Beyond" paper [NM 15]).

gp635» Satan is in the darkness concerning this fact, "he believes *not* that he shall return out of darkness" (Job 15:22). This verse in the typical reading speaks of a "wicked one" (V. 20). Yet since a wicked man is merely a shadow of what is in him (a spirit of Satan with its law of confusion), then Satan himself is in the dark. He believes he will not return from the bottomless pit (Rev 20:1-3). **That makes Satan extremely dangerous: that is why Satan goes completely mad at the end of the age** (Rev 12:12; and see God's Wrath papers [PR 6]).

Review of GP 8

gp636» In this part we learned the meaning of the cherubs. The *right* cherub represents the right hand or right side of the Power of God — the good side of God. The *left* cherub represents the left hand or left side of God — the evil side of God. The BeComingOne is actually foreshadowed by the cherubs and the mercy seat in the most holy place. The right side of God is Jesus Christ, while the left side of God is that one called Satan. Both Jesus Christ and Satan are represented by the cherubs and the mercy seat. Jesus Christ the man was represented by the mercy seat. The cherubs and the mercy seat represent the BeComingOne, and the truest sense of the BeComingOne is the finished God — the true God — who is the good God. The true God will change Satan and then put this *reformed* spirit back into Himself. Satan when he is put back into the Power will then be a good spirit or power with the memory or knowledge of his former evil ways. The knowledge of evil was needed so as to give the true knowledge of good to ALL, since good and evil must be compared in order for us to know either. In the beginning all went *out of* God. This included Satan. But at or before the end all will be brought back into the God, so that God will be all in all. The physical cherubs and the mercy seat were one piece, thus pointing to the future oneness of the Real cherubs and mercy seat. Satan will thus be brought back into the God. The meaning of the cherubs indicates this to us.

God has all power	
("I form the light, and create darkness; I make peace, and create evil, I the BeComingOne do all these things" [Isa 45:7])	
All went out of the all powerful God to learn good <u>and</u> evil	
Right Side of God	**Left Side of God**
system of love (harmony) – light	system of hate (disharmony) – darkness

---

[24] Strong's # 126 (from #104) = always, continual, perpetual, not necessarily "forever." See NM24.

God has all power

("I form the light, and create darkness; I make peace, and create evil, I the BeComingOne do all these things" [Isa 45:7])

All went out of the all powerful God to learn good *and* evil

Right Side of God	Left Side of God
affection (of good: "good is good")	affection (of evil: "evil is good")
anger (of evil – Mark 3:4-5; Ps 7:11; Eph 4:26)	anger (uncontrolled)
hate (evil – Ps 97:10; Prov 8:13; Amos 5:15)	hate (good – Ps 34:2; Micah 3:2-4)
good (all in harmony with God's laws)	evil (all in disharmony with God's laws)
graciousness (respectful, polite)	ungraciousness (rude, vulgar)
peaceful (calming)	unpeaceful (agitating, reckless)
kind	unkind (harsh, malevolent)
helpful	troublemaker
forgiving	unforgiving
thankful (grateful)	unthankful (ungrateful)
reconciliatory	revengeful
lawful	lawless
rebuke (for edification)	rebuke (for berating or belittling)
truthful	liar
fairness (impartial)	unfairness (partiality)
brave (gives life for truth, justice)	coward (fearful, hides)
temperance (life in balance)	overindulgence (life of extremes)
honorable	dishonorable
unpretentious (reserved, humble)	pretentious (arrogant, boastful)
elegant (graceful)	crude (vulgar)
patient	impatient (rash, reckless)
light	darkness
sympathetic	unsympathetic (callous, indifferent)

Both sides create the knowledge of good and evil

"like God [*elohim*] knowing good and evil"

"God all in all" – 1 Cor 15:28

GP 9: God's Symbolic Throne – Power of God

Outline of Scriptures
What is the Meaning of the Throne?

gp637» Those who have read the scripture of God's symbolic throne have more than likely come away mystified. The description of this symbolic throne is found in Ezekiel chapters 1 and 10, Isaiah chapter 6, and Revelation chapters 4 and 5. Various other places in the Bible have further information on this mysterious throne of God. The description of this throne is truly "out of this world." We will in this paper tie-in the scriptures of Ezekiel, Isaiah, and Revelation. By this we will manifest that all these scriptures are describing the same throne, but each set of scripture is qualifying and amplifying each other set of scripture.

gp638» The synthesizing of Biblical scripture is a key to understanding the Bible. We must synthesize the Biblical verses of God's symbolic throne in order to understand it. By synthesizing these verses we are conforming to one of the major principles in Biblical study (see "Premises for Belief" paper [BP 5] in the *Beginning Papers*). This principle is the one of "here a little, and there a little" (Isa 28:10). After we synthesize the verses on God's symbolic throne, we will give the meaning of this throne and its specific elements. By doing this *we will prove that God's symbolic throne represents the God's full power, authority, and control of everything.*

gp639» We will now begin to synthesize scripture on this symbolic throne. We will use the outline form mostly because of the complexity of synthesizing these scriptures by any other method. The outline form is easy to check and to review which is another reason we will use it.

Outline of Scriptures

Throne's Setting

gp640»

- The appearance of the symbolic throne of God occurs with a whirlwind, great clouds, great noise, great fire, and brightness of light. [Ezek 1:4, 13, 14, 24; 3:13; Dan 7:9-10; Rev 4:5; Psa 97:2-4]

    [This pictures the Last War with its atomic weapons, its clouds, and its lightning. See God's Wrath papers.]

- As in the midst of this fire appears the throne. [Ezek 1:4, 5; Rev 4:5]

- In the midst of the throne are *four living creatures*. [Ezek 1:5; Rev 4:6 (KJV "beasts")]

Biblical Description of the Four Living Creatures

gp641»

- They have a likeness of a man. [Ezek 1:5]

- Each one has *four faces* on each of the four sides of the head. [Ezek 1:6, 10]

- One face was like a *man*; one face was like a *lion*; one face was like an *ox* (calf); one face was like an *eagle*. [Ezek 1:10; Rev 4:7 (note Jer 11:19)]

- Every living creature had *six* wings. [Rev 4:8]

gp642» [[Notice that Ezekiel 1:6, 8 seems to say they had only *four* wings. Let's straighten out this apparent contradiction: "And every one [living creature] had four faces, and every one had four wings" (Ezek 1:6). Yet these four wings are the four wings on each creature's four sides: "their wings on their four sides; and they four [sides] had their [four] faces and their [four] wings" (Ezek 1:8). But these four wings, one on each of the four sides, are *two* pairs of wings, for these wings are in pairs: "two wings on every one [set or pair] joined one to another, and two [pair, thus 4 wings] covered their bodies," (Ezek 1:11) and "every one [set of wings] had two wings, which covered on this side, and every one had two [or each set of wings had two wings, thus these *two* pair of wings made 4 wings covering the four sides of their body], which covered on that side, their bodies" (Ezek 1:23).

Besides these two pairs of wings (4 wings) that covered their bodies, there were two wings that were stretched over their head: "and their *wings* were stretched upward" (Ezek 1:11). Remember, the other four wings (two pairs) "covered their bodies," but this set was "stretched upward." Hence these living creatures had 6 wings: two pairs of wings (four) — one wing per each of the four sides of the body — and a pair of wings stretched overhead.]]

- Each creature had four hands under each of the four wings that covered their bodies. [Ezek 1:8]

- The general appearance of these four living creatures were like: "the color of burnished brass;" or "burning coals of fire;" or "the appearance of flames" (KJV, "lamps"); or "as the appearance of a flash of lightning." [Ezek 1:7, 13, 14]

[In other words, these living creatures appeared as a burning flame with sparks of lightning coming out at times. Another way to describe such an object is to say it looked like the sun or a star. The stars are burning flames and are symbolic of angels (Rev 1:20). Angels are spirits that are each represented as a "flame of fire" (Heb 1:7).]

Cherubs

gp643» Notice in Ezekiel 10, where it also describes the symbolic throne, that the cherubs in this chapter are one and the same with the four living creatures: "and the cherubs were lifted up. This is the living creature that I saw by the river of Chebar [Ezek 1:1, 4-5] ... This is the living creature that I saw under the God of Israel by the river Chebar; and I knew that they were the cherubs" (Ezek 10:15, 20).

gp644» *The cherubs that Ezekiel are describing in chapter 10 are similar to the four living creatures* he described in chapter one. Notice the similarities between the cherubs of Ezekiel 10 and the four living creatures of Ezekiel 1 and Revelation:

- Each cherub of the cherubs has *four faces*. [Ezek 10:21]

- One face like a *cherub*; one face like a *man*; one face like a *lion*; one face like an *eagle*. [Ezek 10:14]

- "The likeness of their faces was *the same* faces which I saw by the river of Chebar" (Ezek 10:22; note Ezek 1:10). But if you compare these faces with Ezekiel 1:10 you see they are not exactly the *same* faces. A Biblical contradiction? No, for the word "same" comes from a Hebrew word meaning "they," and not "same." Corrected it should read: "And the form of their faces, they (are) the faces ..." Thus, these four faces were similar, but not exactly the same (Check this with the Hebrew text, and *Young's Literal Translation of the Holy Bible*). [Ezek 10:22]

[Remember what we are doing now is tying-in the scriptures of the symbolic throne. Each description in the Bible adds information to our general overall view of this throne.]

- Each cherub had four wings, one for each side or face. Each wing had a man's hand under each wing. This is the same as each living creature's wing (Ezek 1:6, 8). [Ezek 10:21, 8]

gp645» Thus, we see the similarities of the four living creatures and the cherubs. Yet everywhere in the Bible where it describes the cherubs, it says there are two cherubs, not four. Thus, there is no reason to say that there were four cherubs in this throne like there were four living creatures. There are only two cherubs in Ezekiel's cherubs, but the cherubs are the living creature. Each living creature is like each cherub in appearance.

gp646» We know cherubs are angels, for when it describes the angel Satan in Ezekiel 28, it calls him an "anointed cherub" (Ezek 28:14). Further we have just shown you how the general appearance of the four living creatures are like fiery flames — thus symbolic of angels (GP 3). The four living creatures were symbolic of angels as the cherubs are symbolic of angels.

Seraphs

gp647» Now Isaiah 6 also describes God's symbolic throne. In Isaiah 6:2 it speaks of the seraphs with their six wings. The word "seraphs" means, "burning nobles." The seraphs looked like a burning creature of noble status. As we manifested before, a burning flame in the Bible is symbolic of an angel. Thus the seraphs were spirit beings.

Isaiah 6 doesn't say how many Seraphs there were. But the seraphs are somewhat like the four living creatures ("beasts") of Revelation chapter 4:

- The seraphs and the beasts both have six wings. [Isa 6:2; Rev 4:8]
- Both speak about the same words around the symbolic throne. [Isa 6:3; Rev 4:8]

gp648» Thus, we can reasonably conclude that the seraphs, and the four living creatures of the book of Revelation are one and the same. Further the four living creatures are the same four living creatures as the ones in Ezekiel one. And the four living creatures of Ezekiel one are the same as the cherubs of Ezekiel 10 as shown previously.

Throne of God

gp649» *The seraphs, four living creatures, and the cherubs are all metonymical terms which help to describe the same symbolic throne of God.*
Now let us continue to synthesize these scriptures.

- The four living creatures and the cherubs had four wheels. [Ezek 1:15-16; 10:9]
- Each wheel looked like they were in each other. [Ezek 1:16; 10:10]
- Eyes were in the wheels. Notice the four living creatures ("beasts") were filled with eyes (Rev 4:8). [Ezek 1:18; 10:12]
- Everywhere the cherubs, or the wheels, or the four living creatures went, they all went *together* as a unit "for the spirit of the living creature was in them." They all went together as a unit, for all the descriptions of this throne are metonymical descriptions of the same thing. [Ezek 1:19-21; 10:16-17]

gp650» Since the general appearance of this throne is like a burning flame (Dan 7:9; Ezek 1:7, 13, 14) which is symbolic of angels or spirits, and since the throne is a unit that goes and moves together because of the spirit in it; *then this symbolic throne is of a spiritual dimension.*

- The sound or noise of the cherubs and living creatures were "as the voice of the Almighty God when he speaks." [Ezek 10:5; 1:24]
- Above the four living creatures, or the cherubs, or the seraphs was the throne. [Ezek 1:26; 10:1; Isa 6:1-2; Rev 4:2, 6]
- Above the whole throne and immediate area was a rainbow. [Ezek 1:28; Rev 4:3]
- Similar things happen around the seraph's throne, and the cherub's throne. [Ezek 10:6-7, 2 with Isa 6:6]
- SITTING ON THE THRONE was one with "the appearance of a MAN." [Ezek 1:26]
- "The BeComingOne (YHWH) sitting upon a throne." [Isa 6:1 (6:5); 2Chron 18:18; note Ezek 10:19]
- The God sits on the throne. [Rev 7:10; 19:4; 12:5; 22:1, 3; Psalm 47:8: Heb 1:8 Psa 45:6]
- The MOST HIGH sits on the throne. [Psalm 9:2, 4]
- The BRANCH on the throne. [Zech 6:12-13 (Isa 11:1-4)]
- JESUS CHRIST on the throne. [Acts 2:30; Rev 3:21 (Rev 1:4 with 4:5)]

    [Compare Revelation 1:4 with 4:5 to see that each throne named has the seven Spirits of God before it because they are the same throne. As Revelation 1:4 says it is the throne of "him which is, and which was, and which is to come." Comparing this with Revelation 1:8 we see this throne is Christ's.]

- The LAMB on the throne. [Rev 5:6; 7:17; 22:3]
- The SON OF MAN on the throne. [Matt 19:28; 25:31]
- The ANCIENT OF DAYS on the throne. [Dan 7:9]
- An ANGEL on the throne. [Rev 10:1 with 4:3 and Ezek 1:27]

gp651» *Christ sitting on the throne.* All these Biblical names of those sitting on the throne are metonymical names of the ONE Christ the BeComingOne. All the above scripture quoted are in context and in a sense concerned with the same throne of God at the very instant of the Last War and the Day of the Lord (note Ezek 1:4; Rev 1:10 & 4:1; with 11:15; etc.). *This throne is describing Christ the BeComingOne's throne with all its spiritual manifestations.*

More Detail on the Throne

gp652» The F*our Living Creatures* of God's throne picture the four beasts of Daniel 7, for the word "beasts" of Daniel 7 in the King James Version (KJV) should have been translated as "living creatures." The four living creatures of Daniel 7 are the kingdoms of Satan. Thus the kingdoms of Satan belong to the total power and authority of God.

gp653» The **seraphs** of the throne are just another way of describing the four living creatures and cherubs (see outline above).

gp654» The **wheels** of the throne are chariot wheels. These wheels can be synthesized with the four chariots of Zechariah 6:2-3. These are symbolic again to the four beasts of Daniel 7 (see "Last War and God's Wrath" paper [PR 5]).

gp655» The **eyes** of the throne (Rev 4:8; Ezek 1:18; 10:12) are the seven eyes of Christ the Lamb (Rev 5:6), or the seven eyes of Christ the Stone or Rock (Zech 3:9), or the seven eyes of Christ the Plummet (Zech 4:10). And these eyes are "the seven Spirits of God sent forth into all the earth" (Rev 5:6; note Zech 4:10). And the seven Spirits of God are the "seven lamps of fire burning before the throne" (Rev 4:5; note 1:4). Spirits are angels (Heb 1:7), and lamps or flames of fire are symbolic of angels or spirits (Heb 1:7). Thus the seven Spirits of God are the seven angels of God (note Rev 1:20). And these seven angels are the seven angel-Spirits of the Church (Rev 1:20). Thus, the eyes of God's throne are the Spirits or angels of God's Church. God's throne or power and authority includes the seven angels of God's Church. In other words, God's power includes his Church and the angels thereof.

gp656» The **faces** of the throne are symbols of the various sides or faces or facets of God. Christ the BeComingOne is a "son of man," thus the face of a man on the cherubs or living creatures. Christ the BeComingOne is an angel, or spirit, thus the face of a cherub. Christ the BeComingOne is symbolized as a Lamb, thus the face of the calf or ox. Christ the BeComingOne is symbolized as a lion (Rev 5:5, "the lion of the tribe of Judah"), thus the face of a lion. Christ the BeComingOne is symbolized as an eagle (Ezek 17:3, with 17:22, its higher meaning), thus the face of an eagle.

gp657» Also Satan, who is part of the throne, is symbolized by an eagle (Ezek 17:7, its higher meaning; Obadiah 1:4; Luke 17:37). And he is symbolized as a lion (1Pet 5:8). And further Satan is a cherub (Ezek 28:14). Thus, these faces also represent Satan. Of course, Christ *the* BeComingOne is/will-be the fulfilled completed God and thus the faces of Satan will be in Christ the BeComingOne at the End, in the sense and way we have explained previously.

Putting Scripture Together

gp658» By studying Ezekiel chapter 1 and 10, and Isaiah 6, and Revelation 4 and 5, and then reading this outline and looking up all the verses quoted (studying and comparing) one will see the great similarities and that indeed these scriptures do pertain to the same throne of God.

gp659» The simplest explanation for the given facts is usually the right answer. These scriptures are not speaking of different thrones, but the same one. These scriptures fit together as the scriptures of Daniel 7 and Revelation 13 & 17 on the "Beast" fit together (see the Beast-System Paper [PR 2]).

gp660» The Bible is made plain only when one synthesizes all scripture on any one topic. By putting the scripture together that pertains to God's throne we get all the facts on it together, and thereafter are ready to understand it. But if we conclude that these scriptures are speaking of different thrones, then we are confused. When we understand that the four living creatures, the cherubs, and the seraphs are merely metonymical names of the overall throne of God, we are on the way to understanding God's mysterious throne.

Throne and the Glory of God

gp661» Notice how Ezekiel generalized on his vision of this throne:

- "I saw the visions of God [*elohim*] ... this was the appearance of the likeness of the glory of the BeComingOne" (Ezek 1:1, 28; note 2:23 and 43:2-3).

This whole vision Ezekiel had was of the glory of God or visions of God. In the truest sense, the Glory of God, is the totally fulfilled God, the BeComingOne who has become. The details of the vision are merely particular manifestations of God. Yet since these visions were mainly of the true God's throne, and its immediate surroundings, and because thrones are symbols of power or authority; then these visions were of the true God's power and authority.

Satan's Throne versus God's Throne

gp662» A parallel would be the scripture on the Beast of Revelation with its 10 horns and 7 heads, etc. The "Beast" represents Satan's spiritual "power, and his throne [KJV, 'seat'], and great authority" (Rev 13:2). Just as the "Beast" represents Satan's power and authority, so too does God's symbolic throne represent God's power and authority. It represents his SPIRITUAL power and authority, for the throne is of a spiritual dimension as we previously indicated in this paper.

What is the Meaning of the Throne?

gp663» As we just noted this throne is symbolic of the BeComingOne's power and authority. The various details of this throne add to our knowledge of God's power and authority.

Power: All

gp664» Just how much power and authority does the BeComingOne hold? Christ the BeComingOne has been *given* ALL the power in heaven and earth (Matt 28:18). As of now Christ does not hold all the power for Satan now has the power of death and destruction (Heb 2:14). "**But now we see not yet all things put under him**" (Heb 2:8). The true and complete God is the "Almighty" (Rev 1:8). This God is All-powerful, He holds ALL the power and authority. The true God, which is the fulfilled Spiritual Body of Christ, will be complete, the "God, all in all," only at the End (1Cor 15:24-28).

gp665» This *all-mighty* Power includes authority over the kingdoms of men: "to the intent that the living may know that *the most High rules in the kingdom of men*, and gives it to whomever he will" (Dan 4:17). And again, "by me kings reign, and princes degree justice. By me princes rule, and nobles, even all the judges of the earth" (Prov 8:15-16). So the BeComingOne somehow has power and authority over the kingdoms of the world.

Predestinated Power

gp666» The kingdoms of the world in this age *are* directly under the authority of Satan as Revelation 13:2 shows (see the "Beast-System Paper" [PR 2]). But these kingdoms under Satan are under the true God's predestinated overall power and authority. Before the beginning of the present universe, God predestinated everything which has happened, which will happen, and which is happening (see the "Predestination Paper" [NM 8]). Then *out of* the pre-creation God Power came everything including the angel or messenger of God who spoke for the BeComingOne. All came out of the God Power, but *all* were at that time predestinated to return to that God Power and become the BeComingOne Power. This is known as the Great Cycle (see GP 6). Since the pre-creation God Power predestinated all to return to Him, He in effect has not lost control of the cosmos. In this old age the God has given the right to rule this age to Satan and his kingdom and the rulers therein: "you [Pilate] could have no power at all against me, except *it were GIVEN you from above*" (John 19:11). Pilate and all physical and spiritual rulers of this evil age were given their power by the predestination of the God before the cosmos began. Even Christ the man's death was predetermined by God (Acts 4:27-28). But remember, all was predestinated <u>before</u> the cosmos, <u>before</u> law (as we know it), and <u>before</u> sin (as we know it). We know it was not possible to create good without in some way creating evil because good is a comparative quality to evil (GP7). Therefore how can anyone call predestinating evil, evil, when it was done before evil and before sin?

To Review

gp667» Hence we are perceiving that the throne, or the power and authority of the God includes both parts or sides or hands of the God. At *this* time, or in this age the left side of God rules through Satan. In the next age the right hand or side of God will rule in the Kingdom of God. But in this age of Satan's direct rulership of man, the God (the BeComingOne) is the over-all ruler for He has predestinated ALL through His PERPETUAL power (note Rom 1:20, in Greek). He is the Almighty God. The BeComingOne is in control of the situation, but has in this age predestinated some of his overall power to Satan for a purpose. This purpose being that man needs a period of madness in order to have future happiness (see GP 7).

Review of GP 9

gp668» We have seen basically that the throne of God represents the power of the true God — the BeComingOne (YHWH) — in its totality. The symbolic throne of God represents all of God's power: both the good and the bad. But let us not forget that the true and completed God is good, but in Him there will be the memory of the evil that was "allowed" by God and predestinated by the pre-creation Power. In the beginning all went *out of* the pre-creation Power to learn about evil so that all would be able to know and enjoy the good. The true God is the finished and completed God, the God all in all.

General Review

gp669» In GP 1 we started our search: who or what is God? From the Bible we learned about the apparent paradoxes of God: "I make peace, and create evil: I the LORD do all these things" (Isa 45:7). God who is Love (1John 4:8) has somehow and for some reason created evil; He has even killed (Deut 32:39). But how can God be Love and also a killer?

We next learned that there are two basic laws and one basic fact we must understand in order to rightly perceive the true nature of God: the Law of Contradiction and the Law of Knowledge plus the fact that the God cannot lie.

We then went on and explained the Law of Contradiction.

We further showed the many attributes and titles of God and put forth that "time" is very important in our understanding of the paradoxes of God.

We also showed you the very NAME of the true God: YHWH, or Jehovah, or Yehowah, or He (who) will-be, or the BeComingOne, or the One who was, who is, and who is coming. God's NAME and its meaning is the real secret in revealing the answer to the Paradoxes of God. God's NAME is an *imperfect* (incomplete) verb and not as would be expected a *perfect* (complete) verb or a noun. Names are very important in the Bible and many times describe some facet of a person. The true NAME of the true God is important for it is the secret in explaining the apparently unexplainable scriptures about God.

In GP 1 we also looked into the meaning of "with God all things are possible," the "*one* Yehowah," the so-called unchangeableness of God, and other matters concerning the God. What GP 1 does is set the stage in our search for who or what is God.

In GP 2 we learned that Jesus Christ's Father was the BeComingOne (YHWH) of the Old Testament: He was the Jews' God.

In GP 3 we learned that the angel of the BeComingOne and the BeComingOne of the Old Testament were closely connected. Since angels are messengers, this means the angel of the BeComingOne is a messenger of the BeComingOne or this angel is the WORD of the BeComingOne. Therefore, the words that the angel of the BeComingOne spoke belonged to the Great BeComingOne Power — the true God. This angel stood in the NAME of the true God (Exo 23:20-21); he represented the great NAME. This angel was in a sense the very WORD of God. The Word (logos) of God before Christ's resurrection was a spirit, the chief-spirit, the chief-angel, the angel of the BeComingOne. The age before Jesus Christ was subjected to angels, even the commandments given on Mount Sinai were from an angel (Acts 7:38).

We have shown *in GP 4* that *before* Jesus Christ was resurrected, he was a human being because he was born from a woman. Thus, Christ before his death and resurrection was a man; he was Jesus Christ the man. He was called Son of man because he was born of mankind through the means of Mary his mother. Jesus the man was not just any human being. Christ was a Son of God, both physically (through the Holy Spirit's union with Mary) and Spiritually (through the medium of God's Spirit inside of him). Christ was a mediator between man and God; he was the Son of God and the Son of man. He is the "one *mediator* between God and men" (1Tim 2:5). Jesus Christ the man actually had the Spirit or Angel of the BeComingOne (YHWH) inside him leading him in the right way. It was because of this Spirit that Christ the man was sinless. God was not Jesus Christ the man, but God (through the power of His Spirit) was inside of Christ the man. When Jesus Christ the man died, his Spirit was then separated from him (Luke 23:46). The Spirit or angel of God did not die *as* Christ the man or *with* Christ the man, for Spirit cannot die. The angel of the BeComingOne separated himself from Christ the man when Christ died.

To say it in slightly a different way, in GP 4 we have shown that Jesus Christ before he was resurrected was a man with the Spirit or angel of the BeComingOne inside him leading him in the way of love. Jesus Christ the man was born from woman and by a miracle of God. Thus, Christ the man was from mankind (through Mary) and from God because of the miraculous conception by the power of God. Jesus Christ the man was a son of man, and a son of the God. He is the "one *mediator* between God and men" (1 Tim 2:5). Christ the man wasn't God, but God's WORD and power were inside of him. The angel of the BeComingOne was inside Jesus Christ the man. When Christ died the angel of the BeComingOne separated from Christ the man's body. Thus, Christ the man died, but his angel inside of him stayed alive, for the angel (spirit) separated himself from Christ the man when Christ died (Luke 23:46).

In GP 5, we have seen that after Jesus Christ the man's death and his burial for three days, he was resurrected and became ONE with the Spirit or Angel of the BeComingOne: **two became one**. The Spiritual marriage of mankind back to God *began* when Jesus Christ the man went into the BeComingOne, the God. Since the beginning of creation when all went *out of* God, God and man were separate. But through Jesus Christ the man, mankind is beginning to go back into God, or into the BeComingOne (YHWH). Through the angel with the NAME, the BeComingOne incorporated Jesus Christ the man into Himself: the Spiritual WORD became flesh. The two, the man Jesus Christ and the Angel of the BeComingOne ("LORD"), as ONE are called: Jesus Christ, God, or in another sense he is/will be Jesus Christ the BeComingOne. Jesus Christ the man has become Jesus Christ *the* God, in one sense, because ALL will eventually go into the Spiritual Body of Jesus Christ by the End (see GP 6). But as of now we do not see ALL in Jesus Christ the God (see Heb 2:8). In two senses Jesus Christ is "the beginning of the creation of the [true] God" (Rev 3:14): the Spirit of Jesus was the First, the beginning of the "old" creation of God; but Jesus Christ the man and his Spirit as ONE is the beginning of the "New" creation.

In GP 6 we learned how the rest of mankind will follow in Christ the man's footsteps. All of mankind each has their own angel which each will eventually be infused with. As Christ the man Spiritually married his angel, so too will each of mankind Spiritually marry his own angel so that two will become ONE. Since the beginning of creation mankind has been out of God. But through the power of Christ and God all will come back into God so "may be the God, all things in all" (1Cor 15:28).

In GP 7 we learned the reason why God created evil (Isa 45:7) in this age. We saw that in order to understand the good and to enjoy the coming utopia, mankind and angelkind must have a time of evil. Good and evil are opposite qualities that need to be compared against each other in order to understand either. A person who grew up with all the good things that the earth has to offer doesn't know the worth of these things until he actually loses them. After he loses the good things he then begins to understand the worth of the good things. If God just automatically at first put the creation into an everlasting utopia, the creation itself would not have the understanding of the worth or value of the utopia. In fact as we learned in GP 7 mankind would not have any understanding of good, if they never had learned evil. But by God putting the creation through an evil period God is actually teaching the creation the value of good and the evil of evil. The creation now is actually learning about good and evil. It is through the evil spirits in the minds of mankind that evil is spread on earth. It will be through the good spirits that mankind will live in good.

In GP 8 we learned the meaning of the cherubs. The *right* cherub represents the right hand or right side of God — the good side of God. The *left* cherub represents the left hand or left side of God — the evil side of God. The BeComingOne is actually foreshadowed by the cherubs and the mercy seat in the most holy place. The right side of God is Jesus Christ, God, while the left side of God is that one called Satan. Both Jesus Christ and Satan are represented by the cherubs and the mercy seat. Jesus Christ the man is represented by the mercy seat. The cherubs and the mercy seat represent the BeComingOne, and the truest sense of the BeComingOne is the finished God — the true God — who is the good God. The true God will change Satan and then put this *reformed* spirit back into Himself. Satan when he is put back into the God will then be a good spirit or power with the memory or knowledge of his former evil ways. The knowledge of evil was needed so as to give the true knowledge of good to ALL, since good and evil must be compared in order for us to know either. In the beginning all went *out of* God. This included Satan. But at or before the end all will be brought back into the God, so that God will be all in all. The physical cherubs and the mercy seat were one piece, thus pointing to the future oneness of the real cherubs and mercy seat. Satan will thus be brought back into the God. The meaning of the cherubs indicates this to us.

We have seen **in GP 9** that the throne of God represented the power of the true God — the BeComingOne (YHWH) — in its totality. The symbolic throne of God represents *all* of the true God's power: both the good and the bad. But let us not forget that the true and completed God is good, but in Him there will be the memory of the evil that was "allowed" by God and predestinated by the pre-creation Power. In the beginning all went *out of* the pre-creation Power to learn about evil so that all would be able to know and enjoy the good. The true God is the finished and completed God, the God all in all.

GP 10: God Is ...

God is Love
God, Predestination, and His Essence
God is Omnipresent
Who or What is God

gp670» It is difficult to put into a few words who God *is* because the Bible does not say who God is, but who God *was*, who God *is*, and who God *will be*. It is the ultimate-goal of God that all will live in happiness. The ultimate state is what is becoming and will become by the end of the creation. The creation is still going on. The Almighty by giving us a time to learn good and evil is creating in us happiness, pleasure, goodness, love, and all else that will serve us well in our endless future.

God Is Love

gp671» Ultimately the true God in his totality[25] will be love for "God is love" (1John 4:8, 16). And what is love? "Love is patient; love is kind and envies no one. Love is never boastful, nor conceited, nor rude; never selfish, nor quick to take offense. Love keeps no score of wrongs; does not gloat over other men's sins, but delights in truth. There is nothing love cannot face; there is no limit to its faith, its hope, and its endurance. Love will never come to an end" (1Cor 13:4-8). God's nature is as these verses describe.

gp672» Further, all the verses that describe how a real Christian should behave are more qualifications on love. A person who can follow all these qualifications on love, is love or a living being of love.

- Thus, love (God is love) does *not* give evil for evil (Rom 12:17). Love does not bless *and* curse at the same time (James 3:10).
- But love is "peaceable, and easy to be entreated, full of mercy and good fruits, without partiality, and without hypocrisy" (James 3:17).
- Love does *not* worry or fear (Matt 6:25-29).
- Love, loves its enemies yet *not* their ways (Matt 5:44; Prov 8:13).
- Love does *not* hate his brother (the person himself), yet if his brother's ways are of evil he hates his brother's ways, yet not the person himself (Prov 8:13 & Luke 14:26).
- Love *does* in deeds what it utters in tongue (1John 3:18 & James 1:22).
- Love does not test others with objects that might lead them away from the truth, to a reasonable degree (Rom 14:20-21),
- yet Love knows nothing in itself is bad (Rom 14:14 & Titus 1:15).

---

[25] Of course his "totality" also includes his other qualities

See the "Freedom and Law" paper [NM 17] for more information on "love" and the way of love.

God, Predestination, and his Essence

God is the Creator We are the Clay

gp673»
- You turn *things* around! Shall the potter be considered as equal with the clay, That what is made would say to its maker, 'He did not make me'; Or what is formed say to him who formed it, 'He has no understanding'? (Isa 29:16)

- I form the light, and create darkness: I make peace, and create evil: I the LORD do all these *things*. 8 Drip down, O heavens, from above, And let the clouds pour down righteousness; Let the earth open up and salvation bear fruit, And righteousness spring up with it. I, the LORD, have created it. 9 Woe to *the one* who quarrels with his Maker-- An earthenware vessel among the vessels of earth! Will the clay say to the potter, 'What are you doing?' Or the thing you are making *say*, 'He has no hands'? 10 Woe to him who says to a father, 'What are you begetting?' Or to a woman, 'To what are you giving birth?' 11 Thus says the LORD, the Holy One of Israel, and his Maker: Ask Me about the things to come concerning My sons, And you shall commit to Me the work of My hands. 12 It is I who made the earth, and created man upon it. I stretched out the heavens with My hands And I ordained all their host. (Isa 45:7-12)

gp674» God has made everything. He predestinated everything before the cosmos was created by him (NM8 & NM9). In GP1 we list some of the verses where God said that he even predestinated some to evil. Now this is very difficult to understand. How can God be love yet predestinate some to evil? How can this be? Yet the Bible clearly speaks about predestination. Not only does God predestinate good, but also evil (NM 8, GP 1).

Free Will?

gp675» There is no easy way of explaining predestination if you believe in free will. But once you understand that free will only exists under the all-powerful free and ultimate will of God, you will understand that your free will is limited. What most think of as free will is just another philosophical belief, not a Biblical teaching. We have some free will, but only under and after the ultimate free will of our God. God is not a fool as to give real free will to each in his creation. This knowledge should not be used as an excuse for our sins, since we do have relative free will under the free will of God. See the Predestination Paper (NM8) for more information.

Paul Explained Predestination

gp676» Paul explained predestination in this way:
- "It does not, therefore, depend on man's desire or effort, but on God's mercy. For the Scripture says to Pharaoh: 'I raised you up for this very purpose, that I might display my power in you and that my name might be proclaimed in all the earth.' Therefore God has mercy on whom he wants to have mercy, and he hardens whom he wants to harden. One of you will say to me: 'Then why does God still blame us? For who resists his will?' " (Rom 9:16-19, NIV)

- "Does not the potter have power over the clay, from the same lump to make one vessel for honor and another for dishonor? 22 What if God, wanting to show His wrath and to make His power known, endured with much longsuffering the *vessels of wrath prepared for destruction*, 23 and that He might make known the riches of His glory on the vessels of mercy, which He had prepared beforehand for glory" (Rom 9:21-23, NKJV).

Let me explain predestination in another more detailed way. You must read the following in context of all this book.

God and Predestination

gp677» There is One God, who is all-powerful and His Name is the *BeComingOne* (Ex 3:14ft, *God*, chap. 1). Before the creation of the universe, God was the highly intelligent pre-creation Power who set up his creation to do exactly as he planned (Eph 1:4; 1Peter 1:20; John 17:24). He thus predestinated everything <u>before</u> the cosmos, <u>before</u> good (as we know it), <u>before</u> evil (as we know it), <u>before</u> law (as we know it), and <u>before</u> sin (as we know it), thus one cannot find sin in God's predestination because it was done <u>before</u> sin. Yet the real God is all-powerful and is responsible for all that takes place in the creation (2Chron 20:6; Isa 44:24; Rom 9:19) and his power is perpetual (Rom 1:20).

Cosmos Created out of Spirit

Ultimate Building "Blocks"

gp678» God was in someway "alone" before the creation (Adam as a type for God, Gen 2:18). God's very essence is spirit, that is, God is spirit (John 4:24). Because spirit is invisible God is invisible (Col 1:15; John 1:18). From God's own invisible essence he created all things because all came out of Him (Rom 11:36; 1Cor 8:6; 15:28). The Spirit of God is the ultimate building block of the present universe and for the coming new universe, when God, in some sense, will be the all in all (1Cor 15:28). The reason we cannot see "spirit" is because it is our ultimate building block. If God, whose essence is spirit was/is/will be everywhere (Jer 23:24; Psa 139:7; Acts 17:27), then he must, he has to be, in some sense everything that was/is/will be. God did not create the universe out of nothing; God created it out of Himself, that is, out of His spirit. In other words, all came *out of* him as Romans 11:36 and other scriptures read in the Greek. By the end of creation God will have created all things new (Rev 21:5).

Word and Jesus Christ

gp679» God created everything by His Word (John 1:1). The Word was the first-angel or Spiritual messenger who spoke the powerful words belonging to the God (GP 3 & GP 4). Since God's essence or spirit is everywhere (Jer 23:24; Psa 139:7; Acts 17:27) and in fact there is nothing else but God (Isa 45:6), in order for God to speak (in the way we understand speech) he must speak through someone who is an individual with spatial position within the ONE who fills all space. Since the Bible calls those who speak or carry messages *angels*, the Word must have been an angel. In fact the Word was the very first-angel or archangel or angel of God's Presence (see GP 3). This archangel who spoke in the Old Testament was not only the first-angel, he was the angel who carried God's very Name (Ex 23:20-21). The Word was made flesh by incorporating Jesus Christ the man into himself as explained in this book (GP 4 & 5). The Word will make all things ever created or ever to be created through him (John 1:3). Apart from him nothing will be created (John 1:3). Christ revealed the invisible Spirit through his behavior (John 14:9-10). Christ reveals God now, for God and Christ the man were fused together as a new creation (GP 5). Christ reveals God now by revealing himself (John 1:18; 14:7, 9).

Father and Jesus Christ

gp680» God who created and will create everything through his Word, is also called the Father since he fathered all things through his great power; he has life in himself, for he is life itself (John 5:26; Acts 17:28). The Father gave all his glory and power to Jesus Christ after Jesus Christ died and rose and was infused with the Spiritual Word (Matt 28:18; John 13:31-32; 17:4-5; GP 5). Jesus Christ in a sense is now the Father (Isa 9:6; GP 5) because he went into the glory of the Father (GP 5). Jesus Christ is now our God, the BeComingOne, since he was infused into the angel with the Name (YHWH), and since all will come back into Jesus Christ's Spiritual Body (GP 6) so that God will be all in all (1Cor 15:28). **The ONE who is the Father of everything and in a sense is everything, now speaks and works through Jesus Christ:**

- Philip said to Him, Lord, show us the Father, and it is enough for us. 9 Jesus said to him, Have I been so long with you, and *yet* you have not come to know Me, Philip? He who has seen Me has seen the Father; how *can* you say, 'Show us the Father'? (John 14:8-9)

Evil Predestinated?

gp681» We know from scripture that God, the super intelligent pre-creation Power, chose Jesus Christ to be the Savior of the world before the foundation of the creation (1Pet 1:19-20; Rev 13:8), and thus before sin. The Bible by saying this projects to us that God knew beforehand that his creation would need saving. The question is, why didn't God create a universe that did not need saving? Some think mistakenly that God could have created a universe without death, without pain. Why didn't he? Because he knew that in order to create good, happiness, and pleasure he must also create evil, unhappiness, and pain (NM 19). The fact that you cannot have pleasure without knowing about pain and the fact that you cannot know happiness without first knowing unhappiness is understood when you understand the Law of Knowledge. The simple fact is that God could not create good, without in someway creating evil. God created evil through predestination before good (as we know it), before evil (as we know it), before law (as we know it), and thus <u>before</u> sin (as we know it), and therefore God did not sin in his predestination.

Should we then be angry with God?

gp682» Remember all will come back into God (1Cor 15:28; GP 6). Therefore, at the end of creation no one can stand up and say he is better than anyone else, for all will have contributed to the madness, and soon to come, all will contribute to the harmony (GP 7, GP 8, GP 9). No, we should not be angry with God because would we want to live forever without the understanding of immortality, or pleasure, or happiness?

Time and the God

gp683» One secret to unlocking the paradoxes in the Bible pertaining to God is to know the Name of the God, and the significance of that Name. God's Name is the *BeComingOne* or *He (who) will-be*. The God who is everywhere and thus in a sense is everything, or at least his Power is everywhere, and since he is all-powerful, then his power is responsible for everything that was, is, and will be. When the BeComingOne speaks it pertains to the time that **was**, or that **is**, or that **is to come**, since he is becoming and his essence and works are in what was, what is, and what will be. Although God did create evil, he created evil through predestination <u>before</u> time or history (as we know it). To better understand this read and study the following chart.

gp684» Chart of Father and Time Below:

Time	Father and Time				
Before Creation	Pre-Creation Power **Father of All Things** predestinates everything before the cosmos				
Beginning	Beginning of Creation				
Creation Period [1 thru 7th day] Father gives all Power to his Right and Left Side, but all future power given to the Word, and through the Word to Jesus and his Church	[Power to the Right Side for all that is good]		Word of the BeComingOne Creates all things	[Power to the Left Side for all that is evil]	
	God is Light Right Cherub 2/3 of all angels		*God separates all things between light and darkness during a 6000 Year Period*	**Satan is Darkness** Left Cherub 1/3 of all angels	
	First-Angel	God's Angels		angel of Satan	Satan's angels
	Angel of God acts throughout OT in the affairs of the patriarchs of the Messiah	Influences and guides God's Prophets and OT Saints	All Father's power exists as everything diffused throughout the Creation	Tempts Adam and Eve to sin, is the father of lies and sin; misleads all mankind	Evil minds of Satan become the "other-minds" in first 6,000 years
	Angel Begets Jesus supernaturally		All power diffused between good and evil	Tempts Jesus throughout his life	Tempts all mankind
	Jesus is the **First** **Resurrection**		All power predestinated to return to the Father by the end of creation	Satan thrown out of the Godhead	
	Establishes his Church	Churches of Jesus Christ	Father still in control through predestination	Satan dwells in the Anti-Christ	Angels of Satan destroy world
	Jesus as King of Kings rules with the Saints	Christians Born of God in **Second Resurrection**	1000 Year Sabbath 7th Spiritual Day Kingdom of God rules on earth Earth is renewed	Satan punished in hell-fire for 1000 years. Mankind deceived by the evil angels during the first 6000 years are dead during the 1000 year Kingdom	
100 Years [8th Day] Father is All Typically	100 year Great Last Day 8th Spiritual period **Third Resurrection** All Become One in Good Spirit and in the System of Love; all evil behavior taken out of the Creation; heaven and earth still belong to first creation				
Endless Age [9th Day] Father exists as ONE with New Creation	New Heaven and Earth Created **Father is all in all** All return to the Father's Power through Jesus Christ's Spirit except at that time **billions of individuals** will have been created with the knowledge of good and evil Endless Age of God's Kingdom Continues forever				
Note: See *New Mind Papers* [NM 16] for explanation of spiritual days (1st through 9th day)					

God is Omnipresent: Everywhere

gp685» Besides the typical sense of God's omnipresence, which is that the God's spirit is everywhere in the sense that everything came out of God's spirit when the universe was created, and everything is a manifestation of that pre-creation spirit, there is an antitypical sense of God's omnipresence. As shown in this book, the true God is the BeComingOne. It is the BeComingOne who will incorporate ALL into Himself, so that will be "the God, all in all" (1Cor 15:28). It is the true God, which has ALL in Him, and it is this God that is omnipresent in the truest sense. At the true end of creation, God is everywhere because God is everything, "the God, all in all" (1 Cor 15:28). "I am the BeComingOne [YHWH] and there is none else" (Isa 45:6).

God is Omnipotent: Almighty

gp686» The typical sense of God's omnipotence (all-powerfulness) is that God predestinated everything through his power. But at the end of the true creation God is omnipotent because all will be in the God, thus, this true God will have *all* the power. At that time all people and powers will be in the One Spirit — the Spirit of LOVE. All at that time will be in the God: God will be many in ONE. All the powers will be in this true God.

God is Omniscient: Knows All

gp687» The typical sense of God's omniscience (all knowledge) is that God knows all because He predestinated all, so of course, He knows all because He predestinated all that happens before the true end of creation. But at the true end of creation ALL will be in the true God, therefore, all the individuals, with all of their total knowledge, will be in the true God. Thus, the true God has *all* knowledge because *all* those with knowledge will be in Him.

Who or What is God?

gp688» The following short summary is based on the Bible and all of this book:

- The **God (YHWH) is unlike any thing else**; there is none like him (Isa 46:9), and that was why Israel was not allowed to make any graven image or any likeness to depict Him (Exodus 20:4).

- **All came out of the pre-creation Power, the Father of all** (1Cor 8:6; Rom 11:36). This means that all have come out of the pre-creation Power, all were made out of the Father's Power and His "substance" or "essence."

- During the creation period (from day one to the End) the Father gave himself the Name, BeComingOne [YHWH] (Ex 3:14-15), for He is all that **was**; all that **is**, and all that **Will Come**, the **Almighty** (Rev 1:8); there is **none else but the BeComingOne** (Isa 45:18); there is no life outside of Him (John 5:26; Acts 17:28).

- **All came out of Him through predestination to learn about good and evil**, about time, about death, and about life, thus to learn about good and be able to appreciate it forever (GP 7). God predestinated everything that will be <u>before</u> the creation, <u>before</u> law, and <u>before</u> sin; God's predestination is without sin.

- **Because the true God is the BecomingOne**, because the God is all-powerful, because the God wishes all to be saved (1Tim 2:3-4; 2Pet 3:9), because the God will bring all back into himself through Jesus Christ (GP 6), this means that:

- all of creation, both physical and spiritual (Col 1:20; Eph 1:8-10,23; Phil 2:10; 3:21), will become one as individuals within the Spiritual power of Christ by the end (Eph 1:23; 1Cor 15:24-28), so that all will be in the true God, **God all in all:** all will be in subjection to the ONE ALL (1Cor 15:28) under the system of love, for the true God is Love (1John 4:8).

- **Adam prefigured:** From one Adam came all of the individuals of mankind; from one mind-substance Power and essence is coming the **many in the ONE God.** God is reproducing Himself as Adam reproduced himself.

- "**BeComingOne, himself, the Gods.**" [Deut 4:35, 39]

The true God is the BeComingOne that has become the ONE-ALL.

GP: Appendix

More Details

Yehowah / Yahweh / Jehovah / Lord
Massoretic Text
More Language Details on God's NAME
More on "I will be"

Hebrew Words Written Without Vowels

gp689» At first the Hebrew language, as with other Semitic languages, was written only with consonants and was written from right to left. When the Hebrews read, they added the vowels in their mind to the words. In Moses' time there was apparently no method of writing vowels in Hebrew. Two thousand years after Moses a system of vowel points was developed that was added below, between, and sometimes on top of the letters:

- "The present pronunciation of this consonantal text, its vocalization and accentuation, rest on the tradition of the Jewish schools, as it was finally fixed by the system of punctuation (§ 7 *h*) introduced by Jewish scholars about the seventh century A. D." [*Gesenius' Hebrew Grammar*, p. 12]

Therefore when Moses wrote down God's NAME he did not write any vowels.

Is the Correct Pronunciation of the NAME Possible?

gp690» Moses did not write down the vowels for God's NAME, since in his time there was no method to write vowels. But it is said that the correct vowels for God's NAME were passed down orally through the years and are preserved in today's vowel point system. But may be unlikely that the exact sound of the Biblical Hebrew has been preserved for us today because there were different schools with different methods and interpretations, and there were Jews with different ways of pronouncing the Hebrew words (*Gesenius' Grammar*, p. 38, footnote 2; see § 7 *i*; § 8 "Preliminary Remark"; p. 42 footnote 3; etc.). And of course there were no tape recorders in Moses' time. But we will examine this question anyway to help we can better understand the problem over the last three millenniums.

Yehowah or Yahweh or Jehovah or LORD

gp691» In the King James Version of the Bible, we see the word "LORD" was used throughout the Old Testament for the NAME of God. As we have indicated in GP 1, LORD is a mistranslation. "LORD" was translated from a Hebrew word "YHWH," which means — the BeComingOne, or he (who) will-be. In square-shaped letters of the Hebrew language the NAME looked like this: יהוה (read right to left). The square-shaped letters are the ones we see in today's copies of the Hebrew Old Testament. But the more ancient Hebrew letters looked somewhat like the ancient Phoenician or ancient Greek letters. Because of different scribal styles or schools, the ancient Hebrew alphabet varied slightly through the ages. In one style of the old-Hebrew alphabet God's NAME, YHWH, looked something like this:

𐤄𐤅𐤄𐤉

gp692» *Consonants Only*. Hebrew is read from right to left *vis-a-vis* English's left to right. Originally, the Old Testament was written with only the consonants. "As the Hebrew writing on monuments and coins mentioned in [2] *d* [dated c. 850 B.C. to c. 138 A.D.] consists only of consonants, so also the writers of the Old Testament books used merely the consonant-signs (§ 1 *k*), and even now the written scrolls of the Law used in the synagogues must not, according to ancient custom, contain anything more. The present pronunciation of this consonantal text, its vocalization and accentuation, rest on the pronunciation of the Jewish schools, as it was finally fixed by the system of punctuation (§ 7 *h*) introduced by Jewish scholars about the seventh century A.D.; cf. § 3 *b*" (§ 2 *i*, pp. 11-12, *Gesenius' Hebrew Grammar*, Oxford, 1910 [1980 reprint]). The Hebrews' written language was thus a "shorthand" language. The vowels were dropped to shorten the space and the time needed to write documents. Other ancient languages were also written only with their consonants. Yet today when we look at the Hebrew texts of the Bible, we see square-lettered Hebrew with *vowel-points* under them. Vowel-points are little dots or lines written under, inside, and over the consonants.

gp693» *No Paragraphs, No Verses, No Spaces*. Up to the finding of the Dead Sea Scrolls sometime around 1945 there were no vowels in these older manuscripts, there were no verses, and there were no paragraphs. But one copy of Isaiah of the Dead Sea Scrolls had "paragraph divisions correspond almost exactly to those in the modern Hebrew Bible" (St. Mark' Monastery Isaiah Scroll, IQIs[a], Willaim Sanford LaSor, *The Dead Sea Scrolls*, 1972, pp 29-30). In most of the older manuscripts there were not any separations or spaces between words, all the consonants ran together (Ginsburg, *Introduction to the Massoretico-Critical Edition of the Hebrew Bible*, pp. 158ff).

gp694» *Meticulous Transcription*. The Scribes did not have printing presses or computers; they copied the Bible by hand. In order to preserve the original words as best as possible, the Scribes were very meticulous, they counted words on each page (C.D. Ginsburg, *Introduction to the Massoretico-Critical Edition of the Hebrew Bible*, p. 109) and numbered the letters (Ginsburg, p. 113) and made lists in order to check each manuscript for error (see later).

Spelling of the Name of God

gp695» *Vowel Letters, Vowel Signs*. The Scribes and readers of the Bible learned from each other the correct pronunciation of each word. But the Masoretes, sometime near 600-700 A.D., began to place graphic-signs for vowels, which led to different systems of vowel-points seen in different Hebrew texts (Ginsburg, pp. 449ff; *Gesenius' Gram.* § 3*b*, 7*h,i*). Today most scholars from the West only study one system of vowel-points. Much earlier than this some scribes made use of vowel-letters (see later), although there seemed to be no uniform tradition (Ginsburg, p.299ff; *Gesenius' Gram.*, §7*a-g*).

Yehowah or Yahweh

gp696» Today (1989) we have only two Hebrew-Greek-English Interlinear Bibles. One Interlinear Bible (Pub. 1976/1986) was edited by Jay P. Green, and uses the so-called *Letteris Bible* (published by the British and Foreign Bible Society in 1866); the other Interlinear Bible (Pub. 1979/1985) was edited by John R. Kohlenberger III and uses the *Biblia Hebraica Stuttgartensia* (BHS) text (published 1967 / 77 by the German Bible Society in cooperation with the United Bible Societies, which reproduces the Leningrad Codex B19*a* [L]) with only a few deviations and is but a version of the *Biblia Hebraica* (BHK), edited by Kittel-Kahle (1905/1947). The Leningrad Codex was previously known as the St. Petersburg Codex B19*a*. This Codex is recognized as the oldest complete Hebrew Old Testament text of the Bible; it has vowel signs and is dated about 1009 A.D.

Yehowah

gp697» The *Letteris Bible* has vowel signs, and the Name of God is spelled: YEhOwAh. The vowels are **e**, **o**, and **a**. The vowel points for Yehowah looked as follows:

- **e**   The short or half vowel "e" was called the Sewa and was two dots, one above the other: ְ . It was placed under the consonant י (Yod), together they looked like this: יְ . The Sewa sounds like an "eh," or the "e" in emit, or no sound at all when used as a syllable divider.

- **o**   The "o" was a dot " ֹ " called the Holem and was placed above the " ו " (Waw) The Holem sounds like the "o" in roll or mold. The Waw and Holem together looked like this וֹ .

- **a**   The "a" was the vowel " ָ " called the Qames or Kamets and was placed under the ו (Waw) just before the ה (He). It looked something like a small compressed capital " T " and was placed under its letter. It sounds like the "a" in father. Waw used to be more commonly called Vav. This is one reason Jehovah had the "v" in it instead of the "w."

gp698» In the square-shaped Hebrew alphabet Yehowah looked like this:

$$\text{יְהֹוָה}$$

This spelling of God's NAME is also common in major Jewish-Hebrew texts. It is found in *The Pentateuch and Haftorahs*, edited by J.H. Hertz, Chief Rabbi, and published by the Soncino Press, 1956; the spelling is found in the *Interlinear Hebrew-English Old Testament* (Genesis-Exodus), by George R. Berry; the spelling is found in the C.D. Ginsburg's Hebrew Bible; the spelling is also found in some verses of the *Biblia Hebraica Stuttgartensia* (BHS), such as Gen 3:14; 9:26; Ex 3:2; 13:3,9,15; 14:1,8; etc.

Yehwah

gp699» In the *Biblia Hebraica Stuttgartensia* (BHS) God's NAME is spelled: YEhwAh. The vowels are **e** and **a**. The vowel mark called the Holem is missing. In the square-shaped Hebrew alphabet Yehwah looked like this: יְהוָה . Notice this is not Yahweh, but Yehwah. But as noted above Yehowah does appear in some verses in the BHS text. Yahweh does not.

Theory of Yahweh

gp700» But in many Biblical dictionaries, encyclopedias, and some translations of the Bible we see: **Yahweh**. This spelling has the same consonants, but with the vowels **a** and **e** instead of **e**, **o**, and **a**, or **e** and **a**. The spelling, Yahweh, does not appear in any Hebrew text. I repeat, Yahweh does not appear in any Massoretic text, or any ancient manuscript, or papyri, or on any coin. The same consonants, YHWH, appear in ancient writings, but not the vowels.

gp701» There is a popular theory that says that the Hebrew word "Yehowah" does not have its original vowel points, and that the original vowel points would make YHWH to be "Yahweh" instead of Yehowah. But there is no real proof of this spelling as we will show. This is a very popular theory. But it is only a theory. Just because a theory is popular doesn't make it a correct theory. It started out as a theory of a few, most notable was Gesenius, the great grammarian. Some of his students embraced this theory, and helped to make it dogma.

gp702» The reason many think that Yehowah is not the correct rendering of the Hebrew word is because over 2000 years ago, according to some, some of the Jews began substituting another word that meant "Lord" (the Hebrew, *'adhonay*, or Greek, *kurios*) when they read the Hebrew NAME for God in public. It is said that some of the Jews began doing this because they became very cautious about misusing the NAME of God due to a superstitious misunderstanding of the commandment given to Moses: "You shall not take the name of the Yehowah your God in vain" (Exodus 20:7). These Jews were extremely careful about taking the NAME of Yehowah in vain — they didn't use it at all, for they substituted the word "Lord" for "Yehowah." Therefore we see that one version of the Greek translation of the Old Testament (the *Septuagint*, LXX) had the Greek word, *Kurios* ("Lord") translated in place of Yehowah (YHWH).

gp703» According to tradition, this Greek translation was completed in Egypt in about the third century BC. F.F. Bruce in his, *The Canon of Scripture*, states that the original Greek text probably only contained the Law or the first five books of the Bible (p. 43). There are also copies of the Greek text of the Old Testament that have the ancient Hebrew letters for God's NAME instead of the Greek, *Kurios* (see below, God's NAME in Greek ...).

Gesenius and Yahweh

gp704» Gesenius, the famous 19th century expert in Oriental literature, popularized this theory:

- "Whenever, therefore, this *nomen tetragrammaton* [the four letter NAME of God] occurred in the sacred text, they were accustomed to substitute for it *'adhonay*, and thus the vowels of the noun *'adhonay* are in the Masoretic text placed under the four letters יהוה, but with this difference, that the initial Yod [י in יְהוָה] receives a simple and not a compound Sh'va [Sheva v. Hateph Patah or the vowel **e** v. **a**].... As it is thus evident that the word יְהוָה does not stand with its own vowels, ..." (see *Gesenius' Hebrew and Chaldee Lexicon*, Translated by Tregelles, Eerdmans Pub., 1974 printing, p. 337 under YHWH).

gp705» Notice carefully that the vowels, that were according to this theory, transposed from *'adhonay* to Yehowah, were not '**e**' (Sheva) '**o**' and '**a**,' but were '**a**' (Hateph Patah) '**o**' and '**a**.' Right here you should stop and think. From the beginning of their theory they use a sleight-of-hand to set this theory on its way. They say that the vowels from *'adhonay* were substituted for the real vowels in YHWH. (This is very suspicious because this is exactly opposite to the Written-Read or the *Kethib-Qere* method.) Yet Yehowah does not even have the vowels from *'adhonay*, for Yehowah does not read Y**a**howah, but Y**e**howah. After this sleight-of-hand they go on and make up a word, Yahweh, and say this is the true pronunciation. Yahweh, with its vowels, does not, I repeat, does not appear in any ancient document; only the constants YHWH appear. Arrogantly, a theory is made up that the NAME for God, יְהוָה, has the wrong vowels, and that the vowels were taken from the Hebrew,*'adhonay*, a word that meant lord or "my lords." (Read the discussion in *Gesenius' Hebrew-Chaldee Lexicon*, and see GP 1.) In reality Yahweh (or Yehwah [BHS] or Yehowah [Letteris]) does not have the vowels for *'adhonay*. The vowels in each word are different, thus the theory is nonsense. If you change one vowel in a word, you most often change the meaning of the word. If you change one vowel in the Hebrew אל (*'l*) you get either the meaning of "not" (*'al*) or "God"(*'el*) or "these" (*'el*) or "towards" (*'el*), which correspond to Strong's numbers 408, 410, 411, and 413. Notice 410, 411, and 413 are spelled the same, but have very different meanings; these different meanings are ascertained by context (Ginsburg, p. 451). There is a lot of craftiness going on here by the advocates for the spelling of Yahweh.

Gesenius admits the spelling "Yehowah" fits the evidence

gp706» But at the same time Gesenius made this argument for the spelling, Yahweh, he wrote, "**Also those who consider that Yehowah was the actual pronunciation, are not altogether without ground on which to defend their opinion. In this way can the abbreviated syllables Yeho and Yo, with which many proper names begin, be more satisfactorily explained.**" As the editor of said, "This last argument goes a long way to prove the vowels Y**eho**wah to be the true ones" (*Gesenius' Hebrew and Chaldee Lexicon*, Tran. by S. P. Tregelles, 1949, Eerdmans Pub p. 337).

gp707» To repeat, Gesenius said that those who hold that Yehowah is the actual pronunciation, "are not altogether without ground on which to defend their opinion. In this way can the abbreviated syllables **Yeho** and **Yo**, with which many proper names begin, be more satisfactorily explained."

Ginsburg lists some evidence for the use of "Yehowah"

gp708» From Ginsburg *Introduction to the Massoretico-Critical Edition of the Hebrew Bible* we quote:

- "There are, however, a number of compound names in the Bible into the composition of which three out of the four letters of the Incommunicable Name have entered. Moreover, these letters which begin the names in question are actually pointed Jeho [Yeho], as the Tetragrammaton itself and hence in a pause at the reading of the first part of the name it sounded as if the reader was pronouncing the Ineffable Name. To guard against it [according to a theory] an attempt was made by a certain School of redactors [editors] of the text to omit the letter *He* so that the first part of the names in question has been altered from *Jeho* into *Jo*." [P. 369ff]

gp709» Ginsburg then lists proper names which have the first three consonants of the Tetragrammaton (YHW [יהו]) which are mistranslated with their vowels into English as **Jeho** but should have been translated as: **Yehow**. Notice the third letter is left out of the English translations. Ginsburg first lists, the names with *Jeho*, then the same name altered by using *Jo* instead of *Jeho*.:

- Jehoachaz (Yehoachaz) appears 20 times in the Bible; Joachaz 4 times
- Jehoash (Yehoash) 17 times; Joash 47 times
- Jehozabad (Yehozabad) 4 times; Jozabad 9 times
- Jehohanan (Yehohanan) 9 times; Johanan 24 times
- Jehoiada (Yehoiada) 42 times; Joiada 5 times
- Jehoiachin (Yehoiachin) 10 times; Joiachin 1Time
- Jehoiakim (Yehoiakim) 37 times; Joiakim 4 times
- Jehoiarib (Yehoiarib) 2 times; Joiarib 5 times
- Jehonadab (Yehonadab) 8 times; Jonadab 7 times
- Jehonathan (Yehonathan) 79 times; Jonathan 42 times
- Jehoseph (Yehoseph) 1Time; is found as Joseph in all other passages
- Jehozadak (Yehozadak) 8 times; Jozadak 5 times, no distinction in the KJV
- Jehoram (Yehoram) 29 times; Joram 20 times
- Jehoshaphat (Yehoshaphat) 83 times; Joshaphat 2 times

So there were about 349 times where proper names were written in the Bible, using the first three consonants and first two vowel of God's NAME, which most agree is referring to Yehowah (Ginsburg, pp. 370-75). The consonant and vowel left out was the last letter and last vowel of God's NAME. That is the **a** and the **h**. It so happens that when an **ah** is used at the end of a verbal word, in many instances, in the Biblical Hebrew, it adds **emphasis** to the meaning of the verb.

Fourth Letter in God's NAME

Cohortative Verb?

gp710» The fourth consonant-letter of God's NAME, **Yehowah**, is the last **h**. In Hebrew when a word takes on a new letter (sometimes with a vowel), either as a prefix or suffix, the new letter adds a secondary meaning to the root word. Notice the suffix in God's NAME: the "ah" in Yehow**ah**. This is important. God's NAME has the suffix "ah" because God's NAME may be in the *cohortative* or is like a cohortative. Words in the Hebrew cohortative are imperfect verbal words with the suffix "ah" which has the effect of emphasizing the word (*Gesenius' Hebrew Grammar*, Oxford 2nd English Edition, § 48c, d, e, & i; Driver *Hebrew Tenses*, Chap IV). As explained previously in this book, God's NAME is an imperfect verbal word that may be called a proper noun because of the way it is used and explained in the Bible (Exo 3:12-16). And it was repeated twice by God for emphasis because when words are repeated twice in the Bible it was for emphasis to show the importance of the of the idea.

God's NAME is *Emphasized* – He will be!

gp711» Remember that when God first revealed his NAME He repeated it twice: "**I will be** that **I will be**." It is known that when words are repeated in Hebrew it has the effect of ***emphasizing*** the word (see Introduction in the *Emphasized Bible*, and *Gesenius' Hebrew Grammar*, § 133 k,l). For example in Genesis 2:17, the Hebrew word for "death" is repeated twice, and can be literally translated, "dying, you shall die." But when translated into English it becomes "you shall *surely* die." Or in Exodus 26:33 in Hebrew it has, "holy of the holies," and is translated as "the most holy" or "the most holy place." Therefore when God repeated his NAME twice (**I will be** that **I will be**), He was giving *emphasis* to his NAME.

gp712» God repeated his NAME twice for emphasis, "**I will be** that **I will be**." He again says that his NAME is **I will be**. He then changes it to **He will be** or **Yehowah** only because this is the only grammatically correct way for Moses or anyone else to address God. Moses couldn't grammatically say, "**I will be** has sent me," but he could correctly say, "**He (who) will be** has sent me."

What is a Cohortative Verb?

- The Hebrew cohortative "**lays stress on the determination underlying the action, and the personal interest in it**" (*Gesenius' Hebrew Grammar*, Oxford's 2nd English Edition, § 108a and § 48k, § 110c).

- "The cohortative, then, marks the presence of a strongly-felt inclination or impulse: in cases where this is accompanied by the ability to carry the wished-for action into execution, we may, if we please, employ *I, we will* ... in translating" (Driver, *Hebrew Tenses*, p. 53; "..." are in text).

- It is similar to the Arabic *energetic*, "which expressed a strongly-felt purpose or desire," "an emphatic command," or was used "to add a general emphasis to the assertion of a future fact" (*Hebrew Tenses*, Driver, p. 241).

- Notice Exodus 34:14 correct translation: "For you shall worship no other god: for the BeComingOne [YHWH], whose **name** is Zealous, is a zealous GOD." Zealous is from a Hebrew verb (*qanah*) that describes action that is intent on reaching a desired outcome. His name is zealous because He is intent on becoming, "I will be that I will be" and thus it is in the cohortative form. "The verb expresses a very strong emotion whereby some quality or possession of the object is desired by the subject [GOD]." (See p. 802 in the *Theological Wordbook of the Old Testament*, Vol. 2; p. 896 # 2127 in Jeff A. Benner, *The Torah: A Mechanical Translation*, 2019) This same Hebrew word is sometimes translated as "jealous" because, depending on context, can mean zeal for one's own property.

gp713» Grammarians have found a pattern or "rule" — the Hebrews added "ah" to the end of imperfect verbs to add emphasis to these verbs (*Gesenius' Hebrew Grammar*, § 48c, d, e, i, k; and § 46). We emphasize a word in writing by italicizing it or underlining it; in speech we emphasize a word by the way we stress the word. Names like "cohortative" or "imperative" are arbitrarily chosen by grammarians to explain apparently slight variations of the emphatic use of the "ah" suffix on imperfect verbs in the Hebrew language.

gp714» In our books, in order to write something, we have picked the spelling of **Yehowah**, which is the spelling found in major Jewish-Hebrew texts of the Old Testament (See "More Details" below). Nehemia Gordon in the last ten year or so has make some good arguments that indeed **Yehovah may be the correct spelling.** (see www.nehemiaswall.com/nehemia-gordon-name-god)

The above gives some evidence that Yehowah or Yehovah may have the original vowels.

Yah

gp715» There are 149 proper names in the Hebrew Bible which according to the Massoretic text end with **Yah** (Jah) (Ginsburg, pp. 387-96). For example, Abi**jah**, Uri**jah**, Hezeki**jah**, etc. The **Yah** in the 149 proper names (Jah in most English Bibles) are at the end of the words. Yeho**wah** has "ah" at the end of it. Hebrew has certain ways of ending words. Because Yehowah is similar to a cohortative verb, it ended with, "ah" (GP 1, "Cohortative Verb"). Yehowah fits the cohortative verbal rules, it fits the rule for verbs being used as nouns, and it also fits the Biblical text (Ex 3:9-16; gp92; see all GP 1). Yah is merely an abbreviation for **Yeho**wah: **Yah**.

gp716» Yehowah or Yehwah has the vowel-points written by "the" Massoretes. The spelling of Yahweh is found nowhere in any Massoretic text. But there is more against this theory.

Hebrew New Testament

gp717» The Jews of Christ's time were Hebrew and spoke and read in Hebrew or Aramaic (He Walked Among Us, pp.234ff). "The Israelites never wrote their sacred literature in any language but Aramaic and Hebrew, which are sister languages. The Septuagint was made in the 3rd century, B.C., for the Alexandrian Jews. This version was never officially read by the Jews in Palestine who spoke Aramaic and read Hebrew. Instead, the Jewish authorities condemned the work and declared a period of mourning because of the defects in the version.... Greek was never the language of Palestine. Josephus' book on the Jewish Wars was written in Aramaic. Josephus states that even though a number of Jews had tried to learn the language of the Greeks, hardly any of them succeeded.... Indeed, the teaching of Greek was forbidden by Jewish rabbis. It was said that it was better for a man to give his child meat of swine than to teach him the language of the Greeks" (Holy Bible From the Ancient Eastern Text, George M. Lamsa, Translator, Aramaic text, pp. ix & x; see Josephus' Antiquities of the Jews, Book 20, Chapter 11, Paragraph 2; The Life and Times of Jesus The Messiah, Alfred Edersheim, Bk. 1, Chap. 1, footnote #34; Ginsburg, p. 306). And there is some proof that at least some of the New Testament was originally written in Hebrew. In the fourth century, Jerome in his *Concerning Illustrious Men*, wrote:

- "Matthew, who is also Levi, and who from a publican came to be an apostle, first of all composed a Gospel of Christ in Judaea in the Hebrew language and characters for the benefit of those of the circumcision who had believed. Who translated it after that in Greek is not sufficiently ascertained. Moreover, the Hebrew itself is preserved to this day in the library at Caesarea, which the martyr Pamphilus so diligently collected. I also was allowed by the Nazarenes who use this volume in the Syrian city of Beroea to copy it" (Translated from Latin for the series "Texte und Untersuchungen zur Geschichte der altchristlichen Literatur," Vol. 14, Leipzig, 1896, edited by E.C. Richardson).

Also, recently a fragment of Mark was found written in Hebrew (*Bible Review*, 1989?). Nehemia Gordon has also found other fragments of NT Hebrew texts.

God's NAME in Greek Text Written in Hebrew

gp718» There is also some evidence today that there were Greek versions of the Old Testament that used the Hebrew word for God (YHWH) everywhere it should have been translated (*Bible Review*, "Glossary: New Testament Manuscripts," Feb. 1990, p. 9 top picture and inset text; *The Dead Sea Scrolls and the New Testament*, 1972, chapter 2, p. 30; Foreword, pp. 10ff, *The Kingdom Interlinear Translation of the Greek Scriptures*, 1969; see Appendix 1A, 1C, & 1D, pp. 1561ff of the *New World Translation of the Holy Scriptures — with References*, 1984 revised ed.). It is not only a possibility, but a probability that some used a Greek text that had the equivalent to the Hebrew YHWH in it instead of the Greek *Kurios* ("Lord"). But for some reason, either by historical accident or conspiracy to rid the church of Jewish tradition, this version did not prevail and thus we see many of today's translations are influenced by an Egyptian Greek version (*Septuagint*) of the Old Testament. Just how much this Greek version influenced theology can be seen by the following quote from Augustine in about the fourth century A.D.:

- There have, of course, been other translations of the Old Testament from Hebrew into Greek. We have versions by Aquila, Symmachus, Theodotion, and an anonymous translation which is known simply as the 'fifth edition.' Nevertheless, the Church [Catholic] has adopted the Septuagint as if it were the only translation. [*City of God*, by "Saint" Augustine, book 18, chapter 43]

Jehovah

gp719» The reason you see "Jehovah" used by some today is because it is a common translation of Yehowah. Even such names as "Jehoachaz," "Jehozabad," and "Jehohanan" should be rendered as "Yehoachaz," "Yehozabad," and "Yehohanan." Most English translations have a "J" in these words instead of a "Y."

gp720» The first known use of "Jehovah" is found in the book, *Pugeo Fidei*, on page 559, where it is spelled "Jehova" and where the square-lettered YHWH is found next to "Jehova." This was written or published by a Spanish monk, Raymundus Martini, in 1270 A.D (see photographic copy of the page in *Aid to Bible Understanding*, p. 885).

gp721» The reason "J" is found in Jehovah instead of "Y" is the same reason "J" was written in the King James Version instead of "Y" for such words as Jehoachaz, Jehozabad, and Jehohanan. The translators at that time felt that this translation was correct. Comparative studies with other related languages in the last two centuries has refined the art of translation. "Y" is now used to transliterate the Hebrew **Yod** (׳) instead of "J." Because the Jewish race was dispersed, either usage may be right, depending on local Jewish pronunciation norms.

gp722» The reason "v" is found in Jehovah instead of "w," is because in the past, at least some of the linguists believed that the Hebrew **waw** (ו) should be pronounced as the "v" and because some of the Jews pronounced it that way. In older Grammars and Biblical works *waw* was called *vav* (see "A Comparative Table of Ancient Alphabets," just before page 1 in *Gesenius's Hebrew and Chaldee Lexicon to the Old Testament Scriptures*, Wm. B. Eerdmans Pub, reprint of 1857 edition, reprinted 1974; *Gesenius' Grammar*, see §6a). *Gesenius' Hebrew Grammar* in the German language (1817-1909) had "w" for the Hebrew "w" (which is pronounced as a "v" in German), so the "w" in Gesenius' Grammar should be pronounced as a "v" in English.

Yehowah

gp723» From the above evidence and from the rest of GP 1 we see that **Yehowah** is the most likely correct transliteration from the Hebrew, and the "BeComingOne" is a correct translation of the true meaning of the Hebrew word into English. There is no good reason to use Yahweh instead of Yehowah. The spelling of Yahweh comes from an arrogant-intellectual mindset.

Massoretic Text

gp724» *Note*: **The quotes in the following section** were published in 1965 by Harry M. Orlinsky, Professor of the Bible Hebrew Union College, and were included in the "Prolegomenon" of Ginsburg's *Introduction to the Massoretico-Critical Edition of the Hebrew Bible* (the KTAV Publishing House's 1966 printing).

gp725» First "the" Massoretic Text is not one text. It is a collated and compiled text from many different texts. On the whole the variations between the texts are minor. The variations being mostly spelling, order of words, and a few additions by the scribes in order to clarify. After the invention of the printing press, there were no less than twenty-two printed texts of the Hebrew Bible printed between 1477 and 1521, eight of these containing the entire Bible (Ginsburg, p. X). Since then there have been the following editions of the Bible:

- Bomberg Rabbinic Bible (1524-26), edited by J. ben Chayim Bibles of Johannes Buxtorf (1611 & 1618-19)
- Joseph ben Abraham Athias's Bible (1661)
- Daniel Ernest Jablonski's Bible (1699)
- Johann Heinrich Michaelis's Bible (1720)
- Everard van der Hooght's Bible (1705)
- Benjamin Kennicott's Edition of the Bible (1776, 1780) August Hahn's Bible (1831)
- Meir Halevi Letteris' Bible (1852)
- The Letteris Bible (1866, British and Foreign Bible Society)
- Kittel's Biblia Hebraica, 1905-6, 1912/36 2nd & 3rd Ed (BHK).
- *Biblia Hebraica Stuttgartensia* (BHS), 1967/77
- and others...

gp726» The *Biblia Hebraica* (BHK) appeared with much fanfare because "it was supposed to represent the pure text achieved by Aaron ben Moses ben Asher, the great Masorete of the tenth century" (p.XIII).

gp727» "We are now ready to deal with the crux of the whole matter, something that the numerous editors of 'masoretic' editions of the Bible have overlooked, namely: **There never was, and there never can be, a single fixed masoretic text of the Bible!** It is utter futility and pursuit of a mirage to go seeking to recover what never was" (XVIII).

The Massoretic Text?

gp728» "There never was and there can never be 'the masoretic text' or 'the text of the Masoretes.' All that, at best, we might hope to achieve, in theory, is 'a masoretic text,' or a text of the Masoretes,' that is to say, a text worked up by Ben Asher, or by Ben Naftali, or by someone in the Babylonian tradition, or a text worked up with the aid of the masoretic notes of an individual scribe or of a school of scribes. But as matters stand, we cannot even achieve a clear-cut text of the Ben Asher school, or of the Ben Naftali school, or of a Babylonian school, or a text based on a single masoretic list; indeed, it is not at all certain that any such ever existed.... At the same time, it cannot be emphasized too strongly that none of these manuscripts or of the printed editions based on them has any greater merit or 'masoretic' authority than most of the many other editions of the Bible, than, say, the van der Hooght, Hahn, Letteris, Baer, Rabbinic and Ginsburg Bibles" (pp. XXIII-XXIV).

Written-Read, Kethib-Qere

gp729» In the margins of the Massoretic text(s) they have notations about certain word variations. The written text (Kethib or Kethiv) was how the text was received; the notes in the margin were how some believed it should be read (Qere or Keri). "It is now scarcely possible to deny that the system of Kethib-Qere readings had its origin in variant readings; by the same token, the theory that the Qere readings are but corrections (really a euphemism for 'emendations') of the Kethib readings has no real justification" (p. XXIV). Examples by Orlinsky followed to page XXIX. "It is now admitted by the best textual critics that in many instances the reading exhibited in the text is preferable to the marginal variant, inasmuch as it sometimes preserves the archaic orthography [spelling] and sometimes gives the original reading" (Ginsburg, p. 184).

gp730» There is no single manuscript that contains all of the Kethib-Qere variations: "In order to exhibit, therefore, all the Keris [marginal readings] irrespective of the different Schools, it is absolutely necessary to collate all the existing MSS. which at present is almost an impossible task" (Ginsburg words, p. 185-86).

- "In summary: none of the 'masoretic' editions of the Bible published to date has genuinely masoretic authority for hundreds of Kethib-Qere that they offer the reader" (p. XXIX).

Ben Asher V. Ben Naftali

gp731» "The vast majority of the scholars who have attempted to work up 'the' masoretic text of the Bible have scarcely bothered with the system of Ben Naftali.... A few scholars, e.g., Ginsburg and Baer, did pay attention to Ben Naftali, even if they usually preferred Ben Asher's readings... But the question asks itself: What is there inherently in the masoretic work of Ben Asher school that gives it greater authority than that of the Ben Naftali school?" (p. XXIX-XXX).

gp732» "All the Masoretes, from first to last, were essentially preservers and recorders of the pronunciation of Hebrew as they heard it" (p. XXXII).

Tiberian Massoretes

gp733» "Due to the efforts of the Tiberian Massoretes their system of punctuation had displaced all the others by the end of the 9th century. But by this no absolutely uniform text of the Bible was yet established. These Tiberian Massoretes among themselves continued to hold different views on many issues" (p. XXXV).

gp734» Note. The following quotes (gp229, gp231-235) are from C.D. Ginsburg's *Introduction to the Massoretico-Critical Edition of the Hebrew Bible*:

Vowel-Letters Theory

gp735» "To facilitate still further the study of the unpointed consonants on the part of the laity, the Scribes gradually introduced into the text the *matres lectionis* which also served as vowel-letters. But in this branch of their labours as is the case in the other branches, the different Schools which were the depositories of the traditions themselves were not uniform."(p. 299) It should also be noted that vowel-letters when used were used before there were vowel-points. Vowel-points superseded the system of vowel-letters.

gp736» According to the *Gesenius's Hebrew Grammar*,

- "the partial expression of the vowels by certain consonants (א י ו ה), which sufficed during the lifetime of the language, and for a still longer period afterwards...."(§7b)

- "When the language had died out, the ambiguity of such a writing [using vowel-letters] must have been found continually more troublesome; and as there was thus a danger that the correct pronunciation might be finally lost, the vowel signs or vowel points were invented in order to fix it.... To complete the historical vocalization of the consonantal text a phonetic system was devised, so exact as to show all vowel-changes occasioned by lengthening of words, by the tone, by gutturals, &c.... The pronunciation followed is in the main that the Palestinian Jews of about the sixth century A.D."(§7h,i)

From §7b of *Gesenius' Grammar* we see that the consonant:

- י = ê and î,

- ו = ô and û,

- ה = "in the inflection of the verbs לָה the long vowels **a, e,** and **è**.

Thus, even using the theory of the vowel-letter system, God's NAME reads, Yehowah.

Children Reading the Bible

gp737» Just before the time of Christ, schools were or had been established and "at the age of five, moreover, every boy had to learn to read the Bible. As a consequence it was strictly enacted that the greatest care was to be taken that the copies of the sacred books from which the Sopherim imparted instruction should be accurately written. It is to these facts that Josephus refers when he declares 'our principal care of all is to educate our children.' "(p. 304-05)

Josephus, Titus, Vespasian, and Severus to the Massorah

gp738» "Josephus tells us that Titus presented him with Codices of the Sacred Scriptures from the spoils of the Temple, and we know that there were others [MSS.] in the possession of distinguished doctors of the Law, which exhibited readings at variance with the present textus receptus.... Josephus records that among the trophies which Vespasian brought from the Temple to Rome was the Law of the Jews. This he ordered to be deposited in the royal palace circa 70 A.D. About 220 A.D. the emperor Severus who built a synagogue at Rome which was called after his name, handed over this MS. to the Jewish community, and though both the synagogue and the MS have perished, a List of variations from this ancient Codex has been preserved. This List I [Ginsburg] printed in my Massorah from the able article by the learned Mr. Epstein. Since then I have found a duplicate of this List in a MS of the Bible in the Paris National Library No. 31 (folio 399a) where it is appended as a Massoretic Rubric. The List in this Codex, though consisting of the same number of variations and enumerated almost in the same order, differs materially from the one preserved in the Midrash as will be seen from the following analysis of the two records, exhibits the primitive Rubric. The heading of the Paris List is as follows: These verses which were written in the Pentateuch Codex found in Rome and carefully preserved and locked up in the Synagogue of Severus, differs as regards letters and words" (pp. 409-411). Examples of differences followed this quote (pp. 411-20).

Massorites

gp739» "We thus see that the registration of anomalous forms began during the period of the second Temple. The words of the text, especially of the Pentateuch were now finally settled, and passed over from the Sopherim or the redactors to the safe keeping of the Massorites. Henceforth the Massorites became the authoritative custodians of the traditionally transmitted text. Their functions were entirely different from those of their predecessors the Sopherim. The Sopherim as we have seen, were the authorised revisers and redactors of the text according to certain principles [This is a popular theory; the Bible was a Holy book, and thus was not allowed to be tampered with; any revisions or editing was at most minor.], the Massorites were precluded from developing the principles and altering the text in harmony with these canons. Their province was to safeguard the text delivered to them by 'building a hedge around it,' to protect it against alterations or the adoption of any readings which still survived in MSS. or were exhibited in the ancient Versions. For this reason they marked in the margin of every page in the Codices every unique form, every peculiarity in the orthography, every variation in ordinary phraseologies, every deviation in dittographs &c. &c.

gp740» "In the case of the Pentateuch, the Massoretic work was comparatively easy since its text, as we have seen, was as a whole substantially the same during the period of the second Temple as it is now.... The present text, therefore, is not what the Massorites have compiled or redacted, but what they themselves have received from their predecessors and conscientiously guarded and transmitted with the marvelous checks and counter checks which they have devised for its safe preservation" (pp. 421-22). Examples are then given of the care the Massorites took (pp. 423ff).

gp741» Ginsburg gives information on the vowel-points (pp. 451-68).

More Language Details

Yehowah, Similar to Participles

gp742» God's NAME is a verb used as a noun. The English language has verbals that act as adjectives or nouns. The English present participle is the *ing* form of verbs used as adjectives; the gerund is the *ing* form of verbs used as a noun. A Greek participle is a verb or verbal used as an adjective or noun, and is thus a verbal adjective or is a verbal "noun" or verbal substantive when it is used with the article. A Greek participle partakes of both the noun and verb. In Matthew 11:3, John the Baptist sent two of his disciples to ask Jesus, "Are you The **Coming One**, or do we look for another." John wanted to know if Jesus was the Messiah, The Coming One. John was expecting the Messiah (Matt 3:11). The Greek word with its definite article in Matthew 11:3 is ὁ ἐρχόμενος, or Strong's # 2064. It is classified as a verb, participle, present tense, masculine, and singular (*Analytical Greek New Testament*, Friberg, p. 33). The Greek participle partakes "of both noun and verb" (A. T. Robertson's Grammar, p. 372; see Friberg, p. 810). Robertson classifies this participle as a "future participle" (p. 1118). The same word is in Revelation 1:8 but is translated as, "who is to come" in "Lord the God, who is, who was, and **who is to come**, the almighty" (see Rev 1:4; 4:8; 11:17). This can also be correctly translated:

- "Lord, the God, the is, the was, and **the Coming-One**, the almighty."

Is is in the present tense, **was** is in the imperfect tense, and **Coming-One** is a verb in its present participle tense, but A.T. Robertson classifies this particular participle as a "future participle" (p. 1118). The Hebrew word **Yehowah** is a verb used as a noun, while the Greek participle **coming** (#2064) or **Coming-One** is a verb used as a noun; it is a verbal substantive. In Matthew 11:3 the "coming one" is synonymous for the Messiah.

Hebrew Participle

gp743» It should be noted that Hebrew has different shades of the participle: some act in a more verbal character, some more as adjectives, and some as nouns depending on context or syntax (*Gesenius' Gram.* §50 & §116a,g,f). The Hebrew participles "occupy a middle place between the noun and the verb." A *participle active* is dissimilar from an imperfect verb: participle active expresses simple duration of an activity; an imperfect expresses progressive duration (*Gesenius' Gram.* §116c; Driver, p. 35ff).

Yehowah, The NAME, is a Verb

gp744» After Moses asked God His NAME, He answered with **I will be** repeating it twice, then He told Moses to tell Israel that His NAME was **I will be**, and right after this He told Moses to tell Israel that His NAME was **Yehowah** [יְהוָה]. As we saw above "I will be" was in the imperfect tense. Also "Yehowah" is in the imperfect tense. The Hebrew YHWH is a verb. God's NAME comes from a verb. The stem or root of God's NAME is, HWH, which is a *to be* verb. By looking at *Gesenius' Hebrew Grammar* § 40 *c*, we see that the normal method of converting the *to be* verb (HWH) into the imperfect, 3rd person, masculine gender form, is to add the Y [י] to the front of the verb. This makes God's NAME mean *he will be* according to the Hebrew grammar rules. But we see in Genesis 27:29 and Ecc. 11:3 (*Gesenius' Hebrew Grammar* § 75 *s*), YHW [יְהוּ], does mean *will be* or even, *he will be*. Notice in these two scriptures they don't have the last letter, H [ה], of God's NAME as written by Moses. Most experts affirm that YHWH is from Hebrew verb [HWH] and that it is in the imperfect, 3rd person, masculine gender, and when used as a noun means *He who will be* (Brown, Driver, Briggs, Gesenius Hebrew and English Lexicon, p. 218 Col. 1).

NAME: An Imperfect Verb

gp745» **Yehowah** is an imperfect verb in the third person singular pronoun form of the verb *HWH*. The Hebrew *HWH* [הוה] is Strong's # 1933 and means "to be, become, or come to pass" (*Hebrew and English Lexicon*, Brown, Driver, Briggs, & Gesenius, under הוה). It is felt by some to be a more ancient form of the verb *HYH*, and is found in Genesis 27:29 (*Analytical Hebrew and Chaldee Lexicon*, Zondervan, p.171; and other Hebrew Lexicons). **Yehowah** is the correct form for an imperfect verb in its third person, singular, masculine of the verb, *hwh*, according to the table in *Gesenius' Grammar*, §40.

gp746» When Moses wrote God's NAME he used a less common form of the verb *to be*. The common form was, *hyh*. If Moses used the *to be* verb "hyh," then God's NAME would have been expressed as, *'hyh* when spoken by God, or *yhyh* when spoken by us. For God's NAME Moses used the less common form of the verb *to be*; Moses may have used *hwh* instead of *hyh* in his books in order to differentiate God's NAME from the more common, *hyh*. The meaning of either *yhyh* or YHWH, is **He Will Be**.

NAME: Imperfect Verb, Not Future Tense

gp747» Some call the Hebrew imperfect verb a future tense word, but this is not correct. From *Gesenius' Hebrew Grammar* (Oxford, 1980 reprint) we see that:

- "The Hebrew (Semitic) *Perfect* denotes in general that which is *concluded*, *completed*, and *past*, that which is *represented* as accomplished, even though it is continued into present time or even be actually still future. The *Imperfect* denotes, on the other hand, the *beginning*, the *unfinished*, and the *continuing*, that which is just happening, which is conceived as in process of coming to pass, and hence, also, that which is yet future; likewise also that which occurs repeatedly or in a continuous sequence in the past (Latin Imperfect)." [§ 47.1, note 1].

gp748» More on the Hebrew Imperfect verb from S.R. Driver's *Hebrew Tenses*,

- In marked antithesis to the tense [perfect] we have just discussed, the imperfect in Hebrew, as in the other Semitic languages, indicates action as *nascent* [beginning], as evolving itself actively from its subject, as developing. The imperfect does not imply *mere* continuance as such (which is the function of the participle), though, inasmuch as it emphasizes the process introducing and leading to completion, it expresses what may be termed *progressive* continuance." [p. 27]

More on "I will be"

gp749» From *Aid to Bible Understanding*, a 1971 Jehovah Witnesses' book, we see under "Jehovah":

- "God's reply in Hebrew was "'*Eh'yeh asher 'eh'yeh*." While some translations render this as '**I am that I am**,' the Hebrew verb (*ha'yah*) from which the word *'eh'yeh* is drawn does not mean simply *to exist*. Rather, it means *to come into existence, to happen, occur, become*, ... Thus, the footnote of the *Revised Standard version* gives as one reading '**I will be what I will be**' (similar to Isaac Leeser's translation 'I will be that I will be') while the *New World Translation*, reads '**I shall prove to be what I shall prove to be**.' " [p. 888, col. 2]

In the Jehovah Witnesses' translation of the Hebrew verb, *'ehyeh* (from Strong's # 1961), in their *New World Translation*, they add "prove to" to their "I shall be" by way of extending the meaning of the Hebrew word, not by way of its most common usage of the verb in the Bible. This extending of the meaning is not necessarily wrong, for God will prove to be all that He says he will be.

Index

1000 years
    man in .... GP 7:12 | Pg 208

144,000 .... GP 1:22 | Pg 88, GP 5:27 | Pg 177

abortion .... GP 7:11 | Pg 207

Abraham
    angel .... GP 3:3 | Pg 117

age
    new .... BP 1:13 | Pg 35
    old .... BP 1:13 | Pg 35

All
    Christ .... GP 6:5 | Pg 189
    God .... GP 6:5 | Pg 189
    God's Name .... GP 6:5 | Pg 189
    when .... GP 6:5 | Pg 189

all glory .... GP 6:4 | Pg 188

all power .... GP 9:7 | Pg 240

all saved .... GP 6:1 | Pg 185

all Spirit .... GP 6:4 | Pg 188

all Yehowah .... GP 6:5 | Pg 189

all yhwh .... GP 6:5 | Pg 189

almighty .... GP 9:7 | Pg 240
    God .... GP 6:4 | Pg 188
    God is .... GP 1:10 | Pg 76
    Jesus .... GP 6:4 | Pg 188

analogy

    marriage and Christ .... GP 5:5 | Pg 155

Angel .... **GP 3:2 | Pg 116, GP 6:6 | Pg 190**
    Abraham .... GP 3:3 | Pg 117
    all, for .... GP 6:7 | Pg 191
    Balaam .... GP 3:4 | Pg 118
    Gabriel .... GP 3:5 | Pg 119
    God's presence, of .... GP 3:5 | Pg 119
    Hagar .... GP 3:2 | Pg 116
    Jacob .... GP 3:3 | Pg 117, GP 3:5 | Pg 119
    Jesus, inside of .... GP 4:7 | Pg 134
    Joshua .... GP 3:7 | Pg 121
    Manoah .... GP 3:4 | Pg 118
    messenger, is .... GP 3:1 | Pg 115
    Michael .... GP 3:6 | Pg 120
    Moses .... GP 3:3 | Pg 117
    Name given to .... GP 3:9 | Pg 123
    our own .... GP 6:6 | Pg 190
    Zechariah .... GP 3:6 | Pg 120

angel of Becoming-One
    Jesus, in .... GP 4:9 | Pg 136

angels
    better than .... GP 5:13 | Pg 163
    spirits, and .... GP 6:5 | Pg 189
    stars, and .... GP 6:5 | Pg 189

anti-matter .... GP 1:1 | Pg 67

antitypical meanings .... BP 4:3 | Pg 53

appreciation
    what is it .... GP 7:5 | Pg 201

archangel
    Michael .... GP 3:6 | Pg 120

Asher .... **GP: Appendix | Pg 262**

atomic inferno... BP 1:11 | Pg 33

Aztecs.. GP 1:2 | Pg 68

bad news.. BP 1:10 | Pg 32

Balaam

    angel.. GP 3:4 | Pg 118

Basic Law of Knowledge .... GP 7:3 | Pg 199, GP 7:15 | Pg 211

Becoming-One

    Jesus was/is/will-be... GP 8:3 | Pg 219

    Word... GP 3:10 | Pg 124

Becoming-One Papers

    how to read them .... BP 5:1 | Pg 55

becomingness of Jesus...................................... GP 5:12 | Pg 162

beginning

    Word, was the.. GP 5:24 | Pg 174

Ben Asher V. Ben Naftali .... GP: Appendix | Pg 262

Bible .... GP 1:3 | Pg 69

    three tests... BP 3:5 | Pg 47

Bible Paper (Beginning Papers).............. BP 3:1 | Pg 43, BP 3:3 | Pg 45

Biological Catastrophe

    Biological .... BP 1:13 | Pg 35

birth of Jesus

    promised beforehand .... GP 4:3 | Pg 130

black holes.. GP 1:1 | Pg 67

blame for evil .... GP 8:11 | Pg 227

blind

    light and darkness.. GP 7:3 | Pg 199

body

    death and spirit .... GP 4:14 | Pg 141

body, new .... GP 6:10 | Pg 194

brain cell

    mindset .... BP 2:5 | Pg 42

Bruce, F.F. .... **BP 3:8 | Pg 50**
chart
    Goal of creation.. GP 9:1 | Pg 234
cherubim
    yhwh is... GP 1:39 | Pg 105
cherubs .... **GP 8:4 | Pg 220, GP 9:3 | Pg 236**
    face each other .... GP 8:6 | Pg 222
    one, are... GP 8:6 | Pg 222
    Yehowah is THE .... GP 1:37 | Pg 103
    yhwh is... GP 1:37 | Pg 103
Children
    Reading the Bible.................................. GP: Appendix | Pg 263
children of God .... **GP 5:26 | Pg 176**
Children Reading the Bible .... **GP: Appendix | Pg 263**
Christ .... **GP 4:7 | Pg 134**
    ALL the power of his Father .... GP 6:1 | Pg 185
    and the Word... GP 10:3 | Pg 247
    Came From God .... GP 4:8 | Pg 135
    into the Father... GP 5:12 | Pg 162
    Jesus not called before death............................. GP 4:1 | Pg 128
    mystery .... GP 6:2 | Pg 186
    suffered, why... GP 7:10 | Pg 206
    temple.. GP 4:10 | Pg 137
    tempted .... GP 4:10 | Pg 137
    tested .... GP 4:10 | Pg 137
    will fulfill all things .... GP 6:5 | Pg 189
    words from God .... GP 4:12 | Pg 139
Christ & Father
    were two .... GP 4:8 | Pg 135
Chrysippus .... **GP 7:12 | Pg 208**
Cohortative.. **GP: Appendix | Pg 257**

verb with emphasis .... GP: Appendix | Pg 257

cold and hot .... GP 7:4 | Pg 200

color green .... GP 7:16 | Pg 212

commission

    Jesus' .... GP 6:1 | Pg 185

complementary knowledge .... GP 7:10 | Pg 206

Consonants Only .... GP: Appendix | Pg 253

Cortez .... GP 1:2 | Pg 68

cosmos

    created out of spirit .... GP 10:3 | Pg 247

creation

    new .... GP 5:9 | Pg 159

    predestination before the creation .... GP 10:3 | Pg 247

creator

    God is .... GP 1:11 | Pg 77

    God of all .... GP 5:24 | Pg 174

cycle, great .... GP 6:9 | Pg 193

dating method

    radioactive dating .... BP 1:5 | Pg 27

David

    seed, his .... GP 4:5 | Pg 132

death

    Jesus' (why) .... GP 4:15 | Pg 142

    life, and .... GP 7:5 | Pg 201

death and immortality .... GP 1:7 | Pg 73, GP 1:8 | Pg 74

death of Christ .... GP 4:13 | Pg 140

death of Jesus

    not called `Christ' before .... GP 4:1 | Pg 128

decay rates, constant

    no proof .... BP 1:6 | Pg 28

deformities .... GP 6:11 | Pg 195

dimensions
- physical & spiritual .... GP 7:9 | Pg 205
- physical and spiritual .... GP 7:9 | Pg 205

dual meaning of names .... GP 1:21 | Pg 87

duality .... BP 4:1 | Pg 51

earth is young system .... BP 1:9 | Pg 31

Elijah
- John, and .... GP 5:25 | Pg 175

elohim
- name of God(s) .... GP 1:36 | Pg 102
- Plural .... GP 1:36 | Pg 102

Elohim, Yehowah .... GP 1:42 | Pg 108

emphasized
- God's Name, is .... GP: Appendix | Pg 258

evil
- and predestination .... GP 10:4 | Pg 248
- God created it .... GP 7:6 | Pg 202
- know evil to know good? .... GP 7:1 | Pg 197, GP 7:2 | Pg 198
- know it to know good .... GP 7:2 | Pg 198
- predestinated .... GP 10:4 | Pg 248
- problem of .... GP 1:12 | Pg 78
- Problem Of Evil .... GP 1:12 | Pg 78
- seek it? .... GP 7:6 | Pg 202
- who is to blame? .... GP 8:11 | Pg 227
- why .... GP 7:8 | Pg 204
- why know evil .... GP 7:2 | Pg 198
- why know it .... GP 7:2 | Pg 198

evolution .... BP 1:5 | Pg 27

Exodus 3:12 v. Exodus 3:14 .... GP 1:24 | Pg 90

experience teaches .... GP 7:2 | Pg 198

eyes .... GP 9:5 | Pg 238

Ezekiel .... GP 9:3 | Pg 236

faces .... GP 9:5 | Pg 238

fact, basic

    God does not lie .... GP 1:5 | Pg 71

Father

    and Jesus Christ .... GP 10:4 | Pg 248

    and time chart.. GP 10:5 | Pg 249

    Jesus as the.. GP 5:12 | Pg 162

    legal... GP 4:22 | Pg 149

    proof God is Father... GP 2:1 | Pg 112

    see Him? .... GP 2:2 | Pg 113

    yhwh is .... GP 2:2 | Pg 113

Father & Christ

    were two... GP 4:8 | Pg 135

Finegan, Jack .... BP 3:8 | Pg 50

first, the... GP 8:2 | Pg 218

flesh

    God made, when... GP 4:12 | Pg 139

    Jesus came in... GP 4:7 | Pg 134

    salvation of.. GP 5:10 | Pg 160

    Word became .... GP 5:27 | Pg 177

forces

    two .... GP 7:6 | Pg 202

four beasts .... GP 9:2 | Pg 235

four living creatures................................ GP 9:2 | Pg 235

free will .... GP 10:2 | Pg 246

Gabriel

    angel... GP 3:5 | Pg 119

general review (Part 3) .... GP 3:12 | Pg 126

general review (Part 5) .... GP 5:32 | Pg 182

general review (Part 9) .... GP 9:8 | Pg 241

glory

    all .... GP 6:4 | Pg 188

Glory of God .... GP 5:30 | **Pg 180**

    Christ into .... GP 5:12 | Pg 162

    Christ, and .... GP 5:12 | Pg 162

    throne, and .... GP 9:6 | Pg 239

God

    age, His .... GP 7:11 | Pg 207

    all back into .... GP 6:3 | Pg 187

    all out of .... GP 6:9 | Pg 193

    All Things Possible .... GP 1:10 | Pg 76

    almighty .... GP 1:10 | Pg 76

    and omnipotent .... GP 10:6 | Pg 250

    and omnipresent .... GP 10:6 | Pg 250

    and omniscient .... GP 10:6 | Pg 250

    and Time .... GP 10:5 | Pg 249

    Angel of God .... GP 3:2 | Pg 116

    angry with God? .... GP 10:4 | Pg 248

    Attributes .... GP 1:9 | Pg 75

    Christ the man, inside of .... GP 4:6 | Pg 133

    created all .... GP 5:24 | Pg 174

    creator .... GP 1:11 | Pg 77

    definition of .... GP 1:4 | Pg 70

    did not die on the cross .... GP 4:12 | Pg 139

    elohim .... GP 1:36 | Pg 102

    elohim is plural .... GP 1:36 | Pg 102

    everywhere, is .... GP 1:9 | Pg 75

    evil, created .... GP 7:6 | Pg 202

    faces of .... GP 9:5 | Pg 238

    glory of .... GP 5:30 | Pg 180

    Gods .... GP 1:35 | Pg 101

good, is	GP 1:13 | Pg 79
great cycle	GP 6:9 | Pg 193
I Am	GP 1:28 | Pg 94
image of	GP 5:8 | Pg 158
immortal	GP 4:12 | Pg 139, GP 5:15 | Pg 165
immutability of	GP 1:32 | Pg 98
Importance of a Name	GP 1:20 | Pg 86
invisible	GP 1:10 | Pg 76, GP 5:28 | Pg 178
is love	GP 10:1 | Pg 245
Jesus before his death, not	GP 4:8 | Pg 135
Jesus Christ, and	GP 5:1 | Pg 151
Jesus, and	GP 5:13 | Pg 163
kills, destroys, etc	GP 1:14 | Pg 80
knowledge, has all	GP 1:9 | Pg 75
left & right sides?	GP 1:12 | Pg 78
left side	GP 1:14 | Pg 80, GP 8:7 | Pg 223
lie, does not	GP 1:5 | Pg 71, GP 1:13 | Pg 79
life, and	GP 5:25 | Pg 175
life, is	GP 1:9 | Pg 75
love, is	GP 1:13 | Pg 79, GP 10:1 | Pg 245
made flesh (when)	GP 4:12 | Pg 139
Name is emphasized	GP: Appendix | Pg 258
Name, Imperfect Verb	GP: Appendix | Pg 265
names of	GP 1:19 | Pg 85
Negative Aspects of God	GP 1:14 | Pg 80
New Testament's	GP 8:13 | Pg 229
Nothing Else Besides God	GP 1:9 | Pg 75
nothing impossible for?	GP 5:15 | Pg 165
omnipotent	GP 10:6 | Pg 250
omnipresent	GP 1:9 | Pg 75, GP 10:6 | Pg 250
omniscient	GP 1:9 | Pg 75, GP 10:6 | Pg 250

    one is.. GP 1:38 | Pg 104
    one versus only... GP 1:39 | Pg 105
    one, is... GP 1:36 | Pg 102
    Only God .... GP 1:41 | Pg 107
    paradox, and .... GP 1:18 | Pg 84
    paradoxes .... GP 1:4 | Pg 70, GP 1:42 | Pg 108
    power, all.. GP 6:4 | Pg 188
    power, His... GP 9:7 | Pg 240
    Predestinates Wrath and Mercy....................... GP 1:17 | Pg 83
    predestination... GP 10:2 | Pg 246
    received not.. GP 5:26 | Pg 176
    Revealed His Name To Moses .... GP 1:25 | Pg 91
    right side.. GP 1:13 | Pg 79
    sides of... GP 8:8 | Pg 224
    The Name .... GP 1:23 | Pg 89
    The Paradox.. GP 1:18 | Pg 84
    throne, his... GP 9:4 | Pg 237
    time, and .... GP 10:4 | Pg 248
    titles of... GP 1:19 | Pg 85
    Titles or Names Of....................................... GP 1:19 | Pg 85
    unchangeableness of.................................... GP 1:32 | Pg 98
    unchangeableness, the real .... GP 1:34 | Pg 100
    who is.. GP 10:6 | Pg 250
    With God Nothing Shall Be Impossible .... GP 5:15 | Pg 165

God and predestination
    should we be angry...................................... GP 10:4 | Pg 248

God Does Not Lie.... **GP 1:5 | Pg 71**

God Has All Knowledge .... **GP 1:9 | Pg 75**

God is
    BeComingOne .... GP 10:6 | Pg 250

God Is Almighty.... **GP 1:10 | Pg 76**

God Is Everywhere .... GP 1:9 | Pg 75

God Is Invisible .... GP 1:10 | Pg 76

God Is Life .... GP 1:9 | Pg 75

God Is Love .... GP 1:13 | Pg 79

God Keeps His Word .... GP 1:13 | Pg 79

God, gods .... GP 1:35 | Pg 101

God's age .... GP 7:11 | Pg 207

God's Name

    imperfect verb .... GP: Appendix | Pg 265

    meaning of .... GP 1:27 | Pg 93

    pronounced as .... GP 1:27 | Pg 93

    spelling of .... GP 1:27 | Pg 93

    what is it .... GP 1:23 | Pg 89

gods

    Israel, of .... GP 1:36 | Pg 102

    you are .... GP 6:8 | Pg 192

gods versus one God .... GP 1:39 | Pg 105

good

    God is .... GP 1:13 | Pg 79

GP: Appendix .... GP: Appendix | Pg 252

Great cycle

    all out of God .... GP 6:9 | Pg 193

Greek NT

    Hebrew Name .... GP: Appendix | Pg 260

Hagar

    angel .... GP 3:2 | Pg 116

harmony

    disharmony .... GP 7:7 | Pg 203

Hebrew

    in NT .... GP: Appendix | Pg 259

Hebrew Name

Greek NT .... GP: Appendix | Pg 260

Hebrew New Testament .... GP: Appendix | Pg 259

Hebrew Participle .... GP: Appendix | Pg 265

higher meaning

    look to.. BP 4:3 | Pg 53

holy

    most... GP 8:5 | Pg 221

Holy One

    metonym.. GP 5:20 | Pg 170

Holy Spirit... GP 5:17 | Pg 167

    a metonym .... GP 5:21 | Pg 171

    has same Name............ GP 1:22 | Pg 88, GP 4:2 | Pg 129, GP 4:4 | Pg 131, GP 5:20 | Pg 170

    Jesus conceived by....................................... GP 5:33 | Pg 183

hot and cold .... GP 7:4 | Pg 200

hypostases .... GP 5:20 | Pg 170

I Am... GP 1:28 | Pg 94

I will be.. GP: Appendix | Pg 266

image of God .... GP 5:8 | Pg 158

    male & female .... GP 8:9 | Pg 225

immortal

    God is .... GP 5:15 | Pg 165

Immortality and Death .... GP 5:15 | Pg 165

immutability of God

    unchangeableness .... GP 1:32 | Pg 98

imperfect verb

    God's Name.. GP: Appendix | Pg 265

impossible

    God, and.. GP 5:15 | Pg 165

invisible

    Father?, the.. GP 2:2 | Pg 113

God .... GP 5:28 | Pg 178

God is .... GP 1:10 | Pg 76

Israel

God of .... GP 1:36 | Pg 102

Jacob

angel .... GP 3:3 | Pg 117, GP 3:5 | Pg 119

Jechoniah .... **GP 4:22 | Pg 149**

Jehovah .... **GP: Appendix | Pg 253**

Jesus

angel inside of .... GP 4:7 | Pg 134

angel of Becoming-One inside of .... GP 4:9 | Pg 136

before all .... GP 5:14 | Pg 164

born of virgin .... GP 4:4 | Pg 131

commission .... GP 6:1 | Pg 185

complete, not yet .... GP 8:4 | Pg 220

David's seed .... GP 4:5 | Pg 132

first .... GP 8:3 | Pg 219

flesh, came in .... GP 4:7 | Pg 134

flesh, his .... GP 5:7 | Pg 157

God before death, was not .... GP 4:8 | Pg 135

God, the .... GP 5:13 | Pg 163

last .... GP 8:3 | Pg 219

mercy seat, is .... GP 8:6 | Pg 222

middle man .... GP 4:5 | Pg 132

name, new .... GP 5:6 | Pg 156

power, all .... GP 6:4 | Pg 188

power, has all .... GP 6:1 | Pg 185

pre-existence .... GP 5:14 | Pg 164

received not by his own .... GP 5:26 | Pg 176

right cherub .... GP 8:5 | Pg 221

right side of God .... GP 8:2 | Pg 218

son of God, son of man................................... GP 4:5 | Pg 132

son of man through Mary................................. GP 4:3 | Pg 130

Spirit inside of.. GP 4:7 | Pg 134

Spirit, when did he receive............................... GP 4:11 | Pg 138

the Becoming-One... GP 8:3 | Pg 219

throne, on... GP 9:5 | Pg 238

Jesus Christ

glory of God.. GP 5:12 | Pg 162

God inside of... GP 4:6 | Pg 133

names, meaning of... GP 4:1 | Pg 128

prophesied to come.. GP 4:3 | Pg 130

Jesus Christ the God .... GP 5:1 | Pg 151, GP 5:13 | Pg 163

Jesus Christ's death................................... GP 4:13 | Pg 140

why... GP 4:15 | Pg 142

Jesus Christ's Father................................. GP 2:1 | Pg 112

Jesus is becoming..................................... GP 5:12 | Pg 162

Jesus' pre-existence?................................. GP 4:15 | Pg 142

John 1:1-18

details.. GP 5:24 | Pg 174

John the baptist

Elijah, and.. GP 5:25 | Pg 175

Josephus .... GP: Appendix | Pg 263

Joshua

angel... GP 3:7 | Pg 121

Kethib-Qere .... GP: Appendix | Pg 262

kill

God does.. GP 1:14 | Pg 80

knowledge

basic law of............................... GP 7:3 | Pg 199, GP 7:15 | Pg 211

complementary... GP 7:10 | Pg 206

new, not... GP 7:12 | Pg 208 true .... GP 7:6 | Pg 202

Kurios

    Lord... GP 3:2 | Pg 116

last, the .... GP 8:3 | Pg 219

law

    basic law of knowledge .... GP 1:5 | Pg 71

    basic, two .... GP 1:5 | Pg 71

    contradiction, of .... GP 1:5 | Pg 71

Law of Contradiction .... GP 1:5 | Pg 71

Law of Knowledge .... GP 1:5 | Pg 71, GP 7:3 | Pg 199

    blind: light & darkness .... GP 7:3 | Pg 199

    how children learn .... GP 7:16 | Pg 212

    more details .... GP 7:15 | Pg 211

    not new .... GP 7:12 | Pg 208

    table .... GP 7:13 | Pg 209

left side of God .... GP 8:7 | Pg 223

lie

    God does not .... GP 1:5 | Pg 71, GP 1:13 | Pg 79

life

    death and time .... GP 7:8 | Pg 204

    death, and .... GP 7:5 | Pg 201

    God is .... GP 1:9 | Pg 75

    God, and .... GP 5:25 | Pg 175

life, death, time .... GP 7:8 | Pg 204

light and darkness .... GP 5:25 | Pg 175

living creatures .... GP 9:2 | Pg 235, GP 9:5 | Pg 238

Lord

    Kurios, yhwh .... GP 3:2 | Pg 116

love .... GP 1:13 | Pg 79

    God is .... GP 1:13 | Pg 79, GP 10:1 | Pg 245

Love Is .... GP 1:13 | Pg 79

Love is Not .... GP 1:13 | Pg 79

Magnetic Fields

    their disintegration .... BP 1:10 | Pg 32

man

    1000 years, in the .... GP 7:12 | Pg 208

    Christ, to be like .... GP 6:1 | Pg 185

    God's age, from .... GP 7:11 | Pg 207

    school, in .... GP 7:7 | Pg 203

Manoah

    angel .... GP 3:4 | Pg 118

marriage

    spiritual .... GP 5:5 | Pg 155

Mary

    virgin birth of Jesus .... GP 4:4 | Pg 131

Mary, mother of Jesus .... GP 4:3 | Pg 130

Massoretes

    Tiberian .... GP: Appendix | Pg 262

Massoretic Text .... GP: Appendix | Pg 261

Massoretic Text? .... GP: Appendix | Pg 261

Massorites .... GP: Appendix | Pg 264

McDowell, Josh .... BP 3:1 | Pg 43, BP 3:8 | Pg 50

meaning of God's Name .... GP 1:27 | Pg 93

mercy seat

    Jesus is .... GP 8:6 | Pg 222

messenger

    angel, is .... GP 3:1 | Pg 115

Metonymy .... GP 5:17 | Pg 167, GP 5:21 | Pg 171, GP 5:26 | Pg 176, GP 9:4 | Pg 237-GP 9:6 | Pg 239

    Holy Spirit is a .... GP 5:21 | Pg 171

middle man

    Jesus .... GP 4:5 | Pg 132

mind

    new .... GP 7:6 | Pg 202

mindset .... BP 2:1 | **Pg 38**

    brain cell problem .... BP 2:5 | Pg 42

    Ptolemy .... BP 2:1 | Pg 38

Mindset Paper (Beginning Papers) .... BP 2:1 | **Pg 38**

Moses .... GP 5:28 | **Pg 178**

    angel .... GP 3:3 | Pg 117

most holies .... GP 8:5 | **Pg 221**

mother of Jesus

    Mary .... GP 4:3 | Pg 130

mystery, great .... GP 6:2 | **Pg 186**

Naftali .... GP: Appendix | **Pg 262**

Name

    all .... GP 6:5 | Pg 189

    all, and the .... GP 6:4 | Pg 188

    angel, given to .... GP 3:9 | Pg 123

    Becoming-One .... GP 8:3 | Pg 219

    BeComingOne .... GP 1:27 | Pg 93

    Cohortative .... GP: Appendix | Pg 257

    dual meaning of .... GP 1:21 | Pg 87

    Emphasized .... GP 1:25 | Pg 91, GP: Appendix | Pg 258

    God, of .... GP 1:19 | Pg 85, GP 1:23 | Pg 89

    Great Significance of .... GP 1:21 | Pg 87

    imperfect verb .... GP: Appendix | Pg 265

    in the New Testament .... GP 1:28 | Pg 94

    Jesus Christ .... GP 4:1 | Pg 128

    new (Jesus) .... GP 5:6 | Pg 156

    Pronounced .... GP 1:27 | Pg 93

    right side of God, and .... GP 8:2 | Pg 218

    Spelling of .... GP 1:27 | Pg 93 time and paradoxes .... GP 1:42 | Pg 108

    Time, Name, Paradoxes .... GP 1:42 | Pg 108

Name of God

    Israel forgot it .... GP 1:21 | Pg 87

    correct spelling of .... GP 1:27 | Pg 93

    emphasized, is .... GP: Appendix | Pg 258

    meaning of .... GP 1:27 | Pg 93

    significance of .... GP 1:21 | Pg 87

    Spelling of .... GP: Appendix | Pg 254

    what is it? .... GP 1:23 | Pg 89

Name, Forgotten .... GP 1:29 | Pg 95

Names

    Dual Meaning Of Names .... GP 1:21 | Pg 87

    God and Jesus Christ (similar) .... GP 5:2 | Pg 152

Neri .... GP 4:23 | Pg 150

new age .... BP 1:13 | Pg 35

new body .... GP 6:10 | Pg 194

new creation .... GP 5:9 | Pg 159

new mind .... GP 7:6 | Pg 202

new soul .... GP 5:10 | Pg 160

New Testament

    God .... GP 8:13 | Pg 229

    Hebrew .... GP: Appendix | Pg 259

notes of Part 4 .... GP 4:22 | Pg 149

nothing

    God, besides .... GP 1:9 | Pg 75

old age .... BP 1:13 | Pg 35

omnipotent

    God is .... GP 10:6 | Pg 250

omnipresent

    and God .... GP 10:6 | Pg 250

God is . . . . GP 1:9 | Pg 75, GP 10:6 | Pg 250

omniscient

God is . . . . GP 1:9 | Pg 75, GP 10:6 | Pg 250

one God . . . . GP 1:36 | Pg 102

One Versus Only . . . . GP 1:39 | Pg 105

one Yehowah . . . . GP 1:38 | Pg 104

only God . . . . GP 1:39 | Pg 105

paradox

God, and . . . . GP 1:18 | Pg 84

time and Name . . . . GP 1:42 | Pg 108

time, and . . . . GP 1:18 | Pg 84

Paradoxes . . . . GP 1:4 | Pg 70

and God . . . . GP 1:42 | Pg 108

answers . . . . GP 8:12 | Pg 228

God, on . . . . GP 1:4 | Pg 70

Time Answers The Paradoxes . . . . GP 1:18 | Pg 84

Participle

Hebrew . . . . GP: Appendix | Pg 265

Paul

example, an . . . . GP 4:11 | Pg 138

predestination . . . . GP 10:2 | Pg 246

physial dimension

spiritual . . . . GP 7:9 | Pg 205

physical dimensions

spiritual, and . . . . GP 7:9 | Pg 205

pleasure

spiritual and physical . . . . GP 6:12 | Pg 196

power

all . . . . GP 9:7 | Pg 240

Christ . . . . GP 6:1 | Pg 185

Jesus has all . . . . GP 6:1 | Pg 185 predestinated .... GP 9:7 | Pg 240

pre-existence

    Jesus (how) .... GP 5:14 | Pg 164

pre-existence of Jesus

    not so .... GP 4:15 | Pg 142

pre-existence theory .... GP 4:18 | Pg 145

predestination

    and evil .... GP 10:4 | Pg 248

    and God .... GP 10:2 | Pg 246

    before creation .... GP 10:3 | Pg 247

    God, and .... GP 1:17 | Pg 83

    good and evil .... GP 1:17 | Pg 83

    power, and .... GP 9:7 | Pg 240

Premises for Belief (Paper) .... BP 5:1 | Pg 55

Pritchard, J. .... BP 3:8 | Pg 50

problem of evil .... GP 1:12 | Pg 78

promise of the Seed .... GP 4:3 | Pg 130

proof

    yhwh is the Father .... GP 2:1 | Pg 112

prophecy

    of Jesus Christ's birth .... GP 4:3 | Pg 130

Ptolemy

    mindset .... BP 2:1 | Pg 38

radioactive dating method .... BP 1:5 | Pg 27

radiohalos .... BP 1:7 | Pg 29

Reading

    Children Reading the Bible .... GP: Appendix | Pg 263

reincarnation .... GP 7:12 | Pg 208

resurrection

    young, when .... GP 6:11 | Pg 195

review of Part 1 .... GP 1:45 | Pg 111

review of Part 3 .... GP 3:12 | Pg 126

review of Part 4 .... GP 4:23 | Pg 150

review of Part 5a .... GP 5:32 | Pg 182

review of Part 7 .... GP 7:17 | Pg 213

review of Part 8 .... GP 8:16 | Pg 232

review of Part 9 .... GP 9:7 | Pg 240

right & left side of God

    table .... GP 8:16 | Pg 232

right cherub

    Jesus .... GP 8:5 | Pg 221

salvation

    all to have .... GP 6:1 | Pg 185

    flesh, of. .... GP 5:10 | Pg 160

Satan

    does not know future .... GP 8:15 | Pg 231

    Jesus?, inside of .... GP 8:13 | Pg 229

    Peter, in .... BP 4:3 | Pg 53

    scriptures on .... GP 8:15 | Pg 231

school

    man in .... GP 7:7 | Pg 203

    mankind in .... GP 7:7 | Pg 203

science of Chaos .... BP 1:12 | Pg 34

seed

    promised .... GP 4:3 | Pg 130

seed of David .... GP 4:5 | Pg 132

seraphs .... GP 9:3 | Pg 236, GP 9:5 | Pg 238

sexual organs .... GP 6:10 | Pg 194

Shealtiel .... GP 4:22 | Pg 149

simultaneity

    death and immortality .... GP 1:7 | Pg 73, GP 1:8 | Pg 74

son of God

    Jesus .... GP 4:5 | Pg 132

    promised .... GP 4:3 | Pg 130

son of man

    Jesus .... GP 4:5 | Pg 132

    Jesus was through Mary .... GP 4:3 | Pg 130

soul

    new .... GP 5:10 | Pg 160

sound and silence .... **GP 7:4 | Pg 200**

Spelling

    of the Name of God .... GP: Appendix | Pg 254

spelling of God's Name .... **GP 1:27 | Pg 93**

Spelling of the Name .... **GP 1:27 | Pg 93**

Spirit

    all .... GP 6:4 | Pg 188

    body (when it leaves it) .... GP 4:14 | Pg 141

    death, and .... GP 4:14 | Pg 141

    Jesus (when he received it) .... GP 4:11 | Pg 138

    Jesus, inside of .... GP 4:7 | Pg 134

    ultimate building blocks .... GP 10:3 | Pg 247

    works, and .... GP 4:10 | Pg 137

spirits

    angels, and .... GP 6:5 | Pg 189

spiritual dimensions

    physical, and .... GP 7:9 | Pg 205

stars

    angels, and .... GP 6:5 | Pg 189

Stoic writer Chrysippus .... **GP 7:12 | Pg 208**

tabernacle

    cherubs in .... GP 8:4 | Pg 220

Tetragrammaton .... **GP: Appendix | Pg 257**

Three Orders of Salvation

    two in one .... GP 8:11 | Pg 227

throne
    details, more .... GP 9:5 | Pg 238
    eyes .... GP 9:5 | Pg 238
    faces .... GP 9:5 | Pg 238
    wheels .... GP 9:5 | Pg 238

throne of God .... GP 9:4 | Pg 237
    meaning of .... GP 9:6 | Pg 239

Tiberian Massoretes .... GP: Appendix | Pg 262

time .... GP 7:8 | Pg 204
    and God .... GP 10:5 | Pg 249
    Christ's name .... GP 4:1 | Pg 128
    contradictions, and .... GP 1:8 | Pg 74
    God, and .... GP 10:4 | Pg 248
    life and death .... GP 7:8 | Pg 204
    paradox, and .... GP 1:18 | Pg 84
    prophecy, and .... GP 1:8 | Pg 74
    what is it .... GP 7:8 | Pg 204

time and language .... GP 7:8 | Pg 204

time, Name, paradoxes .... GP 1:42 | Pg 108

titles
    God and Jesus Christ (similar) .... GP 5:2 | Pg 152
    God, of .... GP 1:19 | Pg 85

Titus .... GP: Appendix | Pg 263

Tree of knowledge .... BP 1:3 | Pg 25

Tree of Life
    Way to through JC .... GP 8:14 | Pg 230

Trinity .... GP 5:17 | Pg 167
    fourth person in? .... GP 5:20 | Pg 170

true knowledge .... GP 7:6 | Pg 202

Truth

    Truth is... GP 5:16 | Pg 166

    what is it?... GP 5:16 | Pg 166

two forces .... **GP 7:6 | Pg 202**

two in one

    in three orders .... GP 8:11 | Pg 227

two into one .... GP 5:5 | Pg 155, GP 6:6 | Pg 190, GP 6:11 | Pg 195, GP 8:9 | Pg 225

    new creation .... GP 5:9 | Pg 159

two thirds

    one third .... GP 7:11 | Pg 207

Unger, Merrill F.... BP 3:8 | Pg 50

Vespasian .... GP: Appendix | Pg 263

virgin birth

    Mary and Jesus .... GP 4:4 | Pg 131

Vowel-Letters .... GP: Appendix | Pg 263

wheels .... GP 9:5 | Pg 238

why, reason .... GP 7:1 | Pg 197

will of God.. GP 5:27 | Pg 177

wisdom

    Proverbs 8:22ff... GP 4:7 | Pg 134

    spirit .... GP 4:7 | Pg 134

Word

    and Jesus Christ .... GP 10:3 | Pg 247

    Becoming-One, of.. GP 3:10 | Pg 124

    beginning, in the... GP 5:24 | Pg 174

Word became flesh .... GP 5:9 | Pg 159, GP 5:27 | Pg 177

Word made flesh

    meaning of .... GP 4:12 | Pg 139

Word of God... GP 3:10 | Pg 124

    Jesus, in .... GP 4:9 | Pg 136

works

Jesus, and .... GP 4:10 | Pg 137

Written-Read....................................... GP: Appendix | Pg 262

Written-Read, Kethib-Qere .... GP: Appendix | Pg 262

Yahweh .... GP: Appendix | Pg 253

Yehowah .... GP 8:12 | Pg 228, GP: Appendix | Pg 253

    one is .... GP 1:38 | Pg 104

    THE cherubim... GP 1:37 | Pg 103

    Yehovah.. GP 1:25 | Pg 91

Yehowah alone

    created... GP 1:42 | Pg 108

    dwells as the cherubs..................................... GP 1:42 | Pg 108

    gave life .... GP 1:42 | Pg 108

    has the Name... GP 1:42 | Pg 108

    is many in one... GP 1:42 | Pg 108

Yehowah, Elohim....................................... GP 1:42 | Pg 108

yhwh.................................. GP 1:36 | Pg 102, GP 8:12 | Pg 228

    all .... GP 6:5 | Pg 189

    Father, is .... GP 2:2 | Pg 113

    Lord... GP 3:2 | Pg 116

    One .... GP 1:36 | Pg 102

    one is .... GP 1:36 | Pg 102

Zechariah

    angel.. GP 3:6 | Pg 120

Zerubbabel... GP 4:22 | Pg 149

Acknowledgment

I thank my wife Shirley Clare, my daughter Rhonda and others for their help with editing the grammar, spelling and for my wife's patience in the long hours I spent on my projects. I also thank all biblical scholars who wrote helps (concordances, interlinear Bibles, grammars, computer programs, creation v. evolution books, etc.) and critiques of doctrine, for they made my work easier. Lastly, I thank all scholars of serious works (philosophy, science, etc) for their work for no one person can think through all opinions pertaining to subjects: we need to compare our knowledge with others in order to ascertain the truth of the matter. Spiritually, I want to thank our creator for the Spirit and knowledge given to me, for without this I would not have recognized the obvious hints throughout the Bible.

Walter R. Dolen

2021

About the Author

Walter Dolen is an author/editor of several books, using the scientific method[26] including: *My God is the BeComingOne: God Papers*; *New Mind Papers*; *New Chronology Papers*; *BeComing-One Bible*; *Harmony of the Gospels*; *Harmony of the Good News*; *Male & Female*; *Prophecy Papers*; *Einstein: Light, Time and Relativity, Male & Female*; etc. These books were researched and written between 1969 and 2021. Walter has worked with his hands (carpenter/builder), with his mind (publisher/ writer/ building designer) and with his soul (President of the Becoming-One Church).

For more information about the author see his web site:

www.walterdolen.com or www.walterdolen.ws

---

[26] (1) Perceive a problem; (2) examine and analyze all the available evidence; (3) examine and imagine different hypotheses in attempt to solve the problem in a logical manner; (4) form a theory that answers the problem; (5) test the theory; (6) always have an open mind for better theories or answers to the problem; (7) change the theory if new evidence is inconsistent to your prior theory.

www.ingramcontent.com/pod-product-compliance
Lightning Source LLC
Chambersburg PA
CBHW080322170426
43193CB00017B/2872